Anonymous

Census of Nova Scotia, Taken March 30, 1861,

Under Act of Provincial Parliament--Chap. XIV--XXIII VIC.

Anonymous

Census of Nova Scotia, Taken March 30, 1861,
Under Act of Provincial Parliament--Chap. XIV--XXIII VIC.

ISBN/EAN: 9783337175429

Printed in Europe, USA, Canada, Australia, Japan

Cover: Foto ©Suzi / pixelio.de

More available books at **www.hansebooks.com**

REPORT

OF THE

SECRETARY

OF THE

BOARD OF STATISTICS

ON THE

CENSUS OF NOVA SCOTIA,

1861.

BOARD OF COMMISSIONERS:

The Hon. ADAMS G. ARCHIBALD, The Hon. JONATHAN McCULLY,
The Hon. WILLIAM ANNAND.

HALIFAX, N. S.

PRINTED BY ORDER OF THE GOVERNMENT.

1862.

BOARD OF STATISTICS.

REPORT.

CENSUS OFFICE,

Halifax, December 31, 1861.

To THE HONORABLE ADAMS G. ARCHIBALD, ⎫ Members
" THE HONORABLE JONATHAN McCULLY,   ⎬ of the Board of
" THE HONORABLE WILLIAM ANNAND,   ⎭ Statistics.

All the abstracts being completed, and placed in the hands of the printer, in compliance with the request of the Honorable the Chairman of your Board, I have the honor to present my report of the Census of Nova Scotia for 1861.

Before entering upon the results, I trust it will not be considered out of place to make a few observations, in reference to the machinery by which the information detailed in the various abstracts, has been collected and condensed.

After carefully examining the forms used in Great Britain and Canada, it was decided to adopt so much of both, as was applicable to this Province; and after such further additions as were necessary, a form of schedule was prepared, called the "Householder's Schedule," one of which, in conformity with the English practice, and partially that of Canada, was delivered by the Enumerators to each family, before the day fixed for taking the Census, viz.: the 30th March.

In Canada the Census is taken by Townships; but in many parts of this Province, there being no regularly defined Townships, the only practical mode was to take it by Polling Districts; and while upon this part of the subject, I would respectfully suggest the propriety, before another Census is taken, of having every County laid off into Townships, or Census Districts, with boundaries properly defined and established. There are two very strong objections to taking the Census by Polling Districts: first, the great disparity between the Districts, both as respects area and the number of inhabitants; and secondly, the want of permanent boundaries, as scarcely a session of the Legislature passes without the boundaries of some Polling District being changed.

The selection of suitable persons to act as Enumerators, became a very important part of my duty. The Legislature being in session, I availed myself of the opportunity thus afforded, of obtaining information from the members, as to competent persons to employ; and I have much pleasure in bearing testimony to their cordial co-operation, and valuable assistance.

The Enumerators were furnished with printed instructions accompanying the schedules, and much credit is due to most of the parties engaged, for the prompt and efficient manner in which their duties were discharged; more particularly when it is considered, that this was the first time of taking the Census in this Province by the mode adopted.

In a work of this kind, it is necessary to bear in mind that the information obtained is chiefly voluntary. Many of the Enumerators state, that in numerous instances they found persons unwilling, and some even refusing, to give the necessary information, professing to believe that the object of taking the Census was for the puropose of imposing taxation. This, however, is not to be wondered at, as the same prejudice, creating the same difficulty, is found to exist in all other countries. It is said this feeling prevailed to such an extent in the United States when the Census before the last was taken, that it became necessary in some districts to put in force the act of Congress for refusal to reply to the interrogatories of the Enumerators. A writer has remarked, in referrnce to this matter, that "People are slow to see that questions relating to themselves and their households, can have any bearing on the general good, and forget that in accounts of large numbers, the individual is wholly lost sight of in the average, but that the average can only be obtained by an accurate knowledge of all that pertains to the individual." I have great pleasure in stating here, that much credit is due to the clergy of several denominations, for their exertions through the press and otherwise, in disabusing the public mind in reference to such prejudices.

Some idea may be had of the labor to be performed in this office, from the following statement, viz.: About 55,000 Householder's Schedules were returned to the office, each of which had to be carefully examined, and statistical information under six different heads, extracted therefrom and put into as many abstract forms. These do not include buildings, places of worship, mills, &c., which were returned by the Enumerators in a separate schedule.

The mode of proceeding in the analysis was as follows :

1st.—Personal Census.

The most difficult and tedious part of the work was the classification of the ages, deaths, marriages, deaf and dumb, blind, lunatics, idiots, &c., distinguishing between male and female, married and single, widowers and widows; also the number between 5 and 15 years of age, and above 15, who could not read and write, which arrangement in one abstract, occupies no fewer than 150 columns. Next comes the classifications of origin, religions, trades and occupations, deaths and causes of deaths, each requiring separate abstracts.

2nd.—Agricultural Census.

The agricultural tables contain a large and valuable amount of information, which occupy 55 pages of closely printed matter, and which will be found treated of at length hereafter.

Although the work has necessarily cost a considerable amount, the expense will contrast very favorably with that of Canada in 1851, compared with the population. My estimate, exclusive of printing and binding the Report and Abstracts when compiled, was $12,500. In this estimate I did not include the alphabetical arrangement, and binding the schedules, which at your suggestion has been done, making 118 volumes; these will form a valuable record for reference. The whole amount, including some allowance, in addition to that fixed, to Enumerators in large districts, and binding the schedules, will not exceed the estimate more than $400. The experience of the office suggests the propriety of making some alteration in the mode of making the returns by the Enumerators. In Canada a commissioner is appointed for each County, whose duty it is to appoint the Enumerators, receive from them the schedules when filled up, prepare abstracts therefrom, and return the abstracts to the head office; instead of the schedules being returned by the Enumerators, as was done here. I would recommend that in future a person be appointed in each County, as in Canada, thoroughly acquainted with every locality. The Sheriff, as a general rule, would be a suitable person. The commissioner so appointed, to select with great care the Enumerators, furnish them with the schedules, and give them full information relative to their duty in taking the Census. The schedules after being filled up, to be returned to the commissioner, who, with the Enumerators, will carefully examine and correct them ; after which they should be returned by the Commissioner to the head office. I deem it essentially neceasary, for the purpose of insuring correctness and uniformity, that all the abstract work should be done in the head office. The Secretary, in his report of the Census of Canada for 1851, complains that great discrepancies were discovered in the abstracts furnished by the commissioners.

I would suggest that the next Census should contain a return of the value of Agricultural Implements possessed by each land-holder. Such a return would afford a valuable source of information, as showing the amount of that description of personal property.

Mr. Hutton, in his report of the Census of Canada for 1851, says: "The returns of a Population Census acquire their chief utility, from being contrasted with those of former periods; as from this comparison we learn the increase or decrease of the population, and the proportionate relation of the two sexes. It has been found, that although Great Britain has increased upwards of ten millions during the last half century, yet throughout this period the sexes have preserved their relative proportion, viz., 30 males to 31 females." The Census of Canada for 1851 shows the reverse, there being in Upper Canada 33 males to 30 females, and in Lower Canada about 51 males to 50 females; while in Nova Scotia the two sexes are nearly equal. In 1851 the females exceeded the males only about 1 in 200, and in 1861 the males exceed the females about 1 in 500. The difference in the relative proportion of the sexes in the Countries named, may be reasonably accounted for upon the principle of emigration. More males than females emigrate from Great Britain, causing the females to predominate there; while in Canada the males predominate, owing to larger accessions of males than females to the population by immigration. In Nova Scotia the relative proportion of the sexes is but slightly affected in this respect.

The following table shows the increase in the population during the past ten years, with the rate per cent. of increase in the several Counties.

COUNTIES.	Population.		Increase.	Rate per cent. increase.
	1851.	1861.		
Halifax (City)	19949	25026	5077	25.44
" (Outside City)	19163	23995	4832	25.21
Total in County	39112	49021	9909	25.33
Colchester	15469	20045	4576	29.58
Cumberland	14339	19533	5194	36.22
Pictou	25593	28785	3192	12.47
Sydney	13467	14871	1404	10.42
Guysborough	10838	12713	1875	17.30
Inverness	16917	19967	3050	18.02
Richmond	10381	12607	2226	21.44
Victoria, Cape Breton	27580	9643 20866	2929	10.62
Hants	14330	17460	3130	21.14
Kings	14138	18731	4593	32.48
Annapolis	14286	16953	2467	17.26
Digby	12252	14751	2499	20.39
Yarmouth	13142	15446	2304	17.53
Shelburne	10622	10668	46	.43
Queens	7256	9365	2109	29.06
Lunenburg	16395	19632	3237	19.74
Totals	276117	330857	54740	19.82

The Counties of Kings and Cumberland show an increase of over 30 per cent., Colchester and Queens nearly 30, Halifax 25, and the others, Shelburne excepted, varying from 10 to 21—the average increase being nearly

20 per cent. The increase in England and Wales during the same period
was 12 per cent. The County of Shelburne exhibits comparatively no increase. Upon ascertaining this fact I wrote to the Honble. Mr. Locke, and
Thomas Coffin, Esqr., two of the representatives of the County, both of
whom, although evidently surprised at the result, assured me that they had
every confidence in the integrity of the Enumerators, and their ability to
perform the work assigned them.

The average number of each family in the Province is 6.07; in Canada
the average in 1851 was 6.26, and in Great Britain the same year 4.73.

The following table shows the relative proportion of the two sexes under
50 years of age to be nearly preserved, comparing the Census of 1851 with
1861, classified in periods of 10 years.

	1851.		1861.	
	M.	F.	M.	F.
Under 10 years of age	44000	43452	45563	44561
From 10 " to 20	33791	33444	40843	39715
" 20 " to 30	20277	22385	27998	30148
" 30 " to 40	14615	14665	17447	18618
" 40 " to 50	10616	10271	12893	13056
Above 50 years	14378	14228	20489	18844
	137677	138445	*165233	164942

Under 10 and from 10 to 20 years, the males, both in 1851 and 1861, are
in the ascendant; from 20 to 30 and from 30 to 40 years the females exceed
the males in both decennial returns; while from 40 to 50 only, is this relative proportion slightly disturbed, in 1851 the males exceeding the females
345, and in 1861 the females outnumbering the males 163. Above 50
years of age, the relative proportion is still preserved, the males in both
periods exceeding the females, although more in the latter than in the former
period. The Census Tables of 1851 include all over 50 years of age
under one head, while those of 1861 continue the classification in periods of 10
years, by which it is shown that from 50 to 80 the males continue in excess
of the females; the greatest difference, however, being from 60 to 70 years.
From 80 to 90 the females are again in advance of the males, and from 90
to 100 they are equal, numbering 112 of each sex. Over 100 years of age
there are 7 males and 14 females, viz.: of males 3 married, 1 single, and 3
widowers; and of females 1 single and 13 widows. The Census Tables
again, in 1851, include all under 10 years of age in one column, while those
of 1861 divide them into periods of 1 year each, up to 5, and include from
5 to 10 under one head, at all of which periods the males exceed the females.
A reference to the Abstracts will show, that the relative proportions vary
very much in different Counties, compared with the general result; in some
Counties the males, and in others the females predominating at the various
ages or periods into which they are divided.

In Upper Canada, in 1851, where the males exceeded the females about
10 per cent in the aggregate, they were also in advance in every period into
which the abstracts were divided. In Lower Canada, however, where the
relative proportion of the two sexes in the whole population is nearly similar
to that of Nova Scotia, the like result is also exhibited as regards the various
classifications of ages, at some periods the males, and at other periods the
females being in the ascendant.

The married portion of the population next claims attention. The Counties of Colchester, Cumberland and Digby, each return 1 married female
under 15 years of age. There are 615 of this class between 15 and 20,

* In column ages not given, not included.

Inverness contributing 7, the smallest, and Kings 75, the largest number, compared with the population of the respective Counties. There are also returned for the Province 31 married males under 20 years of age; between 20 and 30 the married males number considerably more than half the married females; while between 30 and 40 the number of each sex occupying this relation is nearly equal, the females, however, still leading in numbers; but about this period a change takes place, the married males between 40 and 50 outnumbering the females over 1000. From 50 to 100 years of age, the number of married males continues in advance of the females of this class, in about the same ratio as the latter exceeded the former previous to 50; and, it is a curious fact, that the number of married males over 100 years of age is just equal to the number of married females under 15 years. The Counties of Halifax, Pictou and Lunenburg each return 1 of this class at this advanced age. There is another curious feature relative to the married portion of the population, viz.: the number of both sexes that marry so much earlier in life in some Counties than in others. Take for example King's, Lunenburg, Colchester and Cumberland, with a population about equal, all of which return a much greater number of married of both sexes under 30 years of age, than Inverness and Cape Breton, having a population nearly corresponding with the above Counties. They also return a greater number of this class than Pictou, with a population much larger. Similar comparisons would apply to other Counties. The disparity between the number of widows and widowers, is another remarkable feature ascertained by the Census; there being 8382 widows, and but 3165 widowers, or over 160 per cent. more of the former than of the latter. Nearly the same inequality is found to exist throughout the various classifications of ages in the Census abstracts; this is the more singular, from the fact that there is only 12 per cent. more deaths of males than females. The disparity can only be reasonably accounted for upon the principle that a much greater number of widowers than widows marry again, and that they do not generally select widows as partners. The Census of 1851 shows the same preponderance of widows over widowers. In Canada the difference is not so great, being under 100 per cent., although the relative mortality of the two sexes is nearly equal; widows must be more fortunate in obtaining husbands there.

The total number of deaths in one year, previous to the 30th March, 1861, was 4679, being 1.41 per cent. of the entire population. The mortality of the two sexes, as before remarked, was nearly equal, viz.: 2480 males, and 2199 females. A similar equality is observable in the various periods of classification, excepting between 20 and 30, and between 70 and 80, the deaths of males in the former period exceeding those of the females 67, and in the latter period 55. One-third of the total number of deaths is of persons under 5 years of age, and over two-fifths of this number, or nearly one-seventh of the total number of deaths, takes place under 1 year of age. The Census of 1851 shows the annual mortality at that time to be 2802, being about 1 per cent. of the population. The increased mortality as exhibited in the present Census, is owing to the ravages of that, in this Province comparatively new, and fatal disease, Dyptheria, it having carried off over 1000 during the year. The mortality in Upper Canada in 1851, was under 1 per cent., and in Lower Canada 1½ per cent. In New Brunswick in 1851, it was similar to that of Lower Canada.

The returns of the Deaf and Dumb show nearly the same number, compared with the population, as in 1851. Some Counties return a less number than in 1851; but this may be accounted for by there being a number in the Deaf and Dumb Institution at Halifax, from the country, and all of which are included in the number from Halifax. There is 1 of this class in every 1100 of the population. In Canada in 1851, there was 1 in 1372, and in the United States 1 in 2395 of the entire population. The proportion of Deaf and Dumb in Great Britain, is 1 to 1590 of the population, in France, 1 to 1212, in Prussia, 1 to 1364, and in Switzerland, 1 to every

2

503. The average proportion of this class throughout the civilized world, is estimated at about 1 in 1550 of the population.

The report of the Institution for the Deaf and Dumb for 1860, kindly furnished me by the Rev. James Cochran, M. A., the Secretary, who has always taken a deep interest in its management, shows that 42 of this unfortunate class attended the school during the year, 6 of whom belonged to Halifax, 7 were from New Brunswick, and 29 from various parts of this Province—viz.: 7 from the County of Pictou, 4 from Colchester, 4 from Annapolis, 3 from King's, 4 from Cape Breton, 2 from Queen's, and 1 each from Cumberland, Hants, Digby, Sydney, and Guysborough Counties.

In 1851 there were 136 Blind persons returned; the present Census returns 185; showing a somewhat larger proportionate increase than that of the population. There is no means of ascertaining from the returns, how many of these 185 were born blind, or how many became so from disease or old age; it is probable that not more than one-half, if so many, were born blind. I would suggest the propriety, in taking the next Census, so to arrange the schedules that such distinctive information may be obtained.

The number of Lunatics returned shows that this class of unfortunates, during the last decade, has increased in a greater ratio than the population. In 1851 there were 166, being only 1 in 1660 of the whole population; while the returns for 1861 show 340, including those in the Hospital for the Insane, being 1 in 970 of the population. A reference to the abstract at the close of the Census report, will show the number of Lunatics belonging to the several Counties, including those in the Asylum. It is difficult to account for this disparity, otherwise than by supposing that they were not all returned in 1851. The number of Idiots does not exhibit a like proportionate increase with that of Lunatics. There were 299 Idiots returned in 1851, and 317 in the present Census. Probably some who were returned in 1851 as Idiots, are now returned as Lunatics.

There are 5927 colored persons in the Province. The ratio of increase of this class of persons, for the past ten years, has been the same as the increase of the general population.

The returns of the Indians show an increase of 33 per cent. during the last decade. There were 1056 returned in 1851; while the present returns give 1407. The names, as far as they could be obtained, were taken by the Enumerators, and all at the same time, so that the present Census is reliable. Owing to the migratory habits of this portion of the population, it is difficult to obtain anything like a correct return, unless taken simultaneously. The prevailing opinion is, I believe, that the Indians are not increasing in the Province; if this opinion is well founded, the full number could not have been given in 1851.

The following table, compiled from the Enumerator's schedules, shews the number of Acadian French in the various Counties.

Counties.	No. of Persons.
Richmond	5733
Digby	4848
Yarmouth	3522
Inverness	2104
Sydney	2050
Halifax	1107
Guysborough	709
Cumberland	424
Cape Breton	362
Total	20859

ORIGIN OF THE POPULATION.

The total population of Nova Scotia is 330,857. Of this number 294,706 were born in the Province, leaving 36,151 who have derived their origin from other places; the proportion born out of the Province being 10.92 per cent. of the whole.

Of this part of our population, Scotland furnishes the largest proportion, viz.: 16,395, or over 45 per cent. of the whole. The natives of Ireland stand next in number, viz.; 9313, and those of England next. viz: 2993.

Of the natives of Scotland, the Counties of Pictou, Inverness, Victoria and Cape Breton, have attracted the largest numbers. Of the natives of Ireland, 4478, or nearly one-half, are to be found in the County of Halifax, the remainder being pretty equally divided amongst the other Counties of the Province.

That the increase of our population is not derived, to any great extent, from immigration into the Colony since the last Census, will appear, from the following considerations. If such had been the case, the largest percentage of increase might be expected in those Counties the population of which contained the largest proportion of natives of other countries. The Counties which contain the largest proportion not native born, are Victoria, Cape Breton, Halifax and Inverness, the percentage to the population in these Counties being, respectively, 22.57, 20.62, 18.23, and 15.03; while the percentage of increase in these Counties is as follows, viz.: for Victoria and Cape Breton, which in 1851 were returned as one County, is 10.62, Halifax 25.33, and Inverness 18.02. Taking the Counties of Pictou and Cumberland, whose population contain about an equal proportion of those who have not derived their nativity from this country, viz.: a little over fourteen per cent. each, it will be found, that while the former has increased its population since 1851 by about 12½ per cent., the increase of the latter has amounted to over 36 per cent.; and the Counties of Lunenburg, Yarmouth, and Digby, which have the smallest proportion of this element in their population, viz.: Lunenburg, 1.18, Yarmouth, 2.48, and Digby, 4.42 per cent., have increased 19.74, 17.53, and 20.39 per cent., respectively.

RELIGIOUS DENOMINATIONS.

In the instructions accompanying the Householder's Schedule, it was directed that particular care should be taken to designate the religious profession of each member of the family, excepting those under 14 years of age, it being assumed that all children under that age would be of the same religious persuasion as the head of the family; and in transferring the numbers from those schedules for the purpose of classifying them under the different denominational heads, this assumption was in all cases kept in view. In some few instances, it was found that the religious profession of those above fourteen years of age in a family was not given; in such cases, if under twenty years of age, they were classified in accordance with the foregoing rule; if over that age, they were put down as amongst those whose religion was not given. This rule might not in every case be found to give a strictly correct statement of the religious persuasion of the family. Instances might occur in which the father might belong to one denomination, and the mother to another; part, or the whole of the children might follow the profession of the mother, and yet, under this rule, be classified with that of the father. The rule observed, however, will be found open to as few objections, as any that under the circumstances could have been adopted.

I cannot attempt to give any reliable statement shewing the comparative ratio of increase in the different denominations since the last Census was taken, as, owing to some error or omission in making up the returns of 1851, the sum of the religious denominations given does not agree with the

amount of the total population of the Province, as shewn in the Census
tables. This will the more clearly appear, by a reference to the following
statement of the religious denominations, as furnished by the Census of
1851.

Church of England	36,482
Roman Catholic	69,634
Kirk of Scotland	18,867
Presbyterian Church of Nova Scotia	28,767
Free Church	25,280
Baptist	42,243
Methodist	23,596
Congregationalist	2,639
Universalist	580
Lutheran	4,087
Sandimanians	101
Quakers	188
Other denominations	3,791
Making	256,255

The total population of the Province at that time was 276,117, leaving
19,862 not included or accounted for, showing an evident error in the
religious classifications of that year. The discrepancy is more apparent in
some Counties than in others. In the County of Cumberland, for instance,
out of a population of 14,339, there are 4,275 who are not classed under
any denominational head. In the Counties of Lunenburg, Cape Breton
and Victoria, and Richmond, the numbers given in the religious classification, exceed the population of the respective Counties, the first by 639,
the next two, by 199, and the last by 43. Digby and Annapolis are the
only Counties in which the religious denominations appear to have been
correctly classified in that year.

In the table accompanying this report, all the population is accounted
for, and the members of each denomination, as far as could be ascertained,
classed under their respective heads; those to whom, in the returns, no
religious persuasion was assigned, being placed in the column marked
" No creed given."

DEATHS AND CAUSES OF DEATHS.

Although it is very desirable that the statistical returns of the various
causes which affect the health of the community, should be accurately
ascertained, a difficulty has always existed in arriving at correct conclusions
in this matter, from the inability of a large portion of the inhabitants
of a country to specify the exact disease of which their relatives
died; and this is particularly the case upon the introduction of any
class of epidemics new to the country, or when the death had occurred at
an early period of the year upon which the returns were demanded.
Another difficulty arises from the fact that many diseases are known by
different names in different localities, rendering it necessary to condense
the materials supplied by the Enumerators, in order that the information
thus given to the public may be placed in the clearest light, and in as concise
a form as possible. The following tabular statement gives the diseases to
which the deaths occurring during the year have been attributed, with the
number of deaths from each disease.

DEATHS AND CAUSES OF DEATHS.

Class of Disease.	Nature of Disease.	Deaths	Class of Disease.	Nature of Disease.	Deaths.
Epidemic, Endemic, and Contageous Diseases.	Cholera	10	Diseases of the Respiratory and Circulating Organs.	Asthma	14
	Cramp	9		Bronchitis	11
	Intermittent Fever	22		Consumption	767
	Dyptheria	1003		Croup	122
	Dysentery	2		Cough	3
	Typhus Fever	66		Disease of Lungs	14
	Hooping Cough	57		Disease of Heart	67
	Influenza	13		Inflammation of Lungs	114
	Measles	152		Inflammation of Chest	3
	Mumps			Inflammation of Heart	1
	Scarlet Fever	210		Pleurisy	75
	Small Pox	49		Quinsy	15
	Hives			Sore Throat	153
		1592			**1359**
Diseases of the Nervous System.	Apoplexy	21	Diseases of Urinary & Generative Organs.		
	Brain Fever	52			
	Disease of the Brain	74		Disease of Bladder	12
	Epilepsy	5		Diabetes	1
	Paralysis	41		Inflammation of Kidneys	6
	Insanity	7		Puerperal Fever	3
	Convulsions	84		Child-bed	36
		284			**58**
Diseases of the Digestive Organs.	Bilious Fever	60	Diseases of Uncertain Seat.	Abscess	8
	Disease of Liver	42		Cancer	26
	Disease of Stomach	7		Colds	35
	Indigestion	13		Scrofula	5
	Debility	25		After Amputation	1
	Jaundice	26		Mortification	4
	Inflammation of Bowels	93		Dropsy	70
	Inflammation of Stomach	28		Old Age	149
	Disease of Bowels	42		Erysipelas	35
	Worms	26		Intemperance	2
	Teething	9		Rheumatism	40
		371		Rickets	
				Tumor	8
				Carbuncle	1
Violent and Accidental Deaths.	Burns and Scalds	22			**384**
	Frozen	1			
	Drowned	95			
	Murdered	1			
	Poisoned	3	Diseases of Org's of Sight & Hearing.	Disease of Eye	2
	Other Accidents	53		Disease of Ear	2
		175			**4**
				Causes not specified	452
				Total of Causes specified	4227
				Total	**4679**

It would appear from the foregoing statement, that the mortality from epidemics is greater than from any other cause, the deaths being 1592, or over one-third of the whole.

DYPTHERIA.—This epidemic has been very fatal in several parts of the Province, the number of deaths from it being greater than from any other disease ; the largest mortality has been in the Counties of Richmond, King's, Lunenburg and Cumberland.

MEASLES.—The deaths from this cause number 152. The disease has been pretty general over the country.

SCARLET FEVER.—This disease has caused more deaths than any of the epidemics, except Dyptheria. It has been most fatal in the Eastern Counties.

SMALL POX.—The number returned as dying from this cause is put down at 49, more than half of which have occurred in the County of Halifax.

TYPHUS FEVER.—The deaths from this cause have amounted to 66. They have occurred in most parts of the Province. This disease does not appear to have raged as an epidemic during the past year.

CONVULSIONS.—The deaths returned from this cause are 84 ; but it is probable that under this head other diseases are included, of which this affection is in early life an attendant.

CONSUMPTION.—From this disease, the most fatal to which the population is subject, 767 deaths are returned, a greater number than were returned from Upper Canada in 1851, with a population nearly three times as great. The Counties which have returned the largest number of deaths from this disease in proportion to the population, are Annapolis and Shelburne, and those which have returned the smallest number are Guysborough, Cape Breton and Queen's ; in the former Counties twice as large a proportion have died from this disease as in the latter.

CROUP.—From this disease the deaths have been 122. As in other countries, it has been more equally distributed than most other diseases ; but it appears to have been most fatal in the rural districts.

SORE THROAT.—The number returned as dying from this disease, is 153 ; it is probable, however, that some of those who are thus returned, died from Dyptheria.

Although the rate of mortality for the whole Province appears by the returns to be somewhat greater than it was either in Canada or in New Brunswick, or even in this country in 1851, yet, having reason to believe that the whole number of deaths in the City of Halifax was not returned, as it is well known that Dyptheria and Small Pox had prevailed there during the year for which the return of deaths was made up, I have compared the return made, with the record of interments in the different Cemeteries of the City, and find that the whole number of interments is 550 ; which would show that there were 226 deaths more than were returned, and would make the percentage of mortality for the city very great. This is an illustration of the extreme difficulty of getting, from the poorer classes in cities, correct returns of the deaths during the prevalence of contagious diseases. This remark, however, will not apply to the rural districts, and should not cast a doubt upon the correctness of the returns from those quarters, the circumstances of each family being so well known, that a death could scarcely occur in a community of this kind, and not be known to nearly every individual in it.

PROFESSIONS, TRADES AND OCCUPATIONS.

It has been generally admitted, that this department of the Census presents more difficulties in the way of getting at correct returns, than any other, and I do not know that Nova Scotia has any right to claim exemption from difficulties that have, in other countries, more or less attended ove⸗

attempt to obtain correct information with regard to the employments of the population.

Nova Scotia has been frequently represented as a country whose soil and climate are not congenial to agricultural pursuits. A glance at the returns, however, will reveal the fact that 37,897, or nearly one-fourth of the entire male population, style themselves farmers, and 9,306 are classed as farm laborers; while in Upper Canada, which may be regarded as emphatically an agricultural country, but three-eighths of the male population claim to be so considered in the Census of 1851 ; and New York, in 1855, returned 321,930, or about one-fifth.

The class which stands next in numbers, in our Province, to the farm laborers, is the fishermen. In connection with this part of the returns, a somewhat singular circumstance demands attention. In abstract No. 5, it will be seen that 7650 return themselves as fishermen; while in abstract No. 6, under the head "men employed in the fisheries," it will be found that 14,322 are so engaged. Some explanation of the apparent anomaly may be given in this way : There are a number of persons in the Province whose ordinary occupation is farming, or some other pursuit on the land, but who are occasionally engaged in the fisheries, and keep boats for this purpose. When called upon to state their occupation, these persons would call themselves by that which they ordinarily followed ; but when required to return the number of men employed in the boats, would include themselves, and some members of their families who had already been classed as following other pursuits. This will, in part, explain, but can scarcely account for the whole of the difference in the numbers of fishermen, as given in abstracts 5 and 6. It may, however, be regarded, and serve as an illustration of, the difficulty of obtaining absolutely perfect information for a work of this kind.

The trades and occupations which, after those already named, give employment to the greatest number of our population are, mariners, 5242, and Carpenters and Joiners, 4463; Merchants, Shopkeepers. and Traders are represented by 1947, Shoemakers by 1976, Blacksmiths, 1518, Coopers, 1145, and Shipwrights, 1122. We have also 864 Teachers, and 385 Clergymen and Ministers, 170 Physicians, and 147 Lawyers. Lastly, we have 665 Miners, a class whose number will in all probability be greatly augmented, before the arrival of the next period for enquiring into the progress we have made in population and wealth, and those arts which contribute to the comfort and happiness of man.

AGRICULTURE.

It will be perceived, by referring to the Census by Trade and Occupation, that there are in the Province of Nova Scotia, 37,897 Farmers, and 9,306 Farm Laborers. As in most instances the heads only, of families, have given their occupation, there must be a great number of male adults and others engaged in farming pursuits (the families in the rural districts being large), and could an approximate calculation be made of the number, it would be found, that a very considerable proportion of the total population of the country depends on this occupation as a means of subsistence. In many cases, where undivided attention has been directed to it, persons have become possessed of large and valuable properties, and have been well rewarded for their industry, adding to the wealth and prosperity of their native or adopted country.

When we compare the state of a country at two different periods, and find that the annual produce of its land and labor is evidently greater at the latter than at the former, that its lands are better cultivated, its manufactures more numerous and more flourishing, and its trade more extensive, we may be assured that its capital must be increased during the interval between those periods. To form a correct judgment of it, we must

compare the state of the country, at periods somewhat distant from one
another.   The progress is frequently so gradual, that at short intervals the
improvement is not only not apparent, but from the decline, either of
certain branches of industry, or of certain districts of country, owing to
fluctuations of trade, or other local causes, there may arise a belief that the
industry and wealth of the whole is declining; when in fact the general
state of the country may be one of great prosperity.

An illustration of this will be furnished by the following Comparative
Table of the Agricultural Produce of Nova Scotia for the years 1851 and
1861.

Comparative Table of the Agricultural Produce of Nova Scotia, as shown by the Census for the years 1851 and 1861.

COUNTIES	Tons Hay.		Bushels Wheat.		Bushels Barley.		Bushels Buckwheat.		Bushels Oats.	
	1851.	1861.	1851.	1861.	1851.	1861.	1851.	1861.	1851.	1861.
1. Halifax	19083	20972	5130	3413	8406	12969	11104	8353	34984	60245
2. Colchester	30633	34807	30880	27360	6858	8968	30591	38611	108234	102976
3. Cumberland	25150	31582	34004	54412	9885	19519	45642	70013	70823	134588
4. Pictou	21626	27494	88180	83467	22103	24703	13151	17676	263368	392213
5. Sydney	11309	23335	31934	43863	9378	13992	5607	4431	182946	189273
6. Guysborough	8382	9517	1807	3412	906	2964	4781	4784	35702	51880
7. Inverness	19176	29862	28951	14354	18084	31924	813	2414	152890	238906
8. Richmond	4362	4827	897	1181	3153	2714	4	16	33119	46752
9. Victoria }	16254	7583	16900	2343	24776	11743	75	235	188438	117935
10. Cape Breton }		8673		6172		19735		829		176181
11. Hants	26112	23680	26385	22217	8072	9109	13138	8279	108822	129624
12. King's	28117	30788	11403	25034	4917	7459	14901	8809	94573	134084
13. Annapolis	23985	28434	11081	15398	17098	17863	13984	11105	42953	53882
14. Digby	8496	10906	1420	2943	5387	10777	4910	6173	11748	19643
15. Yarmouth	11399	15908	728	1130	3983	7894	3206	1056	6696	7944
16. Shelburne	5496	5869	4	177	1401	9000	46	18	2129	3003
17. Queen's	5732	7439	916	1277	4059	7412	1886	1937	10870	16097
18. Lunenburg	17558	20012	4892	3730	50951	71078	1913	3269	19421	19931
	287837	334367	297187	312081	199067	290078	170301	196340	1284437	1978137

Note.—The Census being taken in March 1851, the Returns show the product of 1850.

Comparative Table of the Agricultural Produce of Nova Scotia, as shown by the Census for the years 1851 and 1861.—Continued.

COUNTIES	Bushels Rye		Bushels Indian Corn		Bushels Potatoes		Bushels Turnips		Produce of the Dairy.			
									Butter, lbs.		Cheese, lbs.	
	1851	1861	1851	1861	1851	1861	1851	1861	1851	1861	1851	1861
1. Halifax	102	526	177	42	58800	111811	24604	44674	144970	220605	957	2090
2. Colchester	327	3308	1998	186	182545	358002	24822	48310	317306	398029	11337	20726
3. Cumberland	2109	4817	514	320	128034	336077	41295	55815	291718	383054	13611	17869
4. Pictou	85	1292	413	208	157039	284169	98849	54530	370471	471486	58330	73418
5. Sydney	25	1174	3782	131	52938	140206	11702	12990	348420	357856	90129	166765
6. Guysborough	9	44	85	22	31336	60653	12145	9003	95567	154144	1176	4173
7. Inverness	17	1804	988	100	69364	240451	14928	7849	317044	461172	55064	182839
8. Richmond		57	3	1	22083	64055	1332	4333	58096	82449	1351	4442
9. Victoria	33	134	124	20	72947		20718	4939	339086	196179	16300	19168
10. Cape Breton		528		64	114554	166772		10434		210587		12982
11. Hants	1242	1536	3043	362	112407	196384	31550	26037	500005	250035	14410	18224
12. King's	29808	23718	18947	4370	574897	838551	29594	66090	222392	200000	92860	84961
13. Annapolis	17085	10433	11779	8256	564899	950192	73450	57800	195112	250977	171964	216770
14. Digby	990	500	379	690	90595	198556	39954	51674	78703	146190	3038	8996
15. Yarmouth	2637	606	169	209	94717	198822	36357	41253	249828	237134	92539	130464
16. Shelburne	10	28	290	28	51196	78423	4598	5104	58027	115805	24640	1507
17. Queen's	1761	1584	378	207	31406	56940	4903	13809	69654	110154	2102	1797
18. Lunenburg	8038	11082	403	149	72929	153054	20847	4730	99829	300812	1494	8418
	65498	60706	37425	15820	3084299	5422964	467127	554356	3615800	4552712	680099	901296

LAND.—In the Census of 1851, the quantity of Land yielding crop was returned under two heads only, viz.: Dyked Marsh, of which there was 40,012 acres, and Other Improved Land, 799,310 acres, making together 839,322 acres. The present returns divide it into four different classes, viz.: Dyked Marsh, Salt Marsh, Cultivated Intervale, and Cultivated Upland. Of the first of these classes, there appears by the returns to be 35,487 acres. This is less, by 4,525 acres, than the quantity given in 1851. It would be a mistake, however, to suppose that there is less of this description of land in cultivation now, than there was at the former period. The difference in the figures may be accounted for, from the fact that a large quantity of land now returned under the head of "Salt Marsh," was in 1851 given as "Dyked Marsh," there being in the returns of that year no other distinctive head under which to place it. Of Salt Marsh, the amount returned is 20,729 acres, making, together with the Dyked Marsh, a total of 56,216 acres, being an increase of 16,204 acres over the total amount of Marsh given in 1851. Of Cultivated Intervale and Cultivated Upland, the number of acres given are 77,102, and 894,714, respectively, making a total of 1,028,032 acres under cultivation in 1861, against 839,322 acres in 1851, being an increase of 188,710 acres. This increase is by no means general throughout the Province, some Counties having increased the quantity of cultivated land but little, while in the County of Shelburne there is a decrease of considerable amount. This decrease, supposing the return of 1851 to have been correct, can only be accounted for, on the supposition that the inhabitants have turned their attention to other branches of industry. The largest increase is in the Counties of Annapolis, King's. Sydney and Lunenburg. The total estimated value of the cultivated land by the present return is $18,801,365. The average value given per acre is. of Dyked Marsh $62.06, of Salt Marsh $26.04, of Cultivated Intervale $27.45, and of Cultivated Upland $15.58. By reference to the abstracts, it will be seen that the estimated value of the same description of land varies very largely in different parts of the Province. That there is a substantial difference in the value of the same description of land in different localities, caused by difference of productiveness, nearness to, or distance from, markets, and other local causes, there can be no doubt. This, however, cannot wholly account for the great discrepancy that appears in the returns. It is very evident that in many localities the prejudices of the people, to which reference has already been made, has caused owners of land to give an under-estimate of the value of their soil, thus materially reducing the general average value below what might be considered a correct return.

HAY.—Colchester, as in 1851, returns a larger quantity of Hay than any other County. King's and Cumberland are the next largest hay-producing Counties. The increase throughout the Province, as compared with the quantity returned in 1851. amounts to 46,450 tons, and it will be seen, by reference to the abstracts. that the increase is not confined to particular Counties, but is pretty general throughout the Province.

WHEAT.—The present returns show a large increase in the Wheat crop, in a few Counties, viz.: Sydney, Cumberland, King's and Annapolis; while in others they shew a decrease in the quantity raised, compared with 1851. This is, no doubt, owing in a great measure to the weavil having affected this grain in some parts of the Province more than in others. The total increase is 14,924 bushels. The Counties of Pictou, Cumberland, and Sydney, raise the largest quantities of wheat, and it is found, that the districts bordering on the Gulf of St. Lawrence are well adapted for the cultivation of this valuable cereal, on account of the nature of the soil and temperature of climate. Wheat of the finest quality can be produced there, weighing 60 lbs. and upwards per bushel, and in some cases giving large returns per acre, and when skilfully manufactured, furnishing flour equal to any imported from the United States.

BARLEY.—The County of Lunenburg produces 71,078 bushels of this description of grain, being more than one-fourth of all grown in Nova Scotia. In 1851, this County returned 50,361 bushels, showing an increase, compared with that period, of 20,717 bushels. There are other Counties which show a much more extensive cultivation of this grain than in 1851. Inverness produces the largest quantity next to Lunenburg. The total increase is 73,481 bushels. Dawson, in his work on Agriculture, suggests that its culture should be more widely extended.

BUCKWHEAT.—The returns show a total of 195,340 bushels of this grain grown in 1860—the Counties of Colchester and Cumberland together producing 117,524 bushels. In some parts of the Province it is not much cultivated; it is generally raised as a first crop on new and mountainous land.

OATS.—There is a considerable increase in this grain, viz.: 593,700 bushels. More attention is paid to its cultivation in Pictou, than in any other County. It is also cultivated largely in the Counties of Colchester, Sydney, Inverness and Cape Breton. It is considered highly nutricious and wholesome food, and more attention should be paid to its culture. If raised extensively, it would be found a good article for exportation to the United States.

RYE.—There is a decrease in this grain of 1732 bushels. It is not much cultivated, except in some of the Western Counties. Formerly there was a good deal of winter rye sown, but it appears not to be grown now; the straw not being serviceable as fodder, may be one cause.

INDIAN CORN.—There is also a decrease of 21,946 bushels in this grain. It appears to be more cultivated in the Western than in the Eastern Counties. It requires a light, deep soil, and warm season.

POTATO.—The returns show an increase in this valuable article of food, of 1,838,075 bushels, being nearly 100 per cent., the increase being very general throughout the Province. Notwithstanding the disease to which it has been subject for some years past, great attention has been paid to its cultivation, and in the Western Counties it has been found a source of great profit, so much so, that its cultivation has to some extent taken the place of wheat and some other grains. It has been found to succeed better there than in some other parts of the Province. A very remunerative market has been obtained in some of the United States.

TURNIPS.—It will be observed that the increase in this useful root is 87,191 bushels, being very small, compared with that of the potato. Dr. Forrester, in his publication on Agriculture, urges that greater attention should be paid to the culture of this and other root crops. They are frequently destroyed by insects, but with proper care and attention the crop is reasonably secure.

PEAS AND BEANS.—There appears a small decrease in the production of these articles of food. It is said they afford a large amount of nutriment, and are serviceable for fattening some description of stock. It would be well if their cultivation were increased.

PRODUCTS OF THE DAIRY.—Butter has increased 918,821 lbs., and Cheese 249,227 lbs. The amount of butter returned, as produced in 1860, is 4,532,711 lbs., and cheese 901,296 lbs.; the milch cows number 110,504. It will thus be seen that the yield is only 41.02 lbs. butter, and 8.15 lbs. cheese, per cow. This appears but a small return, as cows of good breed and in good condition, have given from 100 to 150 lbs. each in a season; if, therefore, 75 lbs. were computed as the average produce of each cow, it would amount to 8,287,800 lbs., and a corresponding increase in cheese. It was observed in making abstracts from the returns of Stock and Produce, that in many the number of cows was given without any return of butter. It is probable that many parties supposed that only the quantity of butter sold, should be returned, and that they omitted the amount consumed in each family, and the same thing as regards cheese.

HORSES.—There has been an increase in the number of these useful animals, of 13,138, and the value of good horses has also increased. As the country grows, and the condition of the population improves, it may be inferred that more horses are required for business and pleasure. More horses are now used in the cultivation of land, being better adapted than oxen for the cultivation of old lands where the fields have become level; oxen being principally used for rough and stony places.

NEAT CATTLE.—It is observable that the number is now less, by 5,064, than ten years since. There are, no doubt, more horses used now, where oxen were formerly employed for the same purpose; and in the Western part of the Province there are not so many cattle raised as formerly, either for working, or for market, for the reasons given in noticing the production of potatoes and the increase in that article, as more money has been made by selling potatoes, than would have been by raising and selling neat cattle.

COWS.—Milch cows have increased largely, and exceed the number in 1851, by 23,648. This increase is not confined to any particular County, but may be noticed in all. There is more demand for butter and cheese than formerly, as prices have advanced, and it is perhaps found more profitable to keep more cows and fewer neat cattle. A greater increase would ensue in butter and cheese, if more attention were paid to the comfortable housing of cows, and feeding them on more succulent food than is customary.

SHEEP.—There is an increase of 50,473 in these animals, so valuable on account of their wool and flesh, and the benefit of their manure to pasture lands. They are considered as profitable stock, and if greater care were taken to procure good breeds, and to feed and house more comfortably in winter, greater advantages would be derived than at present.

The following comparative statement shows the number of horses, neat cattle, cows, sheep and swine, owned in the Province in 1861, as compared with 1851:

Comparative Table of Live Stock for the years 1851 and 1861.

COUNTIES	Horses		Neat Cattle.		Milch Cows.		Sheep.		Swine.	
	1851.	1861.	1851.	1861.	1851.	1861.	1851.	1861.	1851.	1861.
1. Halifax	1742	2202	6456	7741	5185	9645	12845	16720	3605	3042
2. Colchester	3606	3923	15276	12585	7492	8249	22148	27494	4410	3737
3. Cumberland	2920	3253	11092	10514	5483	7074	20677	22122	4343	4266
4. Pictou	4563	4942	18892	19095	10039	13300	29930	30452	8234	5079
5. Sydney	1428	1605	9388	13000	6326	8769	20827	27113	2771	4651
6. Guysborough	659	1048	3211	5096	2810	3929	9495	11759	1928	2270
7. Inverness	2946	4596	11237	12608	8347	11906	24127	36143	3331	5483
8. Richmond	713	1611	2652	7628	2450	3437	8982	13793	973	1907
9. Victoria	2755	1537	13428	5051	10138	6997	28000	16825	3287	1849
10. Cape Breton		3007		6165		6762		24670		4075
11. Hants	2476	2919	10232	8293	8967	9974	16577	19655	3100	2309
12. King's	2981	2900	14876	11173	5216	5760	19384	18100	4603	3940
13. Annapolis	1914	2152	12946	10807	5159	6190	17424	19503	2622	2540
14. Digby	695	637	6063	5490	2568	3041	11709	10393	1323	1494
15. Yarmouth	692	801	6022	6162	3304	3940	12849	10936	1094	1616
16. Shelburne	351	282	3295	3019	2326	2417	9341	8361	1450	1255
17. Queen's	263	400	2231	3496	1555	2300	5540	4594	993	806
18. Lunenburg	669	691	9142	10491	3744	5855	11934	16780	2089	3190
	29199	45007	156472	151701	89856	110504	292580	329563	51533	52217

It has been observed, in copying the agricultural returns from the schedules made by the head of each family, how small the amount of stock and produce raised appears in many instances, from a given quantity of land, and how inadequate they must be for the support of families comprising a great many individuals. It is evident that in such cases, families derive a portion of their subsistence from other sources, and are not dependent entirely upon their farms, nor do they give their undivided attention to the cultivation of the soil. This shews that there is still great room for improvement, and that more attention should be devoted to that important branch of industry.

It may be noticed that there is a progressive improvement in many of the Eastern Counties, and that their productions are rapidly increasing, and that to the Westward considerable attention is being paid to raising fruit, which is becoming a profitable article of export.

FISHERIES.

In the early settlement of Nova Scotia, the various descriptions of fish, which form so large an item in the exports from this Province, abounded in the waters around its shores; and having, up to that period, been scarcely disturbed in their feeding grounds, they were taken with much greater facility, and with infinitely less labor than at the present time. But notwithstanding the increased difficulty in carrying on this branch of business, it is gratifying to know that it is still prosecuted with unabated ardor and increasing success, as will be seen from the following statement, shewing the advancement made since the returns furnished by the Census of 1851.

Comparative Table, showing the number of Vessels and Boats employed, and the quantities of Fish cured in Nova Scotia, as given in the Census Returns of 1851 and 1861.

COUNTIES.	Vessels 1851	Vessels 1861	Boats 1851	Boats 1861	Men Employed 1851	Men Employed 1861	Quintals Dry Fish 1851	1861	Bbls. of Mackerel 1851	1861	Bbls. Shad 1851	1861	Bbls. of Herring 1851	1861	Bbls. Alewives 1851	1861	Bbls. of Salmon 1851	1861	No. Smoked Salmon 1851	1861	Boxes of Herring 1851	1861
1. Halifax	96	175	1437	1939	1309	2366	14684	44645	29835	15137	1	456	5083	44199	182	968	25	360		758	93	307
2. Colchester	3		28	118	50	163	229	56		56	56	3691	112	387		437	15	33		74	300	43
3. Cumberland	3	4	25	89	41	98	680	260	36	44	145	652	678	752	162	1240	97	33		21	150	49
4. Pictou		3	6	81	13	34	34	757		268	563		50	1550	12	58	75	149		74		25
5. Sydney	6	3	180	213	179	297	1033	1382	1829	657		9	1250	1613	32	152	184	155		85		4
6. Guysborough	71	85	833	1080	1294	971	15834	29734	20054	12519	4	81	8460	36959	815	2700	601	829		30		44
7. Inverness	74	38	247	424	643	931	11901	23366	5401	718			2287	7617	2172	1671	193	147		23		31
8. Richmond	99	109	522	984	1316	1707	32255	53905	15373	7384	25		4398	9361	851	415	42	26		4	6	33
9. Victoria	21	3		413		333	21458	7513	9426	4303			6113	2352		29	344	213				
10. Cape Breton		23	654	679	1381	735		26429		30	28			4157	53	368		408	139		41	45
11. Hants	1		8	81	11	79	87	23		132	546	1078	340	86		151	6	3				70
12. King's	7	6	32	50	83	71	994	1088	2	107	856	1274	849	956	164	210	30	14		36	107	1808
13. Annapolis	6	3	62	184	105	118	602	2324	1088	6357	30	53	529	4333	16	77		30		103	2115	23040
14. Digby	34	56	82	295	281	707	10901	14114	1385	4688	50	209	5213	13717	10	11		1			7362	9309
15. Yarmouth	71	83	49	266	553	851	20270	38553	1128		43		1398	6455	611	1927		2	2	4630	9309
16. Shelburne	100	90	410	780	1373	1580	35417	61375	4610	3407		53	6680	23801	61	516	50	16	12	100	367
17. Queen's	27	55	110	278	457	794	8998	25110	1441	315	47		4880	5400		458		6	187	275	305
18. Lunenburg	196	158	458	909	1299	2487	21057	64791	9417	5999	43		4878	29665	202	1177	7	46	1178	30	77
	812	906	5161	8816	10394	14422	196643	396429	100047	66108	2536	7449	53200	194170	5343	12765	1669	2481		2738	15409	35557

Note.—The reader will remember that though the Census was taken in 1861, the return gives the number of vessels and boats employed, and the quantity of fish caught, in 1860.

In the year 1851, there were employed in the fisheries of the Province, 812 vessels, 5161 boats, and 10,394 men. The returns given by the present Census, shew that 900 vessels, 8816 boats, and 14,322 men, are engaged in prosecuting this important branch of industry, being an increase of 88 vessels, 3655 boats, and 3028 men; and they also shew that the quantity of fish cured has kept pace with the increased number of persons employed in the business. Of Dry Fish, there were cured in 1851, 196,434 quintals, and in 1860, 396,425 quintals, being 199,991 quintals more than were returned by the previous Census. Of Herrings, there were taken in the year 1851, 53,200 barrels, and in 1860, 194,170 barrels, the increase being 140,970 barrels. Of Alewives, there were taken in the year 1851, 5343 barrels, and in 1860, 12,565 barrels; the increase being 7,222 barrels. Of Shad, there were taken in 1851 3536, barrels, whilst the present returns shew, that of this valuable fish, 7,649 barrels have been secured; the increase, as compared with the former period, being 4,113 barrels. Of Smoked Herring, there were returned in 1851, as the produce of the fishery, 15,409 boxes; in 1860, the number of boxes cured amounted to 35,557, being an increase, as compared with the previous Census returns, of 20,148 boxes. The increase that has taken place in this branch of industry is not confined to a few Counties only; all parts of the Province in which the business has been carried on, having contributed their share in bringing about this result.

The only kind of fish in which there is a decrease of the catch, as compared with the returns of 1851, is the Mackerel. In that year there were caught 100,047 barrels, whilst the returns for the present Census shew but 66,108 barrels, the deficiency being 33,939 barrels; but this circumstance ought not to be regarded as any indication that this branch of the business is being prosecuted with any less vigor than heretofore, the migratory habits of this fish rendering the pursuit one of considerable uncertainty.

There are returned by the present Census 2481 barrels, and 2738 Smoked Salmon, against 1669 barrels for 1851, the increase being 812 barrels. There being no return of Smoked Salmon for the former year, I have no means of comparing the quantity cured in this way, as shewn by the present returns, with that of any former period. I may, however, remark here, that I do not think the quantity shewn by the present returns represents the entire catch of this valuable fish, as considerable numbers are sent during the season, fresh, to the United States from Halifax and some of the Western Counties.

Salmon are taken in the season, in every County in the Province, and it might be worthy of consideration whether inducements could be held out for the introduction into this country of the system of artificial breeding of this fish, which has been so successfully prosecuted in other places.

Gratifying as are the results of this enquiry, inasmuch as they shew so creditable an advance during the past decade, in our most important article of export, it must be borne in mind, that the success which has been achieved, has been almost exclusively with the inshore fishery—the deep sea or bank fishery being as yet, as far as this Province is concerned, almost wholly untouched.

LUMBER AND TIMBER.

These articles have always formed important items in the trade of the North American Colonies, both with the mother country, and in their interchanges with their Colonial brethren of more Southern climes. In Nova Scotia, when the land was to a large extent covered with the primeval forest, this business formed the winter occupation of a large portion of its inhabitants, and it is still pursued, to a greater or less extent, in most parts of the Province.

4

The Census Report for 1851 gave no return of the quantity of lumber manufactured at that time; I have therefore no data upon which to institute a comparison between the returns of the present Census and those of any previous period. A glance at these returns, however, will show the quantity manufactured last year, and the localities where the business is chiefly carried on. It will be seen that Cumberland returns the largest quantity of Deals, being more than two-thirds of all manufactured in the Province. Queen's returns the largest quantity of Pine boards, more than half of the whole quantity manufactured being from that County. The manufacture of Spruce and Hemlock lumber seems to be more evenly spread over the country than that of any other, as these woods, being of more rapid growth, and less sought after in the earlier periods of the timber trade than the Pine, now form a large portion of the Nova Scotia forests—Lunenburg supplies the largest proportion, the quantity being double that of any other County. Of square timber, Pictou, Colchester, and Halifax, return the largest proportion, the quantity from these three Counties being nearly one-half of all made in the Province during the Census year.

VESSELS.

From the situation of Nova Scotia on the Map of the American continent, and its almost insular position, maritime pursuits have, from an early period in its history, formed the occupation of a large portion of its population; and though she cannot compare with some of the other North American Colonies as regards the number of vessels built for sale in other countries, yet, no mean comparison might be instituted, as regards the number owned by her people, and sailed by them in most parts of the world. But, as the object of a work of this kind is more particularly to show the advancement or retrogression in the different branches of productive industry, made within given periods of time, I shall content myself with giving such information, from the materials I have at hand, as may facilitate the labors of others, who may choose to enter upon these enquiries.

I was desirous at the commencement of this work, of getting, through the Enumerators, the number of vessels and the amount of tonnage owned throughout the Province; but from the fact of many of the vessels being owned in small shares by a number of persons, some of whom resided in different polling districts from the others, I had not sufficient confidence in the accuracy of returns that might be furnished in this way, to warrant me in making it obligatory upon the Enumerators to supply them. Upon enquiry at the office of the Registry of Shipping, in Halifax, I found that no more accurate information could be afforded me respecting the shipping in this port, than was supplied for the Trade Returns, as given to the Legislature last year, and it was inferred that this would apply equally to the other ports of the Province; I have therefore appended a statement from those returns, showing the number of vessels owned, with the amount of tonnage, at that time.

Statement of the number and tonnage of Vessels registered in Nova Scotia, on 30th September, 1860.

PORTS.	Vessels Registered.	
	No.	Tons.
Annapolis	10	826
Arichat	264	16031
Baddeck	4	170
Digby	212	15768
Guysborough	64	3195
Halifax	1581	78696
Liverpool	136	10514
Lunenburg	163	6732
Parrsborough	64	5543
Pictou	141	21503
Pugwash	5	378
Shelburne	27	1467
Ship Harbor	16	656
Sydney, C. B.	77	4408
Windsor	196	29058
Yarmouth	158	39798
	3118	234743

These returns can only be regarded as an approximation to the amount of tonnage owned at that time in the Province, though sufficiently accurate for most practical purposes, inasmuch as there may have been vessels sold or lost, that had not been reported to the department.

The returns for the present Census will show the state of the ship-building trade, as compared with 1851. In that year there were returned, as having been built within the previous 12 months, 486 vessels, of the aggregate tonnage of 57,776. Since that period, owing to heavy losses sustained, consequent upon fluctuations peculiarly incident to this branch of business, there has been a falling off in the number of vessels built, and the present returns show that but 211 vessels, whose aggregate tonnage is 26,049, were launched in 1860. But the number returned as being in the course of building on the 30th of March last, would seem to indicate a revival in the business, as there were 295 vessels, estimated to measure in the aggregate 47,922 tons, on the stocks. The Counties which have returned the largest amount of tonnage as building, are Hants, which returns 7220 tons, and Yarmouth, which returns 6381 tons.

I have now brought this work to a close, and though defects and inaccuracies may be discovered in it, I have spared no pains to make it as perfect as the means at my disposal would enable me to do. If not altogether such as was expected, it must be borne in mind that this was a first attempt to make a complete Census of the Province; and I trust the information obtained has been put in such a shape, as to make it available to all who may have occasion to consult the work, and that sufficient materials have been collected to enable those who may be engaged in a subsequent work of this kind, to trace with greater accuracy the operation of those causes that have tended to advance or retard the prosperity of the the country.

Respectfully submitting the above,
I have the honor to be,
Gentlemen,
Your obedient humble servant,
STEPHEN FULTON,
Secretary.

APPENDICES

TO THE

REPORT

OF THE

SECRETARY OF THE BOARD OF STATISTICS

ON THE

CENSUS OF NOVA SCOTIA.

1861.

TABLE OF CONTENTS.

PERSONAL CENSUS

BY AGES.

No. 1.—PERSONAL CENSUS

COUNTY OF

POLLING DISTRICTS.	Males.	Females.	Total.	Number of Families.	Average Number of each Family.	Under one year of age. M.	F.	Deaths under 1 yr. age since 30th March, 1860. M.	F.
	1	2	3	4	5	6	7	8	9
1. Ward 1, (City.)	1881	2318	4199	718		54	63	1	4
2. do. 2. do.	1731	1925	3656	560		42	41	1	1
3. do. 3. do.	1690	1900	3590	671		49	39	3	4
4. do. 4. do.	1235	1311	2546	526		35	39	4	1
5. do. 5. do. { 1st Section	1635	1875	3510	626		54	49	4	4
2nd do	2233	2477	4710	897		64	58	2	3
6. do. 6. do.	1375	1440	2815	471		37	38	2	3
Total in City.	11780	13246	25026	4469	5.60	335	327	17	20
7. Ferguson's Cove	398	323	721	119		11	9		
8. Portuguese Cove	339	311	650	104		5	14		1
9. Sambro	316	254	570	96		15	8		1
10. Prospect	741	629	1370	207		28	31	1	1
11. Haggets Cove	498	482	980	142		10	24	1	1
12. French Village	383	332	715	105		15	14	1	
13. Drysdales	181	193	374	55		3	5		1
14. North West Arm	171	159	330	60		7	7		
15. Piers' Mill	195	203	398	61		9	1	1	
16. Hammond's Plains	398	372	770	139		17	16		2
17. Windsor Road	427	387	814	140		9	8	1	
18. Truro Road	296	290	586	96		5	5	1	
19. Gay's River	315	301	616	100		5	8		1
20. Wise's Corner	296	260	556	90		10	11		1
21. Middle Musquodoboit	608	575	1183	209		24	6	1	
22. Upper Musquodoboit	478	457	935	158		11	20		
23. Caledonia	123	107	230	36		3		1	1
24. Salmon River	503	450	953	148		15	4	4	
25. Sheet Harbor	352	322	674	103		20	20	1	
26. Pope's Harbor	602	539	1141	157		11	22	2	1
27. Jeddore	965	895	1860	284		28	24		3
28. Chezetcook	893	870	1763	291		29	24	3	1
29. Lawrencetown	236	226	462	69		6	6		
30. Preston	313	328	641	130		11	16	2	2
31. Dartmouth	1487	1668	3155	559		45	49	3	
32. Black Point	429	366	795	127		18	13	2	
33. Eastern Passage	378	375	753	130		9	9		1
	24101	24920	49021	8384	5.84	714	701	42	38

COUNTY OF

	1	2	3	4	5	6	7	8	9
1. Truro	1457	1477	2934	502		56	46	2	5
2. Old Barns	461	466	927	170		14	16		1
3. Lower Stewiacke	835	753	1588	265		15	14	1	3
4. Upper Stewiacke	918	931	1849	319		37	28	2	2
5. Upper Onslow and Kemptown	770	810	1580	277		23	30	1	1
6. Onslow	393	379	771	148		8	19		
7. Earltown	596	620	1216	195		8	22		
8. New Annan	610	621	1231	189		14	23	1	1
9. Waugh's River	589	564	1153	178		21	18	1	
10. Tatamagouche	735	665	1400	208		13	17	2	4
11. Upper Londonderry	822	751	1573	278		26	22		
12. Lower Londonderry	1100	1032	2132	370		30	34		
13. Economy and Five Islands	878	813	1691	288		23	24	3	
	10163	9882	20045	3387	5.91	297	313	13	17

BY AGES...1860—61.

HALIFAX.

Over 1 and under 2 yrs. of age.		Deaths between 1 and 2 years, since 30th M'h, 1860.		Over 2 and under 3 years of age.		Deaths between 2 and 3 years, since M'ch 30, 1860.		Over 3 and under 4 years of age.		Deaths between 3 and 4 years, since M'ch 30, 1860.		Over 4 and under 5 years of age.		Deaths between 4 and 5 years, since M'ch 30, 1860.	
M.	F.	M.	F.	M.	F.	M.	F.	M.	F.	M.	F.	M.	F.	M.	F.
10	11	12	13	14	15	16	17	18	19	20	21	22	23	24	25
57	45		1	49	57	1		68	38	1		52	47		1
36	32	2	1	29	52			40	44	1		34	43		
35	45	•1	1	26	34	1	1	30	56			38	28	1	
34	37	1	1	23	34	1	2	32	36		1	32	23	1	
45	48		2	53	42			55	51	2		41	42	1	
66	67	2		58	48	1	2	54	55	2		57	43	1	1
29	32	2	3	33	37		1	35	28			33	32		
302	306	8	9	271	304	4	6	314	308	6	1	287	258	4	2
7	2			14	6			16	9			11	9		
9	13	1	1	12	12			12	12			17	11		
10	8			9	11			11	4			14	8		
14	15		1	20	25		1	25	23			28	20		
12	22			13	18	2	1	14	21		1	18	20		
10	16			18	12		1	11	10			15	12		
4	7			5	6			4	5			6	5		
5	5			6	8			4	6			4			
5	8			4	2			9	5			6	3		
13	14	2		19	11		1	14	15			10	13		
15	15			17	9			11	11			11	12		
13	15			12	6		1	11	13	1		8	8		
8	12			13	8			7	13			9	8		
3	8			17	16			9	4			11	7	2	
22	18	1	1	18	17		1	24	25	2		10	18	1	
21	10	1		15	18	2		20	19	1	1	10	12		
2	4			4	1			5	1			3	4		
17	10			17	14		1	20	11			14	21	1	
10	8			13	10			11	5			14	14		
20	24			20	18		3	24	15			23	17		
32	29	1	1	42	25	1		30	30			29	22	1	
29	29			36	30	1	1	27	32		1	31	30	1	
8	6			5	6			7	5			5	4	1	
5	4		1	14	16		1	13	9			14	10		
35	36		2	45	37			49	38	2		34	44		
14	12		1	12	14		1	17	10		2	17	12		1
9	17	1	2	13	13		1	12	16	1		13	13		1
654	673	15	19	704	673	10	20	731	675	13	6	672	615	11	4

COLCHESTER.

M.	F.	M.	F.	M.	F.	M.	F.	M.	F.	M.	F.	M.	F.	M.	F.
45	43	1	1	38	38		1	40	33	1	2	43	31		1
17	15	1		14	19			19	18	1		6	14		
36	28			20	25	1		28	23		1	17	17		
19	29	1	2	20	36	1		26	17	1	1	25	33	1	3
29	27	1		22	40			21	26			22	23		
15	10	2	1	14	7		1	8	13			15	8		
15	12			20	20			16	16			7	16		
18	22		2	25	18	1		21	19	1		17	25	1	
19	16			17	13	1		20	24	1	1	21	16		
12	23			27	21	1	1	27	21			27	17		
18	23	4	3	29	20	1		14	23	1		19	22	1	
35	33	2		33	31	3	3	40	38		1	34	20	1	2
36	21			30	19			24	25			21	26	1	2
314	303	12	9	309	307	7	6	304	296	6	6	274	268	5	7

No. 1.—PERSONAL CENSUS

COUNTY OF

POLLING DISTRICTS.	Over 5 and under 10 years of age.		Deaths between 5 and 10 y'rs. since M'ch 80, 1880.		Over 10 and under 15 years of age.				Deaths since M'ch 80, 1880.	
					Males.		Females.			
	M.	F.	M.	F.	MD.	S.	MD.	S.	M.	F.
	26	27	28	29	30	31	32	33	34	35
1. Ward 1. (City)	238	212	3	3		217		219	1	
2. do. 2. do.	192	178	2	1		196		175	1	
3. do. 3. do.	189	206		2		214		225		1
4. do. 4. do.	143	139		1		142		140	1	
5. do. 5. do. { 1st Section	223	203		1		170		194		
{ 2d do.	266	286	3	2		276		272		
6. do. 6. do.	171	160	1			190		156		
Total in City	1421	1384	9	10		1405		1381	3	1
7. Ferguson's Cove	52	41				42		50		
8. Portuguese Cove	53	49				48		37		
9. Sambro	51	33				42		30		
10. Prospect	116	96	1			89		73	2	
11. Hagget's Cove	73	79		1		79		66	1	
12. French Village	59	54				60		38		
13. Drysdales	32	30				24		23		
14. North West Arm	31	20	2			18		25	2	
15. Piers' Mills	27	26	1			31		30		
16. Hammonds Plains	57	65	2	2		53		51	1	1
17. Windsor Road	45	46				50		36		
18. Truro Road	35	55				33		30		1
19. Guy's River	45	51				48		38		
20. Wise's Corner	49	38				36		33	1	1
21. Middle Musquodoboit	97	77	3	5		78		61	3	8
22. Upper Musquodoboit	67	56	1	1		61		62		
33. Caledonia	16	16				13		11		
24. Salmon River	65	72				68		54		
25. Sheet Harbor	45	46				40		42		
26. Pope's Harbor	102	85	1	5		89		62		
27. Jeddore	139	147	1			115		125		
28. Chezetcook	117	125	1	4		128		108	1	1
29. Lawrencetown	28	31				43		39		
30. Preston	42	44	3			38		47		1
31. Dartmouth	208	204				176		181		
32. Black Point	69	69				62		51		
33. Eastern Passage	57	61	1			54		44		
	3197	3100	26	28		3023		2827	14	14

COUNTY OF

1. Truro	176	197		1		175		179		
2. Old Barns	64	63		1		55		60		
3. Lower Stewiacke	109	112	2	1		104		91		
4. Upper Stewiacke	117	124	3			118		109	1	1
5. Upper Onslow and Kemptown	102	108	1	1		100		97		2
6. Onslow	49	43	1	1		46		38		
7. Earltown	74	68	1	2		80		68		1
8. New Annan	80	98				73		78		2
9. Waugh's River	89	89	3	1		86	1	72		
10. Tatamagouche	123	88	1			108		104	1	
11. Upper Londonderry	117	99	1	1		100		85		1
12. Lower Londonderry	142	144	1	3		149		130	2	
13. Economy and Five Islands	115	105	4	2		95		102		
	1357	1338	18	14		1289	1	1213	4	7

BY AGES...1860—61.

HALIFAX, Continued.

Over 15 and under 20 years of age.								Over 20 and under 30 years of age.							
Males.			Females.			Deaths since M'ch 30, 1860.		Males.			Females.			Deaths since March 30, 1860.	
MD.	S.	WDR	MD.	S.	WD.	M.	F.	MD.	S.	WDR	MD.	S.	WD.	M.	F.
36	37	38	39	40	41	42	43	44	45	46	47	48	49	50	51
	188		3	305			1	81	224		164	364	17	2	4
	176		4	235		3	1	64	228	1	104	289	3	2	5
	227		4	234			2	69	236	1	118	224	13	3	
	160		8	141		1		73	171	2	115	136	11	1	1
	186		6	216				73	200	3	149	240	9	1	1
	247		5	325			3	134	273	1	214	271	5	5	3
	158		4	160		1	2	43	156	1	89	185	7	1	3
	1342		34	1616		5	9	537	1488	9	953	1709	65	15	17
	51			41				15	67		29	30	1		
	28		1	24				10	41	1	35	24	1		
	32		4	22			1	23	20		33	10	1		
	87		4	75	1	1		43	90	2	59	46	3	2	
	57		5	43	1			21	52		40	34			
	38		3	33				20	32		24	21			
	21		4	21				17	13		16	17	5		
	18		2	12				8	16		14	10			
	13			28			1	8	12		9	28	1		
	52		6	29	1	1	3	21	36		28	13	1	3	1
	50		2	41	1			12	50		34	39			1
	26		1	24				14	45	1	13	31			1
	33			31				5	29		17	29			
	32			28			1	10	26	1	23	16	1		1
	64		3	67		2	1	24	55	1	41	60		4	3
	60			43				20	43		36	40	1		2
	11			12				2	21		8	14			
	60			50				13	66		32	47			1
	25		2	25		1		15	58		30	25	1		
1	68		4	69		1	2	32	73		43	41	2	5	2
	112		6	79		1		46	104	1	82	61	1	2	
	98		5	120		2	1	41	88	2	70	67	1	3	2
	31			35				9	19		18	15			2
	35			27		3		15	24	1	17	17			2
1	166		9	198		1		67	153		123	200	5	1	
	49		5	29				30	27	2	42	7	1	1	
	28		1	43				20	40		38	16	1		
2	2087		10	2865	2	19	19	1098	2788	21	1907	2667	92	36	35

COLCHESTER, Continued.

Over 15 and under 20 years of age.								Over 20 and under 30 years of age.							
Males.			Females.			Deaths since M'ch 30, 1860.		Males.			Females.			Deaths since March 30, 1860.	
MD.	S.	WDR	MD.	S.	WD.	M.	F.	MD.	S.	WDR	MD.	S.	WD.	M.	F.
2	170		4	195	1	1		86	173		111	155	2	2	
	45			43				26	47	1	47	29			
	115		9	75		1	1	36	108		48	72	2	3	
	113			96		2		36	115	2	67	104			7
	81		1	81				30	86		59	62	2	2	
	43		1	37		1		20	42		36	35	1	1	
	69			53				13	100	1	34	94			
	77		1	51		1		28	84		46	58		1	3
2	55		5	62				24	66		33	60	1		2
	96		1	62				22	85		50	74	1	1	
	85		1	73		1	4	40	110	1	58	69		1	2
	116		7	117		2	3	49	119	1	94	71	2	4	2
1	116		5	91				58	96		88	74		2	2
5	1181		35	1036	1	9	8	468	1231	6	771	957	11	17	18

POLLING DISTRICTS.	Over 30 and under 40 years of age.							
	Males.			Females.			Deaths since March 30, 1860.	
	MD.	S.	WDR	MD.	S.	WD.	M.	F.
	52	53	54	55	56	57	58	59
1. Ward 1. (City)	198	44	3	208	88	23	2	
2. do. 2. do.	121	71	8	163	85	21		
3. do. 3. do.	122	49	4	169	56	34	4	1
4. do. 4. do.	103	24	2	110	24	23	2	
5. do. 5. do. { 1st Section	164	30	4	164	43	31		
2d do.	183	47	9	196	54	32	1	1
6. do. 6. do.	122	24	4	132	37	17	1	
Total in City	1013	289	34	1142	387	181	10	2
7. Ferguson's Cove	32	9		29	2	2		
8. Portuguese Cove	34	7		27	2			
9. Sambro	28	1	1	29	3	1		
10. Prospect	52	21	5	55	5	2		
11. Hagget's Cove	57	7	1	47	4	4	1	
12. French Village	33	6	1	34	6			
13. Drysdale's	16	2		14		1		
14. North West Arm	13	2	1	14	1	1	1	
15. Piers' Mills	14	10		19				
16. Hammonds Plains	41	5		29	6	4	1	
17. Windsor Road	35	19	2	28	11	1		
18. Truro Road	24	9		33	3			1
19. Gay's River	18	10	2	18	3	1		
20. Wise's Corner	23	7	1	23	1	1		
21. Middle Musquodoboit	54	13		58	18	2		
22. Upper Musquodoboit	48	5	1	52	11	1		1
23. Caledonia	13	10		9	8			
24. Salmon River	38	12		38	5	2		
25. Sheet Harbor	35	5	1	31	3	3		
26. Pope's Harbor	51	6		56	4	4	2	
27. Jeddore	88	8	1	83	12	5	2	1
28. Chezetcooke	82	9	4	82	5	6	2	2
29. Lawrenctown	13	5	1	12	3	1	1	1
30. Preston	25	5		36	4		1	
31. Dartmouth	121	21	3	131	34	9		
32. Black Point	37	4		42	9	1		
33. Eastern Passage	44	6	3	34	7	2		
	2082	513	62	2205	557	235	21	8

	MD.	S.	WDR	MD.	S.	WD.	M.	F.
1. Truro	112	32	4	132	29	2	2	1
2. Old Barns	44	4	2	50	7	2		
3. Lower Stewiacke	70	15	2	68	19	5	1	
4. Upper Stewiacke	79	13	3	80	16	4		1
5. Upper Onslow and Kemptown	76	12		61	19	1	2	1
6. Onslow	43	4	2	33	7		1	1
7. Earltown	38	22		41	35	4		
8. New Annan	51	6	1	58	15	1		1
9. Waugh's River	48	10	2	51	12	1	1	1
10. Tatamagouche	54	10	1	56	11	3	1	
11. Upper Londonderry	68	21		74	15	3	1	
12. Lower Londonderry	109	18	3	100	18	7	1	
13. Economy and Five Islands	84	13		82	12	1		
	876	180	20	886	215	34	10	6

BY AGES...1860—61.

HALIFAX, Continued.

Over 40 and under 50 years of age.								Over 50 and under 60 years of age.							
Males.			Females.			Deaths since March 30, 1860.		Males.			Females.			Deaths since March 30, 1860.	
MD.	S.	WDR	MD.	S.	WD.	M.	F.	MD.	S.	WDR	MD.	S.	WD.	M.	F.
60	61	62	63	64	65	66	67	68	69	70	71	72	73	74	75
147	14	9	119	42	29	2		109	8	8	69	13	43		
140	30	15	109	40	40		2	77	28	19	65	23	42	3	
130	23	7	125	25	43	1	1	108	12	10	65	14	31	3	2
95	11	5	88	9	34	1	1	55	9	16	45	7	36	2	1
144	11	7	115	27	32	3	3	76	6	8	58	15	27	1	3
177	19	8	161	24	43	5	1	110	9	14	101	15	41	1	
97	13	3	83	12	18	2		73	10	4	66	14	13	1	2
930	120	54	800	179	239	14	8	608	82	79	469	101	233	11	8
15	2	1	21	1	5			27	2	1	19		4		
23	3		20	1	1	1		15	2	2	11		1		
29	2		19		2	1	1	10		2	9		4		
46	4	2	47		4	1	1	32	4	1	13		5		
34	2	4	23	2	1	2		17	1		13	1	1		
23	1		22	1	1			12		3	12		4		
10	1		9		1			8		1	11		1		
12		1	13	4	1	1		10		2	6		1		1
20	1	1	22					10	1		4		1		
18	2	1	25	1	2	3		15		1	11	1	4		
33	1	1	35		4		1	21		1	13	4	2	1	
18	1		20	1	2			14		4	9	3	5		2
25	4		23	1	2		1	18	4	1	15	1	1		
17	4	1	19	1	2		1	18		1	8		4	1	
42	6	2	33	3	4	1		30	3	1	26	4	5		
32	3		32	1	3		2	25		1	15		3		1
5			6	3				5	1		6	1			
36	3	2	28	6	2		1	23		1	23		7		
22	1	1	19	6	2	1		12	2		6	1	5		
35			25		5			15	2	2	17		4	1	1
60	8	1	53	2	4	1		43	4	2	43	3	5		
56	8	6	49	3	2	4	1	42	1	3	33	1	4	2	1
16	3		21	1	2			18	1		10	1	2		
19	1		21	2	3			10		2	10		5		
126	14	5	123	16	18		1	88	10	1	56	10	27		
25	2	2	17		1			16	1		11				
20	4	1	18	3	4	1		15	5	2	14		4		2
1747	201	86	1563	238	317	31	18	1177	126	114	893	132	342	16	16

COLCHESTER, Continued.

MD.	S.	WDR	MD.	S.	WD.	M.	F.	MD.	S.	WDR	MD.	S.	WD.	M.	F.
100	9	1	107	18	6			75	9	3	61	2	10	2	
44	6	1	27	5	2			13	1	2	19	4	1		
46	5	1	41	5	5	1		33	6	5	34	5	7		
64	5	3	64	6	5	2	1	46	1	2	42	1	11		
61	1	1	57	11	1			40	3	1	32	11	8		
24	1	2	32	3	2			27	1	1	18	4	4	2	
35	5	1	28	7	6	1		24	2	3	25	6	5		
38			26	1	3			28			26	3	4		
36	3	1	28	4	2		1	23	2	2	20	2	5		
52	2	4	47	4	5			29	1	4	19	1	7		1
50	5	3	49	7	5			51	8	2	38	4	7		1
92	6	2	77	10	6			44	4	3	30	3	11	1	
53	7	1	41	8	2			39	1	3	40	1	8		1
695	55	21	624	89	50	4	2	472	39	31	404	47	88	5	3

No. 1.—PERSONAL CENSUS

COUNTY OF

Over 60 and under 70 years of age.

POLLING DISTRICT.	Males.			Females.			Deaths since March 30, 1860.	
	MD.	S.	WDR	MD.	S.	WD.	M.	F.
	76	77	78	79	80	81	82	83
1. Ward 1. (City)	64	8	10	38	11	53	2	2
2. do. 2. do.	74	24	33	30	7	38	1	
3. do. 3. do.	57	2	13	34	5	45	2	1
4. do. 4. do.	37	3	4	15	1	27	3	2
5. do. 5. do. { 1st Section	42	3	8	27	4	36	1	
2d do.	101	8	14	43	7	50	3	4
6. do. 6. do.	50	6	7	24	5	24		3
Total in City	425	54	89	211	40	273	12	12
7. Ferguson's Cove	14		1	6		2		
8. Portuguese Cove	10	1		3		4	1	
9. Sambro	6	1	4	3	1	2		
10. Prospect	14	2	1	11	1	1	1	
11. Hagget's Cove	8		2	6		1		
12. French Village	12	2	3	6		4	1	
13. Drysdale's	4	2		8	1	3		
14. North West Arm	7	1	2	4		2		1
15. Piers' Mills	7	1	1	5	2	3		
16. Hammonds Plains	10	1	2	8	1	1		
17. Windsor Road	12	4	2	8		8	1	
18. Truro Road	7	2	5	3		5	1	1
19. Gay's River	12	2	1	10		1		
20. Wise's Corner	7		2	7	1	1	1	
21. Middle Musquodoboit	21		5	13		2	1	1
22. Upper Musquodoboit	14	1	3	11	2	3		1
23. Caledonia	3		1	1		1		
24. Salmon River	19		3	10	2	2	2	
25. Sheet Harbor	11	1	1	9		3	1	
26. Pope's Harbor	12	1	4	6	1	8		
27. Jeddore	40	1	6	16	2	6	1	1
28. Chezetcooke	25		8	12	3	9		1
29. Lawrencetown	8	2	3	1	2	1		
30. Preston	11		2	10	1	10		1
31. Dartmouth	63	6	12	39	4	37	1	
32. Black Point	17	2		8	1	3	1	
33. Eastern Passage	13	3	2	7	2	1		
	812	90	165	442	67	404	25	19

COUNTY OF

	76	77	78	79	80	81	82	83
1. Truro	62	6	8	36	2	13	1	1
2. Old Barns	16		2	6	2	5		1
3. Lower Stewiacke	37	6	3	25				
4. Upper Stewiacke	36	2	10	23	3	8		2
5. Upper Onslow and Kemptown	24	4	7	24	3	7	2	4
6. Onslow	15	1		11	4	5		
7. Earltown	28	1	4	23	4	10	1	
8. New Annan	24	2	3	21	2	7		1
9. Waugh's River	19	2	1	12		3	1	
10. Tatamagouche	21	1	3	11	1	9	1	
11. Upper Londonderry	26	3	7	23	2	7		1
12. Lower Londonderry	30	5	2	24	1	3	1	
13. Economy and Five Islands	32		3	21	1	2		
	370	33	53	260	25	86	7	10

BY AGES...1860—61.

HALIFAX, Continued.

	Over 70 and under 80 years of age.							Over 80 and under 90 years of age.							
	Males.			Females.		Deaths since March 30, 1860.		Males.			Females.			Deaths since March 30, 1860.	
MD.	S.	WDR	MD.	S.	WD.	M.	F.	MD.	S.	WDR	MD.	S.	WD.	M.	F.
84	85	86	87	88	89	90	91	92	93	94	95	96	97	98	99
16	3	7	2	2	27	2	....	....	....	3	1	1	7	1	....
15	10	14	6	4	36	1	1	4	1	8	1	1	9	....	....
22	4	4	6	1	11	1	3	1	1	1	2	1	4	1	1
9	2	7	4	....	21	2	1	....	1	4	....	....	4	....	....
14	2	7	7	3	26	2	2	1	....	....	3	....	9	....	1
21	1	8	8	4	31	5	1	4	....	2	1	1	10	....	....
14	3	5	5	3	20	1	1	1	1	....	....	....	1	....	....
111	25	52	38	17	172	14	9	11	4	21	5	4	43	3	2
5	1	....	1	....	2	....	....	....	....	....	....	2	....	....	....
3	....	1	4	....	2	....	....	2	....	....	....	....	2	....	....
4	....	1	3	....	5	1	....	....	....	....	....	....	1	....	....
6	5	2	3	....	8	1	1	1	....	1	....	....	....	2	1
5	....	4	3	....	1	....	....	....	1	1	....	....	1	....	....
6	1	....	1	....	....	....	....	....	1	....	....	....	3	1	....
7	....	1	....	....	1	....	....	....	....	....	....	....	....	....	....
1	....	2	....	....	3	....	....	....	....	....	....	....	....	....	....
3	....	2	3	....	3	....	....	....	....	....	....	....	....	1	....
5	....	3	3	....	6	....	1	....	....	1	1	....	2	1	....
10	2	3	3	1	5	....	1	....	....	1	1	....	....	....	....
3	....	3	2	....	2	....	....	2	....	1	1	....	....	1	....
10	....	2	7	....	2	1	....	4	....	....	1	....	....	1	....
6	1	2	4	....	1	....	....	2	....	....	....	....	1	....	1
6	1	4	5	....	6	3	1	3	....	....	1	....	2	....	....
9	....	3	3	....	2	1	....	1	1	....	1	....	....	1	....
2	....	2	1	....	....	....	....	....	....	....	....	....	....	....	....
4	....	3	4	....	3	....	....	1	....	2	....	....	3	....	1
4	1	1	2	....	1	....	....	2	....	....	....	....	1	....	....
7	1	2	2	1	3	2	....	....	....	1	....	....	1	....	....
15	2	1	8	....	7	1	1	2	....	3	1	....	4	....	1
9	1	8	5	1	6	1	1	1	....	2	....	....	2	....	....
1	....	1	2	....	....	....	....	1	....	....	....	....	1	....	....
19	....	3	7	....	8	....	1	2	....	1	1	....	2	....	....
18	1	11	11	4	16	1	....	2	....	5	....	....	6	....	....
4	....	1	3	....	2	....	....	1	....	....	....	....	2	....	....
4	....	1	2	....	5	....	....	....	....	1	....	....	....	1	....
287	42	119	130	24	272	26	16	36	8	41	12	4	77	12	6

COLCHESTER, Continued.

84	85	86	87	88	89	90	91	92	93	94	95	96	97	98	99
18	2	7	9	2	5	....	2	1	1	2	2	1	4	....	2
8	....	2	4	1	4	....	....	2	....	2	....	....	....	....	1
8	....	4	4	....	10	....	....	3	....	....	....	....	1	....	....
14	1	4	7	3	8	2	....	2	....	1	1	1	5	1	....
12	1	5	9	....	4	1	1	3	1	1	1	....	3	1	....
5	....	1	2	....	3	1	....	1	....	3	1	....	2	....	....
14	1	1	8	3	4	....	....	7	....	....	1	....	1	....	1
14	....	2	5	1	1	....	....	2	....	....	1	1	....	....	1
4	....	4	5	....	4	1	....	2	1	1	1	....	2	....	....
5	1	....	3	....	4	....	....	1	....	....	2	....	2	....	....
11	2	3	5	1	9	1	1	3	....	1	1	....	5	2	3
11	....	6	4	....	10	....	....	3	....	2	1	....	4	....	....
15	2	4	5	....	3	....	....	1	....	3	....	....	3	....	....
139	10	43	70	11	69	6	4	30	3	17	12	3	32	4	8

No. 1.—PERSONAL CENSUS

COUNTY OF

POLLING DISTRICT.	Males.			Females.			Deaths since March 30, 1860.	
	MD.	S.	WDR	MD.	S.	WD.	M.	F.
	100	101	102	103	104	105	106	107
1. Ward 1. (City)							1	1
2. do. 2. do.					1			
3. do. 3. do.			1			1		
4. do. 4. do.						1		1
5. do. 5. do. ⎰ 1st Section								
⎱ 2d do.	1		2			2		
6. do. 6. do.				1		2		
Total in City	1	1	2		7	6	1	1
7. Ferguson's Cove								
8. Portuguese Cove	1							
9. Sambro								
10. Prospect								
11. Hagget's Cove								
12. French Village				1		1		
13. Drysdale's								
14. North West Arm								
15. Piers' Mills								
16. Hammonds Plains					1		2	2
17. Windsor Road					1			
18. Truro Road								
19. Gay's River								
20. Wise's Corner						1		
21. Middle Musquodoboit								
22. Upper Musquodoboit								
23. Caledonia								
24. Salmon River								
25. Sheet Harbor						1		
26. Pope's Harbor								
27. Jeddore				1		1	1	
28. Chezetcooke				1		2		2
29. Lawrencetown								
30. Preston								
31. Dartmouth						1		
32. Black Point								
33. Eastern Passage								
	2	1	6	1	1	14	3	3

COUNTY OF

1. Truro	1						1	
2. Old Barns	1		1				1	
3. Lower Stewiacke				1				
4. Upper Stewiacke								
5. Upper Onslow and Kemptown								
6. Onslow								
7. Earltown	2		1			1		
8. New Annan						1		
9. Waugh's River	1							
10. Tatamagouche			1					
11. Upper Londonderry						2	1	
12. Lower Londonderry	1		1	1				
13. Economy and Five Islands			1			1		
	6		6	1		4	3	

BY AGES. 1860—61.

HALIFAX, Continued.

	Over 100 years of age.							Ages not given		Deaths. Ages not given		Males			
	Males.			Females.		Deaths since M'ch 30, 1860.						Married	Single	Widowers	Total
MD.	S.	WDR.	MD.	S.	WD.	M.	F.	M.	F.	M.	F.				
108	109	110	111	112	113	114	115	116	117	118	119	120	121	122	123
								2	7		2	614	1227	40	1881
				2				1	2			495	1138	98	1731
								5	3			509	1141	40	1690
								1	3			372	823	40	1235
								3	2			515	1080	40	1635
									4			731	1445	57	2233
								52	37	1		404	946	25	1375
				2				64	58	1	2	3640	7800	340	11780
								2	2			108	287	3	398
												98	237	4	339
												100	208	8	316
												194	533	14	741
								5	2			143	343	12	498
												106	269	8	383
												62	117	2	181
												51	112	8	171
												62	129	4	195
												110	270	9	398
1								9	9			128	289	10	427
												82	200	14	296
												92	217	6	315
												83	205	8	296
												180	415	13	608
								3				150	320	8	478
								1				31	89	3	123
												135	357	11	503
								1	1			101	247	4	352
											1	153	440	9	602
								1	9			295	654	16	965
								1	4			256	603	34	893
						1		2	1			66	164	6	236
							1	1				102	202	9	313
		1					1	1	2			485	964	38	1487
									1			130	294	5	429
												115	254	9	378
1		1				3	3	*91	†89	1		37258	16228	615	24101

COLCHESTER, Continued.

						1						457	975	25	1457
								2	3			155	293	13	461
								2	1			234	585	16	835
								4				278	615	25	918
								1	2			246	509	15	770
								1				136	247	9	392
								6	5			162	422	12	596
								2	4			186	417	7	610
								7	2			159	419	11	589
								4	1			186	535	14	735
								1				248	557	17	822
								1	1	1		340	740	20	1100
								4	2			283	580	15	878
						1		†35	§20	1		3070	6894	199	10163

* 14 md., 77 s. † 16 md., 89 s., 4 wd. ‡ 28 md., 11 s., 1 wdr. § 11 md., 9 s.

No. 1.—PERSONAL CENSUS

COUNTY OF

POLLING DISTRICTS.	Females.				Grand Total.	Deaths.		
	Married.	Single.	Widows.	Total.		Males.	Females.	Total.
	124	125	126	127	128	129	130	131
1. Ward 1. (City)	604	1514	200	2318	4199	19	18	37
2. do. 2. do.	482	1252	191	1925	3656	17	12	29
3. do. 3. do.	523	1195	182	1900	3590	21	20	41
4. do. 4. do.	386	767	158	1311	2546	20	12	32
5. do. 5. do. { 1st Section...	527	1178	170	1875	3510	15	18	33
{ 2d do.	730	1533	214	2477	4710	31	21	52
6. do. 6. do.	407	932	101	1440	2815	14	18	32
Total in City......	3659	8371	1216	13246	25026	137	119	256
Poors' Asylum						50	18	68
7. Ferguson's Cove	105	201	17	323	721			
8. Portuguese Cove...............	101	199	11	311	650	3	2	5
9. Sambro.	100	138	16	254	570	2	3	5
10. Prospect......................	192	410	27	629	1370	12	6	18
11. Hagget's Cove.................	138	335	9	482	980	7	4	11
12. French Village................	102	217	13	332	715	3	1	4
13. Drysdales.....................	62	119	12	193	374		1	1
14. North West Arm...............	53	98	8	159	330	6	2	8
15. Piers' Mills..................	62	133	8	203	398	3	1	4
16. Hammonds Plains...............	111	236	25	372	770	15	11	26
17. Windsor Road..................	129	237	21	387	814	4	3	7
18. Truro Road....................	82	194	14	290	586	4	7	11
19. Guy's River...................	91	203	7	301	616	2	2	4
20. Wise's Corner.................	84	164	12	260	556	5	6	11
21. Middle Musquodoboit..........	179	374	22	575	1183	22	21	43
22. Upper Musquodoboit	150	294	13	457	935	7	9	16
33. Caledonia.....................	31	75	1	107	230	1	1	2
24. Salmon River.................	135	296	19	450	953	7	4	11
25. Sheet Harbor	99	206	17	322	674	4		4
26. Pope's Harbor.................	153	359	27	539	1141	14	15	29
27. Jeddore	294	568	33	895	1860	13	8	21
28. Chezetcook	256	582	32	870	1763	22	19	41
29. Lawrencetown.................	65	154	7	226	462	3	3	6
30. Preston	102	197	29	328	641	10	9	19
31. Dartmouth	492	1057	119	1668	3155	9	3	12
32. Black Point...................	129	227	10	366	795	4	5	9
33. Eastern Passage	114	244	17	375	753	5	7	12
	7270	15888	1762	24920	49021	374	290	664

COUNTY OF

1. Truro.........................	462	971	44	1477	2934	13	17	30
2. Old Barns.....................	156	296	14	466	927	3	4	7
3. Lower Stewiacke...............	230	486	37	753	1588	10	6	16
4. Upper Stewiacke...............	284	606	41	931	1849	17	20	37
5. Upper Onslow and Kemptown	245	539	26	810	1580	11	10	21
6. Onslow	134	228	17	379	771	9	4	13
7. Earltown	162	427	31	620	1216	3	4	7
8. New Annan.....................	188	415	18	621	1231	6	11	17
9. Waugh's River	156	390	18	564	1153	9	6	15
10. Tatamagouche.................	189	445	31	665	1400	8	6	14
11. Upper Londonderry............	249	465	37	751	1573	14	17	31
12. Lower Londonderry............	339	650	43	1033	2132	18	14	32
13. Economy and Five Islands....	282	511	20	813	1691	10	6	16
	3076	6429	377	9882	20045	131	125	256

BY AGES...1860—61.

HALIFAX, Continued.

Deaf and Dumb		Blind		Lunatics		Idiots		Cannot Read				Cannot Write				Married since March 30, 1860.	Colored persons included in population.	Indians not included in population.
								Over 5 and under 15 years of age.		Above 15 years of age.		Over 5 and under 15 years of age.		Above 15 years of age.				
M.	F.	M.	F.	M.	F.	M.	F.	M.	F.	M.	F.	M.	F.	M.	F.			
132	133	134	135	136	137	138	139	140	141	142	143	144	145	146	147	148	149	150
	2	1				1		96	93	136	179	98	101	162	235	11		
2	2	2	1	14	21	2	2	103	82	151	168	128	105	173	265	13	26	
6	2	1	1	2				142	146	163	254	195	226	242	379	8	221	
1	1	3	1					117	124	159	233	166	176	211	359	3	138	
								152	169	155	226	179	208	190	312	5	64	
3	2	1	1	1		1		203	186	189	248	263	262	250	391	6	325	
25	13	3	1		1		1	135	102	99	126	171	135	119	163	5	72	
37	22	11	5	17	22	4	3	948	902	1052	1434	1200	1213	1347	2104	51	846	
1	1							77	74	112	85	81	78	129	116			
			1					62	47	47	46	76	55	69	74	1	1	
								43	29	28	28	76	48	83	107	7		
1							1	152	120	166	128	163	141	240	231	10		
								62	56	80	55	99	102	115	114	7		
1	1							70	55	63	62	107	79	111	127	9	1	
1	1							38	39	38	53	46	41	55	70		47	
					1			33	23	25	25	37	25	35	38	1	14	2
								29	24	12	17	37	37	20	31	1	6	
2				2			1	51	55	54	58	72	80	85	96	10	235	
1				1			1	45	43	81	73	52	58	90	95	4	87	
		1			1			22	42	40	47	66	66	76		1	105	
						1	1	23	22	13	12	40	45	20	25	1	3	
2	1				1	1	1	23	18	16	8	45	43	29	29	2		
1	1	1						40	28	14	14	85	67	25	36	12	2	5
			1					45	34	34	26	63	53	40	37	5		
					1			9	3	5	7	24	15	7	19	1	6	
1	2				3			69	62	99	76	102	96	155	155	8	24	
1				1			1	41	37	52	48	53	56	77	100	10	5	
3	1				2			110	84	145	132	128	94	192	171	7		
		2	1	1	1			166	190	229	159	200	218	311	269	43	4	
6	5			1			1	205	195	385	355	221	207	420	410	22	12	
							2	49	38	38	40	53	51	48	52	4		
							2	42	53	75	106	54	63	99	120	2	455	
2				2	1			181	163	214	246	212	201	228	287	7	197	34
						2	2	66	48	83	73	77	55	104	108	4		
1						2	2	53	54	70	47	78	81	91	105	2	2	
61	39	15	13	25	29	14	6	2753	2537	3270	3460	3528	3368	4291	5202	232	2022	71

COLCHESTER, Continued.

M.	F.	M.	F.	M.	F.	M.	F.	M.	F.	M.	F.	M.	F.	M.	F.			
2	1	1	2	2		2		45	42	25	15	104	115	52	79	27	25	46
	1							46	52	39	38	60	58	46	46	2		
1					1			26	25	26	22	72	62	46	55	9		
	1	1	1			2		47	46	9	12	104	97	40	49	22		15
	1	1				1		67	52	38	42	109	130	84	112	8	35	
	1	2		1		1		23	12	4	6	50	43	14	21	8	1	
	1							49	50	41	59	84	84	89	178	7		
								40	50	20	19	86	105	49	77	9		
				2	1	1	3	78	75	41	56	120	117	98	137	10		
		1	1					69	56	29	29	99	92	67	81	2		
		1		3	2		1	68	44	13	8	127	91	44	54	14	11	
1	1	1	1	2		1	2	58	66	34	25	138	132	56	73	8	4	
				1	2		3	84	79	35	33	135	139	54	83	16		
2	9	8	3	11	9	5	12	700	649	354	364	1294	1255	739	1045	142	76	61

No. 1.—PERSONAL CENSUS

COUNTY OF

POLLING DISTRICTS.	TOTAL POPULATION. Males	Females	Total	Number of Families	Average Number of each Family	Under one year of age M.	F.	Deaths under 1 yr. age since 30th March, 1860 M.	F.
	1	2	3	4	5	6	7	8	9
1. Amherst	1398	1369	2767	460	......	44	46	2	6
2. Westchester	396	378	774	124	......	5	9		
3. Head of Amherst	951	845	1796	278	......	39	19	1	1
4. River Philip	950	928	1878	296	......	27	35	3	1
5. River Hebert	916	797	1713	254	......	15	23	1	1
6. Maccan	438	400	838	142	......	10	14	1	
7. Pugwash	1610	1555	3165	493	......	53	32	2	3
8. Wallace	1233	1267	2500	401	......	34	47	3	2
9. Wentworth	358	338	696	116	......	8	9	2	
10. Advocate Harbor	567	507	1074	181	......	13	26		1
11. Mill Village	1166	1166	2332	396	......	33	34	4	1
	9983	9550	19533	3141	6.21	281	294	19	16

COUNTY OF

	1	2	3	4	5	6	7	8	9
1. Pictou	1403	1430	2833	509	......	30	34	1	6
2. Carriboo	594	598	1192	189	......	16	7		1
3. Cape John	725	699	1424	229	......	12	28	3	1
4. West side River John	627	688	1315	221	......	30	20		
5. West branch River John	458	459	917	141	......	9	20	2	
6. Rogers Hill	557	570	1127	189	......	10	9	1	1
7. Hardwood Hill	581	558	1139	184	......	14	16		2
8. Green Hill and West River	492	491	983	166	......	14	10	1	2
9. Mount Thom	613	629	1242	198	......	19	18		
10. Gairloch	434	503	937	159	......	11	12	3	1
11. New Larig	310	305	615	99	......	6	5		
12. Albion Mines	1059	1029	2088	353	......	42	42		
13. New Glasgow	1161	1127	2288	386	......	34	24	3	3
14. Little Harbor	431	427	858	134	......	6	12		
15. McLellan's Mountain	503	578	1081	158	......	14	9	1	
16. East branch East River	623	675	1298	215	......	21	20	1	
17. Hopewell, W. branch East River	769	854	1623	276	......	20	14	2	2
18. Middle River	566	554	1120	165	......	10	12		
19. Gulf Shore	547	565	1112	162	......	9	9		
20. Barney's River	625	649	1274	198	......	14	19		
21. Merrigomish	765	779	1544	243	......	18	12	1	2
22. Blue Mountain, St. Mary's, &c	406	369	775	127	......	22	7	3	2
	14244	14536	28785	4701	6.12	381	359	22	23

COUNTY OF

	1	2	3	4	5	6	7	8	9
1. Arisaig	717	733	1450	212	......	16	14		
2. Cape George	544	625	1169	169	......	12	14		
3. Morristown	471	496	967	148	......	9	12	1	
4. Antigonish	1415	1460	2875	434	......	35	35	2	1
5. Lochaber	846	919	1765	254	......	24	25		2
6. Upper South River	562	637	1199	164	......	12	14	2	1
7. St. Andrew's	1037	1117	2154	308	......	31	24	3	3
8. Tracadie	812	837	1649	255	......	21	26	5	1
9. Harbor Bouche	813	830	1643	253	......	24	24	3	3
	7217	7654	14871	2197	6.76	184	188	16	11

BY AGES...1860—61.

CUMBERLAND.

Over 1 and under 2 yrs. of age		Deaths between 1 and 2 years, since 30th M'h, 1860.		Over 2 and under 3 years of age.		Deaths between 2 and 3 years, since M'ch 30, 1860.		Over 3 and under 4 years of age.		Deaths between 3 and 4 years, since M'ch 30, 1860.		Over 4 and under 5 years of age.		Deaths between 4 and 5 years, since M'ch 30, 1860.	
M.	F.	M.	F.	M.	F.	M.	F.	M.	F.	M.	F.	M.	F.	M.	F.
10	11	12	13	14	15	16	17	18	19	20	21	22	23	24	25
36	23	1	3	36	52	1		33	28	3	1	30	23	2	
13	17	2		10	18	1	1	15	11		1	17	13		
28	36		2	40	23			29	26			30	31		
37	32		1	33	37	1		32	27			26	30		
35	35			30	30	1	1	20	32	1	1	31	17	1	
11	15		1	13	11	1	1	13	11			19	12		1
51	47	2	2	51	45	1	3	42	54	1		55	44		
25	38			29	37	1	6	39	36	2	10	44	34	3	4
15	14	1		13	6		3	6	9	3	1	10	12		1
26	17			28	14			25	11			23	15	1	
35	35	2	3	26	32	2	2	36	38		3	42	34		
312	309	9	11	309	305	9	17	290	283	10	17	327	265	7	6

PICTOU.

M.	F.	M.	F.	M.	F.	M.	F.	M.	F.	M.	F.	M.	F.	M.	F.
35	34	3		32	39	1		31	38	1		37	35	1	
17	16			16	18			9	15		1	16	14	1	
29	14			23	16	1	1	14	22			21	22		
14	16			27	22		1	18	22		1	22	24		
9	5			16	14			13	20	1		9	5		1
9	21			9	15	1		19	13			13	11		
10	10			16	17			21	16			14	14		2
16	10			6	8			11	13	1		11	12		1
14	12			17	15			16	16	1		11	20		1
7	8			9	8			16	10			10	7		
4	7			8	5			6	5			7	6		
34	32	1		32	33		2	34	37	2		30	26		
27	31			27	27			29	26			29	28		
10	6			13	13			14	5			11	17		
8	13		1	14	15			15	14	1		14	13		
10	10			15	12			17	17			20	12		
13	18	1		13	27			19	20			16	28		
11	9			13	16			12	5			11	16		
24	13	1		12	13			13	9	1		18	15		1
14	13			16	17			15	18			13	17		
13	25	1		18	15	2	2	20	15			21	17		
8	16			17	13	1		16	9		1	13	13		
336	339	7	1	369	378	6	6	378	365	8	3	367	372	2	6

SYDNEY.

M.	F.	M.	F.	M.	F.	M.	F.	M.	F.	M.	F.	M.	F.	M.	F.
4	12	1		14	25	2		14	14			12	17	1	
11	12		1	17	20			13	10		1	14	23		1
9	16			13	16			13	12			8	17		
20	43	1	4	38	35	2	1	44	33			45	42	1	
23	15	1	1	28	23			23	23			19	31	1	2
13	19	1	2	13	14		1	14	11	1		16	15		
28	25			22	33	1		25	25	2		26	21	1	2
22	14	1	1	20	17	1	1	16	20	1		15	23	1	
16	21		2	28	28	2		20	21		4	30	20	1	
155	177	5	11	193	211	8	3	182	169	4	5	185	209	6	5

No. 1.—PERSONAL CENSUS

COUNTY OF

POLLING DISTRICTS.	Over 5 and under 10 years of age.		Deaths between 5 and 10 y'rs. since M'ch 30, 1863.		Over 10 and under 15 years of age.				Deaths since M'ch 30, 1860.	
					Males.		Females.			
	M.	F.	M.	F.	MD.	S.	MD.	S.	M.	F.
	26	27	28	29	30	31	32	33	34	35
1. Amherst	176	181	6	7		175		184		2
2. Westchester	61	46	1	1		49		40	1	1
3. Head of Amherst	128	128				118	1	116		1
4. River Philip	132	137	1	1		119		147		1
5. River Hebert	124	123	1			107		84	1	1
6. Maccan	60	46	3	3		58		41	2	3
7. Pugwash	221	236	3	3		226		214	2	
8. Wallace	157	193	10	3		163		148	3	4
9. Wentworth	60	44	2	1		50		51		4
10. Advocate Harbor	74	73				73		74		
11. Mill Village	132	187	5	6		142		131	3	2
	1325	1394	32	25		1280		1230	12	19

COUNTY OF

	M.	F.	M.	F.	MD.	S.	MD.	S.	M.	F.
1. Pictou	189	155	2	2		214		149		
2. Carriboo	77	73	3	3		94		80	1	
3. Cape John	131	116	1			116		86		
4. West side River John	76	95	1			85		103	1	
5. West branch River John	67	69	2	1		56		57		
6. Rogers Hill	72	59	2	3		72		82	1	1
7. Hardwood Hill	82	67				71		84	1	
8. Green Hill and West River	68	47		1		74		68	1	
9. Mount Thom	78	81				88		82		
10. Gairloch	53	61				55		67		
11. New Larig	25	29		1		42		40		
12. Albion Mines	164	133		1		130		138	1	1
13. New Glasgow	136	123				133		126		
14. Little Harbor	52	55				62		56		
15. McLellan's Mountain	64	61				53		96		
16. East branch East River	76	81				53		82		
17. Hopewell, W. branch E. Riv.	88	95		2		100		118		
18. Middle River	69	56				66		78		
19. Gulf Shore	62	53				60		68	1	2
20. Barney's River	90	78	2			81		86	1	
21. Merrigomish	95	96	1			104		102		1
22. Blue Mount'n, St. Mary's, &c.	62	54	1	2		65		50		
	1876	1737	15	18		1931		1896	8	5

COUNTY OF

	M.	F.	M.	F.	MD.	S.	MD.	S.	M.	F.
1. Arisaig	74	71	2	1		102		80		1
2. Cape George	61	70		3		60		56	2	1
3. Morristown	46	57	1			60		54		
4. Antigonish	159	147	2			60		54	1	1
5. Lochaber	99	111	2			171		177	1	
6. Upper South River	56	90	3	2		101		140	1	
7. St. Andrew's	97	110	1	4		61		80	1	
8. Tracadie	103	87	5	3		151		140		2
9. Harbor Bouche	99	108	4	5		95		100	1	2
						119		90		1
	794	851	19	18		920		926	6	7

BY AGES...1860—61.

CUMBERLAND, Continued.

			Over 15 and under 20 years of age.						Over 20 and under 30 years of age.						
Males.			Females.			Deaths since March 30, 1860.		Males.			Females.			Deaths since March 30, 1860.	
MD.	S.	WDR	MD.	S.	WD.	M.	F.	MD.	S.	WDR	MD.	S.	WD.	M.	F.
36	37	38	39	40	41	42	43	44	45	46	47	48	49	50	51
.....	157	.....	2	167	.....	1	1	65	199	3	96	145	2	1	2
.....	43	.....	2	47	.....	1	.....	21	48	.....	33	25	1	2	
1	129	.....	3	99	.....	.....	.....	45	104	1	83	61	3	.....	2
.....	85	.....	5	84	.....	.....	1	58	118	1	92	65	1	2	2
1	90	.....	1	84	.....	2	1	48	146	.....	66	78	2	.....	1
1	33	.....	6	54	.....	1	.....	26	61	.....	34	33	1	1	4
.....	190	.....	2	192	.....	.....	4	52	183	.....	106	138	1	4	1
.....	137	.....	1	147	.....	.....	3	43	128	3	80	117	4	1	1
.....	35	.....	.....	33	.....	1	.....	15	35	.....	23	28	.....	.....	2
1	55	.....	3	53	.....	.....	.....	30	65	.....	51	31	.....	.....	1
1	152	.....	11	119	.....	5	.....	73	124	.....	118	110	2	5	.....
5	1106	.....	36	1079	.....	11	10	476	1211	8	782	831	17	16	16

PICTOU, Continued.

MD.	S.	WDR	MD.	S.	WD.	M.	F.	MD.	S.	WDR	MD.	S.	WD.	M.	F.
.	172	.....	.....	176	.....	1	.....	39	182	.....	74	199	3	3	3
.	63	.....	.....	77	.....	.....	.....	12	77	.....	26	84	.....	1	1
1	78	.....	2	69	.....	.....	.....	21	69	.....	44	78	.....	1	.....
.	76	.....	3	71	.....	1	.....	24	65	1	53	77	1	1	1
.	54	.....	.....	41	.....	.....	.....	6	67	.....	14	60	.....	1	1
.	75	.....	1	67	.....	.....	.....	6	71	1	25	69	1	1	2
.	75	.....	.....	76	.....	1	.....	7	83	2	21	58	1	2	3
.....	78	.....	2	50	.....	.....	1	12	51	.....	19	72	.....	.....	.....
.....	85	.....	1	74	.....	.....	.....	10	74	.....	24	78	.....	.....	1
.....	52	.....	.....	63	.....	.....	.....	1	66	.....	17	73	.....	.....	.....
..	45	.....	.....	39	.....	.....	.....	5	59	.....	10	42	1	1	.....
.	144	.....	12	103	.....	2	.....	76	100	.....	97	83	1	.....	2
..	153	.....	1	133	.....	1	1	34	174	2	78	156	1	5	2
.	47	.....	.....	55	.....	.....	.....	7	65	.....	18	56	.....	.....	.....
.	60	.....	1	67	.....	.....	.....	9	83	.....	29	89	1	.....	1
.	83	.....	1	87	.....	.....	.....	15	78	1	29	100	1	2	2
..	106	.....	4	92	1	1	1	29	111	.....	52	114	2	2	1
1	76	.....	.....	70	.....	.....	1	2	118	.....	18	96	.....	1	1
.	76	.....	1	71	.....	2	.....	11	92	.....	30	103	1	.....	.....
.	75	.....	.....	79	.....	2	.....	11	88	.....	29	77	1	1	1
.....	104	.....	3	98	.....	1	.....	16	114	.....	31	113	.....	1	.....
.	39	.....	.....	34	.....	.....	.....	19	37	.....	31	27	.....	2	.....
2	1816	.....	32	1692	1	12	4	372	1924	7	769	1904	15	25	22

SYDNEY, Continued.

MD.	S.	WDR	MD.	S.	WD.	M.	F.	MD.	S.	WDR	MD.	S.	WD.	M.	F.
.....	114	.....	.....	93	.....	.....	.....	10	140	.....	33	157	.....	1	1
.....	61	.....	.....	68	.....	1	.....	5	101	.....	24	107	1	1	.....
.....	57	.....	.....	49	.....	1	2	8	100	.....	22	84	.....	1	1
.....	210	.....	5	167	.....	1	.....	41	218	.....	89	246	1	7	1
.....	113	.....	.....	110	.....	.....	1	23	151	1	45	121	.....	2	3
.....	72	.....	.....	83	.....	.....	.....	6	119	.....	25	114	.....	.....	.....
.....	144	.....	1	149	.....	1	3	22	182	.....	44	170	.....	.....	.....
.....	89	.....	.....	120	.....	1	2	28	132	2	47	107	2	10	1
.....	88	.....	3	100	.....	.....	2	26	109	.....	69	115	.....	1	.....
.....	948	.....	9	939	.....	5	10	169	1252	3	398	1221	4	23	7

No. 1.—PERSONAL CENSUS

COUNTY OF

POLLING DISTRICTS.	\multicolumn{8}{c}{Over 30 and under 40 years of age.}							
	\multicolumn{3}{c}{Males.}			\multicolumn{3}{c}{Females.}			Deaths since March 30, 1860.	
	MD.	S.	WDR	MD.	S.	WD.	M.	F.
	52	53	54	55	56	57	58	59
1. Amherst	97	43	2	113	29	6	2	2
2. Westchester	34	7	2	30	10	3		
3. Head of Amherst	76	15	1	65	15	1		
4. River Philip	87	23		86	11		1	
5. River Hebert	77	25	2	78	11	1	1	
6. Maccan	35	7		36	6	1	1	1
7. Pugwash	130	38		131	20	8		
8. Wallace	107	44	1	116	25	3	3	
9. Wentworth	27	5		30	4	1		
10. Advocate Harbor	50	6		54	6	1		1
11. Mill Village	109	26	1	93	17		1	
	829	239	9	832	154	25	9	4

COUNTY OF

1. Pictou	113	25	5	119	44	19		4
2. Carriboo	28	22		39	11	2	1	
3. Cape John	48	10		60	15	5		2
4. West side River John	58	7		55	13	1		2
5. West branch River John	23	17		42	16	1	1	
6. Rogers Hill	36	20		37	17	1		
7. Hardwood Hill	35	19	3	36	13		1	1
8. Green Hill and West River	23	8	1	38	23			1
9. Mount Thom	47	28	1	53	20	1		1
10. Gairloch	23	14		23	28			
11. New Larig	17	15		23	20			
12. Albion Mines	91	11	2	89	21	9		
13. New Glasgow	92	41	4	79	48	6		
14. Little Harbor	14	20	2	23	16			1
15. McLellan's Mountain	39	15		40	16			1
16. East branch East River	41	10		52	18	1		
17. Hopewell, W. branch East River	70	21	1	68	30	5		
18. Middle River	40	23		40	21	1		1
19. Gulf Shore	31	27		31	26	4		
20. Barney's River	36	20	2	52	24			
21. Merrigomish	44	37	1	51	37	5		1
22. Blue Mountain, St. Mary's, &c	32	3	1	35	10	2	1	
	981	413	23	1085	487	63	4	15

COUNTY OF

1. Arisaig	30	47	1	38	32	2	1	2
2. Cape George	35	28	2	43	42	1		1
3. Morristown	28	22	2	34	28	3		
4. Antigonish	92	58	5	110	60	4	2	2
5. Lochaber	54	19		64	37	4	1	
6. Upper South River	29	33		32	31	1	2	
7. St. Andrew's	52	32	1	77	56	7	1	
8. Tracadie	59	37	3	63	26	8	3	2
9. Harbor Bouche	75	13	3	58	19	3	1	
	454	289	17	519	331	33	11	7

BY AGES...1860—61.

CUMBERLAND, Continued.

	Over 40 and under 50 years of age.								Over 50 and under 60 years of age.						
Males.			Females.			Deaths since March 30, 1860.		Males.			Females.			Deaths since March 30, 1860.	
MD.	S.	WDR	MD.	S.	WD.	M.	F.	MD.	S.	WDR	MD.	S.	WD.	M.	F.
60	61	62	63	64	65	66	67	68	69	70	71	72	73	74	75
121	10	4	121	6	10	1	1	72	1	8	50	7	8	1	2
21	1	3	24	4	2	1		13	1	4	12	1	5		
63	8	4	62	6	2	1	1	29	1	1	16	4	4		
68	6		54	3	3			37	5	2	33	2	6	1	
60	5	1	54	3	4	1		35	9	3	25	4	2		
33	2	1	30	3		2		16	2	2	13	1	3	1	
121	13	3	126	10	10	3	2	72	2	3	51	3	8	1	1
102	18	6	90	7	6	1		50	9	1	45	2	6	1	1
29	3		29	2	1			18	1	1	16	1	2		
49		3	30		3			17		1	15		3		
74	3	3	64	7	9			58	3	4	58	4	9	2	1
741	69	28	684	51	50	10	4	417	34	30	334	29	56	7	5

PICTOU, Continued.

60	61	62	63	64	65	66	67	68	69	70	71	72	73	74	75
95	15	5	100	24	11	3	1	78	3	5	57	11	21		1
30	12		38	9	7	1		41	2	1	32	2	5	2	
57	7		45	8	5			24	2	6	17	2	4		
52	6	1	43	3	4		1	28	4		23	5	2		
42	6		32	4	2			27	1	1	22	3	7		
26	6		39	8	3		1	46	3		29	3	5		
35	2		46	4	4	1		33	2	2	27	1	2		
46	3		41	16	2			26	2	3	23	2	2		
33	4		39	12	3			31	6	2	19	4	10	1	
33	4	1	38	8	5			27	3	3	18	10	4		
23	4		19	5	3			15	2	1	18	1	3	1	
63	3	2	63	6	8	1	1	46	2	2	40	4	6		
69	10	4	72	16	7	1	2	58	1	10	48	9	6	1	2
28	5		29	5	4			21	4	2	18	5	4		
32	2		30	7	4			33	1	1	25	3	7		
46	2		44	5	2			36	2	1	34	8	7		
44	5	2	47	11	4	2	1	45	4	1	42	9	4		
27	3		34	7	4			32	2	2	28	1	11		
31	2	3	23	13	5	1	1	24	3	5	23	6	6	1	1
38	3		34	5	4			40	2	1	33	3	3		
49	5	2	51	7	5			35	2	1	33	3	6		
30			23	3				16			17		6		
929	109	20	930	186	96	10	8	762	53	50	626	95	131	6	4

SYDNEY, Continued.

60	61	62	63	64	65	66	67	68	69	70	71	72	73	74	75
45	7	1	35	8	5	1	1	32	1	2	31	8	10		1
31	8	2	26	16	5			25	3		21	8	11		
20	2	1	19	4	4	1		23	1	4	17	2	2		
90	12	1	64	11	15	3	1	57	5	4	53	13	18	1	1
53	4	1	53	9	4			37	1	2	36	4	10		1
38	8	3	32	9	7	1	1	25	1	9	19	2	4	1	1
75	9	3	65	11	6			48	4	3	48	11	10	1	
44	13	1	41	9	7			34	6	4	23	7	9	2	1
49	4	3	33	7	4	1	1	18	1	4	37	2	12		1
445	67	16	368	84	57	7	4	299	23	32	285	57	86	5	6

No. 1.—PERSONAL CENSUS

COUNTY OF

POLLING DISTRICT.	Over 60 and under 70 years of age.							
	Males.			Females.			Deaths since March 30, 1860.	
	MD.	S.	WDR	MD.	S.	WD.	M.	F.
	76	77	78	79	80	81	82	83
1. Amherst	48	3	12	24	2	13	1	......
2. Westchester	13	2	2	9	1	4	......	......
3. Head of Amherst	24	2	8	18	2	3	......	2
4. River Philip	34	......	4	17	......	9	1	2
5. River Hebert	31	4	4	14	3	6	......	......
6. Maccan	18	2	1	20	......	4	......	1
7. Pugwash	51	5	6	32	2	11	1	1
8. Wallace	53	2	2	34	5	12	3	1
9. Wentworth	20	3	......	10	......	1	......	......
10. Advocate Harbor	14	3	3	10	......	7	1	......
11. Mill Village	50	1	6	26	......	9	1	......
	356	27	48	214	15	79	8	7

COUNTY OF

1. Pictou	50	7	7	28	3	22	......	1
2. Carriboo	38	1	3	22	1	9	1	1
3. Cape John	27	4	6	20	1	6	1	......
4. West side River John	19	1	1	14	1	7	......	......
5. West branch River John	15	1	2	10	......	5	......	......
6. Rogers Hill	28	5	7	16	2	9	......	2
7. Hardwood Hill	35	1	7	19	......	7	......	1
8. Green Hill and West River	20	......	3	11	1	4	1	......
9. Mount Thom	22	2	5	18	3	14	......	......
10. Gairloch	13	4	7	10	2	9	1	......
11. New Larig	14	3	2	6	1	7	......	......
12. Albion Mines	28	......	3	14	1	12	2	......
13. New Glasgow	40	1	5	22	5	17	1	1
14. Little Harbor	23	6	3	13	1	5	......	1
15. McLellan's Mountain	27	......	1	19	......	11	......	1
16. East branch East River	36	1	4	19	2	11	......	......
17. Hopewell, West branch East River	35	2	5	18	2	13	......	......
18. Middle River	24	1	3	17	......	5	2	......
19. Gulf Shore	21	5	2	14	3	3	2	......
20. Barney's River	39	2	3	26	6	5	......	......
21. Merrigomish	36	4	2	20	2	13	......	1
22. Blue Mountain, St. Mary's, &c	13	1	......	9	......	3	......	......
	603	52	81	365	37	197	11	9

COUNTY OF

1. Arisaig	33	......	6	16	4	17	1	......
2. Cape George	25	4	8	16	2	11	3	1
3. Morristown	20	......	8	17	3	8	......	......
4. Antigonish	57	......	8	31	4	27	2	1
5. Lochaber	36	3	3	17	1	14	2	......
6. Upper South River	17	1	2	10	1	8	......	......
7. St. Andrew's	44	2	5	20	5	16	1	1
8. Tracadie	28	3	4	28	4	16	1	1
9. Harbor Bouche	47	6	4	28	2	10	......	......
	307	22	48	183	26	127	10	4

BY AGES...1860—61.

CUMBERLAND, Continued.

Over 70 and under 80 years of age.								Over 80 and under 90 years of age.							
Males.			Females.			Deaths since March 30, 1860.		Males.			Females.			Deaths since March 30, 1860.	
MD.	S.	WDR	MD.	S.	WD.	M.	F.	MD.	S.	WDR	MD.	S.	WD.	M.	F.
84	85	86	87	88	89	90	91	92	93	94	95	96	97	98	99
14	2	3	7	2	13	2	....	3	....	1	....	....	8	1	....
8	....	3	2	....	7	....	....	....	....	....	....	....	2	2	....
13	1	6	7	....	4	....	....	4	....	1	2	....	3	....	....
6	2	2	4	....	3	....	....	2	1	3	....	....	2	....	....
9	....	2	9	....	3	....	....	1	....	1	....	....	5	....	....
10	....	1	3	....	2	2	1	....	....	1	....	....	....	....	....
27	1	6	10	1	9	2	....	1	1	3	1	1	9	2	....
21	....	10	8	5	15	1	2	4	....	1	1	1	3	....	....
3	....	....	4	....	3	....	....	....	....	1	1	....	3	1	....
7	1	....	3	....	4	....	....	....	....	....	....	....	3	....	....
21	2	4	9	....	4	....	....	....	....	3	1	1	4	2	....
139	9	37	66	8	67	7	3	15	2	15	6	3	42	8	....

PICTOU, Continued.

MD.	S.	WDR	MD.	S.	WD.	M.	F.	MD.	S.	WDR	MD.	S.	WD.	M.	F.
11	1	12	5	1	17	2	1	2	1	2	2	....	6	2	....
8	....	6	2	1	5	2	1	2	....	2	1	....	1	....	1
14	....	2	6	....	7	2	....	1	....	1	....	....	1	....	....
9	....	1	3	....	6	1	1	1	....	1	1	....	....	2	....
12	....	3	5	....	5	1	....	1	....	1	....	....	....	....	....
11	....	4	8	4	7	....	....	2	1	1	2	....	5	....	2
5	....	1	3	1	12	1	....	3	....	2	....	....	3	1	....
6	2	5	5	....	7	....	1	2	....	1	1	....	3	1	....
15	1	2	5	....	7	4	1	1	....	1	....	....	1	....	....
10	1	6	6	....	13	2	2	5	....	....	1	1	1	....	....
3	1	3	1	....	7	1	1	....	....	....	....	....	2	....	....
8	2	2	....	2	7	....	2	1	1	1	1	....	4	....	....
15	1	6	7	3	16	1	....	3	....	1	2	1	3	....	....
9	....	3	4	1	4	....	....	2	....	2	....	....	2	....	3
4	....	5	2	....	1	....	1	4	....	1	....	....	3	....	....
10	1	1	3	2	7	1	....	1	....	2	3	....	2	....	....
9	....	5	6	....	4	....	....	2	....	....	....	....	5	....	....
12	1	4	3	1	4	....	....	2	....	....	....	....	1	1	1
5	1	3	4	....	14	1	....	3	....	3	....	....	2	1	....
12	....	3	4	3	5	....	....	4	....	1	....	....	6	....	1
14	2	2	8	....	7	1	....	4	....	2	1	....	3	....	....
5	....	4	....	....	5	....	....	1	....	1	1	....	1	....	1
207	15	83	90	19	167	20	11	46	3	22	20	2	58	12	9

SYDNEY, Continued.

MD.	S.	WDR	MD.	S.	WD.	M.	F.	MD.	S.	WDR	MD.	S.	WD.	M.	F.
6	....	3	3	1	3	....	....	1	....	2	1	....	2	....	1
13	2	2	7	2	4	....	....	1	....	....	....	....	4	....	1
13	....	1	6	1	8	1	....	1	....	1	....	....	1	....	....
19	2	4	8	1	11	2	1	6	....	2	2	....	7	....	....
17	1	5	9	....	4	....	1	3	....	1	1	1	2	1	....
7	....	2	6	....	6	....	....	2	....	2	2	....	2	1	1
18	1	3	7	2	19	1	....	3	....	5	1	2	9	3	2
19	3	2	9	2	7	4	....	2	1	1	....	....	1	....	....
15	1	2	7	....	3	....	....	4	....	1	1	....	1	....	1
127	10	24	62	9	65	8	2	23	1	15	8	3	29	5	6

No. 1.—PERSONAL CENSUS

COUNTY OF

POLLING DISTRICT	Over 90 and under 100 years of age.							
	Males.			Females.			Deaths since March 30, 1860.	
	MD.	S.	WDR	MD.	S.	WD.	M.	F.
	100	101	102	103	104	105	106	107
1. Amherst						1		1
2. Westchester								
3. Head of Amherst								
4. River Philip								
5. River Hebert						1		
6. Maccan								
7. Pugwash			2					
8. Wallace								
9. Wentworth								
10. Advocate Harbor						1	1	
11. Mill Village	1		1					
	1		3			3	1	1

COUNTY OF

POLLING DISTRICT	100	101	102	103	104	105	106	107
1. Pictou						1		
2. Carriboo	1					1		
3. Cape John						1		
4. West side River John								
5. West branch River John								
6. Rogers Hill	2	1	1			2		
7. Hardwood Hill								
8. Green Hill and West River							1	
9. Mount Thom						1		1
10. Gairloch								
11. New Larig				2				
12. Albion Mines							1	
13. New Glasgow								
14. Little Harbor						1		
15. McLellan's Mountain					2			
16. East branch East River	1			2				
17. Hopewell, W. branch E. Riv						1		
18. Middle River				1				
19. Gulf Shore								
20. Barney's River	2				2		1	1
21. Merrigomish					2	1	1	
22. Blue Mount'n, St. Mary's, &c	1							
	7	1	10			9	4	1

COUNTY OF

POLLING DISTRICT	100	101	102	103	104	105	106	107
1. Arisaig						1		
2. Cape George						1		
3. Morristown						1		
4. Antigonish				1				
5. Lochaber						1		
6. Upper South River	1					3		1
7. St. Andrew's				1				
8. Tracadie				1		3		1
9. Harbor Bouche						2	1	
	1		3			12	1	2

BY AGES...1860—61.

CUMBERLAND, Continued.

Columns — Over 100 years of age: Males (MD 108, S 109, WDR 110), Females (MD 111, S 112, WD 113), Deaths since M'ch 30, 1860 (M 114, F 115); Ages not given; Deaths (M 116, F 117); Ages not given (M 118, F 119); Males (Married 120, Single 121, Widowers 122, Total 123).

MD	S	WDR	MD	S	WD	M	F	M	F	M	F	Married	Single	Widowers	Total
108	109	110	111	112	113	114	115	116	117	118	119	120	121	122	123
												420	945	33	1398
												110	272	14	396
								2	3			257	672	22	951
									2			292	646	12	950
												262	641	13	916
												139	293	6	438
								1	1			454	1133	23	1610
								1	1	1	1	380	828	25	1233
												112	244	2	358
												168	392	7	567
												387	757	22	1166
								*4	†7	1	1	2981	6823	179	9983

PICTOU, Continued.

MD	S	WDR	MD	S	WD	M	F	M	F	M	F	Married	Single	Widowers	Total
1		1				3	3					390	976	37	1403
												160	422	12	594
	1					1						193	517	15	725
												191	431	5	627
												126	325	7	458
												157	386	14	557
						1						153	411	17	581
												135	344	13	492
											1	159	443	11	613
												112	303	19	434
												77	227	6	310
						5	5					313	733	13	1059
						2	1					311	818	32	1101
												104	315	12	431
						3	1					148	346	9	503
			1				1					186	428	9	623
						1	1					235	519	15	769
						1						140	417	9	566
												128	404	15	547
							1					180	433	12	625
								1				198	557	10	765
												117	283	6	406
1	1	1			1	‡17	‖13	1		1		3913	10038	298	14249

SYDNEY, Continued.

MD	S	WDR	MD	S	WD	M	F	M	F	M	F	Married	Single	Widowers	Total
												157	545	15	717
												135	395	14	544
												113	340	18	471
												362	1029	24	1415
					1				1			224	600	13	846
												124	419	19	562
				1								262	754	21	1037
								5	3	2	1	214	581	17	812
								4	3			237	559	17	813
					1	1		§9	¶7	2	1	1828	5231	158	7217

* 2 md., 2 s. † 3 md., 4 s. ‡ 8 md., 18 s., 1 wdr. ‖ 5 md., 7 s., 1 w. § 3 md., 6 s. ¶ 2 md., 5 s.

No. 1.—PERSONAL CENSUS

COUNTY OF

POLLING DISTRICTS.	Females.				Grand Total.	Deaths.		
	Married	Single	Widows	Total		Males	Females	Total
	124	125	126	127	128	129	130	131
1. Amherst	413	895	61	1369	2767	25	28	53
2. Westchester	112	242	24	378	774	11	4	15
3. Head of Amherst	259	566	20	845	1796	2	9	11
4. River Philip	291	612	25	928	1878	11	8	19
5. River Hebert	247	527	23	797	1713	10	6	16
6. Maccan	142	247	11	400	838	15	16	31
7. Pugwash	459	1040	56	1555	3165	24	20	44
8. Wallace	376	842	49	1267	2500	33	38	71
9. Wentworth	113	213	12	338	696	11	12	23
10. Advocate Harbor	166	320	21	507	1074	2	3	5
11. Mill Village	380	749	37	1166	2332	32	18	50
	2958	6253	339	9550	19533	176	162	338

COUNTY OF

POLLING DISTRICTS.	Married	Single	Widows	Total	Grand Total	Males	Females	Total
1. Pictou	387	943	100	1430	2833	20	19	39
2. Carriboo	160	408	30	598	1192	13	9	22
3. Cape John	194	477	28	699	1424	9	4	13
4. West side River John	195	472	21	688	1315	8	8	16
5. West branch River John	125	314	20	459	917	6	5	11
6. Rogers Hill	157	380	33	570	1127	6	9	15
7. Hardwood Hill	152	377	29	558	1139	9	9	18
8. Green Hill and West River	140	332	19	491	983	5	8	13
9. Mount Thom	159	435	35	629	1242	7	5	12
10. Gairloch	113	358	32	503	937	6	3	9
11. New Larig	77	205	23	305	615	4	2	6
12. Albion Mines	316	665	48	1029	2088	9	9	18
13. New Glasgow	309	757	61	1127	2288	16	11	27
14. Little Harbor	105	303	19	427	858		5	5
15. McLellan's Mountain	147	404	27	578	1081	2	5	7
16. East branch East River	186	456	33	675	1298	4	2	6
17. Hopewell, W. branch E. Riv.	238	578	38	854	1623	8	7	15
18. Middle River	140	388	26	554	1120	4	4	8
19. Gulf Shore	129	400	36	565	1112	12	7	19
20. Barney's River	179	445	25	649	1274	8	2	10
21. Merrigomish	198	542	39	779	1544	9	7	16
22. Blue Mount'n, St. Marys, &c.	116	236	17	369	775	8	6	14
	3922	9875	739	14536	28785	173	146	319

COUNTY OF

POLLING DISTRICTS.	Married	Single	Widows	Total	Grand Total	Males	Females	Total
1. Arisaig	157	536	40	733	1450	10	8	18
2. Cape George	137	450	38	625	1169	7	10	17
3. Morristown	115	355	26	496	967	6	3	9
4. Antigonish	362	1014	84	1460	2875	27	13	40
5. Lochaber	225	652	42	919	1765	11	14	25
6. Upper South River	126	483	28	637	1199	12	7	19
7. St. Andrew's	263	784	70	1117	2154	17	18	35
8. Tracadie	211	574	52	837	1649	39	16	55
9. Harbor Bouche	238	558	34	830	1643	13	20	33
	1834	5406	414	7654	14871	142	109	251

BY AGES...1860—61.

CUMBERLAND, Continued.

								Cannot Read.				Cannot Write.						
Deaf and Dumb.		Blind.		Lunatics.		Idiots.		Over 5 and under 15 years of age.	Above 15 years of age.			Over 5 and under 15 years of age.	Above 15 years of age.			Married since 80, 1860.	Colored persons included in population.	Indians not included in population.
M.	F.	M.	F.	M.	F.	M.	F.	M.	F.	M.	F.	M.	F.	M.	F.			
132	133	134	135	136	137	138	139	140	141	142	143	144	145	146	147	148	149	150
2	....			1	1	....	....	114	137	75	84	146	157	102	117	30	118	....
....	1	....	....	2	1			65	49	18	27	83	73	54	75	2		....
1	....	....	....		1		1	84	74	39	36	160	149	68	99	16	16	....
....	1	1	....	1	....	1	....	101	101	43	39	163	166	85	100	21	24	7
....	....	1	....			1	....	106	93	107	105	139	99	144	151	11	30	12
....	....	1				....		66	40	38	27	90	64	65	58	8	....	14
1	2	1	2	1	1	....	....	164	155	65	70	288	290	141	222	10	1	15
1	....	....			1	1	1	112	105	65	63	176	172	79	134	13	1	3
....				2				38	30	7	8	67	53	18	22	2	....	....
....	....	1	2	1	2	....		86	62	31	25	104	99	56	73	2	....	....
....	....		1	....		1	1	55	73	62	51	88	116	103	123	34	1	....
5	4	4	4	6	6	9	3	991	919	550	535	1504	1438	915	1174	149	191	51

PICTOU, Continued.

M.	F.	M.	F.	M.	F.	M.	F.	M.	F.	M.	F.	M.	F.	M.	F.			
1	....	1	1	....	1			70	51	39	55	115	90	64	116	14	1	10
					2			34	40	35	37	53	50	54	78	5	....	....
1	....		1			1	....	88	88	38	37	166	149	81	136	10	....	....
2	1				1	1	....	47	61	21	35	93	121	58	113	4	1	....
				1		2	....	45	36	41	57	77	71	71	113	5	....	....
....	1	....		1				39	35	13	36	76	66	24	95	9	....	....
								23	29	14	15	63	54	31	65	5	....	30
		1	2					25	18	1	9	49	27	2	14	10	1	2
3	1	....		1		1	2	2	49	59	23	45	83	86	47	121	5	1
....		1	1	....	1	1		20	18	13	24	42	41	28	78	6	....	....
....		2		....	1	1	....	14	19	19	19	14	36	45	94	8	....	....
				1		1	....	76	70	40	50	147	140	82	162	14	....	....
2	2	1		1	2	....	1	45	34	23	38	72	88	43	138	18	2	75
								30	31	12	27	51	53	42	70	1	....	22
....	1							27	37	13	31	77	84	64	178	12	....	....
....		1		1			2	54	66	31	74	90	109	76	188	12	....	....
1	....	1		1	....			42	41	28	30	86	89	53	161	14	1	....
	1			1				27	28	12	27	54	53	42	99	8	....	....
....	1	1		1	....			41	38	42	140	68	58	68	186	8	....	30
					2			78	59	23	55	121	105	54	151	9	....	....
2	4	....		1	....	1		49	60	38	45	124	122	67	123	7	....	....
		1	1	1	1	1	1	49	46	37	60	86	78	82	143	2	....	....
12	12	10	8	7	11	14	6	972	964	556	946	1807	1779	1158	2622	186	7	169

SYDNEY, Continued.

M.	F.	M.	F.	M.	F.	M.	F.	M.	F.	M.	F.	M.	F.	M.	F.			
....		....		....		1	3	....	108	114	137	336	112	137	151	399	12	....	....
					1	1	....		62	85	81	257	76	105	107	304	7	1	....
									59	73	44	108	66	83	53	122	1	2	....
						1	1	136	136	141	353	155	163	174	424	27	4	22
		1	1			1		110	149	108	257	148	191	177	358	14	....	....
				1		2	1	39	95	48	150	47	107	63	212	4	....	57
1	1	2	2	3	2	5	3	115	157	202	448	158	205	266	565	12	4	17
2	....	1	3	....		4	4	96	111	153	240	130	141	209	352	10	110	....
2								174	147	279	361	178	160	302	420	17	37	....
5	1	4	7	4	6	14	9	899	1067	1193	2490	1070	1208	1502	3156	104	158	96

4

No. 1.—PERSONAL CENSUS

COUNTY OF

POLLING DISTRICTS.	TOTAL POPULATION.			Number of Families.	Average Number of each Family.	Under one year of age.		Deaths under 1 Yr. age since 30th March, 1860.	
	Males.	Females.	Total.			M.	F.	M.	F.
	1	2	3	4	5	6	7	8	9
1. Guysborough	1119	1123	2242	359		39	27	3	6
2. Intervale	481	487	968	154		18	12	1	3
3. Manchester	773	775	1548	240		25	32	3	3
4. Melford	813	770	1583	256		37	28	2	2
5. Crow Harbor	371	356	727	117		13	10		
6. Cape Canso	410	416	826	132		11	16	1	1
7. Country Harbor	450	443	893	148		8	14		
8. Sherbrooke	590	579	1169	196		10	15		
9. Marie Joseph	343	305	648	108		6	11	3	
10. Forks, St. Mary's	591	571	1162	192		19	23	1	
11. Molasses Harbor	464	483	947	143		9	15	1	
	6405	6308	12713	2045	6.21	195	203	15	15

COUNTY OF

POLLING DISTRICTS.	TOTAL POPULATION.			Number of Families.	Average Number of each Family.	Under one year of age.		Deaths under 1 Yr. age since 30th March, 1860.	
1. Plaster Cove	831	879	1710	239		26	16	1	2
2. Judique	861	971	1832	241		19	20	1	
3. River Inhabitants	741	747	1488	206		10	18		
4. Port Hood	523	508	1031	148		4	17	1	2
5. Mabou	1387	1350	2737	407		34	25	2	5
6. Broad Cove (Intervale)	701	693	1394	190		19	8	5	1
7. Broad Cove	414	425	839	108		8	4	2	
8. Margaree	187	196	383	56		4	4		
9. Young's Bridge	484	459	943	120		14	11	1	1
10. Friar's Head	371	366	737	106		12	11		3
11. Cheticamp	732	672	1404	216		22	20	3	3
12. Whycocomagh	1098	1126	2224	337		30	29		2
13. Lake Ainslie	392	455	847	128		11	17	2	
14. River Dennis	612	605	1217	170		14	12	1	
15. North-east Margaree	579	602	1181	186		24	15		
	9913	10054	19967	2858	7	251	227	19	19

COUNTY OF

POLLING DISTRICTS.	TOTAL POPULATION.			Number of Families.	Average Number of each Family.	Under one year of age.		Deaths under 1 Yr. age since 30th March, 1860.	
1. Arichat	475	533	1008	179		14	15	3	2
2. Petite Degrat	925	950	1875	273		21	23	3	1
3. D'Escouse	570	603	1173	200		15	24	3	6
4. Black River	376	366	742	109		8	10		1
5. River Bourgeoise	415	434	849	139		8	15	1	
6. St. Peter's	377	403	780	133		14	7		1
7. L'Ardoise	702	773	1475	232		27	22	3	3
8. Grand River	385	370	755	123		6	9		
9. Red Island	390	384	774	105		6	9	2	1
10. River Inhabitants	466	452	918	138		21	11		2
11. Little Arichat	692	743	1435	228		27	21	5	4
12. Loch Lomond	201	211	412	63		5	5	1	
13. Flamboise	224	187	411	75		3	5		
	6198	6409	12607	1997	6.31	175	176	21	21

BY AGES...1860—61.

GUYSBOROUGH.

Over 1 and under 2 yrs. of age.		Deaths between 1 and 2 years, since 80th M'th, 1860.		Over 2 and under 3 years of age.		Deaths between 2 and 3 years, since M'ch 80, 1860.		Over 3 and under 4 years of age.		Deaths between 3 and 4 years, since M'ch 80, 1860.		Over 4 and under 5 years of age.		Deaths between 4 and 5 years, since M'ch 80, 1860.	
M.	F.	M.	F.	M.	F.	M.	F.	M.	F.	M.	F.	M.	F.	M.	F.
10	11	12	13	14	15	16	17	18	19	20	21	22	23	24	25
26	23	1	1	24	32	1		39	28	1	2	19	32		1
9	7			15	15	3		8	15	2	1	22	15	3	2
17	20	2		18	24		1	22	27		1	26	19		1
19	18	1	1	26	28	2	1	23	19	1		19	18	2	1
11	6		1	12	12	1		9	10	2	1	7	13		
10	14			14	10		2	12	15			12	16		1
12	16	1	2	14	9	1	1	9	14	1	1	11	18	1	
25	13	1	1	17	17			16	19		2	22	14	1	1
14	17			12	5			12	9			9	11		
18	17			13	30		2	19	21			18	15		1
17	12			15	17			15	17			14	17		
178	163	6	6	180	199	8	7	184	194	7	8	179	188	7	8

INVERNESS.

M.	F.	M.	F.	M.	F.	M.	F.	M.	F.	M.	F.	M.	F.	M.	F.
17	19	2		17	22	1		20	19			21	23		
14	18			17	26			14	18			21	17		
20	26			18	15			20	21		1	18	26		
10	16			10	12			19	7			19	12		
25	29	1	2	54	25	1		32	35			39	44	1	1
20	10			14	23			14	17			25	22	1	
11	12			7	13			12	12			10	11		
4	6	1		5	3			4	6			5	5	1	
12	7		1	14	15	1		6	10			18	12		
12	7			10	12			7	12	2		10	7	1	
20	10		1	21	29	1	1	20	20	2	1	17	17	2	1
30	22			36	33			35	24			31	34	2	
13	9			12	19			12	15		1	18	17		
13	14	1		15	18			22	12			20	10		
15	23		1	19	16			19	25		2	15	16		
236	228	5	5	269	281	4	1	256	253	4	5	287	273	8	2

RICHMOND.

M.	F.	M.	F.	M.	F.	M.	F.	M.	F.	M.	F.	M.	F.	M.	F.
11	12			15	4	1		10	21		1	12	13		1
13	19	4	3	21	18	1		25	26	3	3	24	22	2	3
12	5	3	2	15	12	7	1	16	13	3	3	11	24	4	3
17	6			10	7			16	13			7	11		1
2	8	2	2	8	9			9	16			12	17		
6	10			10	7		2	10	12	1		9	8	1	
11	16		1	28	21	1	1	18	17		2	14	26		1
11	7			5	12			9	8			14	10		
5	14			9	13			11	4	1		12	7		1
18	12			11	13			10	17		1	10	13		
19	18	2	3	14	30	2	4	17	21	3	2	17	24	6	3
8	2			2	4			6	6			1	7		1
9	9			11	7			9	6			6	4		
142	138	11	11	159	157	14	6	166	180	11	12	149	186	13	14

No. 1.—PERSONAL CENSUS

COUNTY OF

POLLING DISTRICTS.	Over 5 and under 10 years of age.		Deaths between 5 and 10 y'rs. since M'ch 1860.		Over 10 and under 15 years of age.					
					Males.		Females.		Deaths since M'ch 30, 1860.	
	M.	F.	M.	F.	MD.	S.	MD.	S.	M.	F.
	26	27	28	29	30	31	32	33	34	35
1. Guysborough	142	138	4	2	...	146	...	148	...	1
2. Intervale	58	55	1	2	...	57	...	68	...	1
3. Manchester	99	106	1	2	...	103	...	83	...	2
4. Melford	106	98	1	6	...	112	...	96	1	...
5. Crow Harbor	56	39	3	2	...	50	...	50	1	1
6. Cape Canso	61	48	1	1	...	49	...	52	...	1
7. Country Harbor	67	65	...	3	...	69	...	47	1	...
8. Sherbrooke	81	84	2		...	89	...	74	1	...
9. Marie Joseph	51	46			...	48	...	38	1	...
10. Forks, St. Mary's	77	57	5		...	77	...	62	2	...
11. Molasses Harbor	78	79		1	...	69	...	66	...	
	876	817	18	19	...	869	...	784	7	6

COUNTY OF

	26	27	28	29	30	31	32	33	34	35
1. Plaster Cove	93	136		1	...	114	...	122	1	...
2. Judique	101	114	1	1	...	106	...	117	...	
3. River Inhabitants	108	105	1		...	104	...	91	...	
4. Port Hood	69	75		1	...	64	...	71	...	1
5. Mabou	185	153	1		...	184	...	164	1	...
6. Broad Cove (Intervale)	92	90	3		...	105	...	78	...	
7. Broad Cove	52	56			...	49	...	50	...	
8. Margaree	24	22	1	1	...	22	...	30	...	
9. Young's Bridge	71	78	1	2	...	72	...	66	...	
10. Friar's Head	46	45	3		...	49	...	53	...	2
11. Cheticamp	104	83	2	2	...	104	...	82	1	1
12. Whycocomagh	125	144	2		...	153	...	139	...	1
13. Lake Ainslie	53	55			...	45	...	48	...	
14. River Dennis	72	81			...	73	...	73	...	
15. North-east Margaree	86	84	1		...	79	...	68	...	1
	1281	1321	16	8	...	1323	...	1252	3	6

COUNTY OF

	26	27	28	29	30	31	32	33	34	35
1. Arichat	68	58	3	8	...	58	...	55	...	
2. Petite Degrat	127	111	6	6	...	113	...	123	...	6
3. D'Escouse	61	52	9	7	...	72	...	87	7	4
4. Black River	55	49			...	60	...	36	...	1
5. River Bourgeoise	63	68	4	1	...	58	...	52	1	5
6. St. Peter's	50	58		1	...	48	...	60	1	1
7. L'Ardoise	103	119	2	2	...	91	...	91	2	2
8. Grand River	41	38			...	50	...	38	...	1
9. Red Islands	59	41		1	...	59	...	65	...	
10. River Inhabitants	50	59		1	...	39	...	55	...	1
11. Little Arichat	111	100	8	6	...	76	...	89	2	1
12. Loch Lomond	23	35			...	28	...	30	...	
13. Flamboise	32	18			...	27	...	23	...	
	843	806	33	33	...	779	...	804	13	22

BY AGES...1860—61.

GUYSBOROUGH, Continued.

	Over 15 and under 20 years of age.							Over 20 and under 30 years of age.							
Males.			Females.			Deaths since March 30, 1860.		Males.			Females.			Deaths since March 30, 1860.	
MD.	S.	WDR	MD.	S.	WD.	M.	F.	MD.	S.	WDR	MD.	S.	WD.	M.	F.
36	37	38	39	40	41	42	43	44	45	46	47	48	49	50	51
1	147	....	2	150	....	....	....	44	155	1	71	125	1	1	1
....	60	....	1	66	....	....	2	12	76	....	30	55	....	2	1
....	90	....	1	103	....	....	1	31	111	....	55	83	1	....	....
....	97	....	5	81	....	....	....	34	110	....	56	91	1	....	1
....	46	....	4	44	....	....	....	19	38	....	29	26	2	....	....
....	45	....	....	58	....	2	1	19	55	....	42	34	....	1	....
....	56	....	2	52	....	....	....	27	43	....	40	37	2	....	....
....	58	....	2	67	....	....	1	21	76	....	41	56	2	3	....
....	43	....	2	30	....	....	....	22	42	....	24	18	....	....	....
....	64	....	2	62	....	....	1	27	79	....	49	61	2	1	2
....	55	....	3	62	....	....	....	34	41	....	38	34	2	....	....
1	761	....	24	775	....	2	6	290	826	1	475	620	13	8	5

INVERNESS, Continued.

MD.	S.	WDR	MD.	S.	WD.	M.	F.	MD.	S.	WDR	MD.	S.	WD.	M.	F.
....	124	....	....	102	....	....	....	10	119	....	34	129	1	....	1
....	105	....	....	116	....	....	1	12	185	....	37	191	1	....	1
....	91	....	....	99	....	....	1	9	123	....	33	105	....	....	....
....	78	....	....	50	....	....	....	14	92	....	29	58	1	1	....
....	177	....	2	194	....	....	1	30	236	....	71	216	3	4	4
....	85	....	2	88	....	....	....	13	113	....	37	104	....	1	1
....	58	....	1	52	....	....	....	7	75	....	17	72	....	....	....
....	25	....	1	15	....	....	....	2	33	....	10	34	....	....	....
....	67	....	....	52	....	1	....	6	86	....	25	65	....	....	....
....	50	....	1	43	....	1	1	21	59	2	30	44	....	3	....
....	96	....	....	98	....	....	....	40	98	2	58	70	1	1	2
....	125	....	....	137	....	....	....	28	179	4	58	150	1	1	....
....	41	....	....	42	....	....	....	9	55	....	30	61	1	....	....
....	73	....	....	67	....	....	....	4	105	....	18	94	....	....	....
....	60	....	....	67	....	1	....	23	78	....	38	71	3	....	1
....	1255	....	7	1222	....	3	4	228	1636	8	525	1464	12	11	10

RICHMOND, Continued.

MD.	S.	WDR	MD.	S.	WD.	M.	F.	MD.	S.	WDR	MD.	S.	WD.	M.	F.
....	57	....	2	56	....	1	....	17	47	1	39	68	2	3	....
....	136	....	4	122	....	2	6	42	119	....	60	112	5	5	....
....	77	....	3	59	....	5	3	46	71	3	63	65	2	7	3
....	48	....	1	45	....	....	....	5	37	1	12	67	1	2	....
....	61	....	1	52	....	2	1	16	54	2	27	46	....	....	1
....	44	....	....	48	....	....	....	7	57	....	21	52	....	1	....
....	77	....	....	87	....	1	....	35	87	....	64	79	3	....	1
....	52	....	....	51	....	....	....	4	73	....	18	58	....	1	....
....	64	....	....	52	....	....	1	2	52	....	10	54	2	....	....
....	55	....	1	44	....	....	....	28	82	2	38	49	1	2	1
....	99	....	4	85	....	....	....	37	63	2	65	73	2	3	....
1	30	....	....	24	....	....	....	4	33	....	7	25	....	....	....
....	29	....	....	18	....	....	....	18	28	....	20	23	2	....	....
1	829	....	16	743	....	11	11	261	803	11	453	771	20	24	6

COUNTY OF

POLLING DISTRICTS.	Over 30 and under 40 years of age.							
	Males.			Females.			Deaths since March 30, 1860.	
	MD.	S.	WDR	MD.	S.	WD.	M.	F.
	52	53	54	55	56	57	58	59
1. Guysborough	71	19	1	83	25	3	....	1
2. Intervale	38	7	....	38	15	1	1	1
3. Manchester	50	20	1	62	14	4	1	....
4. Melford	63	16	1	66	17	6	....	1
5. Crow Harbor	38	8	....	32	13	1	1	1
6. Cape Canso	44	4	....	35	6	....	....	....
7. Country Harbor	34	13	1	38	5	2	....	....
8. Sherbrooke	60	12	1	59	7	3	....	....
9 Marie Joseph	28	3	....	34	5	3	....	....
10. Forks, St. Mary's	52	16	3	44	19	1	....	....
11. Molasses Harbor	41	1	....	42	2	1	....	....
	519	119	8	533	128	25	3	4

COUNTY OF

	MD.	S.	WDR	MD.	S.	WD.	M.	F.
1. Plaster Cove	50	40	2	60	37	4	1	2
2. Judique	44	48	2	52	47	2	....	1
3. River Inhabitants	49	30	....	56	24	2	....	1
4. Port Hood	28	18	1	36	21	3	....	1
5. Mabou	112	45	4	111	39	5	1	1
6. Broad Cove (Intervale)	48	22	1	43	31	1	....	....
7. Broad Cove	20	26	....	26	27	1	....	....
8. Margaree	15	10	....	13	7	1	....	....
9. Young's Bridge	32	6	3	32	9	2	....	....
10. Friar's Head	30	7	....	35	8	....	....	....
11. Cheticamp	69	8	3	53	11	1	....	4
12. Whycocomagh	62	36	1	75	44	5	1	1
13. Lake Ainslie	40	12	....	35	24	2	....	....
14. River Dennis	30	44	....	47	40	7	....	....
15. North-east Margaree	44	6	....	49	15	....	1	....
	673	358	17	723	384	36	4	11

COUNTY OF

	MD.	S.	WDR	MD.	S.	WD.	M.	F.
1. Arichat	53	9	1	53	21	6	....	....
2. Petite Degrat	81	9	1	76	21	6	1	2
3. D'Escouse	53	6	2	47	10	3	....	....
4. Black River	25	10	1	30	9	2	1	....
5. River Bourgeoise	35	5	....	40	4	....	....	2
6. St. Peter's	29	13	1	32	11	5	2	1
7. L'Ardoise	72	10	2	68	15	5	....	....
8. Grand River	20	24	....	25	13	3	2	....
9. Red Islands	24	12	....	30	13	1	....	....
10. River Inhabitants	40	13	1	40	10	2	....	....
11. Little Arichat	73	6	3	74	8	7	1	....
12. Loch Lomond	10	5	....	15	4	1	....	....
13. Flamboise	18	4	1	17	3	3	....	1
	533	126	13	547	142	44	7	6

BY AGES...1860—61.

GUYSBOROUGH, Continued.

Over 40 and under 50 years of age.								Over 50 and under 60 years of age.							
Males.			Females.			Deaths since March 30, 1860.		Males.			Females.			Deaths since March 30, 1860.	
MD.	S.	WDR	MD.	S.	WD.	M.	F.	MD.	S.	WDR	MD.	S.	WD.	M.	F.
60	61	62	63	64	65	66	67	68	69	70	71	72	73	74	75
74	6	1	78	10	10	....	1	59	.....	2	50	1	14	....	.....
30	1	1	29	6	2	....	1	18	1	.....	22	.....	4	....	.....
59	5	.....	48	3	4	....	1	32	1	2	35	2	7	1	2
43	1	2	47	8	1	....	.....	40	3	3	27	1	4	....	.....
21	.....	2	22	2	2	....	.....	7	.....	3	12	1	4	....	.....
28	2	1	26	3	3	....	.....	14	2	2	15	1	5	....	.....
29	1	1	30	3	4	....	.....	19	2	2	17	.....	2	1	.....
40	3	.....	36	5	8	1	....	17	3	2	12	1	5	2	.....
18	.....	1	18	3	1	....	.....	14	1	1	12	.....	4	....	.....
34	5	1	37	4	3	....	.....	25	.....	1	25	2	5	....	1
34	1	1	33	.....	5	....	.....	13	1	.....	13	.....	1	....	.....
410	25	11	404	47	43	1	3	258	14	18	240	9	55	4	3

INVERNESS, Continued.

MD.	S.	WDR	MD.	S.	WD.	M.	F.	MD.	S.	WDR	MD.	S.	WD.	M.	F.
55	10	3	50	9	4	....	.....	38	2	2	36	5	4	....	.....
52	7	3	48	11	11	1	1	32	5	.....	35	4	6	....	1
44	6	2	37	3	8	....	.....	31	1	.....	30	2	4	1	.....
46	5	.....	36	10	4	....	.....	18	1	2	12	2	3	....	.....
63	11	2	70	5	15	1	....	67	1	4	52	4	20	2	1
32	2	3	41	6	7	....	.....	30	2	1	32	7	4	....	.....
19	1	1	20	5	.....	....	.....	17	2	1	19	3	1	....	.....
10	2	.....	10	6	4	....	1	10	1	1	6	1	2	....	.....
31	1	1	27	3	2	....	.....	20	.....	2	16	2	10	....	.....
23	1	.....	21	1	6	1	....	18	.....	.....	8	1	3	1	1
38	.....	3	45	2	5	....	.....	23	.....	4	31	1	3	....	1
71	10	.....	69	12	8	....	.....	56	4	4	43	.....	13	....	.....
20	1	.....	17	3	2	....	.....	15	.....	.....	14	3	4	....	1
37	3	.....	23	4	6	2	....	24	5	1	21	1	3	1	.....
39	2	.....	34	4	1	....	.....	25	1	.....	26	.....	3	....	.....
580	62	18	548	84	83	5	2	429	25	29	381	36	83	5	5

RICHMOND, Continued.

MD.	S.	WDR	MD.	S.	WD.	M.	F.	MD.	S.	WDR	MD.	S.	WD.	M.	F.
34	3	2	22	9	9	....	.....	21	2	.....	24	.....	5	....	.....
68	3	4	66	10	8	....	.....	48	3	4	45	5	10	1	1
41	.....	1	40	6	11	1	....	24	.....	1	27	3	17	....	.....
24	1	.....	26	1	1	....	.....	23	.....	.....	16	.....	2	....	.....
29	2	.....	29	1	6	....	.....	26	.....	1	23	1	8	1	.....
25	1	2	21	5	3	....	1	21	3	2	18	1	2	....	.....
54	.....	.....	34	10	10	....	.....	24	.....	1	31	2	5	1	.....
25	2	.....	17	3	3	1	....	13	1	2	12	1	8	....	.....
29	2	2	22	4	3	....	1	11	1	1	20	.....	1	....	1
23	3	2	24	4	3	1	....	17	3	1	19	.....	6	....	.....
53	1	2	42	4	9	....	.....	30	1	4	23	2	13	1	.....
15	.....	.....	14	1	2	....	.....	11	1	1	7	.....	3	....	.....
5	2	.....	8	.....	2	....	.....	9	.....	.....	8	.....	1	1	.....
425	20	15	365	58	70	3	2	278	15	18	273	15	81	5	2

No. 1.—PERSONAL CENSUS

COUNTY OF

POLLING DISTRICTS.	Males.			Females.			Deaths since March 30, 1860.	
	MD.	S.	WDR	MD.	S.	WD.	M.	F.
	76	77	78	79	80	81	82	83
1. Guysborough	49	2	11	36	1	14	3	
2. Intervale	32		4	18		7	3	
3. Manchester	37	3	3	14	2	10	2	
4. Melford	32		4	23	2	15	1	
5. Crow Harbor	15	2	4	6		7		
6. Cape Canso	12	1		5		8		
7. Country Harbor	17	3	3	8		6		
8. Sherbrooke	15		4	11	1	7		
9. Marie Joseph	12		1	6		6	1	
10. Forks, St. Mary's	23	3	3	14	2	7		
11. Molasses Harbor	14		1	11		4		
	258	14	38	152	8	91	10	

COUNTY OF

1. Plaster Cove	38	2	6	22	1	10		3
2. Judique	50	1	7	28	6	16	1	
3. River Inhabitants	27		6	11	2	8	2	
4. Port Hood	10		1	5		13		1
5. Mabou	47		3	35	4	13	2	
6. Broad Cove (Intervale)	31	1	5	8	4	10		1
7. Broad Cove	20	1	3	7		5		
8. Margaree	5			3	1	2		
9. Young's Bridge	13		1	3	2	2		
10. Friar's Head	9		1	7		7		
11. Cheticamp	20		3	14	1	7	1	
12. Whycocomagh	50			30	3	20		1
13. Lake Ainslie	15	1	4	11	1	6		2
14. River Dennis	25		9	22		15		1
15. North-east Margaree	22	1	2	13	4	5		
	382	8	51	219	29	130	6	9

COUNTY OF

1. Arichat	24	2	3	14	1	15	1	
2. Petite Degrat	40	1	7	21	2	10		2
3. D'Escouse	30	2	2	18		9		1
4. Black River	15		2	9		2		
5. River Bourgeoise	16		2	3		2		
6. St. Peter's	14	1	2	8		2		
7. L'Ardoise	25	1	6	16	1	14	1	1
8. Grand River	19		2	18	1	9	1	
9. Red Islands	19		1	4	1	7		
10. River Inhabitants	27		2	14	1	6		
11. Little Arichat	21		1	11	1	7		
12. Loch Lomond	10	1	1	6		3		
13. Flamboise	10		1	4	1	3		
	270	8	31	146	9	88	3	4

BY AGES...1860—61.

GUYSBOROUGH, Continued.

| | Over 70 and under 80 years of age. | | | | | | | | Over 80 and under 90 years of age. | | | | | | |
| | Males. | | | Females. | | | Deaths since March 30, 1860. | | Males. | | | Females. | | | Deaths since March 30, 1860. |
MD.	S.	WDR	MD.	S.	WD.	M.	F.	MD.	S.	WDK	MD.	S.	WD.	M.	F.
84	85	86	87	88	89	90	91	92	93	94	95	96	97	98	99
24	1	4	7	1	5			3	1	2	1		1		1
6	1	3	2		4	2		3		1					
9	1	2	2		7	2				1			1		
17			3		8	3							2		
7		2	2		7		1			1					
4	2	4			3		1	1		1			1		
6		1	2	1	4			2			1		4		
12	1	1	7		7	1	1	1		2	2	1	1	1	
4			1		1					1					
8		2	3		1		1	2		2	1	1	1		1
5		2	3		3		1	3			1		1		
102	8	21	32	2	50	8	5	15	1	11	6	2	12	1	2

INVERNESS, Continued.

12		5	4	1	8		2	1		2			1	1	
11			6		11	2		1		1	1	2	8		
12	1	3	7		5		3	2		1		1	4		
6		3	3	1	5		2	2		3	1		5	1	1
21		4	4		8			5		2			4	2	1
10		4	7	1	8	1	1	4		4	1		1	2	
6	1	4	2	2	4			1		2		1	2		
2		2	2		2			1							
2		3			3								5		
1		2			3	1				1			1		2
7		2	3	1	3	2		2		1			1		
18		1	12	1	12		1	6		2	1	1	7		
9		2	7	2	7			3					2	1	
12		4	6		7	2		4					3	1	1
13	1		5	5	4	1		1	1	1		4	2	1	
142	3	39	68	13	90	9	9	33	1	20	4	9	46	9	5

RICHMOND, Continued.

7		1	2		4					1					
10		1	6		5	3	1	2		1	2		3	1	
4		3	1							2			2		
7		1	5		3			1		3	1		1		
3		1	2		2			1		1			1		
8			4		7								2		
9		2	6	1	5	1		1		3		1	3		
9			2		2			3			1	1	2		
3		2	3		2	1	1	3		1			1		
6			3		4								1		
6		3	2		6		1	2	1	3			2	1	
2		2	2	1	3										
1			1		1					1				1	1
75		16	39	2	44	5	3	13	1	16	4	2	18	3	1

5

No. 1.—PERSONAL CENSUS

COUNTY OF

POLLING DISTRICTS.	Over 90 and under 100 years of age.							
	Males.			Females.			Deaths since March 30, 1860.	
	MD.	S.	WDR	MD.	S.	WD.	M.	F.
	100	101	102	103	104	105	106	107
1. Guysborough						1		
2. Intervale								
3. Manchester								
4. Melford								
5. Crow Harbor							1	
6. Cape Canso								
7. Country Harbor								
8. Sherbrooke								
9. Marie Joseph								
10. Forks, St. Mary's								
11. Molasses Harbor						1		
						2	1	

COUNTY OF

	100	101	102	103	104	105	106	107
1. Plaster Cove				1				
2. Judique	1			2			2	
3. River Inhabitants							1	
4. Port Hood								
5. Mabou								
6. Broad Cove (Intervale)	1							1
7. Broad Cove								
8. Margaree								
9. Young's Bridge								
10. Friar's Head								1
11. Cheticamp							2	
12. Whycocomagh				1				
13. Lake Ainslie								
14. River Dennis	1			1			1	
15. North-east Margaree				1				
	3			4	2		5	1	2

COUNTY OF

	100	101	102	103	104	105	106	107
1. Arichat								
2. Petite Degrat		1						
3. D'Escouse								
4. Black River								
5. River Bourgeoise								
6. St. Peter's						1		
7. L'Ardoise								
8. Grand River				1		1		
9. Red Islands							1	
10. River Inhabitants						1		
11. Little Arichat						2		
12. Loch Lomond								
13. Flamboise								
	1			1		5	1	

BY AGES...1860—61.

GUYSBOROUGH, Continued.

Over 100 years of age.						Deaths since M'ch 30, 1860.		Ages not given	Deaths.				Males.			
Males.			Females.								Ages not given		Married.	Single.	Widowers.	Total.
MD.	S.	WDR	MD.	S.	WD.	M.	F.	M.	F.	M.	F.					
108	109	110	111	112	113	114	115	116	117	118	119	120	121	122	123
								6	5			328	769	22	1119
												139	333	9	481
								5	4			220	544	9	773
								5	1			230	572	11	813
												107	252	12	371
												122	280	8	410
												134	308	8	450
								1	2			166	414	10	590
												98	241	4	343
												171	408	12	591
												144	316	4	464
								*17	†12			1859	4437	109	6405

INVERNESS, Continued.

								1				205	605	21	831
												203	643	15	861
				1				5	2			176	553	12	741
												124	389	10	523
												345	1023	19	1387
									2			169	514	18	701
												90	313	11	414
												45	139	3	187
								3				104	370	10	484
						1						102	263	6	371
												204	510	18	732
				1								291	794	13	1098
								1	1			112	274	6	392
								1			1	137	461	14	612
			1					2				167	409	3	579
						2	1	1	‡13	‖5	1	2474	7260	179	9913

RICHMOND, Continued.

								2	3			157	309	9	475
						1						292	615	18	925
												198	358	14	570
												100	269	7	376
												126	282	7	415
												104	266	7	377
												220	467	15	702
												93	288	4	385
										1		91	292	7	390
						2						141	317	8	466
												222	452	18	692
						1	4					53	144	4	201
												61	160	3	224
						1		§5	¶7	1		1858	4219	121	6198

* 6 md., 10 s., 1 wdr.   † 7 md., 3 s., 2 w.   ‡ 4 md., 9 s.   ‖ 2 md., 3 s.   § 1 md., 4 s.   ¶ 2 md., 5 s.

No. 1.—PERSONAL CENSUS

COUNTY OF

POLLING DISTRICTS.	Females.				Grand Total	Deaths.		
	Married	Single	Widows	Total		Males	Females	Total
	124	125	126	127	128	129	130	131
1. Guysborough	332	742	49	1123	2242	14	17	31
2. Intervale	140	329	18	487	908	18	14	32
3. Manchester	219	522	34	775	1548	12	14	26
4. Melford	228	505	37	770	1585	14	13	27
5. Crow Harbor	107	226	23	356	727	9	7	16
6. Cape Canso	123	273	20	416	826	5	8	13
7. Country Harbor	138	281	24	443	893	6	7	13
8. Sherbrooke	170	374	35	579	1169	13	6	19
9. Marie Joseph	97	193	15	305	648	5	.....	5
10. Forks, St. Mary's	175	379	20	577	1162	9	9	18
11. Molasses Harbor	144	321	18	483	947	1	2	3
	1873	4142	293	6308	12713	106	97	203

COUNTY OF

1. Plaster Cove	206	641	32	879	1710	7	11	18
2. Judique	297	707	57	971	1882	6	6	12
3. River Inhabitants	175	539	33	747	1488	4	6	10
4. Port Hood	122	352	34	508	1031	3	9	12
5. Mabou	345	957	68	1350	2737	19	16	35
6. Broad Cove (Intervale)	171	497	31	693	1394	13	5	18
7. Broad Cove	92	320	13	425	839	2	.....	2
8. Margaree	45	140	11	196	383	3	2	5
9. Young's Bridge	105	332	24	459	943	4	4	8
10. Friar's Head	102	244	20	366	737	13	11	24
11. Cheticamp	204	445	23	672	1404	15	17	32
12. Whycocomagh	288	772	66	1126	2224	7	6	13
13. Lake Ainslie	115	316	24	455	847	4	4	8
14. River Dennis	138	426	41	605	1217	9	2	11
15. North-east Margaree	166	417	19	602	1181	5	5	10
	2479	7079	496	10054	19967	114	104	218

COUNTY OF

1. Arichat	157	355	41	553	1008	12	12	24
2. Petite Degrat	289	614	47	950	1879	33	34	67
3. D'Escousse	189	366	44	603	1173	49	33	82
4. Black River	100	254	12	366	742	3	3	6
5. River Bourgeose	125	286	20	434	849	11	12	23
6. St. Peter's	104	279	20	403	786	10	5	15
7. L'Ardoise	219	508	46	773	1475	11	14	25
8. Grand River	93	250	27	370	755	6	1	7
9. Red Islands	80	277	18	384	774	5	7	12
10. River Inhabitants	139	288	25	452	918	3	6	9
11. Little Arichat	221	476	46	743	1435	34	24	58
12. Loch Lomond	52	147	12	211	412	1	1	2
13. Flamboise	58	117	12	187	411	2	2	4
	1845	4194	370	6400	12607	180	154	334

BY AGES...1860—61.

GUYSBOROUGH, Continued.

Deaf and Dumb		Blind		Lunatics		Idiots		Cannot Read.				Cannot Write.				Married since March 30, 1860.	Colored persons included in population.	Indians not included in population.
								Over 5 and under 15 years of age.	Above 15 years of age.			Over 5 and under 15 years of age.	Above 15 years of age.					
M.	F.	M.	F.	M.	F.	M.	F.	M.	F.	M.	F.	M.	F.	M.	F.			
132	133	134	135	136	137	138	139	140	141	142	143	144	145	146	147	148	149	150
1			1	1				141	133	140	175	197	194	217	297	18	200	26
		1					2	79	89	77	79	100	105	117	186	19	180	
1			1		2	2	1	136	129	132	144	148	143	159	192	15	148	49
	1						1	133	113	137	148	156	150	200	280	19	35	
1	1							100	85	158	176	101	92	186	197	9		
								67	56	75	84	80	67	97	125	2	3	
							2	83	65	62	71	104	84	102	133	15	33	
2								69	50	39	43	105	92	80	107	3		
	1		1				1	68	58	10	11	80	65	11	19	3		
1				1	2	1	1	34	31	27	24	92	78	61	104	11	2	
	1						1	126	118	168	201	132	131	187	239	6		13
6	4	2	2	4	4	7	5	1030	927	1025	1156	1295	1201	1417	1879	120	601	88

INVERNESS, Continued.

Deaf and Dumb		Blind		Lunatics		Idiots		Cannot Read.				Cannot Write.				Married since March 30, 1860.	Colored persons included in population.	Indians not included in population.
2						3	1	106	166	127	256	149	200	175	328	20	4	
1		2	1	1	1	2	1	127	176	141	454	154	193	190	516	15		
1	1		1	1		1		156	169	273	345	177	181	302	393	3		
			1					62	70	34	80	68	76	43	90	4		
1			1	1	4	2	1	173	175	269	453	227	222	369	611	14		
1	2		1		2	1	1	105	112	106	267	150	149	159	348	12		
					1		1	60	87	60	185	61	92	87	203	7		
				1		1		29	39	32	73	33	37	45	89	2		
				1	1	1		75	113	85	183	95	129	122	231	8		
1	1	2	1				2	44	63	79	100	73	84	155	197	15		8
				1	3		1	154	117	212	242	190	160	356	398	11		19
							1	132	168	174	285	138	182	214	336	15	1	30
1	3						1	44	51	66	137	60	75	93	184	7		
	1	1						67	84	88	182	90	129	128	283	9	24	11
	1	1				1	1	118	107	144	229	126	112	170	268	1		
8	9	6	6	3	11	14	12	1452	1697	1890	3470	1782	2021	2599	4475	143	29	68

RICHMOND, Continued.

Deaf and Dumb		Blind		Lunatics		Idiots		Cannot Read.				Cannot Write.				Married since March 30, 1860.	Colored persons included in population.	Indians not included in population.
		1				3		45	47	59	84	47	62	72	110	4	1	
3	7			1	2	1	1	190	198	435	457	203	209	450	530	24	24	
1	1					2		105	112	291	271	115	117	302	330	16		
								39	33	41	82	61	57	67	144	3		
1								98	102	186	221	102	103	197	239	14		
						1		74	84	113	162	75	89	135	191	4		
1		2	5	2	3	9		175	174	301	338	184	192	351	445	11		8
1			1			1		58	57	110	169	62	62	114	189			
						1		89	96	132	185	97	101	146	203	1		19
			3					58	68	125	142	71	87	158	202	9	1	1
1	2				1	1	1	138	147	290	345	158	159	301	400	9	6	
								26	39	31	60	29	53	65	99	5		
								29	21	44	57	30	21	69	82	2		
8	10	1	5	7	6	11	12	1124	1178	2158	2573	1234	1312	2427	3164	102	32	28

No. 1.—PERSONAL CENSUS

COUNTY OF

POLLING DISTRICTS.	TOTAL POPULATION.			Number of Families.	Average Number of each Family.	Under one year of age.		Deaths under 1 yr. age since 30th March, 1860.	
	Males.	Females.	Total.			M.	F.	M.	F.
	1	2	3	4	5	6	7	8	9
1. Washabok	505	539	1044	159		15	10	2	
2. Middle River	451	426	877	124		11	9	2	3
3. Baddeck	769	784	1553	239		14	21		2
4. Munro's Point, St. Ann's	712	728	1440	214		15	22	1	1
5. Englishtown, St. Ann's	619	605	1224	182		17	10	1	3
6. Boulardrie	574	604	1178	173		19	19	5	3
7. Ingonish	281	285	566	86		7	10	2	2
8. Cape North	342	325	667	90		11	8	1	1
9. Bay St. Lawrence	182	171	353	55		5	4		
10. Little Narrows	366	375	741	103		15	7		1
	4801	4842	9613	1425	6.76	120	120	14	16

COUNTY OF

1. Sydney	1198	1269	2467	375		37	32	5	
2. Ball's Bridge	1076	1093	2169	316		24	43	1	2
3. Mira Ferry	439	460	899	143		11	11	1	
4. Sydney Mines	1633	1650	3283	505		44	38	5	7
5. Mainadieu	745	764	1509	234		17	17	1	
6. Louisburg	659	715	1374	230		21	23	2	
7. Gabarus	776	775	1551	243		25	20	1	1
8. East Bay	895	890	1785	273		16	20	2	1
9. Beaver Cove	500	492	992	149		18	18	4	3
10. Howley's Ferry	515	486	1001	155		8	17		
11. Lingan Mines	624	629	1253	176		16	14		3
12. Cow Bay	345	368	713	101		7	11		1
13. Big Pond	302	341	643	103		11	5	2	
14. Christmas Island	605	622	1227	183		17	9	2	4
	10312	10554	20866	3189	6.54	272	278	26	22

NOTE.—158 returned from No. 7 after first Returns were made up.

COUNTY OF

1. Windsor	1093	1178	2271	400		28	25	1	1
2. St. Croix	607	497	1104	182		11	19		1
3. Brooklyn	552	533	1085	196		13	12	1	
4. Scotch Village	1148	1106	2254	424		31	37	2	2
5. Falmouth	579	606	1185	213		19	15		
6. Kempt	1019	946	1965	331		45	40	3	4
7. Rawdon Church	392	367	759	125		13	16		2
8. South Rawdon	321	303	624	101		7	11	1	
9. Noel	971	820	1791	295		34	23		2
10. Nine Mile River	972	948	1920	314		36	30	2	1
11. Maitland	997	970	1967	327		33	34	2	1
12. Chester Road	273	262	535	91		11	10		
	8927	8533	17460	3009	5.81	280	272	11	14

BY AGES...1860—61.

VICTORIA.

Over 1 and under 2 ys. of age		Deaths between 1 and 2 years, since M'ch 30, 1860.		Over 2 and under 3 years of age		Deaths between 2 and 3 years, since M'ch 30, 1860.		Over 3 and under 4 years of age		Deaths between 3 and 4 years, since M'ch 30, 1860.		Over 4 and under 5 years of age		Deaths between 4 and 5 years, since M'ch 30, 1860.	
M.	F.	M.	F.	M.	F.	M.	F.	M.	F.	M.	F.	M.	F.	M.	F.
10	11	12	13	14	15	16	17	18	19	20	21	22	23	24	25
10	15	...	...	15	11	2	...	14	19	...	1	8	15	...	...
9	13	...	...	16	12	...	...	16	11	...	1	14	20	...	...
24	9	...	1	31	27	...	...	28	24	...	1	13	27	2	...
17	19	...	...	19	17	...	2	24	15	...	...	9	19	...	...
17	11	1	1	17	14	...	...	18	17	...	...	13	14	...	...
15	14	...	...	25	13	...	...	15	18	...	...	16	20	...	...
12	7	...	...	8	12	1	...	7	17	...	...	11	10	...	...
11	13	1	...	11	12	...	...	7	10	...	...	11	14	...	...
13	8	...	...	5	2	...	...	4	7	1	...	9	3	...	...
5	6	...	...	10	18	...	...	6	4	1	...	13	10	...	...
133	115	2	1	157	138	3	2	139	142	2	3	117	152	2	...

CAPE BRETON.

M.	F.	M.	F.	M.	F.	M.	F.	M.	F.	M.	F.	M.	F.	M.	F.
31	27	1	1	28	38	...	...	36	35	...	...	31	34	1	1
16	16	1	2	31	31	1	1	34	26	...	2	28	26	1	...
10	12	...	...	14	10	...	...	10	8	...	...	7	18	...	1
28	32	1	4	59	56	1	1	51	38	...	1	39	53	...	...
17	13	...	...	36	23	...	2	24	16	...	1	22	28	...	1
28	17	...	1	17	19	...	...	18	18	...	1	21	19	1	...
11	19	...	...	20	32	...	...	18	18	...	2	24	20	...	...
29	25	...	...	24	37	...	...	26	29	...	...	26	27	...	2
12	14	...	...	16	19	...	...	14	13	...	...	13	12	1	...
22	15	...	...	17	7	...	...	20	14	...	...	22	18	...	...
14	17	...	...	23	17	...	...	16	18	...	...	20	13	...	...
4	13	...	...	12	16	...	...	7	3	...	...	16	14	...	...
2	8	...	...	7	8	...	...	9	9	...	...	3	3	...	...
14	12	...	...	19	11	...	...	15	15	...	...	21	12	1	...
238	240	3	8	323	324	2	4	298	260	...	7	293	297	5	5

HANTS.

M.	F.	M.	F.	M.	F.	M.	F.	M.	F.	M.	F.	M.	F.	M.	F.
18	50	1	...	27	28	1	...	32	29	...	1	25	26	2	...
15	17	1	...	17	12	...	...	17	19	...	...	18	24	...	...
18	12	...	2	15	21	1	1	14	12	...	...	17	20	1	1
29	19	3	...	33	38	2	2	35	24	2	...	34	26	2	2
17	16	...	...	19	16	...	2	22	8	...	...	22	11	...	...
26	20	...	...	33	38	...	1	30	26	...	2	31	27	...	...
13	12	1	...	14	8	...	...	11	11	...	...	11	15	...	...
3	8	...	...	16	10	...	...	11	11	...	...	11	9	...	...
30	28	1	2	34	25	...	1	26	33	3	2	28	18	1	1
30	28	2	1	37	30	1	2	27	40	...	...	32	22	1	...
40	29	2	...	32	28	1	...	33	33	...	1	33	30	...	...
6	10	1	...	8	8	1	...	7	7	...	...	7	11	...	...
245	229	12	5	285	262	7	9	265	253	5	6	269	239	7	4

44 CENSUS REPORT OF NOVA SCOTIA.

No. 1.—PERSONAL CENSUS

COUNTY OF

POLLING DISTRICTS.	Over 5 and under 10 years of age.		Deaths between 5 and 10 yrs. since M'ch 30, 1860.		Over 10 and under 15 years of age.					
					Males.		Females.		Deaths since M'ch 30, 1860.	
	M.	F.	M.	F.	MD.	S.	MD.	S.	M.	F.
	26	27	28	29	30	31	32	33	34	35
1. Washabok	65	81	1			66		56		
2. Middle River	67	51				56		55		
3. Baddeck	109	110	2			102		101		1
4. Munro's Point, St. Ann's	81	77				99		74	1	
5. Englishtown, St. Ann's	90	64		1		76		75		1
6. Boulardrie	70	82	1			63		75		
7. Ingonish	48	48				32		40		1
8. Cape North	45	39				46		51		
9. Bay St. Lawrence	25	24				16		23		
10. Little Narrows	46	38				53		59		
	646	614	4	1		609		609	1	3

COUNTY OF

	M.	F.	M.	F.	MD.	S.	MD.	S.	M.	F.
1. Sydney	175	170	4	2		163		177	1	
2. Ball's Bridge	161	153				166		156		
3. Mira Ferry	48	63		1		73		58		
4. Sydney Mines	233	244	1	1		247		229	1	
5. Mainadieu	98	86	1	4		90		102		1
6. Louisburg	80	93		2		89		90		3
7. Gabarus	116	89	1			90		99		
8. East Bay	125	137	1			134		125	2	
9. Beaver Cove	73	50				78		65		
10. Howley's Ferry	60	63				70		49		
11. Lingan Mines	84	85		1		89		88	1	
12. Cow Bay	55	47				40		54	1	
13. Big Pond	41	45				44		42		
14. Christmas Island	80	80				98		87		
	1429	1405	8	11		1471		1421	6	4

COUNTY OF

	M.	F.	M.	F.	MD.	S.	MD.	S.	M.	F.
1. Windsor	143	136	3	1		130		124		1
2. St. Croix	77	69				83		60	1	1
3. Brooklyn	64	60	2	3		68		73	1	
4. Scotch Village	151	109	3	3		125		149	1	2
5. Falmouth	73	69				54		84		
6. Kempt	141	125	2			140		127	1	
7. Rawdon Church	45	48				47		43		
8. South Rawdon	54	39		1		47		34		
9. Noel	136	108	6	2		129		99	2	1
10. Nine Mile River	114	130				112		121	1	
11. Maitland	144	145		1		127		148		
12. Chester Road	32	35	1	1		40		30		
	1173	1073	17	12		1102		1092	7	5

BY AGES...1860-61.

VICTORIA, Continued.

	Over 15 and under 20 years of age.								Over 20 and under 30 years of age.						
Males.			Females.			Deaths since March 30, 1860.		Males.			Females.			Deaths since March 30, 1860.	
MD.	S.	WDR	MD.	S.	WD.	M.	F.	MD.	S.	WDR	MD.	S.	WD.	M.	F.
36	37	38	39	40	41	42	43	44	45	46	47	48	49	50	51
	72		69			1		11	87		29	75			2
	45		45				1	11	64		26	51			
	100		81					21	98		42	95			
	77		96					19	128		42	120	1	2	1
	75	2	70					24	82		36	107		1	1
	78		70					15	92		35	86			
	44	2	30					20	24		23	26	3		1
1	43	1	38			1	1	10	52		18	33	2		
	20		19					11	28		17	20	1	1	1
	46		54					14	65		17	69		1	
1	600		5	572		2	2	156	720		285	682	7	5	6

CAPE BRETON, Continued.

MD.	S.	WDR	MD.	S.	WD.	M.	F.	MD.	S.	WDR	MD.	S.	WD.	M.	F.
	153		3	160	1	1		22	161		54	152	3	1	
	144		1	138		3	1	27	143		47	146	1	2	1
	61			66			1	9	57		19	57		1	
1	204		9	230		3	2	73	203	1	121	156	3	2	1
	86		5	89			1	21	104		54	95	1	1	
	70			83			1	14	78	1	43	88		2	3
	91			110		1	1	31	128		57	95	1	2	
	96		1	92				13	139		45	89	1	2	2
	54			60				11	62		29	70	3	2	
	60			64				13	66	1	34	55		1	2
	73			75		1		15	101	2	26	88	2	2	2
	39			42			1	10	47	1	24	44			1
	29			46				5	55		14	52			
	84			78				11	75	1	21	108	1	1	
1	1244		19	1333	1	9	9	275	1419	7	588	1295	16	19	12

HANTS, Continued.

MD.	S.	WDR	MD.	S.	WD.	M.	F.	MD.	S.	WDR	MD.	S.	WD.	M.	F.
1	117		9	160			1	58	141		89	146	4		1
	72		2	40		1	1	28	90		43	50	1		2
	76		1	54		1	1	13	63	1	31	57			3
	137		10	108		1	2	62	118	1	88	105	3	2	3
	72		3	82			1	23	54	1	47	61	3	1	
	102			109			1	68	108	3	95	70	1	3	1
	40			37				16	45		32	28		1	
	32			44		1	1	9	42	1	18	19			
	117		5	80		1		43	104		75	67	1	4	1
	110		3	88				25	133		59	111	3		3
	119		11	103		1	1	45	108		79	60	2	2	2
	30		3	33			1	9	32		15	13			
1	1024		47	938		6	10	399	1038	7	671	787	18	13	16

6

No. 1.—PERSONAL CENSUS

COUNTY OF

	Over 30 and under 40 years of age.							
POLLING DISTRICTS.	Males.			Females.			Deaths since March 30, 1860.	
	MD.	S.	WDR	MD.	S.	WD.	M.	F.
	52	53	54	55	56	57	58	59
1. Washabok	33	14	2	33	20	5	2	2
2. Middle River	29	20	1	36	14	1		
3. Baddeck	55	20	1	68	31			
4. Munro's Point, St. Ann's	54	26	1	50	24	1		1
5. Englishtown, St. Ann's	41	24	3	45	16	1		1
6. Boulardrie	35	21		37	21	1		
7. Ingonish	16	6	1	19	2	1		1
8. Cape North	20	9		24	2		1	
9. Bay St. Lawrence	10	2		13	2			
10. Little Narrows	18	9		22	9	2		
	311	151	9	347	141	12	3	5

COUNTY OF

	52	53	54	55	56	57	58	59
1. Sydney	69	21		93	30	12	2	
2. Ball's Bridge	64	31	1	80	28	6	2	1
3. Mira Ferry	19	1		33	8	2	1	
4. Sydney Mines	121	31	2	123	24	5		2
5. Mainadieu	71	17		60	19	8	1	
6. Louisburg	40	26		48	22	4		
7. Gabarus	52	25	1	50	13	2		
8. East Bay	62	22	2	8	20	5	1	1
9. Beaver Cove	34	1	1	34	10	1		1
10. Howley's Ferry	39	12	3	41	10	2		
11. Lingan Mines	37	21	1	48	16	8	1	2
12. Cow Bay	26	8		27	6	2		
13. Big Pond	26	7	2	24	18	2		1
14. Christmas Island	31	13	1	37	24	3		
	691	256	14	777	248	62	8	8

COUNTY OF

	52	53	54	55	56	57	58	59
1. Windsor	84	33	2	94	26	10	1	1
2. St. Croix	42	14	1	47	11	2	1	
3. Brooklyn	41	11	3	49	7			1
4. Scotch Village	83	23	1	111	27	10	2	1
5. Falmouth	43	12	1	49	8	6	1	
6. Kempt	81	15	1	96	14	3	1	1
7. Rawdon Church	37	12	1	29	4			
8. South Rawdon	23	2		31	6	2		
9. Noel	77	28	3	74	20	2	3	2
10. Nine Mile River	82	31	3	90	19	4		1
11. Maitland	83	9	1	90	13	5	1	
12. Chester Road	20	5		23	7			1
	696	195	17	783	162	44	9	8

BY AGES...1860—61,

VICTORIA, Continued.

			Over 40 and under 50 years of age.								Over 50 and under 60 years of age.				
Males.			Females.			Deaths since March 30, 1860.		Males.			Females.			Deaths since March 30, 1860.	
MD.	S.	WDR	MD.	S.	WD.	M.	F.	MD.	S.	WDR	MD.	S.	WD.	M.	F.
60	61	62	63	64	65	66	67	68	69	70	71	72	73	74	75
25	2	....	25	5	2	....	....	26	....	2	20	1	6	....	1
32	4	2	23	2	4	....	....	14	2	....	12	1	3	....	....
52	3	1	49	10	7	....	1	31	3	....	20	....	9	....	....
39	3	3	37	4	6	....	....	36	1	....	31	1	11	1	....
34	1	1	33	1	5	....	....	32	2	1	23	2	12	2	....
36	2	2	39	5	3	....	1	27	2	4	19	....	3	....	....
14	2	1	19	....	1	....	....	12	1	1	6	....	3	....	....
17	2	....	23	....	2	....	....	17	....	....	14	1	1	....	....
9	1	1	7	....	....	....	....	10	1	....	7	1	1	1	....
19	1	1	24	....	3	....	....	17	....	....	17	....	1	....	....
277	21	12	279	27	33	....	2	222	12	8	75	7	50	4	1

CAPE BRETON, Continued.

84	11	2	84	5	11	2	....	65	4	2	47	3	14	3	....
74	8	4	66	5	9	1	....	48	1	5	41	5	8	2	....
40	3	2	40	2	2	....	....	32	1	....	21	1	8	1	....
109	10	3	99	15	20	....	2	79	2	5	69	9	17	....	1
49	4	2	45	5	11	2	....	31	1	2	26	1	5	2	....
57	7	4	44	6	8	....	....	28	3	2	24	2	10	....	....
57	2	....	50	3	6	....	....	34	....	....	35	....	14	1	....
60	4	3	47	5	10	1	....	43	3	1	34	3	10	1	....
30	3	2	29	....	2	....	1	29	1	1	20	....	2	....	....
34	4	1	29	2	2	....	....	23	1	1	23	2	9	....	....
35	3	2	27	1	6	....	....	17	4	3	24	3	10	1	....
21	5	1	19	4	5	....	1	24	2	1	19	....	1	....	1
15	2	2	20	2	2	....	....	14	....	2	9	....	5	....	....
34	5	....	45	4	4	2	....	42	1	3	26	1	6	....	....
699	71	28	644	59	98	8	4	509	24	28	418	30	119	11	2

HANTS, Continued.

77	10	2	77	14	10	1	1	68	6	11	50	8	15	....	1
40	6	5	30	1	3	1	....	27	4	3	21	1	1	....	....
50	3	1	52	6	5	....	3	43	4	4	24	2	4	....	....
92	6	1	87	13	7	1	....	82	9	5	48	4	4	1	1
58	7	2	51	7	5	1	2	35	5	1	23	1	5	....	1
71	5	....	57	2	5	....	1	41	2	1	40	1	5	....	....
26	2	1	26	11	1	....	....	22	1	3	14	2	4	....	....
28	3	1	19	....	1	....	....	12	....	....	13	2	2	....	1
56	7	1	45	7	10	....	....	31	7	6	32	4	6	....	....
70	13	5	49	7	3	1	1	43	6	4	34	6	13	....	....
80	3	....	64	9	11	....	....	47	2	3	26	2	4	1	....
22	3	2	24	3	1	....	....	17	1	....	13	....	1	....	....
670	68	21	581	80	62	5	8	468	47	41	338	33	64	2	4

No. 1.—PERSONAL CENSUS

COUNTY OF

POLLING DISTRICTS.	Over 50 and under 70 years of age.							
	Males.			Females.			Deaths since March 30, 1860.	
	MD.	S.	WDR	MD.	S.	WD.	M.	F.
	76	77	78	79	80	81	82	83
1. Washabok	21		2	17	1	11	1	
2. Middle River	21		5	15	1	7	1	
3. Baddeck	35		2	18	3	7		1
4. Munro's Point, St. Ann's	28	1	5	24	2	9		1
5. Englishtown, St. Ann's	25	1	1	26		7		
6. Boulardrie	26	1	6	18	2	7		
7. Ingonish	6		2	2		2		
8. Cape North	18		1	9		5	1	
9. Bay St. Lawrence	6			6	1	1		
10. Little Narrows	16		2	6		3		
	202	3	26	141	10	59	3	2

COUNTY OF

POLLING DISTRICTS.	MD.	S.	WDR	MD.	S.	WD.	M.	F.
1. Sydney	57	3	9	31	5	16	2	
2. Ball's Bridge	35		1	13	1	15		
3. Mira Ferry	15		3	5	1	6		
4. Sydney Mines	52	6	6	19	1	12	1	1
5. Mainadieu	26	1	7	16	4	1	2	
6. Louisburg	27	1	1	17	1	12	1	1
7. Gabarus	29		1	17	1	5	1	
8. East Bay	33		3	17	1	8		
9. Beaver Cove	23		1	18		6		1
10. Howley's Ferry	18		4	10	1	3		
11. Lingan Mines	25	2	2	16		10		
12. Cow Bay	10	1	1	5		1		
13. Big Pond	9	1	2	12	2	6	1	
14. Christmas Island	18		5	13		14	1	1
	377	15	46	209	18	128	9	4

COUNTY OF

POLLING DISTRICTS.	MD.	S.	WDR	MD.	S.	WD.	M.	F.
1. Windsor	41	8	4	19	4	13	3	
2. St Croix	18	2	6	11	1	8		
3. Brooklyn	10		1	9		12		
4. Scotch Village	41	3	5	26	5	19		1
5. Falmouth	20		2	12		7		1
6. Kempt	46		6	17	1	10		1
7. Rawdon Church	13	3	2	9	1	3	2	
8. South Rawdon	10	1	2	4	1	5		
9. Noel	34	5	5	24		10	1	2
10. Nine Mile River	27	3	7	18	1	13	3	1
11. Maitland	29	5	5	24		8		
12. Chester Road	11	1		3		2		
	300	31	45	176	14	110	9	6

BY AGES...1860—61.

VICTORIA, Continued.

	Over 70 and under 80 years of age.								Over 80 and under 90 years of age.						
Males.			Females.			Deaths since March 30, 1860.		Males.			Females.			Deaths since March 30, 1860.	
MD.	S.	WDR	MD.	S.	WD.	M.	F.	MD.	S.	WDR	MD.	S.	WD.	M.	F.
84	85	86	87	88	89	90	91	92	93	94	95	96	97	98	99
9	....	2	3	1	4	2	....	4	....	....	2	....	3	....	....
6	....	1	4	1	6	....	1	4	....	1	1	....	2	....	....
16	....	4	8	....	4	1	....	3	....	1	2	1	4	1	....
13	....	4	4	3	9	....	....	....	....	6	1	1	4	1	....
12	....	6	3	....	3	....	....	2	....	1	2	2	4	1	....
8	1	2	2	2	7	1	2	2	....	....	....	1	4	1	....
3	....	2	1	....	....	....	....	....	....	1	....	....	1	....	1
5	1	2	1	....	2	....	....	....	1	....	....	....	1	....	....
4	....	....	3	....	....	....	....	1	....	....	....	....	....	....	....
7	....	....	5	....	1	....	....	1	....	2	....	....	....	....	....
83	2	23	34	7	36	4	3	17	1	12	8	5	23	4	1

CAPE BRETON, Continued.

19	....	5	10	....	13	3	1	4	....	1	2	....	4	1	....
13	....	2	9	....	9	3	....	7	....	3	1	....	4	1	1
6	1	1	3	....	4	....	1	1	....	3	....	....	1	....	....
11	2	3	6	....	12	....	1	3	....	2	....	....	6	....	....
12	....	1	7	....	3	....	....	2	1	1	2	1	7	....	....
12	2	2	5	....	13	1	1	5	....	3	3	....	1	....	....
13	1	1	2	1	7	....	1	2	....	....	2	....	3	....	2
15	1	6	5	3	6	1	4	2	....	2	2	....	5	....	....
11	....	....	9	1	3	2	....	2	....	1	1	....	3	....	....
11	....	1	6	....	6	....	....	1	....	....	2	....	4	....	....
12	3	....	2	....	10	....	....	2	....	1	1	....	2	....	....
4	....	2	2	....	8	....	....	1	....	....	....	1	1	1	....
10	....	1	2	....	2	....	....	2	....	....	....	....	2	....	....
5	1	4	4	....	3	....	1	5	....	....	....	1	2	....	....
154	10	29	72	5	99	10	10	39	1	19	14	3	45	3	3

HANTS, Continued.

12	1	6	4	1	13	1	1	1	1	....	1	....	7	....	....
6	....	3	2	....	1	....	....	....	1	1	....	....	1	....	....
13	....	5	5	....	4	1	....	1	....	....	....	....	1	....	....
19	5	7	11	3	6	....	1	4	2	3	2	....	5	....	1
9	....	5	6	....	7	....	....	2	....	2	1	1	2	....	....
10	1	7	7	1	7	....	1	2	....	2	....	....	1	1	....
1	1	5	3	1	....	....	....	3	....	....	....	....	1	....	....
6	....	1	4	....	3	....	1	1	....	1	....	....	3	....	....
17	....	6	7	2	7	2	....	1	1	3	....	....	8	1	2
17	....	2	10	....	14	2	....	2	....	1	....	1	1	1	....
8	....	2	2	....	7	1	1	4	....	....	....	....	3	....	....
4	....	2	4	1	5	1	....	1	1	1	....	....	....	....	....
122	8	51	65	9	74	8	5	22	6	15	4	2	33	3	3

No. 1.—PERSONAL CENSUS

COUNTY OF

POLLING DISTRICTS.	Over 90 and under 100 years of age.							
	Males.			Females.			Deaths since March 30, 1860.	
	MD.	S.	WDR	MD.	S.	WD.	M.	F.
	100	101	102	103	104	105	106	107
1. Washabok								
2. Middle River								
3. Baddeck	1		1					
4. Munro's Point, St. Ann's	1		1			1	1	
5. Englishtown, St. Ann's			1					
6. Boulardrie						1		
7. Ingonish							1	
8. Cape North								
9. Bay St. Lawrence	1					1		
10. Little Narrows								
	3		3			3	2	

COUNTY OF

	100	101	102	103	104	105	106	107
1. Sydney						2		
2. Ball's Bridge						2		
3. Mira Ferry								
4. Sydney Mines			1					
5. Mainadieu	1		1			1		
6. Louisburg	1		1			1		
7. Gabarus						1		
8. East Bay	2		2					
9. Beaver Cove								
10. Howley's Ferry			1					
11. Lingan Mines	2					1		
12. Cow Bay								
13. Big Pond			1					
14. Christmas Island			2			1		1
	6		9			9		1

COUNTY OF

	100	101	102	103	104	105	106	107
1. Windsor								
2. St. Croix								
3. Brooklyn								
4. Scotch Village			1			2		
5. Falmouth								
6. Kempt								
7. Rawdon Church						2	1	1
8. South Rawdon						1		
9. Noel			2					1
10. Nine Mile River								
11. Maitland								1
12. Chester Road								
			3			5	1	3

BY AGES...1860—61.

VICTORIA, Continued.

Over 100 years of age.								Ages not given.	Deaths.		Ages not given.	Males.			
Males.			Females.			Deaths since M'ch 30, 1860.						Married.	Single.	Widowers.	Total.
MD.	S.	WDR	MD.	S.	WD.	M.	F.		M.	F.	M.	F.			
108	109	110	111	112	113	114	115		116	117	118	119	120	121	122	123
													129	368	8	505
													117	324	10	451
													214	545	10	769
									2	3			191	501	20	712
					1				1				170	434	15	619
													149	411	14	574
													71	202	8	281
									1	1			88	251	3	342
													52	129	1	182
													92	269	5	366
					1				*4	†4			1273	3434	94	4801

CAPE BRETON, Continued.

MD.	S.	WDR	MD.	S.	WD.	M.	F.		M.	F.	M.	F.	Married.	Single.	Widowers.	Total.
									5	1			320	859	19	1198
									5	7			268	792	16	1076
					1								122	308	9	439
									2	4			449	1161	23	1633
													213	518	14	745
					1								184	461	14	659
									4	3			218	555	3	776
									1	1			230	646	19	895
													140	354	6	500
													139	362	14	515
					1								145	468	11	624
													96	243	6	345
					1								81	211	10	302
													146	443	16	605
					1	3			‡17	‖16			2751	7381	180	10312

HANTS, Continued.

MD.	S.	WDR	MD.	S.	WD.	M.	F.		M.	F.	M.	F.	Married.	Single.	Widowers.	Total.
					1				6	5		1	344	724	25	1093
													161	427	19	607
													171	366	15	552
													383	741	24	1148
													190	375	14	579
									1	1			319	680	20	1019
									4	6			118	262	12	392
													89	229	6	324
												1	259	686	26	971
													266	684	22	972
									2				296	689	12	997
												1	84	184	5	273
					1				§13	¶12		3	2680	6047	200	8927

* 1 md., 3 s.　† 1 md., 3 s.　‡ 17 s.　‖ 15 s., 1 w.　§ 2 md., 11 s.　¶ 2 md., 10 s.

No. 1.—PERSONAL CENSUS

COUNTY OF

POLLING DISTRICTS.	Females.				Grand Total.	Deaths.		
	Married.	Single.	Widows.	Total.		Males.	Females.	Total.
	124	125	126	127	128	129	130	131
1. Washabok	129	379	31	539	1044	11	6	17
2. Middle River	117	286	23	426	877	3	6	9
3. Baddeck	213	540	31	784	1553	6	6	12
4. Munro's Point, St. Ann's	190	496	42	728	1440	7	6	13
5. Englishtown, St. Ann's	170	403	32	605	1224	6	8	14
6. Boulardrie	150	428	26	604	1178	8	6	14
7. Ingonish	72	202	11	285	566	4	6	10
8. Cape North	90	222	13	325	667	5	2	7
9. Bay St. Lawrence	53	114	4	171	353	3	1	4
10. Little Narrows	91	274	10	375	741	2	1	3
	1275	3344	223	4842	9643	55	48	103

COUNTY OF

1. Sydney	324	869	76	1269	2467	27	5	32
2. Ball's Bridge	258	781	54	1093	2169	18	11	29
3. Mira Ferry	121	315	24	460	899	4	4	8
4. Sydney Mines	446	1129	75	1650	3283	15	24	39
5. Mainadieu	215	499	50	764	1509	10	10	20
6. Louisburg	184	481	50	715	1374	7	13	20
7. Gabarus	213	523	39	775	1551	7	7	14
8. East Bay	231	613	46	890	1785	11	10	21
9. Beaver Cove	140	332	20	492	992	9	6	15
10. Howley's Ferry	143	317	26	486	1001	1	2	3
11. Lingan Mines	144	435	50	629	1253	6	9	15
12. Cow Bay	95	255	18	368	713	2	5	7
13. Big Pond	81	241	19	341	643	3	1	4
14. Christmas Island	146	442	34	622	1227	7	7	14
	2741	7232	581	10554	20866	127	114	241

COUNTY OF

1. Windsor	345	760	73	1178	2271	14	11	25
2. St. Croix	156	324	17	497	1104	5	5	10
3. Brooklyn	171	336	26	533	1085	8	15	23
4. Scotch Village	383	667	56	1106	2254	22	21	43
5. Falmouth	192	379	35	606	1185	3	7	10
6. Kempt	312	602	32	946	1965	10	13	23
7. Rawdon Church	113	243	11	367	759	5	3	8
8. South Rawdon	89	194	17	300	624	2	4	6
9. Noel	262	514	44	820	1791	24	20	44
10. Nine Mile River	263	634	51	948	1920	14	10	24
11. Maitland	296	634	40	970	1967	11	8	19
12. Chester Road	85	168	9	262	535	4	4	8
	2667	5455	411	8533	17460	122	121	243

BY AGES...1860—61.

VICTORIA, Continued.

Deaf and Dumb		Blind		Lunatics		Idiots		Cannot Read.				Cannot Write.				Married since March 30, 1860.	Colored persons included in population.	Indians not included in population.
								Over 5 and under 15 years of age.		Above 15 years of age.		Over 5 and under 15 years of age.		Above 15 years of age.				
M.	F.	M.	F.	M.	F.	M.	F.	M.	F.	M.	F.	M.	F.	M.	F.			
132	133	134	135	136	137	138	139	140	141	142	143	144	145	146	147	148	149	150
	1	2	1	1			1	100	110	147	249	100	110	147	249	7		
3			1		3			78	66	58	86	97	82	106	175	7		
1		1						95	120	73	100	95	120	73	100	1	1	
2			1		1			61	71	75	136	101	109	157	311	15		
						1		108	100	119	190	121	121	202	340	10		
1		1	1			2	4	49	77	79	140	82	119	128	244	10		
	1						1	40	60	67	83	58	73	91	116	5		1
		1		1				55	60	69	94	68	76	98	128	2		3
								49	44	65	74	42	46	66	75	2		13
								68	84	78	99	76	86	98	144			
7	2	6	3	3	2	5	6	694	792	830	1251	840	942	1166	1882	59	1	17

CAPE BRETON, Continued.

M.	F.	M.	F.	M.	F.	M.	F.	M.	F.	M.	F.	M.	F.	M.	F.	Married	Colored	Indians
1		1		1				189	207	209	302	215	234	257	410	17	24	6
		1						55	64	191	250	61	67	219	281	19	3	8
				1				62	63	94	169	105	111	183	236	1		
		1		2	1	1		254	276	347	442	322	319	411	555	20	14	35
	2	1			1		1	155	165	245	363	158	167	246	375	10		
	1	1		3		2		125	161	200	307	149	172	245	353	7		
							2	159	148	225	305	183	154	245	349	9		
2		2		1				176	208	255	371	195	235	316	438	18		31
			1					147	111	232	296	147	111	244	303	10		
			1	1	1	1	1	106	98	194	249	116	103	220	271	3		
1		2			1			108	119	172	230	121	142	206	283	4		
	1			1	2	1		44	51	56	83	54	81	82	133	5		
					1			67	77	105	174	60	74	115	191	8		
		3						148	152	222	358	154	154	232	360	6		68
3	4	8	3	12	4	8	5	1795	1900	2747	3899	2040	2124	3221	4538	137	41	148

HANTS, Continued.

M.	F.	M.	F.	M.	F.	M.	F.	M.	F.	M.	F.	M.	F.	M.	F.	Married	Colored	Indians
		1	1	1				55	52	47	39	75	75	60	68	15	7	
					3	1		39	32	27	26	70	51	47	42	8	112	6
	1		1		1			29	22	11	7	40	33	11	10	6	4	29
	1	1	1	1		1	2	76	58	37	45	111	96	51	76	19		
			1		1			19	18	10	18	30	25	13	22	8	64	3
			1					51	56	10	15	56	70	20	25	11	3	
			1				1	22	23	13	17	30	33	16	23	5	1	
	1		1					44	25	39	32	62	48	52	58	2		
			1	1				62	40	26	27	107	79	57	71	23	4	
4	1	1	2	1		4	4	95	78	53	39	130	142	92	109	11	10	26
2				1				89	98	44	30	164	170	94	120	18		18
3	2			1		1		24	15	20	18	47	45	39	45	11	1	31
9	6	3	8	6	3	10	8	605	517	337	313	922	867	552	669	137	206	113

7

No. 1.—PERSONAL CENSUS

COUNTY OF

POLLING DISTRICTS.	TOTAL POPULATION.			Number of Families.	Average Number of each Family.	Under one year of age.		Deaths under 1 yr. age since 30th March, 1860.	
	Males.	Females.	Total.			M.	F.	M.	F.
	1	2	3	4	5	6	7	8	9
1. Canning	1135	1120	2255	385		29	48	2	1
2. Canard	671	671	1342	232		22	20		1
3. Cetreville	1037	981	2018	382		28	32	1	
4. Lakeville	834	765	1599	273		40	23	2	
5. Somerset	1197	1089	2286	417		42	33	3	1
6. Kentville	774	714	1488	270		25	31	2	2
7. Gaspereaux	590	499	1089	189		23	22	2	2
8. Wolfville	804	773	1577	265		15	23	1	1
9. Lower Horton	651	664	1315	257		26	21	3	2
10. Aylesford	692	659	1351	248		20	19	1	4
11. West Sherbrooke	101	96	197	33		4	2		1
12. Aylesford	690	652	1342	241		22	23	2	1
13. Berwick	444	428	872	147		20	11		2
	9620	9111	18731	3339	5.60	316	308	19	18

COUNTY OF

1. Wilmot	955	881	1836	326		40	33	2	
2. Wilmot, Middleton Corner	730	744	1474	267		18	24	1	2
3. Clarence, Wilmot	720	714	1434	282		25	27		2
4. Bridgetown	722	682	1404	244		18	21	2	
5. Bealisse	589	566	1155	209		18	16		1
6. New Caledonia	615	637	1252	235		18	19		
7. Broad Cove	441	457	898	168		16	14		
8. Clementsport	700	619	1319	231		21	23	2	2
9. Hessian Line	462	479	941	179		24	17		
10. Annapolis Royal	907	896	1803	331		28	24	1	
11. Carleton's Corner	358	349	707	135		10	6		
12. Nictaux	622	616	1238	224		14	20	1	2
13. Dalhousie	268	293	561	91		5	6	2	
14. Maitland	208	161	369	56		9	7		
15. Morse Road	193	169	362	61		9	3	1	
	8490	8263	16753	3039	5.50	273	260	12	9

COUNTY OF

1. Hillsburg	611	580	1191	226		20	19	1	
2. Head of St. Mary's Bay	472	482	954	164		9	17		
3. Digby	922	929	1851	333		19	27	2	
4. Sandy Cove	611	573	1184	212		15	15		
5. Long Island	503	451	954	170		11	23		1
6. Westport	337	341	678	124		6	13	1	1
7. On St. Mary's Bay	772	697	1469	236		37	27		1
8. Weymouth	673	635	1308	219		24	13	1	1
9. Belivoe Cove	530	586	1116	170		14	15		
10. Session House, Clare	777	809	1586	255		23	26	1	1
11. Montegan	775	756	1531	233		24	21	1	4
12. Salmon River	453	476	929	150		15	11	4	
	7436	7315	14751	2492	5.91	217	227	11	9

BY AGES...1860—61.

KING'S.

Over 1 and under 2 ys. of age		Deaths between 1 and 2 years, since M'ch 30, 1860.		Over 2 and under 3 years of age.		Deaths between 2 and 3 years, since M'ch 30, 1860.		Over 3 and under 4 years of age.		Deaths between 3 and 4 years, since M'ch 30, 1860.		Over 4 and under 5 years of age.		Deaths between 4 and 5 years, since M'ch 30, 1860.	
M.	F.	M.	F.	M.	F.	M.	F.	M.	F.	M.	F.	M.	F.	M.	F.
10	11	12	13	14	15	16	17	18	19	20	21	22	23	24	25
33	38	2	6	46	41	4		41	18		1	39	33		
16	22	1	1	15	17	2		18	20		1	21	20	1	1
28	32	1	2	43	28		1	34	22			33	25		2
24	21			31	32	1	1	18	28			25	20	1	
42	41			40	31	2	1	35	41	2	1	38	39		3
21	17		2	18	20			29	11			24	18		
24	16	1		29	18			19	13			19	16	2	
26	15			32	24			16	20	1	1	22	23		
20	21	1		23	18	1	1	13	19			18	14	2	
27	23	1	2	25	29	3		13	21		1	16	18	1	2
3	4			1	5			5	2			2	3		
17	26		1	26	13			28	18	2	1	22	16	1	1
19	12	1	1	14	9			16	11	1		17	12	1	
300	288	8	15	343	285	13	5	285	243	6	6	296	257	9	9

ANNAPOLIS.

M.	F.	M.	F.	M.	F.	M.	F.	M.	F.	M.	F.	M.	F.	M.	F.
23	24	1	2	27	24	2		19	27	2		22	22	1	
24	22		1	31	26		1	20	14	1		26	22		1
21	16			24	20			16	20			22	19		
20	16			21	16			27	15		1	16	14		
13	21			20	20		1	22	13			19	13	2	
19	16			19	21		2	17	21			19	10	1	2
10	13			15	16			12	13			11	17		1
26	14		1	23	17			22	20			27	17	1	
11	14			14	15			19	15			14	20		
21	26	2	1	28	31			29	20			33	20		
8	7			13	7		1	10	9	1		9	9		
23	16			14	15			20	16		1	13	14	1	
7	11			8	6			5	10			8	7		1
13	9			10	5			8	5			7	9		
9	5			6	5		1	5	3			9	7		
248	230	3	5	273	244	2	6	251	221	4	2	255	220	6	5

DIGBY.

M.	F.	M.	F.	M.	F.	M.	F.	M.	F.	M.	F.	M.	F.	M.	F.
15	17			21	17		2	12	20			19	15		
16	11	1	1	7	12			16	18			11	11		
12	26			22	16	4	2	29	26	3	1	22	15	2	
14	17		1	14	12			18	19			16	17		
15	12			17	20			11	12			21	14	2	
5	9			11	6			6	7			9	7		
14	19			36	24			17	22			25	29		
19	21		1	25	23			19	13			19	17		
14	14			17	19			13	18		2	11	17		
21	15	1		23	18		3	20	18			33	12	1	
15	23	1		28	21		2	22	18	1		21	22		
10	12	1		16	11	1		10	18		3	18	16		
170	196	4	3	237	199	5	9	193	209	4	6	225	192	5	

No. 1.—PERSONAL CENSUS

COUNTY OF

POLLING DISTRICTS.	Over 6 and under 10 years of age.		Deaths between 5 and 10 y'rs. since M'ch 30, 1860.		Over 10 and under 16 years of age.					
					Males.		Females.		Deaths since M'ch 30, 1860.	
	M.	F.	M.	F.	MD.	S.	MD.	S.	M.	F.
	26	27	28	29	30	31	32	33	34	35
1. Canning	144	159	4	2		138		130		
2. Canard	75	76	1	1		75		77	2	
3. Centreville	126	140		1		150		102	1	2
4. Lakeville	102	106	1			109		94	1	
5. Somerset	147	138	5	3		151		127	3	4
6. Kentville	101	106	2	3		99		78	3	1
7. Gaspereaux	77	70	1	1		69		49	1	1
8. Wolfville	104	74	3			92		84		1
9. Lower Horton	77	191				75		78		
10. Aylesford	81	82	5	4		90		70	8	1
11. West Sherbrooke	10	16				18		13		
12. Aylesford	82	90	1	3		72		69	1	
13. Berwick	47	77	1	2		60		57	1	1
	1174	1238	24	20		1296		1028	21	11

COUNTY OF

	M.	F.	M.	F.	MD.	S.	MD.	S.	M.	F.
1. Wilmot	121	102	5	5		127		122	2	5
2. Wilmot, Middleton Corner	84	104	2	3		91		103	1	3
3. Clarence, Wilmot	93	97	1			75		77		1
4. Bridgetown	98	92	1	4		91		77		
5. Beslase	90	78	1	1		67		59		
6. New Caledonia	71	84	3			79		71	1	
7. Broad Cove	53	64		1		64		46		
8. Clementsport	96	7	2			88		66	1	
9. Hessian Line	56	62	1			67		54		
10. Annapolis Royal	114	116				120		85	1	1
11. Carleton's Corner	42	29	2	1		33		38		
12. Nictaux	76	78	2	1		85		85	1	3
13. Dalhousie	34	49	1			32		41		
14. Maitland	30	20				25		19		
15. Morse Road	33	29				21		29	2	2
	1091	1087	21	16		1085		972	9	14

COUNTY OF

	M.	F.	M.	F.	MD.	S.	MD.	S.	M.	F.
1. Hillsburg	66	69		3		80		65	1	
2. Head of St. Mary's Bay	59	60				63		61		1
3. Digby	120	97	2	3		116		95		1
4. Sandy Cove	92	75				85		68		1
5. Long Island	71	53				88		50		
6. Westport	41	53				47		39		1
7. On St. Mary's Bay	134	104		1		116		101		
8. Weymouth	81	94				110		66		1
9. Belivoe Cove	77	80				66		73		1
10. Session House, Clare	90	90	1			98		104		
11. Montegan	108	83				87	1	84		
12. Salmon River	75	70	2	1		60		63		1
	1014	937	5	8		1016	1	869	1	7

BY AGES...1860—61.

KING'S, Continued.

| | Over 15 and under 20 years of age. | | | | | | | Over 20 and under 30 years of age. | | | | | | | |
| | Males. | | | Females. | | | Deaths since March 30, 1860. | | Males. | | | Females. | | | Deaths since March 30, 1860. | |
MD.	S.	WDR	MD.	S.	WD.	M.	F.	MD.	S.	WDR	MD.	S.	WD.	M.	F.
36	37	38	39	40	41	42	43	44	45	46	47	48	49	50	51
	127		13	120		2	1	72	121		111	85	4	2	
	80		7	78				29	101	1	49	75	1	1	
	106		7	96				68	85		108	65	1	1	1
	90		6	80			1	36	103	1	81	59	2	1	1
1	137		7	118	1		4	78	124		120	63	4	3	1
	85		6	78	2		2	31	85		60	50		1	2
	52		3	39			1	41	56		64	29	2	1	1
	84		7	106	1			38	130		65	82	1	1	1
	70		7	63	1			47	57		78	42		2	
	74		4	65	5		3	49	68		75	47	1		4
	11		1	11				3	9		8	4			
	67		7	77			3	36	91		60	50			1
	45			36			3	24	51		40	23		1	
1	1028		75	967		12	18	552	1081	2	919	674	16	14	12

ANNAPOLIS, Continued

| | Over 15 and under 20 years of age. | | | | | | | Over 20 and under 30 years of age. | | | | | | | |
| | Males. | | | Females. | | | Deaths since March 30, 1860. | | Males. | | | Females. | | | Deaths since March 30, 1860. | |
MD.	S.	WDR	MD.	S.	WD.	M.	F.	MD.	S.	WDR	MD.	S.	WD.	M.	F.
36	37	38	39	40	41	42	43	44	45	46	47	48	49	50	51
	116		5	90		1	3	56	109	2	86	72			2
	79		5	70			1	30	75	2	59	46	2	2	
	73			67			2	44	65	1	65	54	1		1
	86		6	63	4			35	88		46	79	3	3	1
	60		8	49	1			31	51		48	56	2	2	2
	66		6	67	2			40	62		61	58	1	3	
	46		2	44		1		21	41		41	24	3	3	
	71		3	61	2			34	91		60	50		2	
	41		1	56		1		42	33	1	55	23	1		
	90		2	85		1		36	111	2	61	95	1	1	2
	43			43				10	48		26	31	1	1	2
	80		2	64	1			27	67		54	55		4	
	30		2	41				13	42		21	23			
	15			17		2		12	31		20	8		1	
	16		1	16		2		9	22	1	15	7		2	1
	912		43	833	1	14	11	440	936	9	718	681	15	24	11

DIGBY, Continued.

| | Over 15 and under 20 years of age. | | | | | | | Over 20 and under 30 years of age. | | | | | | | |
| | Males. | | | Females. | | | Deaths since March 30, 1860. | | Males. | | | Females. | | | Deaths since March 30, 1860. | |
MD.	S.	WDR	MD.	S.	WD.	M.	F.	MD.	S.	WDR	MD.	S.	WD.	M.	F.
36	37	38	39	40	41	42	43	44	45	46	47	48	49	50	51
	71		1	61			2	38	66	1	62	41		2	1
	70		2	52			2	13	54	1	33	47	1		1
1	100		7	108				36	114		53	101	1	2	1
1	74		3	61				33	66		55	43	2	1	1
	53		1	56			1	38	42		50	26		1	
	41		5	42				12	44	1	21	30	1	3	1
	89		3	70			1	44	56	3	71	40	3	1	1
	78		3	73				25	78		46	67	2	1	1
	67			69				15	63		38	58		1	1
	84		1	96				25	115		53	103	1		1
	86		2	82				30	120		58	116		1	2
	41		6	65		3	2	31	43		39	38	1	4	
2	854		34	835		3	8	340	861	6	579	710	12	17	11

No. 1.—PERSONAL CENSUS

COUNTY OF

POLLING DISTRICTS.	Over 30 and under 40 years of age.							
	Males.			Females.			Deaths since March 30, 1860.	
	MD.	S.	WDR	MD.	S.	WD.	M.	F.
	52	53	54	55	56	57	58	59
1. Canning	118	20	2	110	5	7	2	1
2. Canard	61	17	1	60	10	5	1	....
3. Centreville	112	15	1	98	14	5	....	2
4. Lakeville	84	11	3	55	15	3	1	2
5. Somerset	104	15	2	105	13	3	1	....
6. Kentville	77	16	....	72	12	4	....	2
7. Gaspereaux	56	13	1	45	7	2	....	1
8. Wolfville	72	20	1	72	23	3	1	....
9. Lower Horton	54	8	1	63	13	....	....	1
10. Aylesford	71	10	1	68	16	1	1	2
11. West Sherbrooke	8	2	....	6	1	....	....	....
12. Aylesford	67	15	2	65	14	6	....	1
13. Berwick	41	5	1	43	7	....	....	....
	925	167	16	862	150	39	7	12

COUNTY OF

	MD.	S.	WDR	MD.	S.	WD.	M.	F.
1. Wilmot	75	19	2	90	14	3	3	....
2. Wilmot, Middleton Corner	73	8	1	71	12	3	1	1
3. Clarence, Wilmot	66	22	1	75	22	4	....	....
4. Bridgetown	52	11	....	56	16	4	1	1
5. Bealisse	56	9	2	52	6	1	1	....
6. New Caledonia	57	5	2	59	12	1	....	....
7. Broad Cove	39	7	1	42	7	4	....	....
8. Clementsport	63	6	....	51	8	3	....	....
9. Hessian Line	44	4	....	48	6	2	....	....
10. Annapolis Royal	75	15	....	78	30	6	....	1
11. Carleton's Corner	25	16	1	29	11	1	1	....
12. Nictaux	63	3	....	55	10	3	2	....
13. Dalhousie	25	3	2	28	3	....	....	....
14. Maitland	19	....	....	21	1	....	....	....
15. Morse Road	18	5	....	17	1	2	1	....
	750	133	12	772	159	37	10	3

COUNTY OF

	MD.	S.	WDR	MD.	S.	WD.	M.	F.
1. Hillsburg	58	10	1	57	8	2	....	....
2. Head of St. Mary's Bay	48	11	....	40	12	2	1	....
3. Digby	58	21	1	79	18	7	....	1
4. Sandy Cove	51	6	....	56	10	2	....	....
5. Long Island	42	2	....	50	1	....	....	....
6. Westport	31	4	....	28	6	4	....	1
7. On St. Mary's Bay	59	6	2	52	4	2	....	....
8. Weymouth	48	11	2	51	11	3	1	....
9. Belivoe Cove	48	9	....	52	17	2	....	....
10. Session House, Clare	59	20	1	56	32	5	1	....
11. Montegan	62	17	....	55	22	3	....	....
12. Salmon River	36	5	....	39	3	1	....	....
	600	122	7	615	144	33	3	2

BY AGES...1860—61.

KING'S, Continued.

	Over 40 and under 50 years of age.								Over 50 and under 60 years of age.							
Males.			Females.			Deaths since March 30, 1860.		Males.			Females.			Deaths since March 30, 1860.	
MD.	S.	WDR	MD.	S.	WD.	M.	F.	MD.	S.	WDR	MD.	S.	WD.	M.	F.
60	61	62	63	64	65	66	67	68	69	70	71	72	73	74	75
86	4	3	69	8	7		1	46	2	1	49	4	8	2	1
50	5		48	5	8			35	1	1	30	6	6		
66	3	3	60	2	5		1	42	5	5	48		14	1	1
51	5	2	62	4	6	1		36	2	2	26	1	5		
94	7	3	78	6	5		2	47		1	49		11	1	1
49	10	2	47	11	7	1		34	5	1	25	6	2	1	
34	3	1	31	2	2			32	3	3	29	3	1		
56	7	1	46	5	6	2		31	3	4	29	5	11		
60	4	2	45	5	4		2	31	2	5	25	5	3		
51	6	1	36	4	2		1	34	2	3	35	5	4	1	
12		1	9					2			3				
41	8	2	34	3		1		36	3		35	3	5		
35	4		28	4	6		1	18	1		15	3	3		1
685	66	21	593	59	58	5	8	424	29	26	398	41	73	6	4

ANNAPOLIS, Continued.

MD.	S.	WDR	MD.	S.	WD.	M.	F.	MD.	S.	WDR	MD.	S.	WD.	M.	F.
82	5	2	60	1	9		4	35	3	1	32	6	4		1
58	6	3	45	4	7	1	1	40	1	2	48	3	4		
54	4	1	39	9	5		1	35	2	1	36	5	6	1	1
49	3	3	58	3	9	1		37	4	2	30	4	9	2	1
38	4	2	41	6	4			37	3		32	2	2		
50	1	2	43	4	4		1	38	5	3	31	2	5		
35	1	1	34	1	4			28	2	1	21	2	5	1	
47	1	2	50	8	2	1	1	38	5	1	33	7	8		
42	3	1	36	4	2			19	3	2	20	3	5		
62	9		55	7	5	1		48	7	3	42	14	11		
24	5		19	10	5	1	1	24	2	2	23	5	4		
56	2	2	48	3	3	1	1	33	1		36		1		
19		1	14	1	1			14		1	10	2	1	1	1
13			10		1			10			4				
12			12	1			1	8		1	6		4		
641	44	20	564	62	61	6	11	444	38	20	403	55	69	5	4

DIGBY, Continued.

MD.	S.	WDR	MD.	S.	WD.	M.	F.	MD.	S.	WDR	MD.	S.	WD.	M.	F.
46	4	1	40	7	4			37		2	27	1	6		
34	3		35	3	4	2		25	2	1	18	4	4		1
75	9	6	75	14	9	1	2	51	4	2	41	5	9	1	
47	2	2	40	3	3	1	1	29	1	2	29	3	8		1
38	1		33		1			24		1	21		4		1
22	3	2	25	3	2			19	1	1	16	1	2	1	
49	2		44	3	6	1		38	1	2	32	3	3		
50	2		51	2	3			36	2	3	24	2	7	1	
41	6	1	32	7	2			28	2		21	2	1		
60	3		48	11	2	3		52	2	3	48	1	8	1	
55	1		44	4	7		1	30	4		28		8		
46		1	37	2	1	1		16			19	1	1		
563	36	15	504	59	44	9	4	385	19	17	324	23	61	4	3

No. 1.—PERSONAL CENSUS

COUNTY OF

POLLING DISTRICTS.	Over 60 and under 70 years of age.							
	Males.			Females.			Deaths since March 30, 1860.	
	MD.	S.	WDR	MD.	S.	WD.	M.	F.
	76	77	78	79	80	81	82	83
1. Canning	39	1	2	14	2	16		
2. Canard	24	4	4	10	2	9		
3. Centreville	43	5	3	19	6	13	2	
4. Lakeville	29	1	5	19	1	5	2	
5. Somerset	48	2	7	21	4	4		
6. Kentville	29	5	2	18		11		
7. Gaspereaux	13	2	1	10	1	12	1	1
8. Wolfville	25	3	4	15	2	17	1	
9. Lower Horton	30	2	1	18	1	5	1	
10. Aylesford	24	2	3	14		5		
11. West Sherbrooke	3				5			
12. Aylesford	29	3	1	13	3	11	1	1
13. Berwick	11	1	4	8	4	4		
	347	31	37	184	26	112	8	2

COUNTY OF

1. Wilmot	39	6	2	19	2	12	1	2
2. Wilmot, Middleton Corner	38	1		19	4	10		1
3. Clarence, Wilmot	40	2	6	25	2	3		2
4. Bridgetown	36	2	4	16	1	6		1
5. Bealiase	22	3	1	16	4	6		
6. New Caledonia	29	1	2	16	3	8	1	
7. Broad Cove	16	2	1	11	1	8		
8. Clementsport	23		4	13	2	12		
9. Hessian Line	11		1	4	1	5		
10. Annapolis Royal	40	3	5	25	6	25	1	
11. Carleton's Corner	19	1	2	8		6	1	2
12. Nictaux	25		3	14	1	6	1	
13. Dalhousie	8		2	5	1	1		1
14. Maitland	5			3		1		
15. Morse Road	4			1		1		
	355	21	33	195	28	110	5	9

COUNTY OF

1. Hillsburg	25	1	2	22	2	5	2	1
2 Head of St. Mary's Bay	18		1	18		4		
3. Digby	43	3	4	16	5	10	1	
4. Sandy Cove	27			12		7		
5. Long Island	18	1		6		8		
6. Westport	17	1	2	11		3		
7. On St. Mary's Bay	22	1	2	13	1	9		
8. Weymouth	28	1	2	14	3	7		
9. Belivoe Cove	22	2	2	12	5	9	1	1
10. Session House, Clare	25		2	23	1	6	1	1
11. Montegan	36		4	28	1	6		
12. Salmon River	18			9		3		
	299	10	22	184	18	77	5	3

BY AGES...1860—61.

KING'S, Continued.

Over 70 and under 80 years of age.								Over 80 and under 90 years of age.							
Males.			Females.			Deaths since March 30, 1860.		Males.			Females.			Deaths since March 30, 1860.	
MD.	S.	WDR	MD.	S.	WD.	M.	F.	MD.	S.	WDR	MD.	S.	WD.	M.	F.
84	85	86	87	88	89	90	91	92	93	94	95	96	97	98	99
11		6	5		10		1	3		1	2		3		
6	1	3	3		3	1	1	4		1			4		
16	1	3	12	1	5	1		3		1			2		
17		4	6		4			1		2			1	1	
18	1	5	10		9	1		1		1			3		1
17	1	1	10	1	5	1	1	2		1		1	4		
10	1	3	5	1	5	1		2		3			3	1	
8		7	2		11	1		2		1					
17	1	3	6		7		1	2		1	1	1			
5			5	1	7			4		1	1		1	1	
5			2		1			1	1						
8	2	4	4		6		2	3		1	1				
5	1	1	4	1	7			1		2			3		
143	9	40	74	5	80	6	6	29	1	15	5	2	24	3	1

ANNAPOLIS, Continued.

MD.	S.	WDR	MD.	S.	WD.	M.	F.	MD.	S.	WDR	MD.	S.	WD.	M.	F.
11		5	7		11	2	3	4	1	1	2		1	2	
5	1	3		1	6		1	3		1	2		3	1	
19			13	1	4		1	3		3			2	1	2
9	2	4	5		10		1	2		1	1		3	2	1
12	1	4	3	1	5			2					2	3	1
5	1	3	4		6	3				1			4	1	
12	1	1	8	2	7		1	1		1			2		
5	1	2	2	1	6			1	1				2		
6		3	2		3	3				1	1		2		
12	4	7	9	2	10	4	1	1	2	2		2	5		
6	1		3		6			2		2	1		3	1	
7	1	2	5	2	6		1	2		1	1		2		
4		2	2		5	1		1	1	1			2	1	
	1												1		
3		2	2		1								1		
116	14	38	65	10	87	13	9	22	5	16	8	2	34	12	4

DIGBY, Continued.

MD.	S.	WDR	MD.	S.	WD.	M.	F.	MD.	S.	WDR	MD.	S.	WD.	M.	F.
7		1	3		4	1		2		1	1		2		
7		1	2		9	1		2					2		
15	5	8	11	4	11	1		4				1	7		1
7		3	4	2	6			1	1	1			1		1
5		3	3		5					2			1		
9			4	2	1			2							1
7	1	2	5		3			1					1		
5		4	3	2	4	1				1		1	5		
7		1	7	1	9			1		1	1		5	2	
11	1	4	6	2	9	2		1		1		1	4		1
8		4	6		3					1			3		
5		2	4					2		2	2		2		
93	7	33	58	13	64	6		15	1	11	5	3	32	2	4

8

No. 1.—PERSONAL CENSUS

COUNTY OF

POLLING DISTRICTS.	Over 90 and under 100 years of age.							
	Males.			Females.			Deaths since March 30, 1960.	
	MD.	S.	WDR	MD.	S.	WD.	M.	F.
	100	101	102	103	104	105	106	107
1. Canning			1	1				
2. Canard								1
3. Centreville						1		
4. Lakeville								
5. Somerset					1	1		
6. Kentville		1						
7. Gaspereaux								
8. Wolfville						2		
9. Lower Horton			1					
10. Aylesford			1					
11. West Sherbrooke								
12. Aylesford	1							
13. Berwick								
	1	1	3	1	1	4		1

COUNTY OF

1. Wilmot						1		
2. Wilmot, Middleton Corner			1			2	1	
3. Clarence, Wilmot			2					
4. Bridgetown								
5. Bealiase	1		1					
6. New Caledonia								
7. Broad Cove	2			1				
8. Clementsport						1		
9. Hessian Line						2		
10. Annapolis Royal						3		
11. Carleton's Corner								
12. Nictaux	2							
13. Dalhousie								
14. Maitland								
15. Morse Road								
	5		4	1		9	1	

COUNTY OF

1. Hillsburg								
2. Head of St. Mary's Bay								
3. Digby				1			1	
4. Sandy Cove		1				2		
5. Long Island								
6. Westport								
7. On St. Mary's Bay								
8. Weymouth						1		
9. Belivoe Cove	1		1					
10. Session House, Clare								
11. Montegan						1		
12. Salmon River								1
	1	1	2			4	1	1

BY AGES—1860—61.

KING'S, Continued.

Over 100 years of age.						Deaths since M'ch 30, 1860.		Ages not given.		Deaths. Ages not given.		Males.			
Males.			Females.									Married.	Single.	Widowers.	Total.
MD.	S.	WDR.	MD.	S.	WD.	M.	F.	M.	F.	M.	F.				
108	109	110	111	112	113	114	115	116	117	118	119	120	121	122	123
												375	745	15	1135
												209	451	11	671
								9	18			552	689	16	1037
												254	501	19	834
								6	4			392	785	20	1197
								3				239	528	7	774
												188	390	12	590
								3				232	554	18	804
												241	396	14	651
								1				238	444	10	692
												34	66	1	101
												221	459	10	690
												135	301	8	444
								*22	†22			3110	6349	161	9620

ANNAPOLIS, Continued.

108	109	110	111	112	113	114	115	116	117	118	119	120	121	122	123
								5	3			302	638	15	955
												248	469	13	730
												261	444	15	720
								1	3			220	488	14	722
												199	380	10	589
												219	383	13	615
												154	281	6	441
				1								211	479	10	700
												164	289	9	462
									1			274	614	19	907
												110	241	7	358
												215	399	8	622
												84	175	9	268
												59	149		208
												54	135	4	193
				1				†6	||7			2774	5564	152	8490

DIGBY, Continued.

108	109	110	111	112	113	114	115	116	117	118	119	120	121	122	123
								4	2			215	387	9	611
												147	321	4	472
								21	32			283	617	22	922
									2			196	407	8	611
								3				165	333	5	503
												110	219	8	337
								4	4			220	540	12	772
									3			192	469	12	673
								3				163	361	6	530
												233	533	11	777
								7	6			223	541	11	775
								1	2			155	293	5	453
								§42	¶51			2302	5021	113	7436

*8 m., 18 s., 1 wdr. †4 m., 17 s., 1 w. ‡1 m., 5 s. ||1 m., 5 s., 1 w. §4 m., 38 s. ¶5 m., 44 s. 2 w.

No. 1.—PERSONAL CENSUS

COUNTY OF

POLLING DISTRICTS.	Females.				Grand Total.	Deaths.		
	Married.	Single.	Widows.	Total.		Males.	Females.	Total.
	124	125	126	127	128	129	130	131
1. Canning	374	691	55	1120	2255	20	15	35
2. Canard	207	428	36	671	1342	10	7	17
3. Centreville	355	579	47	981	2018	8	13	21
4. Lakeville	255	484	26	765	1599	12	5	17
5. Somerset	391	658	40	1089	2286	22	22	44
6. Kentville	238	443	33	714	1488	13	16	29
7. Gaspereaux	187	285	27	499	1089	· 11	8	19
8. Wolfville	236	486	51	773	1577	12	4	16
9. Lower Horton	243	402	19	664	1315	11	7	18
10. Aylesford	238	400	21	659	1351	27	24	51
11. West Sherbrooke	34	61	1	96	197		1	1
12. Aylesford	219	405	28	652	1342	9	15	24
13. Berwick	138	267	23	428	872	6	11	17
	3115	5589	407	9111	18731	161	148	309

COUNTY OF

1. Wilmot	301	539	41	881	1836	24	27	51
2. Wilmot, Middleton Corner	249	458	37	744	1474	11	16	27
3. Clarence, Wilmot	253	436	25	714	1434	3	13	16
4. Bridgetown	218	419	45	682	1404	16	11	27
5. Beeliase	200	344	22	566	1155	10	6	16
6. New Caledonia	220	388	29	637	1252	15	5	20
7. Broad Cove	160	264	33	457	898	4	4	8
8. Clementsport	212	373	34	619	1319	12	6	18
9. Hessian Line	167	290	22	479	941	4	1	5
10. Annapolis Royal	273	557	66	896	1803	11	7	18
11. Carleton's Corner	108	215	26	349	707	8	7	15
12. Nictaux	215	379	22	616	1238	13	8	21
13. Dalhousie	82	201	10	293	561	6	3	9
14. Maitland	58	100	3	161	369	3		3
15. Morse Road	54	106	9	169	362	8	5	13
	2770	5069	424	8263	16753	148	119	267

COUNTY OF

1. Hillsburg	215	342	23	580	1191	7	9	16
2. Head of St. Mary's Bay	148	308	26	482	954	6	6	12
3. Digby	282	591	56	929	1851	19	12	31
4. Sandy Cove	199	345	29	573	1184	2	6	8
5. Long Island	165	267	19	451	954	3	3	6
6. Westport	110	218	13	341	678	5	5	10
7. On St. Mary's Bay	220	451	26	697	1469	2	4	6
8. Weymouth	192	411	32	635	1308	5	4	9
9. Bellvoe Cove	163	395	28	586	1116	4	5	9
10. Session House, Clare	235	539	35	809	1586	12	7	19
11. Montegan	223	500	33	756	1531	4	10	14
12. Salmon River	156	311	9	476	929	16	7	23
	2308	4678	329	7315	14751	85	78	163

BY AGES...1860—61.

KING'S, Continued.

Deaf and Dumb M.	F.	Blind M.	F.	Lunatics M.	F.	Idiots M.	F.	Cannot Read — Over 5 and under 15 years of age M.	F.	Above 15 years of age M.	F.	Cannot Write — Over 5 and under 15 years of age M.	F.	Above 15 years of age M.	P.	Married since March 30, 1860	Colored persons included in population	Indians not included in population
132	133	134	135	136	137	138	139	140	141	142	143	144	145	146	147	148	149	150
	1		3	2			1	65	66	53	50	130	132	75	80	23	11	
						1	1	22	12	4	5	28	13	4	5	6	2	
		1		1				91	88	51	62	122	123	67	94	6	86	20
2	1		1		1	2		65	61	33	15	112	116	61	49	11	6	
1		1			1	1		100	93	41	35	184	162	73	76	13	1	20
					1	1	7	13	11	15	11	16	13	21	23	4	14	
2	1	1		1	1	1	1	18	16	4	7	42	31	16	16	9		11
	1			2		1	1	38	34	26	29	62	57	34	44	6	22	
		1	2		1			50	58	44	36	69	82	52	50	2	63	9
1	1				1			48	45	23	18	79	68	29	27	10	2	
								7	11	4	3	12	14	9	10	3	4	
		1			2	3		22	27	27	10	35	46	31	18	14		20
	1	1		1		5	1	24	35	16	6	45	60	24	18	6	7	
6	6	6	6	8	6	15	12	563	557	341	287	936	917	496	510	113	218	80

ANNAPOLIS, Continued

132	133	134	135	136	137	138	139	140	141	142	143	144	145	146	147	148	149	150
1	1							37	25	23	27	63	59	32	44	13	3	14
			2	1	4		1	64	70	32	27	98	113	57	61	12	18	
		1		1	2		1	9	16	7	5	9	19	6	9	14	20	
3	1		3					57	49	48	51	92	76	58	75	10	140	
2	1	1				3	1	19	21	1		28	26	2		13	96	
					1	1		12	23	19	22	17	23	23	25	10	95	6
1		3						45	42	19	27	55	55	28	39	9	121	
		1		2	1	3		66	55	65	40	108	89	82	80	11	50	11
								50	47	29	27	66	64	42	45	5	62	
				1				55	57	60	70	64	85	77	93	4	114	17
						2		9	7	2	3	9	7	2	3	3	14	
								47	28	17	15	91	83	25	28	16	15	24
1				1	1		1	39	35	10	14	50	54	23	26	5	1	20
								20	8	5	6	27	15	12	15	2		2
								31	21	10	6	37	33	16	26	3		
8	4	7	6	9	5	9	2	560	504	347	340	814	801	485	569	130	749	94

DIGBY, Continued.

132	133	134	135	136	137	138	139	140	141	142	143	144	145	146	147	148	149	150
	1							25	21	20	27	34	33	23	42	13	43	111
1	1	1	1	1		1		53	65	50	39	71	76	77	71	9	47	14
1	2	1	1	3	3	2		88	63	56	44	116	100	76	79	23	101	
1						2	2	68	45	35	38	87	70	50	61	11	12	
					1		1	51	29	10	9	63	40	13	20	5	1	
					1			8	14	4	4	37	41	4	11	11	3	
	1					1	1	186	149	191	165	193	167	192	175	1	9	
1		1	1	1		1	2	81	65	84	91	102	81	100	132	7	146	
							1	87	95	116	123	90	105	126	150	8	73	
1	2				2		2	123	127	215	166	151	150	294	379	17	4	2
1	2	1				1	1	174	150	314	314	180	154	353	397	7	2	1
						2	2	75	72	106	108	91	88	108	118	4	13	
6	8	4	4	6	8	11	12	1019	895	1201	1128	1215	1105	1416	1635	116	454	128

No. 1.—PERSONAL CENSUS

COUNTY OF

POLLING DISTRICTS.	TOTAL POPULATION.			Number of Families.	Average Number of each Family.	Under one year of age.		Deaths under 1 yr. age since 30th March, 1890.	
	Males.	Females.	Total.			M.	F.	M.	F.
	1	2	3	4	5	6	7	8	9
1. Ohio	1128	1166	2294	420	......	36	33	3	4
2. Yarmouth	2005	2147	4152	717	......	56	63	4	2
3. Chebogue	857	830	1687	276	......	23	19	......	2
4. Carleton	357	359	716	113	......	17	9	......	2
5. Plymouth	563	535	1098	189	......	22	18	7	1
6. Tusket	1126	1129	2255	352	......	30	45	7	3
7. Argyle	551	569	1120	196	......	10	19	......	1
8. Pubnico	759	744	1503	231	......	18	18	1	4
9. Kempt	172	137	309	54	......	6	4	......	......
10. West side Tusket River	150	162	312	52	......	4	3	2	......
	7668	7778	15446	2600	5.94	222	231	24	19

COUNTY OF

1. Carleton Village	438	431	869	154	......	18	8	......	1
2. Shelburne	1162	1138	2300	373	......	27	26	......	5
3. Ragged Islands	631	616	1247	206	......	22	27	......	......
4. Louis Head	418	454	872	132	......	8	16	1	1
5. Shag Harbor	588	591	1179	221	......	28	22	3	1
6. Cape Sable Island	722	690	1412	243	......	23	30	......	......
7. Barrington	745	763	1508	303	......	19	19	1	2
8. Port LaTour	639	642	1281	249	......	17	15	1	2
	5343	5325	10668	1881	5.68	162	163	6	12

COUNTY OF

1. Liverpool	1489	1447	2936	501	......	31	43	3	2
2. Bristol	948	917	1865	332	......	38	23	2	2
3. Port Medway	930	903	1833	323	......	34	31	2	2
4. Port Mouton	377	366	743	136	......	5	6	......	......
5. Brookfield	331	285	616	96	......	12	6	......	1
6. Caledonia	542	487	1029	172	......	8	15	......	1
7. Greenfield	182	161	343	54	......	5	10	......	......
	4799	4566	9365	1614	5.80	133	134	7	8

COUNTY OF

1. Lunenburg	1522	1526	3048	519	......	49	53	5	6
2. Ritsey's Cove	712	703	1415	220	......	26	26	2	1
3. Mahone Bay	1358	1341	2699	434	......	44	39	3	1
4. LaHave	481	486	967	148	......	17	13	2	......
5. New Germany	1058	1073	2131	328	......	41	46	2	2
6. Chester	1352	1287	2639	436	......	40	40	2	......
7. Sherbrooke	486	426	912	130	......	24	14	1	2
8. Petite Riviere	1500	1403	2903	488	......	46	54	8	3
9. Bridgewater	1033	996	2029	330	......	29	40	3	3
10. Tancook Island	202	177	379	63	......	12	3	1	......
11. Mill Cove, St. Maagaret's Bay	255	255	510	81	......	11	14	2	1
	9959	9673	19632	3177	6.17	339	342	31	19

BY AGES...1860—61.

YARMOUTH.

Over 1 and under 2 ys. of age.		Deaths between 1 and 2 years, since M'ch 80, 1860.		Over 2 and under 3 years of age.		Deaths between 2 and 3 years, since M'ch 80, 1860.		Over 3 and under 4 years of age.		Deaths between 3 and 4 years, since M'ch 80, 1860.		Over 4 and under 5 years of age.		Deaths between 4 and 5 years, since M'ch 80, 1860.	
M.	F.	M.	F.	M.	F.	M.	F.	M.	F.	M.	F.	M.	F.	M.	F.
10	11	12	13	14	15	16	17	18	19	20	21	22	23	24	25
32	39			34	26	2	2	27	40	2	1	34	36	1	
42	46	1	1	48	60			49	64	3	1	69	50		
23	21		2	25	29			19	26		1	25	24	1	2
12	16		1	11	14			14	11	1		7	18		
17	16		2	18	20			23	16			15	14		
33	35			33	40	2	3	41	32	1		34	28	1	
15	16		1	22	22			16	15			20	20	1	
27	23			21	18	1	1	28	29			24	13		
8	6			5	4			8	8			2	4		
3	6			4	4			6	7			7	6		
212	224	1	7	221	237	5	6	231	248	7	3	237	213	4	2

SHELBURNE.

M.	F.	M.	F.	M.	F.	M.	F.	M.	F.	M.	F.	M.	F.	M.	F.
8	8		1	11	20			18	6			16	10		
37	29	2	1	43	30			31	34	1	2	35	30		
20	14		1	18	28		1	18	23			21	18	1	
8	9			11	7			14	15			12	15	1	
15	14	1		17	22		1	20	21		1	23	17	1	
25	16			26	22	1		18	20	1		17	25		
26	23	2		23	18			20	16			15	26		
10	12			22	16	1		10	25			15	11		1
149	125	5	3	171	163	2	2	149	160	2	3	154	152	3	1

QUEEN'S.

M.	F.	M.	F.	M.	F.	M.	F.	M.	F.	M.	F.	M.	F.	M.	F.
35	37			50	36	5	1	37	28			40	43	1	
22	26	4		27	24	2	3	28	24	1	1	24	24	1	1
24	24	1		39	25	1		25	23	2	2	26	28		1
9	8			8	6			6	12	1		12	9		
12	13	1		9	7			13	9	1		10	8		
17	14	1		14	16			16	18		1	12	14	1	
5	3			8	4			6	6			5	4		
124	125	7		155	118	8	4	131	120	5	4	129	130	3	2

LUNENBURG.

M.	F.	M.	F.	M.	F.	M.	F.	M.	F.	M.	F.	M.	F.	M.	F.
37	34	4	3	46	43	4	1	38	38	3		52	38		2
19	18	2		15	19	3	1	25	22			16	20		2
32	31	2		35	40	2		40	49		1	42	34	1	
12	20		1	12	11			12	20			11	22		
37	40	1		36	49	1	1	38	39			33	37	1	4
35	29	2	1	43	43	1		45	33		2	48	51		2
13	13	1	2	17	17			17	15			25	14		
40	34		2	42	55	2	2	56	54	2	8	40	47	2	1
19	29	1		39	35	1	1	34	27	1	2	29	37	2	6
10	5			8	4		1	9	6			7	9		
9	9		2	6	12		1	6	19			9	11		
263	262	13	11	299	328	14	8	320	322	6	13	312	320	6	17

No. 1.—PERSONAL CENSUS

COUNTY OF

POLLING DISTRICTS.	Over 5 and under 10 years of age.		Deaths between 5 and 10 y'rs. since M'ch 30, 1860.		Over 10 and under 15 years of age.					
					Males.		Females.		Deaths since M'ch 30, 1860.	
	M.	F.	M.	F.	MD.	S.	MD.	S.	M.	F.
	26	27	28	29	30	31	32	33	34	35
1. Ohio	168	171	1	1	...	142	...	168	1	...
2. Yarmouth	246	232	2	4	...	241	...	224	3	1
3. Chebogue	123	108		1	...	110	...	99	...	
4. Carleton	49	59				53	...	49	...	
5. Plymouth	81	66	2		...	59	...	69	...	1
6. Tusket	172	168	1	4	...	161	...	150	1	1
7. Argyle	71	74	1		...	63	...	60	...	1
8. Pubnico	107	113			...	101	...	89	...	1
9. Kempt	31	19			...	26	...	17	...	
10. West side Tusket River	20	27			...	26		22	...	
	1068	1037	7	10	...	982	...	947	5	5

COUNTY OF

POLLING DISTRICTS.	M.	F.	M.	F.	MD.	S.	MD.	S.	M.	F.
1. Carleton Village	63	66	1	2	...	59	...	56	2	1
2. Shelburne	173	151	1	2	...	157	...	152	3	6
3. Ragged Islands	96	80			...	67	...	70	...	
4. Louis Head	52	56			...	59	...	65	...	
5. Shag Harbor	76	76	1		...	57	...	69	...	
6. Cape Sable Island	93	104			...	116	...	84	1	...
7. Barrington	89	73			...	79	...	83	1	...
8. Port LaTour	86	74		1	...	94	...	71	...	
	728	680	3	5	...	688	...	650	7	7

COUNTY OF

POLLING DISTRICTS.	M.	F.	M.	F.	MD.	S.	MD.	S.	M.	F.
1. Liverpool	201	168	6	2	...	185	...	147	...	4
2. Bristol	118	121	2	1	...	114	...	85	1	...
3. Port Medway	125	127	1	2	...	87	...	107	...	
4. Port Mouton	42	57			...	54	...	46	...	
5. Brookfield	46	37			...	40	...	33	1	...
6. Caledonia	78	62	3	2	...	64	...	59	2	3
7. Greenfield	26	22			...	29	...	17	...	
	636	594	12	7	...	573	...	494	4	7

COUNTY OF

POLLING DISTRICTS.	M.	F.	M.	F.	MD.	S.	MD.	S.	M.	F.
1. Lunenburg	196	205	3	2	...	106	...	177	2	2
2. Ritsey's Cove	90	87	1	1	...	71	...	88	...	3
3. Mahone Bay	193	185	1	1	...	172	...	160	...	1
4. LaHave	60	67			...	70	...	57	...	1
5. New Germany	169	165	7	5	...	135	...	148	1	1
6. Chester	173	195	2	2	...	180	...	171	...	1
7. Sherbrooke	87	76		1	...	64	...	54	...	
8. Petite Riviere	210	214	2	7	...	183	...	154	2	3
9. Bridgewater	159	163	4	4	...	129	...	127	1	2
10. Tancook Island	22	25		1	...	25	...	25	...	
11. Mill Cove, St. Margaret's Bay	40	41	1	2	...	40	...	33	...	
	1399	1423	21	26	...	1265	...	1203	6	14

BY AGES...1860—61.

YARMOUTH, Continued.

	Over 15 and under 20 years of age.							Over 20 and under 30 years of age.							
	Males.			Females.		Deaths since March 30, 1860.		Males.			Females.			Deaths since March 30, 1860.	
MD.	S.	WDR	MD.	S.	WD.	M.	F.	MD.	S.	WDR	MD.	S.	WD.	M.	F.
36	37	38	39	40	41	42	43	44	45	46	47	48	49	50	51
.....	148	.....	5	118	.....	4	.....	75	94	2	114	74	3	3	1
1	253	.....	10	298	.....	3	2	113	255	2	186	230	5	5	.....
.....	106	.....	3	89	.....	3		41	88	2	65	70	.....	4	1
.....	44	.....	3	43	.....		2	18	34	1	27	18	1	.....	1
.....	63	.....	3	59	.....	1	.....	29	69	.....	48	53	1	1	1
.....	121	.....	2	138	.....	1	.....	83	114	.....	112	94	1	4	2
1	62	.....	7	59	.....		1	42	49	.....	57	37	.....	.....	.....
.....	81	.....	2	92	.....	1	.....	40	97	.....	83	65	1	.....	.....
.....	16	.....		12	.....		1	14	14	.....	18	5	.....	1	.....
.....	17	.....		19	.....			9	10	.....	15	16	.....	.....	.....
2	911	.....	35	927	.....	10	9	464	824	7	725	662	12	18	6

SHELBURNE, Continued.

MD.	S.	WDR	MD.	S.	WD.	M.	F.	MD.	S.	WDR	MD.	S.	WD.	M.	F.
.....	45	.....	1	52	.....			20	44	.....	31	26	1	.....	1
.....	115	.....	2	123	.....	1		37	133	1	71	104	1	2	1
1	58	.....	5	60	.....	3	.....	41	68	.....	53	39	3	1	.....
.....	61	.....	2	51	.....			11	49	.....	21	41	3	.....	.....
1	71	.....	11	46	.....		2	67	33	.....	69	33	1	1	1
1	98	.....	7	75	.....	3	.....	61	50	1	85	29	4	1	1
.....	93	.....	6	81	.....	1		41	70	.....	75	70	.....	1	2
2	81	.....	3	77	.....			41	54	.....	56	52	1	.....	2
5	622	.....	37	565	.....	8	2	319	501	2	461	394	14	6	8

QUEEN'S, Continued.

MD.	S.	WDR	MD.	S.	WD.	M.	F.	MD.	S.	WDR	MD.	S.	WD.	M.	F.
.....	169	.....	7	186	1	3	.....	70	203	.....	118	135	6	1	3
.....	108	.....	8	122	.....	1	2	44	130	1	86	79	4	.....	1
.....	100	.....	6	85	.....		2	58	128	.....	100	88	1	1	1
.....	46	.....	2	35	.....		1	15	51	.....	26	31	2	.....	1
.....	44	.....	1	30	.....			18	31	.....	25	19	.....	.....	.....
.....	73	.....	.....	56	.....	1	.....	22	79	.....	39	43	.....	.....	1
1	22	.....	3	25	.....			9	21	.....	12	7	1	.....	.....
1	562	.....	27	539	1	5	5	236	643	1	406	402	14	2	7

LUNENBURG, Continued.

MD.	S.	WDR	MD.	S.	WD.	M.	F.	MD.	S.	WDR	MD.	S.	WD.	M.	F.
.....	166	.....	1	181	.....	1	.....	59	189	1	125	171	3	3	.....
.....	65	.....	1	70	.....		1	17	114	.....	55	73	.....	2	1
.....	140	.....	1	148	.....			70	144	.....	121	104	2	.....	3
.....	50	.....	1	56	.....	1	.....	19	74	.....	37	47	.....	1	.....
.....	116	.....	4	110	.....	1	.....	51	107	.....	102	83	.....	2	1
.....	149	.....	8	137	.....	1	3	74	162	2	105	95	6	1	2
1	53	.....	2	46	.....			20	37	.....	31	24	.....	.....	.....
.....	159	.....	7	123	.....	1	2	68	194	.....	140	108	2	.....	2
.....	131	.....	.....	106	.....	4	.....	58	111	2	106	72	3	.....	2
.....	24	.....	3	16	.....			22	15	.....	25	9	1	1	1
.....	30	.....	5	20	.....			21	23	1	29	6	1	.....	1
1	1083	.....	33	1013	.....	9	6	479	1170	6	876	792	18	10	13

9

No. 1.—PERSONAL CENSUS

COUNTY OF

POLLING DISTRICTS.	Over 30 and under 40 years of age.							
	Males.			Females.			Deaths since March 30, 1860.	
	MD.	S.	WDR	MD.	S.	WD.	M.	F.
	52	53	54	55	56	57	58	59
1. Ohio	109	3	1	109	13	7		
2. Yarmouth	183	24	2	196	48	16	1	2
3. Chebogue	73	16	3	75	12	6	2	1
4. Carleton	33	2		33	1			
5. Plymouth	57	7	1	57	9	1		3
6. Tusket	102	10		98	6	2		1
7. Argyle	48	4		43	4	1	1	2
8. Pubnico	76	7	2	57	9	1		1
9. Kempt	18			57				
10. West side Tusket River	14	2		10				
	707	74	9	695	100	23	4	10

COUNTY OF

POLLING DISTRICTS.	MD.	S.	WDR	MD.	S.	WD.	M.	F.
1. Carleton Village	43	5	1	44	9	3	1	
2. Shelburne	96	20	2	96	20	7	1	2
3. Ragged Islands	64	13		64	5	2	1	1
4. Louis Head	33	4	1	34	11	1	3	
5. Shag Harbor	52	8		54	4	4		
6. Cape Sable Island	77	3	1	60	12	4	1	1
7. Barrington	84	7	3	71	14	6	1	2
8. Port LaTour	56	5		56	13	1		
	505	60	8	479	88	29	8	6

COUNTY OF

POLLING DISTRICTS.	MD.	S.	WDR	MD.	S.	WD.	M.	F.
1. Liverpool	116	40	1	123	26	18	1	1
2. Bristol	96	7		96	14			
3. Port Medway	90	21	1	88	11	3		
4. Port Mouton	38	9	2	36	10	3		
5. Brookfield	27	5		30	6	1		
6. Caledonia	46	6	2	44	11	2		
7. Greenfield	13	4		15	2	1		
	432	92	6	432	80	31	1	1

COUNTY OF

POLLING DISTRICTS.	MD.	S.	WDR	MD.	S.	WD.	M.	F.
1. Lunenburg	135	30	3	127	20	12	3	1
2. Ritsey's Cove	65	19	2	59	13	3	1	
3. Mahone Bay	131	29	2	126	24	2		1
4. LaHave	45	9	1	42	10	1		
5. New Germany	96	10		87	12	2		
6. Chester	115	26	3	100	13	7		2
7. Sherbrooke	36	8	1	40	6			
8. Petite Riviere	105	20	2	143	20	5	1	1
9. Bridgewater	121	10	2	114	10	1		2
10. Tancook Island	17		1	17	1			
11. Millcove, St. Margaret's Bay	20	1		20				
	950	162	17	881	129	33	5	7

BY AGES...1860—61.

YARMOUTH, Continued.

Over 40 and under 50 years of age.								Over 50 and under 60 years of age.							
Males.			Females.			Deaths since March 30, 1860.		Males.			Females.			Deaths since March 30, 1860.	
MD.	S.	WDR	MD.	S.	WD.	M.	F.	MD.	S.	WDR	MD.	S.	WD.	M.	F.
60	61	62	63	64	65	66	67	68	69	70	71	72	73	74	75
93	....	2	83	5	2	....	....	51	....	1	43	1	7	2	....
165	6	7	158	10	18	1	2	120	3	3	80	6	24	5	....
51	2	....	56	3	4	....	1	51	....	2	43	1	7	....	1
31	....	1	26	1	1			19	....	....	15	....	1		
35	....	2	21	1	3			20	1	....	27	2	3		
61	7	2	64	3	8	1	1	55	4	7	39	....	4		
41	3	1	37	2	1			32	....	....	32	....	5	1	....
59	2	2	53	5	3			32	....	2	27	1	10	1	....
8	1	....	9	2	1		1	9	....	....	6	....	....		
8	2	....	9	....				8	....	....	8	....	....		
552	23	17	519	32	41	2	5	399	8	15	330	11	61	9	....

SHELBURNE, Continued.

MD.	S.	WDR	MD.	S.	WD.	M.	F.	MD.	S.	WDR	MD.	S.	WD.	M.	F.
34	....		37	2	2	1	....	21	2	2	14	2	3	....	1
78	6	4	76	10	10			54	4	4	47	8	10	....	1
47	4	1	39	6	4		1	21	2	....	18	3	4		
29	1	1	30	4	3			21	1	....	23	2	7		
53	....		52	3	4			33	2	....	24	2	3		
43	....	1	51	5	7	2	1	33	1	1	28	....	2	1	1
47	1	2	47	3	7		1	64	2	1	47	4	10		1
54	1	....	58	5	6	1	1	58	1	....	37	1	10		
385	13	9	390	38	43	4	4	285	15	8	231	22	49	1	4

QUEEN'S, Continued.

MD.	S.	WDR	MD.	S.	WD.	M.	F.	MD.	S.	WDR	MD.	S.	WD.	M.	F.
125	3	4	110	14	13	1	....	67	4	1	52	13	19	1	....
71	5	1	60	3	5			54	1	2	33	3	8		2
56	3	....	48	3	2	1	....	51	3	....	35	6	8		
22	3	....	23	....	4		2	16	....	1	13	....	3		
20	3	1	17	1	2			13	1	1	10	1	1		
29	1	1	32	....	....			31	2	1	27	....	5		
15	....	....	11	....	3			7	....	....	4	....	1		
338	18	7	301	21	29	2	2	239	11	6	174	23	45	1	2

LUNENBURG, Continued.

MD.	S.	WDR	MD.	S.	WD.	M.	F.	MD.	S.	WDR	MD.	S.	WD.	M.	F.
98	14	2	94	8	10	....	1	89	9	2	70	6	17	....	1
58	9	2	45	6	4			38	9	2	36	2	6	1	....
104	5	5	100	9	7	1	2	83	5	6	58	6	10	1	....
35	3	....	34	1	1		1	21	....	1	17	....	5	1	....
90	5	1	66	1	....	1	1	49	1	4	44	....	3		2
92	7	4	88	4	8	2	2	52	6	7	55	3	15		1
38	3	....	30	1	2			15	....	....	17	1	3		
97	10	2	87	8	6		1	70	3	6	54	6	13		
54	5	3	42	2	4			47	2	1	33	4	5		1
13	1	....	7	1	....			5	1	....	8	....	....		
18	....	....	10	....	....			12	....	....	12	....	3		
697	62	19	603	41	42	4	8	481	36	29	404	28	80	3	5

No. 1.—PERSONAL CENSUS

COUNTY OF

POLLING DISTRICTS.	Over 60 and under 70 years of age.							
	Males.			Females.			Deaths since March 30, 1860.	
	MD.	S.	WDR	MD.	S.	WD.	M.	F.
	76	77	78	79	80	81	82	83
1. Ohio	38	....	1	29	1	11	2	1
2. Yarmouth	58	4	7	42	3	26	....	....
3. Chebogue	39	2	2	28	4	10	3	....
4. Carleton	16	....	....	8	....	2	....	....
5. Plymouth	25	....	2	12	....	6	1	1
6. Tusket	32	1	2	28	1	7	2	1
7. Argyle	23	1	2	18	3	4	1	....
8. Pubnico	25	1	2	11	4	6	....	1
9. Kempt	3	....	2	1	1	1	....	....
10. West side Tusket River	6	....	1	6	....	2	....	....
	265	9	21	183	17	75	9	4

COUNTY OF

1. Carleton Village	18	2	2	11	1	6	1	3
2. Shelburne	50	3	7	33	4	17	....	1
3. Ragged Islands	21	....	2	21	1	6	1	....
4. Louis Head	26	....	2	15	3	5	....	1
5. Shag Harbor	18	2	2	19	1	4	....	....
6. Cape Sable Island	17	1	1	11	1	2	....	....
7. Barrington	35	....	3	31	....	11	1	....
8. Port LaTour	31	1	3	17	1	7	1	2
	216	9	22	158	12	58	4	7

COUNTY OF

1. Liverpool	63	6	8	38	6	18	2	3
2. Bristol	32	....	3	24	2	16	1	....
3. Port Medway	31	....	2	21	....	10	....	1
4. Port Mouton	21	3	3	14	2	5	....	....
5. Brookfield	12	1	....	15	....	5	....	....
6. Caledonia	22	....	4	16	1	4	....	....
7. Greenfield	4	....	....	4	....	2	....	....
	185	10	20	132	11	60	3	4

COUNTY OF

1. Lunenburg	57	6	9	39	6	16	2	4
2. Ritsey's Cove	24	2	5	12	2	10	....	1
3. Mahone Bay	43	4	1	33	....	14	....	1
4. LaHave	17	2	3	9	1	5	....	....
5. New Germany	29	....	2	17	1	8	1	....
6. Chester	53	3	9	32	2	9	....	....
7. Sherbrooke	10	....	1	4	....	1	....	....
8. Petite Riviere	46	5	4	24	1	12	2	1
9. Bridgewater	29	1	2	18	2	6	1	....
10. Tancook Island	6	....	....	4	....	2	....	....
11. Mill Cove, St. Margaret's Bay	5	....	....	3	....	3	....	....
	319	23	36	195	15	86	6	7

BY AGES...1860—61.

YARMOUTH, Continued.

| | Over 70 and under 80 years of age. | | | | | | | | Over 80 and under 90 years of age. | | | | | | | |
| | Males. | | | Females. | | | Deaths since March 30, 1860. | | Males. | | | Females. | | | Deaths since March 30, 1860. | |
MD.	S.	WDR	MD.	S.	WD.	M.	F.	MD.	S.	WDR	MD.	S.	WD.	M.	F.
84	85	86	87	88	89	90	91	92	93	94	95	96	97	98	99
27		4	15	1	7	1		1					2		
20	3	1	14	3	21		3	3		1	1	3	5		1
16	2	2	6	2	8	2		2	1	2	2	1	4		
2			1										2		
11	2	2	5		1			1			1				
14		3	7	1	6	1	1	2		1	1		7		
10		1	5		4		1	2		2			2		
6		2	4	1	3			2					2		
1			2			1									
2			2					2							
109	7	15	61	8	50	5	5	15	1	6	5	4	24		1

SHELBURNE, Continued.

MD.	S.	WDR	MD.	S.	WD.	M.	F.	MD.	S.	WDR	MD.	S.	WD.	M.	F.
4		1	3	1	6	1	2			1			2	1	1
17	5	5	10	5	18			4		1	3		8		
12	4	3	6	1	6	2				3			3	1	
8		3	5	1	5		1			2	1		4		1
11			5		4		1						3		
9	1	3	4		6					1			1		1
11		5	7		13		1	2		1			1		
10	1	3	6		7	1		3			1		5		1
82	11	23	46	8	65	4	4	10		9	5		27	2	4

QUEEN'S, Continued.

MD.	S.	WDR	MD.	S.	WD.	M.	F.	MD.	S.	WDR	MD.	S.	WD.	M.	F.
17		6	10	1	17		1	4		3	1	1	11	1	
10		4	6	1	8	3		2		1	1		5		
8		2	5	1	7			1		2	1		5		
7	3	3	7		3			1					3		
9	1		1		2				1		1		1	1	
9		4	3		4			1					1		1
1			2		1			1					1		
61	4	19	34	3	42	3	1	10	1	6	4	1	27	2	1

LUNENBURG, Continued.

MD.	S.	WDR	MD.	S.	WD.	M.	F.	MD.	S.	WDR	MD.	S.	WD.	M.	F.
22	1	9	7	1	12		4	3		3		1	9		
5	2	2	3	4	12			2		4	2		5		
12		5	8	2	12	1		5		6	2		4		
5	1	1	1	4	3	1							1	1	1
5	1	2	1		6	1							2		
16		3	9	2	15	2		4					5		
7	1	3	5	2	4			4		1	2		1		
19	1	8	10	1	12	1	1			2	1		6	1	
9	1	3	6		2	2		3					1		
4			3	2	11										
3			1		1								2		
107	8	36	54	18	80	8	5	21		16	7	1	36	2	1

No. 1.—PERSONAL CENSUS

COUNTY OF

POLLING DISTRICTS.	Over 90 and under 100 years of age.							
	Males.			Females.			Deaths since March 30, 1860.	
	MD.	S.	WDR	MD.	S.	WD.	M.	F.
	100	101	102	103	104	105	106	107
1. Ohio	1							
2. Yarmouth		1				2		
3. Chebogue	1					1		1
4. Carleton								
5. Plymouth					1			
6. Tusket					1	2		
7. Argyle								
8. Pubnico			1			1		
9. Kempt								
10. West side Tusket River								
	2	1	3			6		1

COUNTY OF

POLLING DISTRICTS.	MD.	S.	WDR	MD.	S.	WD.	M.	F.
	100	101	102	103	104	105	106	107
1. Carleton Village								
2. Shelburne								
3. Ragged Islands				1				1
4. Louis Head								
5. Shag Harbor								
6. Cape Sable Island								
7. Barrington								
8. Port LaTour							1	
			2				1	1

COUNTY OF

POLLING DISTRICTS.	MD.	S.	WDR	MD.	S.	WD.	M.	F.
	100	101	102	103	104	105	106	107
1. Liverpool								
2. Bristol								
3. Port Medway	1			1				
4. Port Mouton								
5. Brookfield	1					1		
6. Caledonia						1		
7. Greenfield								
	2			1			2	

COUNTY OF

POLLING DISTRICTS.	MD.	S.	WDR	MD.	S.	WD.	M.	F.
	100	101	102	103	104	105	106	107
1. Lunenburg							2	1
2. Ritcey's Cove								
3. Mahone Bay								
4. LaHave						1		
5. New Germany								
6. Chester	1			1				
7. Sherbrooke								
8. Petite Riviere					2	1	1	
9. Bridgewater						2		
10. Tancook Island						1		
11. Mill Cove, St. Margaret's Bay								
	1		2	1		7	1	1

BY AGES...1860—61.

YARMOUTH, Continued..

	Over 100 years of age							Ages not given	Deaths				Males			
	Males			Females			Deaths since M'ch 30, 1860				Ages not given					
	MD	S	WDR	MD	S	WD	M	F		M	F	M	F	Married	Single	Widowers	Total
	108	109	110	111	112	113	114	115	116	117	118	119	120	121	122	123
									4	3			397	719	12	1128
									10	9		1	676	1304	25	2005
									5	3			276	568	13	857
													112	243	2	357
													178	377	8	563
													349	761	16	1126
							1		10	21			203	341	7	551
													254	515	10	759
													53	117	2	172
													49	100	1	150
							1		*29	†36			2527	5045	96	7668

SHELBURNE, Continued.

							114	115	116	117	118	119	120	121	122	123
													140	291	7	438
							12	3					338	799	25	1162
							3	3					208	413	10	631
								1					120	280	9	418
							4	4					237	349	2	588
													241	472	9	722
							2	1				1	285	445	15	745
								1					235	398	6	639
							‡21	§13					1813	3447	83	5343

QUEEN'S Continued.

							114	115	116	117	118	119	120	121	122	123
								1					462	1004	23	1189
							3	3					311	623	14	948
							7	4					303	620	7	930
													120	248	9	377
										2			100	229	2	331
													160	370	12	542
													51	131		182
							§10	¶10					1507	3225	67	4799

LUNENBURG, Continued.

108							114	115	116	117	118	119	120	121	122	123
1													464	1029	29	1522
													213	482	17	712
													448	885	25	1358
													142	333	6	481
													320	729	9	1058
													407	917	28	1352
													131	349	6	486
													465	1009	26	1500
													321	698	13	1033
													67	134	1	202
													79	175	1	255
1													3057	6741	161	9959

* 12 m., 14 s., 8 wdr.   † 12 m., 24 s.   ‡ 6 m., 15 s.   ‖ 6 m., 6 s., 1 w.   § 3 m., 6 s., 1 wdr.   ¶ 4 m., 6 s.

No. 1.—PERSONAL CENSUS

COUNTY OF

POLLING DISTRICTS.	Females.				Grand Total.	Deaths.		
	Married.	Single.	Widows.	Total.		Males.	Females.	Total.
	124	125	126	127	128	129	130	131
1. Ohio	400	727	39	1166	2294	22	10	32
2. Yarmouth	691	1345	111	2147	4152	28	20	48
3. Chebogue	280	510	40	830	1687	12	15	27
4. Carleton	113	239	7	359	716	1	6	7
5. Plymouth	177	343	15	535	1098	12	9	21
6. Tusket	351	741	37	1129	2255	22	17	39
7. Argyle	203	348	18	569	1120	5	7	12
8. Pubnico	237	480	27	744	1503	4	8	12
9. Kempt	53	82	2	137	309	2	2	4
10. West side Tusket River	50	110	2	162	312	2		2
	2555	4925	298	7778	15446	110	94	204

COUNTY OF

1. Carleton Village	141	267	23	431	869	8	13	21
2. Shelburne	340	727	71	1138	2300	11	21	32
3. Ragged Islands	207	379	30	616	1247	10	5	15
4. Louis Head	129	297	28	454	872	5	3	8
5. Shag Harbor	236	332	23	591	1179	7	7	14
6. Cape Sable Island	241	423	26	690	1412	11	5	16
7. Barrington	285	430	48	763	1508	8	10	18
8. Port LaTour	234	371	37	642	1281	6	10	16
	1813	3226	286	5325	10668	66	74	140

COUNTY OF

1. Liverpool	459	885	103	1447	2936	25	17	42
2. Bristol	316	552	49	917	1865	18	13	31
3. Port Medway	306	561	36	903	1833	9	11	20
4. Port Mouton	121	222	23	366	743	1	4	5
5. Brookfield	100	172	13	285	616	4	1	5
6. Caledonia	161	309	17	487	1029	8	9	17
7. Greenfield	51	100	10	161	343			
	1514	2801	251	4566	9365	65	55	120

COUNTY OF

1. Lunenburg	463	982	81	1526	3048	30	28	58
2. Ritcey's Cove	213	450	40	703	1415	12	11	23
3. Mahone Bay	449	840	52	1341	2699	12	11	23
4. LaHave	141	329	16	486	967	7	4	11
5. New Germany	321	731	21	1073	2151	19	17	36
6. Chester	404	818	65	1287	2639	13	18	31
7. Sherbrooke	131	283	12	426	912	3	5	8
8. Petite Rivière	466	879	58	1403	2903	24	34	58
9. Bridgewater	319	654	23	996	2029	20	23	43
10. Tancook Island	67	106	4	177	379	2	3	5
11. Mill Cove, St. Margaret's Bay	80	165	10	255	510	3	7	10
	3054	6237	382	9673	19632	145	161	306

BY AGES...1860—61.

YARMOUTH, Continued.

Deaf and Dumb.		Blind.		Lunatics.		Idiots.		Cannot Read.				Cannot Write.				Married since 30, 1860.	Colored persons included in population.	Indians not included in population.
								Over 5 and under 15 years of age.		Above 15 years of age.		Over 5 and under 15 years of age.		Above 15 years of age.				
M.	F.	M.	F.	M.	F.	M.	F.	M.	F.	M.	F.	M.	F.	M.	F.			
132	133	134	135	136	137	138	139	140	141	142	143	144	145	146	147	148	149	150
		1	1				1	48	47	13	17	130	135	19	39	28		
1	3		1			2		106	96	82	109	168	157	92	135	23	60	4
1	1			2	1	1	5	70	67	91	95	118	108	101	114	23	181	
				1			1	30	27	7	2	54	57	16	22	7		
1						3		98	77	87	106	117	103	132	182	10		
3	2	2		1		5	4	257	236	362	344	274	253	409	434	23	10	
1								62	63	81	100	72	76	82	106	15	1	1
		1	1		2	2	3	104	98	96	117	135	137	123	235	13	1	24
		1						3	1	1	1	3	1	1	1	7		
								11	14	7	5	13	17	7	5	1		
7	6	5	3	4	2	13	14	789	726	827	806	1084	1044	982	1273	150	253	29

SHELBURNE, Continued.

1								32	27	4	8	62	66	8	26	9	15	9
1	1	1	4		1	2		142	127	123	153	181	170	168	9-8	20	234	5
		1					2	75	65	90	83	92	90	94	113	15	17	14
1	1		1					29	22	16	14	61	57	17	20	3	5	
					1	1		48	53	35	42	86	94	57	155	16	1	
1					1	3		48	53	51	56	132	140	93	151	19	1	
		1						32	19	12	25	67	49	31	86	15	28	16
					1			50	47	39	51	80	68	47	108	13	116	
4	2	2	6		4	6	2	496	413	360	430	761	724	515	871	109	415	44

QUEEN'S Continued.

2			1			1	1	114	99	116	104	218	212	214	297	12	330	
				1				85	59	76	72	145	128	107	139	11	59	22
				1		1	1	111	118	120	109	154	147	167	214	12	32	15
						1		14	29	36	45	27	43	45	79	9	4	
1								29	18	29	15	36	37	34	23	13		22
	2							56	40	33	42	98	67	51	61	12	4	14
								32	24	22	23	36	28	37	39	7		11
3	2	1		2	1	3	1	441	387	423	410	714	662	655	852	76	429	84

LUNENBURG, Continued.

1	3				1	1		236	228	150	145	309	317	403	555	45	3	19
1			3	1	3	1		66	90	15	12	84	118	112	221	11	1	
		1			1	2	4	149	145	170	211	195	209	343	519	30	1	
							1	73	83	66	73	95	102	111	163	9		
	2				1	1	2	213	207	140	121	224	218	164	165	4		6
2	1		1	3	1	1	1	185	206	161	146	264	282	305	315	10	15	13
								80	80	92	93	104	92	135	147	7	6	
1	1					1	2	166	162	172	178	218	234	361	438	26	2	
			1			3	2	210	220	279	266	220	231	325	327	12	17	
								31	30	45	33	41	37	70	64	6		
								49	49	52	50	60	61	72	77	3		
5	7	1	5	4	7	10	12	1458	1500	1354	1328	1814	1901	2401	2991	163	45	38

10

No. 1.—PERSONAL CENSUS BY AGES...1860—61.

GENERAL ABSTRACT.

COUNTIES.	TOTAL POPULATION.			Number of Families.	Average Number of each Family.	Under one year of age.		Under 1 and over 5th March 1861.		Over 7 and under 14 years of Age.		Deaths between 1 and 27 years since 1860.	
	Males.	Females.	Total.			M.	F.	M.	F.	M.	F.	M.	F.
	1	2	3	4	5	6	7	8	9	10	11	12	13
1. { Halifax (City)	11780	13240	25020	4460		353	327	17	20	302	306	8	9
{ " (Outside City)	13333	11674	25995	3915		379	374	25	18	302	367	7	10
Total in County	28110	24920	49021	8384	5.84	714	708	42	38	604	673	15	19
2. Colchester	10558	9882	20045	3387	5.91	207	315	13	17	334	302	12	9
3. Cumberland	9985	9553	19533	3141	6.21	281	294	19	16	312	500	9	11
4. Pictou	14289	14389	28685	4703	6.13	381	359	22	25	536	339	7	1
5. Sydney	7317	7404	14871	2197	6.76	186	188	16	11	185	177	5	11
6. Guysborough	6605	6505	13713	2045	6.21	195	203	12	15	176	164	6	6
7. Inverness	9915	10054	19867	2858	7.	231	237	19	19	236	228	5	5
8. Richmond	6198	6409	12607	1507	6.31	175	176	21	20	142	138	11	11
9. Victoria	4801	4842	9643	1428	6.70	120	120	14	16	133	115	2	1
10. Cape Breton	10313	10654	20866	3189	6.54	273	278	20	22	238	244	3	9
11. Hants	8937	8533	17460	3000	5.81	280	272	13	14	245	239	12	5
12. King's	9637	9114	18751	3339	5.60	316	248	19	16	304	288	8	15
13. Annapolis	8490	8263	16753	3009	5.54	278	264	22	9	348	230	3	5
14. Digby	7436	7315	14781	2498	5.91	217	227	12	9	173	190	4	3
15. Yarmouth	7666	7778	15446	2003	5.94	202	231	24	19	212	204	1	7
16. Shelburne	5345	5325	10668	1884	5.68	162	163	4	12	149	128	5	3
17. Queen's	4799	4566	9365	1616	5.80	133	134	7	8	194	115	7	
18. Lunenburg	9939	9672	19832	3177	6.17	339	342	31	19	263	262	13	11
	180694	166273	330857	54469	6.07	4812	4790	328	306	4408	4840	138	131

GENERAL ABSTRACT, · · · · · · · Continued.

COUNTIES.	14	15	16	17	18	19	20	21	22	23	24	25	26	27	28	29
	M.	F.	M.	F.	M.	F.	M.	F.	M.	F.	M.	F.	M.	F.	M.	F.
1. { Halifax (City)	271	304	4	6	314	308	6	1	287	258	4	2	1421	1384	9	10
{ " (Outside City)	433	369	6	14	417	347	7	5	385	337	7	2	1776	1716	17	18
Total in County	704	673	10	20	731	673	13	6	672	615	11	4	3197	3100	26	28
2. Colchester	308	300	7	6	306	296	6	6	278	268	5	7	1287	1338	18	14
3. Cumberland	309	305	9	17	283	285	10	17	327	263	7	6	1328	1304	32	25
4. Picton	369	328	6	6	375	365	6	3	367	372	2	6	1806	1737	16	19
5. Sydney	198	212	8	3	182	160	4	5	185	208	6	3	796	851	19	18
6. Guysborough	180	199	8	7	194	194	7	8	179	186	7	8	816	817	18	19
7. Inverness	265	281	4	1	256	258	4	5	287	273	8	2	1281	1321	16	8
8. Richmond	159	157	14	6	136	180	11	12	148	183	23	14	843	805	33	33
9. Victoria	137	133	5	2	139	142	2	3	117	152	2		640	614	4	1
10. Cape Breton	328	324	2	4	298	260		3	205	297	5	3	1425	1400	8	11
11. Hants	285	262	7	9	265	253	5	6	269	239	7	4	1173	1071	17	12
12. King's	348	285	13	5	285	243	6	6	209	257	6	8	1174	1238	24	20
13. Annapolis	273	244	2	6	251	225	4	2	205	259	6	5	1091	1087	21	16
14. Digby	237	199	6	9	192	209	4	4	226	193	4		1014	937	5	9
15. Yarmouth	251	237	9	6	233	246	7	3	197	213	4	2	1068	1097	7	10
16. Shelburne	171	163	2	2	149	160	2	3	154	152	3	1	728	680	3	5
17. Queen's	135	118	4	4	131	120	5	4	129	130	3	2	636	594	12	7
18. Lunenburg	299	328	14	8	329	282	6	13	312	339	6	12	1596	1422	21	26
	4939	4800	127	121	4758	4603	104	116	4727	4645	108	97	21997	21452	298	279

COUNTIES	Over 14 and under 15 years of age.						Over 15 and under 20 years of age.							
	Males.		Females.		Deaths since March 10, 1860.		Males.			Females.			Deaths since March 10, 1860.	
	NO.	D.	NO.	D.	M.	T.	NO.	A.	WDS.	NO.	S.	WS.	M.	T.
	30	31	32	33	34	35	36	37	38	39	40	41	42	43
1. Halifax (City)	1409		1382	3	1			1342		34	2210		5	9
" (Outside City)	1618		1446	11	13		2	1345		67	1949	8	14	10
Total in County	3025		2827	14	14		2	2687		104	2860	2	19	19
2. Colchester	1290	1	1312	4	7		5	1181		65	1636	1	9	8
3. Cumberland	1290	5	1290	12	12		5	1100		96	1679		11	10
4. Pictou	1931		1896	8	5		2	3610		82	1692	1	13	4
5. Sydney	928		920	6	7			848		9	920		5	10
6. Guysborough	868		784	7	6		1	761		24	776		9	6
7. Inverness	1362		1382	3	6			1295		7	1284		5	4
8. Richmond	779		804	12	22		1	799		10	744		11	11
9. Victoria	605		608	1	2			603		5	572		2	3
10. Cape Breton	1471		1421	6	4		1	1244		19	1552	1	9	9
11. Hants	1102		1002	7	5		1	1035		47	958		8	10
12. King's	1254		1026	21	11		1	1428		75	980		13	18
13. Annapolis	1003		972	9	14			933		45	853	1	14	11
14. Digby	1015	7	855	1	7		2	854		24	885		4	8
15. Yarmouth	962		947	3	5		3	951		35	927		12	9
16. Shelburne	698		650	2	5		5	622		32	565		8	2
17. Queen's	573		494	4	5		1	562		27	594	3	5	6
18. Lunenburg	1205		1200	6	11		1	1063		33	1013		9	6
	21905	8	20217	138	167		31	19425		615	18875		155	139

COUNTIES.	Over 20 and under 30 years of age.								Over 30 and under 40 years of age.							
	Males.			Females.			Deaths since March 31, 1860.		Males.			Females.			Deaths since March 31, 1860.	
	NO.	A.	WID.	NO.	A.	WD.	M.	F.	NO.	A.	WD.	NO.	A.	WD.	M.	F.
	44	45	46	47	48	49	50	51	52	53	54	55	56	57	58	59
1. { Halifax (City)	537	1486	9	963	1008	65	15	17	1018	287	34	1142	397	181	13	2
" (Outside City)	561	1300	12	934	908	27	11	18	1069	224	28	1003	170	54	11	0
Total in County	1098	2798	21	1907	1007	92	34	33	2082	511	62	2003	567	235	21	8
2. Colchester	468	1331	6	771	907	11	17	18	876	190	20	889	115	34	19	6
3. Cumberland	470	1311	8	782	831	17	16	19	829	238	3	802	114	23	9	4
4. Pictou	271	1924	7	799	1904	12	25	22	581	413	23	1083	897	63	4	15
5. Sydney	169	1252	3	298	1211	4	23	7	434	289	17	519	231	51	11	7
6. Guysborough	260	826	1	475	692	19	8	5	519	119	8	855	23	2	3	4
7. Inverness	298	1636	8	529	1864	12	11	19	672	358	17	723	384	56	4	11
8. Richmond	261	955	11	459	771	30	24	6	533	126	13	547	142	44	7	6
9. Victoria	166	720		285	682	7	8	6	311	112	9	347	141	12	3	5
10. Cape Breton	215	1419	7	568	1200	16	19	13	690	296	14	777	248	62	8	8
11. Hants	399	1098	7	671	797	14	13	16	696	193	17	783	162	44	9	8
12. King's	532	1081	3	929	674	16	14	13	935	167	16	862	150	39	7	13
13. Annapolis	440	506	9	718	681	15	34	11	791	133	18	572	159	37	10	3
14. Digby	340	861	6	579	730	13	17	11	604	122	7	615	166	38	3	2
15. Yarmouth	464	924	7	729	682	12	18	6	783	74	9	693	103	28	4	10
16. Shelburne	319	546	2	461	394	11	6	8	503	60	8	479	88	29	8	4
17. Queen's	380	643	1	496	493	14	2	7	432	92	6	483	80	31	1	1
18. Lunenburg	459	1129	6	876	792	18	19	13	950	188	17	891	122	33	5	7
	7082	20966	112	12208	17514	326	286	321	13814	3649	284	12803	3802	845	127	123

No. 1.—PERSONAL CENSUS BY AGES. 1860—61.

GENERAL ABSTRACT. · · · · · · · Continued.

COUNTIES.	Over 40 and under 50 years of age.								Over 50 and under 60 years of age.							
	Males.			Females.			Deaths since March 30, 1860.		Males.			Females.			Deaths since March 30, 1860.	
	MD.	S.	WDR.	MD.	S.	WD.	M.	F.	MD.	S.	WDR.	MD.	S.	WD.	M.	F.
	60	61	62	63	64	65	66	67	68	69	70	71	72	73	74	75
1. Halifax (City)	909	120	54	800	170	239	14	8	906	92	79	469	109	233	11	8
" (Outside City)	837	80	32	703	59	78	17	10	569	44	35	424	32	109	5	8
Total in County	1746	200	86	1503	238	317	31	18	1475	136	114	893	132	342	16	16
2. Colchester	695	55	21	624	89	99	6	2	472	20	31	406	47	88	5	3
3. Cumberland	744	69	28	684	51	50	10	4	417	34	20	334	29	58	7	5
4. Pictou	922	109	20	890	190	86	10	6	762	53	50	629	90	131	6	4
5. Sydney	445	67	16	368	94	57	7	6	394	33	32	285	57	86	5	6
6. Guysborough	410	20	11	406	47	43	1	5	298	14	18	240	9	35	6	3
7. Inverness	580	62	18	348	81	83	5	2	428	25	22	281	36	82	5	5
8. Richmond	420	20	15	365	58	70	3	2	276	15	18	216	15	82	6	2
9. Victoria	257	21	12	279	27	33		3	223	12	8	112	7	50	4	1
10. Cape Breton	690	73	28	644	59	98	8	4	509	24	28	418	30	110	11	2
11. Hants	670	68	21	581	81	68	5	8	476	47	41	338	33	64	7	4
12. King's	685	66	21	593	50	58	5	8	428	29	26	398	41	73	6	4
13. Annapolis	644	44	20	564	102	61	6	11	441	26	20	405	55	69	5	4
14. Digby	563	56	15	564	59	44	9	4	285	19	17	324	22	61	4	3
15. Yarmouth	582	20	17	519	32	45	3	5	309	8	15	320	11	61	9	
16. Shelburne	395	13	9	390	38	43	4	4	305	15	8	231	22	49	1	4
17. Queen's	338	18	7	304	21	29	3	2	239	11	6	176	23	49	1	2
18. Lunenburg	697	62	19	603	41	42	4	8	481	36	29	406	28	80	3	5
	11479	1093	386	10464	1518	1275	116	99	7988	565	513	6620	683	1593	99	73

GENERAL ABSTRACT, ... Continued.

COUNTIES	Over 60 and under 70 years of age.								Over 70 and under 80 years of age.							
	Males.			Females.			Deaths since March 30, 1860.		Males.			Females.			Deaths since March 30, 1860.	
	MD.	F.	WDR.	MD.	S.	WD.	M.	F.	MD.	S.	WDL.	MD.	S.	WD.	M.	F.
	76	77	78	79	80	81	82	83	84	85	86	87	88	89	90	91
1. Halifax (City)	425	54	89	211	40	273	12	12	111	38	52	39	17	172	14	9
" (Outside City)	387	36	76	231	20	131	13	7	176	17	67	93	7	100	12	7
Total in County	812	90	165	442	60	404	25	19	287	42	119	130	24	272	26	16
2. Colchester	370	18	53	200	28	60	7	10	133	10	43	70	11	69	6	4
3. Cumberland	366	27	48	214	15	79	8	7	133	9	37	66	8	67	7	3
4. Pictou	602	53	81	305	25	197	11	9	207	15	83	90	19	167	20	11
5. Sydney	307	29	48	183	20	120	10	4	127	10	24	68	9	62	8	2
6. Guysborough	258	14	38	132	8	91	10	...	102	6	25	52	5	50	8	5
7. Inverness	382	8	51	219	28	130	6	9	142	3	30	68	15	50	5	9
8. Richmond	270	6	51	145	9	88	3	4	73	...	16	39	3	64	3	3
9. Victoria	202	3	26	147	10	59	3	2	63	3	22	34	5	36	4	3
10. Cape Breton	377	15	49	209	18	138	9	4	154	10	29	72	6	99	10	10
11. Hants	369	33	45	176	14	118	9	6	122	8	40	63	9	74	8	5
12. King's	347	32	37	184	26	112	8	2	143	9	40	14	5	93	6	6
13. Annapolis	356	25	33	195	28	110	5	9	115	14	38	63	10	87	13	6
14. Digby	266	10	22	184	18	77	5	3	99	7	33	58	13	64	6	...
15. Yarmouth	265	9	91	183	17	75	9	4	109	7	15	61	8	50	5	5
16. Shelburne	236	9	32	158	12	58	4	7	92	11	24	46	8	65	4	4
17. Queen's	185	70	20	152	11	60	3	4	62	1	16	34	3	42	3	1
18. Lunenburg	319	28	26	135	15	98	6	7	107	6	30	54	16	83	8	5
	6293	410	823	3736	385	2086	142	110	2388	173	690	1120	174	1301	156	101

COUNTIES.	Over 90 and under 95 years of age.								Over 95 and under 100 years of age.							
	Males.			Females.			Deaths since March 30, 1860.		Males.			Females.			Deaths since March 30, 1860.	
	MD.	S.	WDR.	MD.	S.	WD.	M.	F.	MD.	S.	WDR.	MD.	S.	WD.	M.	F.
	92	93	94	95	96	97	98	99	100	101	102	103	104	105	106	107
1. { Halifax (City)	11	4	21	5	6	43	3	3	1	1	2		1	6	1	1
{ " (Outside City)	25	4	20	7		34	9	4	1		4	1		8	2	2
Total in County	36	8	41	12	6	77	12	6	2	1	6	1	1	14	3	3
2. Colchester	30	3	17	12	3	33	4	8	6		6	1		4	2	
3. Cumberland	15	2	15	6	3	42	8		1		3			3	1	1
4. Pictou	46	3	22	20	2	68	12	9	1	1	10			9	4	1
5. Sydney	25	1	16	8	3	29	3	6	1		3			13	1	2
6. Guysborough	13	2	11	6	2	12	1	3						2	1	
7. Inverness	55	3	20	4	9	46	9	5	3		4	2		5	1	2
8. Richmond	13	1	16	4	2	18	5	1	1		1			5	1	
9. Victoria	17		12	8	3	39	4	1	3		3			2	2	
10. Cape Breton	39	3	19	14	3	45	3	3	6		9			9		1
11. Hants	22	6	15	4	2	33	3	3			3		1	3	1	3
12. King's	29	1	16	5	2	24	3	3	1	1	4	1	1	6		1
13. Annapolis	22	5	16	2	2	34	12	4			4	1		5	1	
14. Digby	12	1	11	5	3	12	2	4	1		2			4	1	1
15. Yarmouth	15	1	6	5	4	24		1	1	1	1			5		1
16. Shelburne	10		9	5		27	2	4			2			3		
17. Queen's	10	1	6	4		27	2	1	1	2				2	2	
18. Lunenburg	23		16	7	3	35	3	1	1		3	1		7	1	1
	411	37	282	137	54	619	87	69	42	9	65	7	3	100	22	18

COUNTIES.	Over 100 years of age.												Deaths.		Males.			
	Males.			Females.			Deaths since M'ch 30, 1860.											
	M.D.	S.	WD.	M.D.	S.	W.D.	M.	F.	M.	F.	M.	F.	Married.	Single.	Widowers.	Total.
	108	109	110	111	112	113	114	115	116	117	118	119	120	121	122	123
1. { Halifax (City)						2			66	58	1	2	3660	7800	340	11780
" (Outside City)	1		1			1	3		27	31		1	3618	8428	275	12321
Total in County	1		1			2	3		91	89	1	3	7258	16228	615	24101
2. Colchester							1		35	20	1		3070	6894	199	10163
3. Cumberland									4	7	1	1	2981	6823	179	9963
4. Pictou	1	1	1				1		17	13	1	1	3913	10088	208	14209
5. Sydney						1	1		3	7	1	2	1828	5231	158	7217
6. Guysborough									17	12			1860	4437	109	6406
7. Inverness				2	1	1			13	5	1		2474	7260	179	9913
8. Richmond						1			6	7	1		1658	4219	129	6106
9. Victoria			1						4	4			1273	3434	94	4801
10. Cape Breton					1	2			17	16			2751	7381	180	10312
11. Hants						1			13	12		3	2680	6047	200	6927
12. King's									22	22			3110	6349	161	9620
13. Annapolis					1				6	7			2774	5564	152	8490
14. Digby									43	31			2302	5021	113	7436
15. Yarmouth						1			29	30		1	2027	5043	96	7068
16. Shelburne									31	18		1	1819	3447	83	5343
17. Queen's									10	17			1507	3225	67	4799
18. Lunenburg	1												3037	6761	161	9959
	3	1	5	2	1	13	7	1	†355	†333	6	11	49033	113384	3105	165584

* 66 md., 310 s., 9 wdrs.   † 59 md., 245 s., 19 wds.

COUNTIES.		Females.			Grand Total.		Deaths.										
						M.	F.	Total	M.	F.	M.	F.	M.	F.	M.	F.	
	124	125	126	127	128	129	130	131	132	133	134	135	136	137	138	139
1. Halifax (City)	3639	8571	1319	13299	26008	187	137	324	37	28	11	5	37	22	4	3
" (Outside City)	3611	7317	505	11678	23056	187	168	345	24	17	4	8	8	7	10	3
Total in County	7250	15888	1702	24973	49024	374	290	664	61	39	15	14	25	28	14	6
2. Colchester	3070	6438	377	9882	20045	131	155	286	2	6	3	11	5	13
3. Cumberland	2958	6243	339	9553	19558	130	168	338	5	4	4	6	6	9	3
4. Pictou	4929	9635	758	14598	29393	175	144	319	13	12	10	8	7	11	14	6
5. Sydney	1824	3400	414	7655	14371	142	109	251	5	1	4	7	4	14	9
6. Guysborough	1823	4145	395	6508	12718	105	97	202	6	6	2	2	4	4	7	5
7. Inverness	3472	7070	400	10006	19960	114	144	288	8	9	6	3	11	14	12
8. Richmond	1945	4104	375	6048	12860	107	134	334	8	10	1	6	5	11	12
9. Victoria	1578	3044	323	4842	9648	50	48	105	7	2	3	3	2	6	6
10. Cape Breton	3741	7203	584	10554	20993	127	114	241	3	4	8	3	13	4	8
11. Hants	3667	5450	411	8533	17480	122	176	345	9	6	3	8	6	8	16
12. King's	3115	5389	407	9711	9761	161	148	309	6	6	8	6	6	15	12
13. Annapolis	2729	5603	424	8563	16533	138	153	291	6	4	7	6	3	9	2
14. Digby	2398	4074	398	7317	14733	82	78	165	6	8	4	4	6	11	12
15. Yarmouth	2335	4945	389	7776	15466	110	94	206	7	4	5	4	13	14
16. Shelburne	1813	3224	396	5350	10808	62	74	140	4	3	6	4	6	7
17. Queen's	1514	2904	353	4800	9087	60	65	138	3	2	5	2	3	1
18. Lunenburg	2604	6207	382	9653	19052	143	161	306	4	7	1	6	2	10	13
	49009	97829	8262	160673	313997	2481	2190	4670	186	152	93	95	121	126	176	189

GENERAL ABSTRACT, • • • • • • • Continued.

COUNTIES.	Coloured Retail.				Coloured White.						
	Over 5 and under 16 years of age.		Above 16 years of age.		Over 5 and under 16 years of age.		Above 16 years of age.				
	M.	F.	M.	F.	M.	F.	M.	F.			
	140	141	142	143	144	145	146	147	148	149	150
1. { Halifax (City)	948	902	1982	1434	1800	1213	1347	2204	61	846	
{ " (Outside City)	1805	1635	2284	2126	2328	2155	2944	3408	181	1176	71
Total in County	2753	2637	3270	3560	3628	3368	4291	6202	282	2022	71
2. Colchester	704	649	384	264	1204	1265	759	1046	142	78	61
3. Cumberland	941	919	593	585	1504	1438	915	1474	140	191	51
4. Pictou	972	964	565	626	1867	1770	1159	2622	169	7	160
5. Sydney	890	1067	1593	2490	1060	1268	1592	2539	104	158	66
6. Guysborough	1030	927	1025	1156	1296	1201	1417	1879	129	696	88
7. Inverness	1482	1607	1869	3470	1792	2021	2699	4475	143	28	68
8. Richmond	1124	1178	2156	2075	1224	1312	2427	3364	102	82	28
9. Victoria	694	793	898	1225	846	942	1106	1682	69	1	57
10. Cape Breton	1768	1993	2747	3800	2040	2124	3025	4538	187	41	118
11. Hants	699	827	392	313	942	867	652	668	185	235	113
12. King's	568	565	344	287	968	817	496	501	113	258	80
13. Annapolis	504	504	347	340	814	802	680	569	131	748	94
14. Digby	1039	895	1351	1128	1218	1165	1455	1655	116	454	124
15. Yarmouth	799	726	829	898	1084	1042	982	1273	199	258	20
16. Shelburne	459	413	380	430	701	736	618	871	108	419	44
17. Queen's	442	387	423	430	714	602	658	832	76	420	44
18. Lunenburg	1458	1501	1354	1288	1814	1801	2965	2061	165	45	28
	18000	18155	19293	23328	24554	24772	29008	38007	2961	5892	1407

APPENDIX NO. 2.

PERSONAL CENSUS
BY ORIGIN.

No. 2.—PERSONAL CENSUS

COUNTY OF

POLLING DISTRICTS.	Total Population.	Natives.	England.	Wales.	Scotland.	Ireland.	Guernsey.	Jersey.
1. Ward 1. (City)....................	4199	3087	142	.....	106	580	4	1
2. do. 2. do.	3656	2417	156	1	110	734	.....	1
3. do. 3. do.	3590	2515	122	2	92	621	.....	.....
4. do. 4. do.	2546	1710	89	4	52	499	.....	2
5. do. 5. do. { 1st Section............	3510	2439	150	8	59	584	1	3
{ 2d do.	4710	3540	220	3	86	557	.....	4
6. do. 6. do.	2815	2076	177	3	68	268	.....	1
Total in City.....	25026	17784	1056	21	573	3843	5	12
7. Ferguson's Cove	721	683	3	.....	3	29	.....	.....
8. Portuguese Cove	650	627	1	.....	3	12	.....	.....
9. Sambro....................	570	562	.....	.....	.....	2	.....	.....
10. Prospect	1370	1330	7	.....	.....	20	.....	.....
11. Hagget's Cove....................	980	966	3	.....	2	2	.....	1
12. French Village	715	702	2	.....	3	2	.....	2
13. Drysdale's....................	374	354	7	1	8	4	.....	.....
14. North West Arm	330	275	9	1	6	31	.....	.....
15. Piers' Mills	398	336	10	.....	19	30	.....	.....
16. Hammond's Plains....................	770	702	4	.....	5	21	.....	.....
17. Windsor Road....................	814	673	31	1	11	62	.....	.....
18. Truro Road	586	492	10	.....	13	49	.....	.....
19. Gay's River	616	560	3	.....	15	32	.....	.....
20. Wise's Corner....................	556	494	4	1	12	36	.....	.....
21. Middle Musquodoboit....................	1183	1085	9	.....	41	26	.....	.....
22. Upper Musquodoboit	935	876	12	.....	25	15	.....	.....
23. Caledonia	230	213	.....	.....	17	.....	.....	.....
24. Salmon River	953	938	4	1	2	7	.....	.....
25. Sheet Harbor....................	674	624	10	.....	2	15	.....	.....
26. Pope's Harbor....................	1141	1126	4	.....	4	1	.....	.....
27. Jeddore....................	1860	1795	13	.....	19	12	.....	.....
28. Chezetcook	1763	1736	2	.....	7	9	.....	.....
29. Lawrencetown	462	456	2	.....	3	1	.....	.....
30. Preston	641	561	1	.....	5	4	.....	.....
31. Dartmouth....................	3155	2628	107	2	78	205	1	4
32. Black Point....................	795	782	7	.....	1	2	.....	.....
33. Eastern Passage....................	753	723	15	.....	6	6	.....	.....
	49021	40083	1336	28	883	4478	6	19

COUNTY OF

	Total Population.	Natives.	England.	Wales.	Scotland.	Ireland.	Guernsey.	Jersey.
1. Truro....................	2934	2666	34	.....	70	74	.....	.....
2. Old Barns....................	927	891	3	.....	11	11	.....	.....
3. Lower Stewiacke....................	1588	1438	40	.....	26	50	.....	.....
4. Upper Stewiacke....................	1849	1774	5	.....	36	18	.....	.....
5. Upper Onslow and Kemptown.........	1580	1453	19	.....	85	9	.....	.....
6. Onslow....................	771	741	2	.....	4	9	.....	.....
7. Earltown....................	1216	904	2	.....	292	4	.....	.....
8. New Annan....................	1231	1065	5	.....	131	21	.....	.....
9. Waugh's River....................	1153	1057	6	.....	63	22	.....	.....
10. Tatamagouche	1400	1274	5	.....	96	11	.....	.....
11. Upper Londonderry	1573	1517	6	.....	16	8	.....	.....
12. Lower Londonderry	2132	1948	41	21	30	37	.....	.....
13. Economy and Five Islands............	1691	1574	4	.....	21	48	.....	.....
	20045	18302	172	21	881	322	.....	.....

BY ORIGIN...1860—61.

HALIFAX.

Isle of Man.	Canada.	New Brunswick.	Newfoundland.	P. E. Island.	Magdalen Islands.	West Indies.	U. States of America.	France.	Spain.	Portugal.	Sardinia.
	29	39	72	8		34	54	4	1		
	21	27	70	9		8	63	4	1		
	7	42	69	27		17	50	1	1		
	8	37	52	28		4	38	1	1		
1	11	45	131	17		11	33	1	1	2	
1	18	46	70	18		28	101	4			
	12	22	23	10		3	32				1
2	**106**	**258**	**487**	**117**		**105**	**371**	**15**	**5**	**2**	**1**
1							1				
	1	2	2				1		1		
		1					5				
			7			3	2				
	1	1				1	2	1			
		1									
	2	3				2	2				
				1			2				
	2		1				29				
	2	13	8	1			8	1			
	1	1		1			19				
		9					4				
		1	2			1	5				
	1	4	1				13				
		6					1				
						1					
		4	9	3		1	4	1			
	1		1	2		1				1	
	1	2		1			7				
	1	2	2				2	2			
		4				3	62		1		
	13	29	18	2		10	45	1			
							3				
	1										
3	**133**	**333**	**538**	**128**		**128**	**588**	**21**	**7**	**3**	**1**

COLCHESTER.

Isle of Man.	Canada.	New Brunswick.	Newfoundland.	P. E. Island.	Magdalen Islands.	West Indies.	U. States of America.	France.	Spain.	Portugal.	Sardinia.
	4	25	2	14			39				
	1	5	1				4				
1	1	19	2	3			4				
	1	7		4			3				
		3	2	3			5				
	1	3					7				
		1	1	9			2				
	1	2					5				
		1					3				
		3	3	2			6				
	1	11					14				
1		18	1	3			32				
	1	15		1			26				
2	**11**	**113**	**12**	**39**			**149**				

No. 2.—PERSONAL CENSUS

COUNTY OF

POLLING DISTRICTS.	Italy.	Turkey.	Other places in the Mediterranean.	Germany.	Norway.	Belgium.	Denmark.	Hungary.
1. Ward 1, (City.)				8	22		1	
2. do. 2. do.				1	7			
3. do. 3. do.	2			4	10	2		1
4. do. 4. do.				1	15			
5. do. 5. do. { 1st Section				2	5			
{ 2nd do.	1				8			
6. do. 6. do.				2	1		1	
Total in City	3			18	68	2	2	1
7. Ferguson's Cove						1		
8. Portuguese Cove								
9. Sambro								
10. Prospect	1							
11. Haggets Cove								
12. French Village	1							
13. Drysdale's								
14. North West Arm								
15. Piers' Mill								
16. Hammond's Plains						1		
17. Windsor Road				2				
18. Truro Road								
19. Gay's River								
20. Wise's Corner								
21. Middle Musquodoboit				2				
22. Upper Musquodoboit								
23. Caledonia								
24. Salmon River								
25. Sheet Harbor				1				
26. Pope's Harbor								
27. Jeddore				9	1			
28. Chezetcook								
29. Lawrencetown								
30. Preston								
31. Dartmouth	1			7	2			
32. Black Point								
33. Eastern Passage								
	6			25	84	3	2	2	1

COUNTY OF

1. Truro	1			4				
2. Old Barns								
3. Lower Stewiacke				2				
4. Upper Stewiacke								
5. Upper Onslow and Kemptown								
6. Onslow								
7. Earltown								
8. New Annan				1				
9. Waugh's River								
10. Tatamagouche								
11. Upper Londonderry								
12. Lower Londonderry								
13. Economy and Five Islands	1							
	2			7				

BY ORIGIN...1860—61.

HALIFAX, Continued.

Holland	East Indies.	Russia.	Africa.	Australia.	New Zealand.	Prussia.	Poland.	Switzerland.	Sweden.	South America.	All other places.	Born at Sea.
1			1			2		1			2	
			1			3		1	1		10	1
								1		2		2
			2			1					1	1
						1	1		1			3
	2	1							1	1		
	2		2		1					3	107	
5	1	6			1	7	1	3	3	6	129	7
						1			1			
			4						1			
												1
	1											
	1										1	
			2									
	7	1	12			1	8	1	3	3	8	130	8

COLCHESTER, Continued.

												1
				1	1							
						1						1
											4	1
												2
				1	1	1					4	5

12

No. 2—PERSONAL CENSUS

COUNTY OF

POLLING DISTRICTS.	Total Population.	Natives.	England.	Wales.	Scotland.	Ireland.	Guernsey.	Jersey.
1. Amherst	2767	2357	30		50	87	1	
2. Westchester	774	711	14		25	8		
3. Head of Amherst	1796	1608	9		9	42		
4. River Philip	1878	1700	35		10	56		
5. River Hebert	1713	1035	58	5	108	222		
6. Maccan	838	791	3		8	25		
7. Pugwash	3165	2782	41	16	133	91		
8. Wallace	2500	2190	34		173	46		
9. Wentworth	696	641	2		13	14		
10. Advocate Harbor	1074	948	13	1	4	26		
11. Mill Village	2382	2065	16		8	171	1	
	19533	16700	256	22	537	799	2	

COUNTY OF

1. Picton	2833	2237	54		324	88		
2. Carriboo	1192	957	2	1	216	4		
3. Cape John	1424	1200	5	1	100	7		
4. West side River John	1315	1209	9		65	16	1	
5. West branch River John	917	728			177	11		
6. Rogers Hill	1127	916	2		201	18		
7. Hardwood Hill	1139	904	13		102	17		
8. Green Hill and West River	983	905	3		45	11		
9. Mount Thom	1242	1036	4		186	5		
10. Gairloch	937	827			102			
11. New Larig	615	547			66			
12. Albion Mines	2088	1514	93	5	343	76		
13. New Glasgow	2288	2082	12		191	8		
14. Little Harbor	858	757	1		86	5		
15. McLellan's Mountain	1081	956	1		116	4		
16. East branch East River	1208	1199	2		95			
17. Hopewell, W. branch E. River	1623	1411	36	3	151	6		
18. Middle River	1124	985	1		128	1		
19. Gulf Shore	1112	1026			77			
20. Barney's River	1274	1005	1		246	4	1	
21. Merrigomish	1544	1370	12		118	33		
22. Blue Mountain, St. Mary's, &c.	775	628	2		124	5		
	28785	24663	253	103	3284	307	2	

COUNTY OF

1. Arisaig	1450	1334			112	1		
2. Cape George	1169	1095			54	11		
3. Morristown	967	903			45	11		
4. Antigonish	2675	2591	1		189	64		
5. Lochaber	1765	1529	2		159	68		
6. Upper South River	1199	1093			94	12		
7. St. Andrew's	2154	1966	2		171	5		
8. Tracadie	1649	1511	2		62	39		
9. Harbor Bouche	1643	1604	2		12	19		
	14671	13626	9		898	230		

BY ORIGIN...1860—61.

CUMBERLAND.

Isle of Man.	Canada.	New Brunswick.	Newfoundland.	P. E. Island.	Magdalen Islands.	West Indies.	U. States of America.	France.	Spain.	Portugal.	Sardinia.
1	4	279	1	55	......	......	4	17	1	......	......
......	......	2	......	1	......	......	......	10	......	......	......
......	......	113	......	15	......	......	......	......	......	......	......
......	1	37	......	30	......	1	7	......	......	......	......
......	1	191	......	12	......	......	42	......	......	......	......
......	......	13	......	1	......	......	......	......	......	......	......
......	......	39	......	46	......	1	11	......	1	......	......
......	2	16	3	23	......	......	11	......	......	......	......
......	3	3	......	9	......	......	7	......	......	......	......
......	......	64	......	3	......	......	5	......	......	......	......
......	2	33	3	17	......	3	10	1	......	......	......
1	13	790	7	215	......	9	120	2	1	......	......

PICTOU.

Isle of Man.	Canada.	New Brunswick.	Newfoundland.	P. E. Island.	Magdalen Islands.	West Indies.	U. States of America.	France.	Spain.	Portugal.	Sardinia.
......	12	14	14	43	......	......	18	......	1	......	......
......	......	......	......	2	......	......	10	......	......	......	......
......	2	......	1	......	......	......	3	......	......	......	......
1	1	8	1	4	......	......	5	......	......	......	......
......	......	1	......	......	......	......	......	......	......	......	......
......	......	......	......	......	1	......	......	......	......	......	......
......	1	11	......	......	......	1	......	......	......	......	......
......	4	2	......	9	2	......	1	......	......	......	......
......	1	......	......	5	......	......	4	......	......	......	......
......	2	......	......	3	......	......	2	......	......	......	......
......	......	......	......	......	......	......	1	......	......	......	......
......	3	4	5	10	......	......	28	......	......	......	......
......	3	11	......	11	1	2	14	......	......	......	......
......	1	......	......	4	......	......	1	......	......	......	......
......	......	......	......	1	......	......	......	......	......	......	......
......	......	1	......	......	......	......	2	......	......	......	......
......	......	5	1	4	......	......	6	......	......	......	......
......	......	3	......	2	......	......	......	......	......	......	......
......	1	......	2	5	......	......	2	1	......	......	......
......	2	2	......	1	......	......	1	......	......	......	......
......	1	5	......	2	......	......	1	1	......	......	......
......	......	2	1	2	......	......	1	......	......	......	......
1	34	69	25	111	4	3	100	2	......	1	......

No. 2.—PERSONAL CENSUS

COUNTY OF

POLLING DISTRICTS.	Italy.	Turkey.	Other places in the Mediterranean.	Germany.	Norway.	Belgium.	Denmark.	Hungary.
1. Amherst								
2. Westchester								
3. Head of Amherst								
4. River Philip				1				
5. River Hebert				38				
6. Maccan								
7. Pugwash			1					
8. Wallace				1				
9. Wentworth						3		
10. Advocate Harbor								
11. Mill Village	1							
	1		1	40	3			

COUNTY OF

1. Pictou								1
2. Carriboo								
3. Cape John								
4. West side River John								
5. West branch River John								
6. Rogers Hill								
7. Hardwood Hill								
8. Green Hill and West River								
9. Mount Thom								
10. Gairloch								
11. New Larig								
12. Albion Mines								
13. New Glasgow								
14. Little Harbor								
15. McLellan's Mountain								
16. East branch East River								
17. Hopewell, W. branch East River								
18. Middle River								
19. Gulf Shore								
20. Barney's River								
21. Merrigomish				1				
22. Blue Mountain, St. Mary's, &c								
				1			1	

COUNTY OF

1. Arisaig								
2. Cape George								
3. Morristown								
4. Antigonish				1				
5. Lochaber								
6. Upper South River								
7. St. Andrew's				1				
8. Tracadie				2		10		
9. Harbor Bouche								
				4		10		

BY ORIGIN...1860—61.

CUMBERLAND, Continued.

Holland	East Indies	Russia	Africa	Australia	New Zealand	Prussia	Poland	Switzerland	Sweden	South America	All other places	Born at Sea
	1											
	1					1						
						1						
												1
	2					2						1

PICTOU, Continued.

Holland	East Indies	Russia	Africa	Australia	New Zealand	Prussia	Poland	Switzerland	Sweden	South America	All other places	Born at Sea
				1							5	1
												1
				1								
												1
												1
												1
												1
											1	
				2							6	6

SYDNEY, Continued.

Holland	East Indies	Russia	Africa	Australia	New Zealand	Prussia	Poland	Switzerland	Sweden	South America	All other places	Born at Sea
												1
2												
											1	
2											1	1

No. 2.—PERSONAL CENSUS

COUNTY OF

POLLING DISTRICTS.	Total Population.	Natives.	England.	Wales.	Scotland.	Ireland.	Guernsey.	Jersey.
1. Guysborough	2242	1989	12		78	100		
2. Intervale	968	859	1		28	70		
3. Manchester	1548	1479	2		2	54		
4. Melford	1583	1447	10		28	74		
5. Crow Harbor	727	710	1			11		
6. Cape Canso	826	776	4		3	24		
7. Country Harbor	893	858	8		11	2		
8. Sherbrooke	1109	1107	7		12	14		
9. Marie Joseph	648	631	5		2	9		
10. Forks, St. Mary's	1162	1042	1		82	21		
11. Molasses Harbor	947	936			3	3		
	12713	11834	51		249	382		

COUNTY OF

1. Plaster Cove	1710	1496	8		151	13	11	
2. Judique	1832	1645			163	1		
3. River Inhabitants	1488	1291			182	5		
4. Port Hood	1031	942			48	26		
5. Mabou	2737	2346	3		319	13		
6. Broad Cove (Intervale)	1394	1138			244	2		
7. Broad Cove	839	721			116			
8. Margaree	383	329			51	2		
9. Young's Bridge	943	829	1		87	18		
10. Friar's Head	737	718			3	3		1
11. Cheticamp	1464	1367			17	1		8
12. Whycocomagh	2224	1539			675			
13. Lake Ainslie	847	660			184	1		
14. River Dennis	1217	923	1		288			
15. North-east Margaree	1181	1023	2		112	31		
	19967	16967	15		2670	116	11	9

COUNTY OF

1. Arichat	1008	883	10		20	45	1	6
2. Petit Degrat	1875	1827	4		2	20		6
3. D'Escouse	1173	1130			4	15	2	9
4. Black River	742	630	2		103	1		
5. River Bourgeois	840	815			15	19		
6. St. Peter's	780	700	2		64	12		
7. L'Ardoise	1475	1395	4		41	17		
8. Grand River	755	532			221			
9. Red Islands	774	635	1		126	3		
10. River Inhabitants	918	810	10		45	21	1	3
11. Little Arichat	1435	1394	1		5	2	1	6
12. Loch Lomond	412	276			126			
13. Flamboise	411	287	1		123			
	12607	11814	35		905	155	5	30

BY ORIGIN...1860—61.

GUYSBOROUGH.

Isle of Man.	Canada.	New Brunswick.	Newfoundland.	P. E. Island.	Magdalen Islands.	West Indies.	U. States of America.	France.	Spain.	Portugal.	Sardinia.
1		3	35	3		3	16				
			7				3				
			8	1			12				
			6	11			7				
			4								
2			8	5			1	2		1	
		3		1		1	7	1			
2		2	4	10			4	2	1	1	
			1								
1		1		2			11				
			1				2				
6		10	74	33		4	53	5	1	2	

INVERNESS.

7		8	1	10			5				
6		2		15							
			1	1				1			
			3	7			5				
		3	2	11			9			1	
				10							
			1	1							
			1								
			2	6							
			6	6							
2		1	2	2		3		1			
				5			5				
							2				
				4							
1		3	4	2		1	2				
16		17	23	80		4	28	2		1	

RICHMOND.

14			12	5	1		5	6			
2			2	7	1		1	2	1		
1		1	1				2	6		1	
			1	5							
		1									
4			2	6			1	3			
							2				
1		2		6							
4			9	6			8				
4		3	1	6				12			
30		7	28	41	2		19	26	1	1	

No. 2.—PERSONAL CENSUS

COUNTY OF

POLLING DISTRICTS.	Italy.	Turkey.	Other places in the Mediterranean.	Germany.	Norway.	Belgium.	Denmark.	Hungary.
1. Guysborough				1				
2. Intervale								
3. Manchester								
4. Melford								
5. Crow Harbor								
6. Cape Canso								
7. Country Harbor					1			
8. Sherbrooke				1			1	
9. Marie Joseph								
10. Forks, St. Mary's				1				
11. Molasses Harbor				1				
			2	3			1	

COUNTY OF

1. Plaster Cove								
2. Judique								
3. River Inhabitants								
4. Port Hood								
5. Mabou								
6. Broad Cove (Intervale)								
7. Broad Cove								
8. Margaree								
9. Young's Bridge								
10. Friar's Head								
11. Cheticamp								
12. Whycocomagh								
13. Lake Ainslie								
14. River Dennis								
15. North-east Margaree								

COUNTY OF

1. Arichat								
2. Petit Degrat								
3. D'Escouse								
4. Black River								
5. River Bourgeoise								
6. St. Peter's								
7. L'Ardoise								
8. Grand River								
9. Red Islands								
10. River Inhabitants								
11. Little Arichat								
12. Loch Lomond								
13. Flamboise								

BY ORIGIN...1860—61.

GUYSBOROUGH, Continued.

Holland.	East Indies.	Russia.	Africa.	Australia.	New Zealand.	Prussia.	Poland.	Switzerland.	Sweden.	South America.	All other places.	Born at Sea.
	1											
		1										
												1
	1	1										1

INVERNESS, Continued.

											7	
												1
											7	1

RICHMOND, Continued.

		1										
												1
					1							1
											1	
		1			1						1	2

13

No: 2—PERSONAL CENSUS

COUNTY OF

POLLING DISTRICTS.	Total Population.	Natives.	England.	Wales.	Scotland.	Ireland.	Guernsey.	Jersey.
1. Washabck	1044	384			189			
2. Middle River	877	624			242	2		
3. Baddeck	1568	1170	5		245	8		
4. Munro's Point, St. Ann's	1440	1015	2		423			
5. Englishtown, St. Ann's	1224	967			264	7		
6. Boularderie	1178	879	2		291	2		
7. Ingonish	566	530	5		32	9		
8. Cape North	887	526	3		112	6		
9. Bay St. Lawrence	353	277			56	9		
10. Little Narrows	741	590			343	1		
	9643	7466	17		2048	38		

COUNTY OF

1. Sydney	2467	2054	27		262	51		1
2. Ball's Bridge	2169	1797	9		332	13		
3. Mira Ferry	899	608			291			
4. Sydney Mines	3283	2528	48		455	145		
5. Mainadieu	1509	1239	6		228	14		
6. Louisburg	1374	956	5		402	6		
7. Gabarus	1561	1192	4		246	2	1	
8. East Bay	1785	1398	2		344	1		
9. Beaver Cove	992	774			218			
10. Howley's Ferry	1001	779	9		203	13		
11. Lingan Mines	1253	1009	92		98	50		
12. Cow Bay	713	573	1		133	3		
13. Big Pond	649	501			146	1		
14. Christmas Island	1227	3098			123	1		
	20868	16563	112		3537	200	1	1

COUNTY OF

1. Windsor	2271	1958	87	2	29	142		
2. St. Croix	1104	1013	14		7	55		
3. Brooklyn	1085	1036	11			25		
4. Scotch Village	2254	2212			1	17		
5. Falmouth	1187	1137	12		3	14		
6. Kempt	1967	1861	14		17	30		
7. Rawdon Church	759	727	4		5	16		
8. South Rawdon	624	575	9	3	6	26		
9. Noel	1791	1716	10		22	21		
10. Nine Mile River	192	1742	24		50	62		
11. Maitland	1967	1867	10		17	51		
12. Chester Road	535	523	3			2		
	17460	16363	201	4	164	470		

BY ORIGIN...1860—61.

VICTORIA.

Isle of Man.	Canada.	New Brunswick.	Newfoundland.	P. E. Island.	Magdalen Islands.	West Indies.	U. States of America.	France.	Spain.	Portugal.	Sardinia.
	1	3	1	1			1				
	4	6		2			2	1			
							2				
	1		6	1			4	1			
			1				3				
			2	12			4	1			
	3	1	3	4						1	
							1				
	5	8	19	20			17	3		1	

CAPE BRETON.

	3	4	10	3			5				
	1	1	7	1			7				
			1	1			2				
	5	5	56	14	2		30				
		1	7	2			1				
			8				1				
		1	2	3							
	2	2	3	59			4				
			1					2			
			9	4							
			2	1			2				
		1		3							
			1	3							
	11	16	106	97	2		52	2			

HANTS.

	6	15	2	8		2	7	1			
		5	1				5				
		3	1	3			1				
		9	1	1			9				
		10		2			9				
		18					18	1			
		2		1			4				
	5										
		3		1			4				
	5	7	5	5			20				
		4		1			16				
		1	2			2					
	16	77	12	22		4	103	2			

No. 2.—PERSONAL CENSUS

COUNTY OF

POLLING DISTRICTS.	Italy.	Turkey.	Other places in the Mediterranean.	Germany.	Norway.	Belgium.	Denmark.	Hungary.
1. Washabok								
2. Middle River								
3. Baddeck								
4. Munro's Point, St. Ann's								
5. Englishtown, St. Ann's								
6. Boularderie								
7. Ingonish								
8. Cape North								
9. Bay St. Lawrence								
10. Little Narrows								

COUNTY OF

	Italy.	Turkey.	Other places in the Mediterranean.	Germany.	Norway.	Belgium.	Denmark.	Hungary.
1. Sydney								
2. Ball's Bridge								
3. Mira Ferry								
4. Sydney Mines					1			
5. Mainadieu								
6. Louisburg								
7. Gabarus								
8. East Bay								
9. Beaver Cove								
10. Howley's Ferry								
11. Lingan Mines								
12. Cow Bay								
13. Big Pond								
14. Christmas Island								
					1			

COUNTY OF

	Italy.	Turkey.	Other places in the Mediterranean.	Germany.	Norway.	Belgium.	Denmark.	Hungary.
1. Windsor	1		5	3		1		
2. St. Croix								
3. Brooklyn				1				
4. Scotch Village								
5. Falmouth								
6. Kempt								
7. Rawdon Church								
8. South Rawdon				2				
9. Noel				1				
10. Nine Mile River								
11. Maitland								
12. Chester Road				2				
	1		5	9		1		

BY ORIGIN...1860—61.

VICTORIA, Continued.

Holland.	East Indies.	Russia.	Africa.	Australia.	New Zealand.	Prussia.	Poland.	Switzerland.	Sweden.	South America.	All other places.	Born at Sea.
												1
												1

CAPE BRETON, Continued.

												1
	1											
												2
											1	
	1										1	3

HANTS, Continued.

No. 2.—PERSONAL CENSUS

COUNTY OF

POLLING DISTRICTS.	Total Population.	Natives.	England.	Wales.	Scotland.	Ireland.	Guernsey.	Jersey.
1. Canning	2255	2093	17		5	57		
2. Canard	1342	1210	22		12	42		
3. Centreville	2018	1798	15		1	106		
4. Lakeville	1599	1476	3		6	45		
5. Somerset	2286	2115	9		9	100		
6. Kentville	1488	1386	19		5	52		
7. Gaspereaux	1089	1046	1			28		
8. Wolfville	1577	1433	22		7	53		
9. Lower Horton	1315	1232	12	1	4	37		
10. Aylesford	1351	1311	4		2	14		
11. West Sherbrooke	197	175				20		
12. Aylesford	1342	1207	6		1	103		
13. Berwick	872	843	7		4	3		
	18731	17325	137	1	56	660		

COUNTY OF

POLLING DISTRICTS.	Total Population.	Natives.	England.	Wales.	Scotland.	Ireland.	Guernsey.	Jersey.
1. Wilmot	1836	1660	10	2	10	87		
2. Wilmot, Middleton Corner	1474	1373	16		9	44		
3. Clarence, Wilmot	1434	1386	10		4	5		
4. Bridgetown	1404	1293	19		9	20		
5. Bellisle	1155	1096	10		5	17		
6. New Caledonia	1252	1202	6		7	18		
7. Broad Cove	898	865	3		5	8		
8. Clementsport	1319	1280	9		6	14		
9. Hessian Line	941	919	8			1		
10. Annapolis Royal	1803	1676	15		8	68		
11. Carleton's Corner	707	673	6		3	5		
12. Nictaux	1238	1187	10		5	16		
13. Dalhousie	561	542			1	14		
14. Maitland	369	359	2		1	1		
15. Morse Road	362	331	8			9		
	16753	15822	132	2	73	327		

COUNTY OF

POLLING DISTRICTS.	Total Population.	Natives.	England.	Wales.	Scotland.	Ireland.	Guernsey.	Jersey.
1. Hillsburg	1191	1154	2		4	8		
2. Head St. Mary's Bay	954	912	1		1	8		
3. Digby	1851	1633	15		21	74		
4. Sandy Cove	1184	1141	5		1	8		
5. Long Island	954	910	1		2	7		
6. Westport	678	639	14	2	7			1
7. On St. Mary's Bay	1469	1438	8			17		
8. Weymouth	1308	1189	18		3	41		2
9. Belivoe Cove	1116	1003	3			16		
10. Session House, Clare	1586	1565				4		
11. Montegan	1531	1519				5		
12. Salmon River	929	906	2			7		
	14751	14099	69	2	39	195		3

BY ORIGIN...1860—61.

KING'S.

Isle of Man	Canada	New Brunswick	Newfoundland	P. E. Island	Magdalen Islands	West Indies	U. States of America	France	Spain	Portugal	Sardinia
	1	44	1	4			33				
	3	33	1			1	14				
	1	74	1	4		1	17				
	1	44		1		1	21				
	3	40		3			7				
	1	7	2				11				
		8					6				
		24	1	5		1	24	1			
	1	8	1			1	17				
		4					16				
		1				1					
1		13					6				
		5				1	9				
1	11	305	7	17		7	181	1			

ANNAPOLIS.

Isle of Man	Canada	New Brunswick	Newfoundland	P. E. Island	Magdalen Islands	West Indies	U. States of America	France	Spain	Portugal	Sardinia
	1	43		10			12				
	1	15	2				9				
		20					8				
		39	3	1		1	17				
		23		1			3				
		10				1	8				
		7	1			1	7				
		16	1				13				
		9					3				
	2	25				1	6	1			
		9	1				9				
		4					8				
		3	1								
		2		4							
		11					2				
	4	236	9	16		4	105	1			

DIGBY.

Isle of Man	Canada	New Brunswick	Newfoundland	P. E. Island	Magdalen Islands	West Indies	U. States of America	France	Spain	Portugal	Sardinia
	1	15					7				
	9	12	1	1			9				
	1	57	3			1	43				
		12		1			16				
		14	1			1	18				
		6				2	7				
	3	1		1			1				
		20		7		2	26				
		2					2				
	6	4				1	2		4		
	1	1					3		1		
		8		1			5				
	21	152	5	11		7	139		5		

No. 2.—PERSONAL CENSUS

COUNTY OF

POLLING DISTRICTS.	Italy.	Turkey.	Other places in the Mediterranean.	Germany.	Norway.	Belgium.	Denmark.	Hungary.
1. Canning								
2. Canard			4					
3. Centreville								
4. Lakeville								
5. Somerset								
6. Kentville	1			3				
7. Gaspereaux								
8. Wolfville				4				
9. Lower Horton				1				
10. Aylesford								
11. West Sherbrooke								
12. Aylesford	1	1		2				
13. Berwick								
	2	1	4	10				

COUNTY OF

	Italy.	Turkey.	Other places in the Mediterranean.	Germany.	Norway.	Belgium.	Denmark.	Hungary.
1. Wilmot								
2. Wilmot, Middleton Corner			2	1				
3. Clarence, Wilmot								
4. Bridgetown			1	1				
5. Bellisle								
6. New Caledonia								
7. Broad Cove								
8. Clementsport								
9. Hessian Line				1				
10. Annapolis Royal				1				
11. Carleton's Corner								
12. Nictaux				8				
13. Dalhousie								
14. Maitland								
15. Morse Road				1				
			3	13				

COUNTY OF

	Italy.	Turkey.	Other places in the Mediterranean.	Germany.	Norway.	Belgium.	Denmark.	Hungary.
1. Hillsburg								
2. Head St. Mary's Bay								
3. Digby								
4. Sandy Cove								
5. Long Island								
6. Westport								
7. On St. Mary's Bay								
8. Weymouth								
9. Belivoe Cove								
10. Session House, Clare								
11. Montegan				1				
12. Salmon River								
				1				

BY ORIGIN...1860—61.

KING'S, Continued.

Holland	East Indies	Russia	Africa	Australia	New Zealand	Prussia	Poland	Switzerland	Sweden	South America	All other places	Born at Sea
					1							
												1
	1		1									
												1
	1		1		1							2

ANNAPOLIS, Continued.

Holland	East Indies	Russia	Africa	Australia	New Zealand	Prussia	Poland	Switzerland	Sweden	South America	All other places	Born at Sea
			1								2	
												1
1												
											1	
1			1								3	1

DIGBY, Continued.

Holland	East Indies	Russia	Africa	Australia	New Zealand	Prussia	Poland	Switzerland	Sweden	South America	All other places	Born at Sea
										1		2
										1		2

14

No. 2.—PERSONAL CENSUS

COUNTY OF

POLLING DISTRICTS.	Total Population.	Natives.	England.	Wales.	Scotland.	Ireland.	Guernsey.	Jersey.
1. Ohio	2394	2352	9		2	6		
2. Yarmouth	4152	3943	36		19	78		
3. Chebogue	1687	1643	5	1	9	14		
4. Carleton	716	708	1		1			
5. Plymouth	1098	1083	7			2		
6. Tusket	2235	2224			4	2		
7. Argyle	1120	1111			1			
8. Pubnico	1503	1485	1			7		
9. Kempt	309	303	2					
10. West side Tusket River	312	310						
	15446	15062	61	1	36	109		

COUNTY OF

1. Carleton Village	869	846			4	2		
2. Shelburne	2300	2241	7	1	18	12		
3. Ragged Islands	1247	1216	3		6	13		
4. Louis Head	872	861			2	5		
5. Shag Harbor	1179	1161	1			4		
6. Cape Sable Island	1112	1376	4		5	8		
7. Barrington	1508	1471	3	1		11		
8. Port LaTour	1281	1362	1		10	1		
	10668	10434	19	2	45	59		

COUNTY OF

1. Liverpool	2936	2633	44	1	34	90		
2. Bristol	1865	1825	8					
3. Port Medway	1833	1730	10			2		
4. Port Mouton	743	738	1			4		
5. Brookfield	616	599	2					
6. Caledonia	1629	900	9	1	1	5		
7. Greenfield	313	339				3		
	9265	8774	74	2	61	234		

COUNTY OF

1. Lunenburg	3048	3004	10	1	11	6		
2. Ritcey's Cove	1415	1411			1	1		
3. Mahone Bay	2699	2689			1	8		
4. LaHave	967	958			5			
5. New Germany	2131	2110	6	1	1	9		
6. Chester	2672	2612	6		1	4		
7. Sherbrooke	912	875	6		3	15		
8. Petite Riviere	2903	2861	8		2	16	1	
9. Bridgewater	2029	1998	5		3	13		
10. Tancook Island	379	379						
11. Mill Cove, St. Margaret's Bay	510	502	3		1			
	19632	19400	44	2	29	72	1	

BY ORIGIN...1860—61.

YARMOUTH.

Isle of Man.	Canada.	New Brunswick.	Newfoun'land.	P. E. Island.	Magdalen Islands.	West Indies.	U. States of America.	France.	Spain.	Portugal.	Sardinia.
	3	2		2		1	16				
	5	12	4	2		7	27	1			
		1				1	10				
		13					4				
	1						3				
	7	5	8				3	1			
	1	12	1				4				
	1		3	1		1	4				
							4				
		1					1				
18	43	16	5			10	76	2			

SHELBURNE.

Isle of Man.	Canada.	New Brunswick.	Newfoun'land.	P. E. Island.	Magdalen Islands.	West Indies.	U. States of America.	France.	Spain.	Portugal.	Sardinia.
			1	1			15				
	2	6	1			2	7				
			2	2		2	2				
			1				3				
		1					11				
		1		1		1	15				
		3		2		2	11				
1							6				
3	11	5	6			7	70				

QUEEN'S.

Isle of Man.	Canada.	New Brunswick.	Newfoun'land.	P. E. Island.	Magdalen Islands.	West Indies.	U. States of America.	France.	Spain.	Portugal.	Sardinia.
	9	13	9	1		24	51		1		
		6				3	12				
	4	19	2	2		2	14				
			1			1	4				
	2						7				
	1	1					8				
16	39	12	3			30	96		1		

LUNENBURG.

Isle of Man.	Canada.	New Brunswick.	Newfoun'land.	P. E. Island.	Magdalen Islands.	West Indies.	U. States of America.	France.	Spain.	Portugal.	Sardinia.
		5	1				2				
		1					3				
		2					2				
	2	9				2	1				
	1		5				9				
			3			1	7				
		2									
3	19	9				3	24				

No. 2.—PERSONAL CENSUS

COUNTY OF

POLLING DISTRICTS.	Italy.	Turkey.	Other places in the Mediterranean.	Germany.	Norway.	Belgium.	Denmark.	Hungary.
1. Ohio								
2. Yarmouth								
3. Chebogue				2				
4. Carleton								
5. Plymouth						1		
6. Tusket								
7. Argyle								
8. Pubnico								
9. Kempt								
10. West side Tusket River								
				2		1		

COUNTY OF

	Italy.	Turkey.	Other places in the Mediterranean.	Germany.	Norway.	Belgium.	Denmark.	Hungary.
1. Carleton Village								
2. Shelburne								
3. Ragged Islands	1							
4. Louis Head								
5. Shag Harbor								
6. Cape Sable Island								
7. Barrington				1				
8. Port LaTour								
	1			1				

COUNTY OF

	Italy.	Turkey.	Other places in the Mediterranean.	Germany.	Norway.	Belgium.	Denmark.	Hungary.
1. Liverpool				1	1	1	4	
2. Bristol				2				
3. Port Medway				1			1	
4. Port Mouton								
5. Brookfield								
6. Caledonia								
7. Greenfield								
				4	1	1	5	

COUNTY OF

	Italy.	Turkey.	Other places in the Mediterranean.	Germany.	Norway.	Belgium.	Denmark.	Hungary.
1. Lunenburg	1	1		5				
2. Ritsoy's Cove				2				
3. Mahone Bay				1				
4. LaHave								
5. New Germany				2				
6. Chester				1				
7. Sherbrooke				4				
8. Petite Riviere				1				
9. Bridgewater				2				
10. Tancook Island								
11. Mill Cove, St. Margaret's Bay				2				
	1	1		20				

BY ORIGIN...1860—61.

YARMOUTH, Continued.

Holland	East Indies.	Russia.	Africa.	Australia.	New Zealand.	Prussia.	Poland.	Switzerland.	Sweden.	South America.	All other places.	Born at Sea.
									1			
	1											
								1				
								1				
	1								2	1		

SHELBURNE, Continued.

			1			1			1			
												1
									1			
			1			1			2			1

QUEEN'S, Continued.

4	2										3	1
									1			
									1			
4	2								1	1	3	1

LUNENBURG, Continued.

						1						
										1		
		1								1		
										1		
		1				1				2		

No. 2—PERSONAL CENSUS BY ORIGIN...1860—61.

GENERAL ABSTRACT.

COUNTIES.																			
1. { Halifax (City)																			
" (Outside City)																			
Total in County																			
2. Colchester																			
3. Cumberland																			
4. Pictou																			
5. Sydney																			
6. Guysborough																			
7. Inverness																			
8. Richmond																			
9. Victoria																			
10. Cape Breton																			
11. Hants																			
12. King's																			
13. Annapolis																			
14. Digby																			
15. Yarmouth																			
16. Shelburne																			
17. Queen's																			
18. Lunenburg																			

COUNTIES.	Italy	Turkey	Other places in the Mediterranean	Germany	Norway	Belgium	Denmark	Hungary	Holland	East Indies	Russia	Africa	Australia	New Zealand	France	Poland	Switzerland	Sweden	South America	All other places	Born at Sea	
1. { Halifax (City)	3		16	68	2		2	1		5	1	6		1	7	1	3	3	6	127	7
" (Outside City)	3		7	16	1	2				2		6			1				2	1	1
Total in County	6		25	84	3	2	2	1		7	1	12		1	8	1	3	3	8	150	8
2. Colchester	2			7									1	1	1					4	5
3. Cumberland	1		1	49	2					2				2						6	6
4. Pictou				1			3						2							1	1
5. Sydney				4		20		3												1	1
6. Guysborough			2	3			1		2	1	1									1	1
7. Inverness																				7	1
8. Richmond												1			1					1	2
9. Victoria																				1	1
10. Cape Breton					1					1										1	3
11. Hants	1		5	9		1				1			2							4	4
12. King's	3	1	4	10						1		1	1							2	2
13. Annapolis			3	13				1				1								2	2
14. Digby			1													1					2
15. Yarmouth				2		1				1							3	1		1	1
16. Shelburne	1			1							1				1			2		1	1
17. Queen's				4	1	1	6			4	2		1					2	1	3	1
18. Lunenburg	1		5	20								1									
	14	2	41	198	8	15	9	1	7	16	3	16	3	2	17	1	5	8	9	158	40

PERSONAL CENSUS
BY RELIGION.

No. 3.—PERSONAL CENSUS

COUNTY OF

POLLING DISTRICTS.	Total Population.	Church of England.	Church of Rome.	Church of Scotland.	Presbyterian Church of L. P.	Baptist.	Wesleyan Methodist.	Free Will and Free Christian Baptists.	Christians, Disciples, & Ref'ed Baptists.
1. Ward 1, (City.)	4199	1082	1983	328	354	134	178		5
2. do. 2. do.	3656	676	1928	248	269	147	161		
3. do. 3. do.	3590	746	1944	158	252	222	169		
4. do. 4. do.	2546	438	1484	37	212	141	188		
5. do. 5. do. {1st Section	3510	791	1817	54	223	187	360		
{2nd do.	4710	1420	1635	88	376	475	573		2
6. do. 6. do.	2815	925	858	40	267	199	350		
Total in City	25026	6078	11649	953	1953	1505	1979		7
7. Ferguson's Cove	721	211	508	2					
8. Portuguese Cove	650	21	622		1				
9. Sambro	570	14	133		3	30	383		
10. Prospect	1370	130	1214	6		20			
11. Hagget's Cove	980	628	12		9	153	165		
12. French Village	715	469	1		2	197	32		
13. Drysdale's	374	99	32		184	34	13		
14. North West Arm	330	188	89	23	14	4	6		
15. Piers' Mill	398	130	113		89	39	25		
16. Hammond's Plains	770	80	77		10	601	2		
17. Windsor Road	814	365	137	15	87	167	38		
18. Truro Road	586	87	204		146	122	26		
19. Gay's River	616	128	54	8	397	2	17		
20. Wise's Corner	556	75	55	50	274	11	53		
21. Middle Musquodoboit	1183	104	4	186	674	31	124		
22. Upper Musquodoboit	935	23		33	829	26	12		
23. Caledonia	230		1		224	1			
24. Salmon River	953	562	69		237	60	16		
25. Sheet Harbor	674	216	130	24	246	12	31		
26. Pope's Harbor	1141	792	197		120	11	12		
27. Jeddore	1860	881	239	9	266	290	174		
28. Chezetcook	1763	471	1201	9	73	9			
29. Lawrencetown	462	110	36	67	214	16	14		
30. Preston	641	127	17	12	22	447	1		
31. Dartmouth	3155	1115	807	118	414	408	168		
32. Black Point	795	610	8		1	151	1		
33. Eastern Passage	753	418	244	8	61	14	8		
	49021	14132	17861	1523	6550	4361	3300		7

COUNTY OF

1. Truro	2934	275	53	133	1781	419	240	3	
2. Old Barns	927	59	28	3	759	53	25		
3. Lower Stewiacke	1588	171	104	24	921	203	33		15
4. Upper Stewiacke	1849	13	9	4	1682	124			
5. Upper Onslow and Kemptown	1580	96	19	226	548	498	160		
6. Onslow	771	13	3	1	370	273	92		
7. Earltown	1216	6	4	651	527	13	11		
8. New Annan	1231	22	59	39	846	135	103		
9. Waugh's River	1153	254	69	102	451	1	229		
10. Tatamagouche	1400	28	24	93	958	120	169		
11. Upper Londonderry	1573	41	3	48	992	391	40		
12. Lower Londonderry	2132	108	68	13	1296	455	139		
13. Economy and Five Islands	1691	65	5	2	885	412	254		2
	20045	1151	448	1339	12016	3097	1495	3	17

BY RELIGION...1860—61.

HALIFAX.

Congregationalists.	Ref and Presbyterians.	Lutherans.	Universalists.	Quakers.	Sandemanians.	Bible Christians.	Campbellites.	Evangelical Union.	Swedenborgians.	Mormons.	Deists.	Other Creeds not classed.	No Creed given.
6	12	39		3	1							25	49
1	2	6		9	4			6				3	195
10	10	31	1	5	5							25	12
2	7	10			26								1
1	2	24		2	7						1	34	7
3	1	111		3	9				1				13
14		31		3	4							7	117
37	34	252	1	25	56			6	1		1	94	395
		6											
	4												3
	5												8
												1	13
													12
												6	
		1		2									
													5
				1									
4													6
31												3	4
40		1	1							1			18
									1				11
													4
		4								1			1
				1									9
													5
													15
8		98		10	7						2		57
		1											
120	44	569	1	39	63			7	4	1	104	541

COLCHESTER.

	4	4									1	3	18
1				1					5			7	103
13		1											3
3									5				25
									1			1	17
													4
		3						9	1				14
			10		8			26					3
8													
			8										50
			1					6	4			1	41
7												15	44
32	4	8	19	1		8		35	6	16	1	27	322

No. 3.—PERSONAL CENSUS

COUNTY OF

POLLING DISTRICTS.	Total Population	Church of England	Church of Rome	Church of Scotland	Presbyterian Church of L. P.	Baptists	Wesleyan Methodists	Free Will and Free Christian Baptists	Christians, Disciples, & Ref'md Baptists
1. Amherst	2767	357	231	17	393	814	931		
2. Westchester	774	8	12	81	65	428	139		
3. Head of Amherst	1796	132	44	23	447	345	576	5	
4. River Philip	1878	90	57	21	285	597	773	11	
5. River Hebert	1713	232	557	52	320	365	122		
6. Maccan	838	11	17		121	197	466		
7. Pugwash	3165	381	127	522	595	739	750		
8. Wallace	2500	115	101	614	449	219	990		
9. Wentworth	696	7	20	73	117	123	343		
10. Advocate Harbor	1074	129	79	1	46	256	555	2	
11. Mill Village	2332	631	212	34	394	323	702		
	19533	2093	1457	1438	3232	4406	6347	18	

COUNTY OF

	Total Population	Church of England	Church of Rome	Church of Scotland	Presbyterian Church of L. P.	Baptists	Wesleyan Methodists	Free Will and Free Christian Baptists	Christians, Disciples, & Ref'md Baptists
1. Pictou	2833	451	429	703	1157	8	32		8
2. Carriboo	1192	30	15	633	498	3	12		
3. Cape John	1424	172	19	535	433	77	128		
4. West side River John	1315	102	30	140	776	21	224		7
5. West branch River John	917	4	10	595	266	9	7		
6. Rogers Hill	1127	13	1	634	460		1	3	
7. Hardwood Hill	1139	65	23	389	635	14	1		
8. Green Hill, West River	983	4			105	873			
9. Mount Thom	1242	42	21	833	302	8	1		
10. Gairloch	937			713	221	1			
11. New Lairg	615		2	586	26				
12. Albion Mines	2088	215	321	609	853	8	78		
13. New Glasgow	2288	10	117	628	1496	14	3		
14. Little Harbor	858	12	118	202	508	17			
15. McLellan's Mountain	1081	1		673	407				
16. East branch East River	1298			557	732	9			
17. Hopewell, W. branch E. Riv	1623	71	36	765	743		6		
18. Middle River	1120	12	1	585	521	1			
19. Gulf Shore	1112	15	771	69	249	1			
20. Barney's River	1274	2	53	483	718	17			
21. Merigomish	1544	11	199	253	1057	19			
22. Blue Mount'n, St. Mary's, &c.	775	1	80	181	513				
	28785	1212	2246	10871	13444	227	493	3	15

COUNTY OF

	Total Population	Church of England	Church of Rome	Church of Scotland	Presbyterian Church of L. P.	Baptists	Wesleyan Methodists	Free Will and Free Christian Baptists	Christians, Disciples, & Ref'md Baptists
1. Arisaig	1450		1449						
2. Cape George	1169	1	1010	3	153				
3. Morristown	967		864	9	63	31			
4. Antigonish	2875	70	2081	6	602	88	1		
5. Lochaber	1765	1	1225	124	379	21			
6. Upper South River	1199		907	61	221	10			
7. St. Andrew's	2154	8	2112		34				
8. Tracadie	1649	158	1323	5	11	106	44		
9. Harbor Bouche	1643	122	1462	12	12	27	8		
	14871	360	12433	220	1477	283	53		

BY RELIGION...1860—61.

CUMBERLAND.

Congregationalists.	Ref'md Presbyterians.	Lutherans.	Universalists.	Quakers.	Sandemanians.	Bible Christians.	Campbellites.	Evangelical Union.	Swedenborgians.	Mormons.	Deists.	Other Creeds not classed.	No Creed given.
			17									3	4
			10										31
19	133		23				1						48
1	4		29	1									9
		27	32										6
			1	4								4	17
1			27										23
1		1	10										
		5	3									4	1
												1	5
						2							34
22	137	33	152	5		2	1					12	178

PICTOU.

8			9				27					1	
												1	
												60	
			15										
							26						
1							14						
			1				11						
							21						1
												9	5
												2	
	1						4						
			5				5					1	
													1
													2
													7
													1
													5
9	1		1	29			108					74	23

SYDNEY.

													1
													27
												15	
													2
												15	30

No. 3.—PERSONAL CENSUS

COUNTY OF

POLLING DISTRICTS.	Total Population.	Church of England.	Church of Rome.	Church of Scotland.	Presbyterian Church of L. P.	Baptists.	Wesleyan Methodists.	Free Will and Free Christian Baptists.	Christians, Disciples, & Ref'md Baptists.
1. Guysborough	2242	337	745	12	32	414	698		
2. Intervale	968	175	674		7	5	95		
3. Manchester	1548	386	605		27	225	225		
4. Melford	1583	554	710	15	81	57	144		
5. Crow Harbor	727	327	119		2	129	150		
6. Cape Canso	820	79	333		21	239	141		
7. Country Harbor	893	345	18	4	60	303	66		
8. Sherbrooke	1460	251	100	1	407	407	3		
9. Marie Joseph	648	619	10		5	3	10		
10. Forks, St. Mary's	1162	55	90	49	783	173	8		
11. Molasses Harbor	947	130	628			17	172		
	12713	3249	4032	81	1425	2062	1712		

COUNTY OF

POLLING DISTRICTS.	Total Population.	Church of England.	Church of Rome.	Church of Scotland.	Presbyterian Church of L. P.	Baptists.	Wesleyan Methodists.	Free Will and Free Christian Baptists.	Christians, Disciples, & Ref'md Baptists.
1. Plaster Cove	1710	100	865	57	528	49	95		
2. Judique	1832		1820		6				
3. River Inhabitants	1488		591	347	529	12			
4. Port Hood	1031	64	819		88	2	58		
5. Mabou	2737	1	1738	11	897	76			
6. Broad Cove (Intervale)	1394		893	123	469				
7. Broad Cove	839		832		7				
8. Margaree	383	11	254		118				
9. Young's Bridge	943		918	13	1		20		
10. Friar's Head	775		771						
11. Cheticamp	1404	9	1254	1	118	22			
12. Whycocomagh	2224	1	127	170	1914	12			
13. Lake Ainslie	847		208	75	562	1	1		
14. River Denis	1217	7	310	189	711				
15. North-east Margaree	1181	8	344	11	299	247	80		
	19967	201	11627	997	6239	121	248		

COUNTY OF

POLLING DISTRICTS.	Total Population.	Church of England.	Church of Rome.	Church of Scotland.	Presbyterian Church of L. P.	Baptists.	Wesleyan Methodists.	Free Will and Free Christian Baptists.	Christians, Disciples, & Ref'md Baptists.
1. Arichat	1008	137	816	10	38	2	5		
2. Petit Degrat	1875	104	1767		2	2			
3. D'Escouse	1177	84	1075	7	1		1		
4. Black River	742	3	77	57	589	10			
5. River Bourgeoise	849	48	692	70	39				
6. St. Peter's	780	11	508	120	134	1			
7. L'Ardoise	1475	11	1354	57	52	1			
8. Grand River	755		13	335	407				
9. Red Islands	774	18	732		24				
10. River Inhabitants	918	140	509	76	80	14	98		
11. Little Arichat	1435	69	1340	12	13		1		
12. Loch Lomond	412			33	379				
13. Flamboise	411		7		331	6	67		
	12607	625	8890	777	2089	36	172		

BY RELIGION...1860—61.

GUYSBOROUGH.

Congregationalists.	Ref'med Presbyterians.	Lutherans.	Universalists.	Quakers.	Sandemanians.	Bible Christians.	Campbellites.	Evangelical Union.	Swedenborgians.	Mormons.	Deists.	Other Creeds not classed.	No Creed given.
													4
													12
80													
10			4									5	3
13													
												6	1
													10
													4
105			4									11	34

INVERNESS.

Congregationalists.	Ref'med Presbyterians.	Lutherans.	Universalists.	Quakers.	Sandemanians.	Bible Christians.	Campbellites.	Evangelical Union.	Swedenborgians.	Mormons.	Deists.	Other Creeds not classed.	No Creed given.
16			2										
2												7	
												10	4
													7
185													1
203			2									17	12

RICHMOND.

Congregationalists.	Ref'med Presbyterians.	Lutherans.	Universalists.	Quakers.	Sandemanians.	Bible Christians.	Campbellites.	Evangelical Union.	Swedenborgians.	Mormons.	Deists.	Other Creeds not classed.	No Creed given.
5													
6													
													6
													1
11													7

No. 3.—PERSONAL CENSUS

COUNTY OF

POLLING DISTRICTS.	Total Population.	Church of England.	Church of Rome.	Church of Scotland.	Presbyterian Church of L. P.	Baptists.	Wesleyan Methodist.	Free Will and Free Christian Baptists.	Christians, Disciples, & Ref'md Baptists.
1. Washabok	1044		980		54	1		9	
2. Middle River	877		11	246	608	12			
3. Baddeck	1553	97	137	80	1161	27	33		
4. Munro's Point, St. Ann's	1440		2	233	1197	2	6		
5. Englishtown, St. Ann's	1224	37	22	60	1102	3			
6. Boulardrie	1178	12	266	189	705	6			
7. Ingonish	566	42	339	33		7	145		
8. Cape North	667	23	157	229	191	41	11		
9. Bay St. Lawrence	353	20	289	4	40				
10. Little Narrows	741	16	57		668				
	9643	247	2260	1074	5726	99	195	9	

COUNTY OF

1. Sydney	2467	627	1085	31	434	65	195		
2. Ball's Bridge	2169	314	784	30	647	279	59		
3. Mira Ferry	899	35	44	5	744	67			
4. Sydney Mines	3283	288	1506	114	1029	134	207	1	
5. Mainadieu	1509	249	610		634	16			
6. Louisburg	1374	179	271		880	9	35		
7. Gabarus	1551	59	545		591	1	355		
8. East Bay	1785	9	1754		12	10			
9. Beaver Cove	992	1	847	17	127				
10. Howley's Ferry	1001	51	401	41	461	47			
11. Lingan Mines	1253	122	983	37	84	10	10		
12. Cow Bay	713	155	68	205	131	154			
13. Big Pond	643		489		153	1			
14. Christmas Island	1227		1222	4	1				
	20866	2089	10609	484	5928	793	861	1	

COUNTY OF

1. Windsor	2271	523	344	27	456	405	506		
2. St. Croix	1104	267	111	1	485	130	99		
3. Brooklyn	1085	277	46		353	136	246		3
4. Scotch Village	2254	284	29		320	440	1037		118
5. Falmouth	1185	132	17		58	623	201		
6. Kempt	1965	230	70		230	560	817		
7. Rawdon Church	759	240	48	15	118	125	161		24
8. South Rawdon	624	147	105	4	68	154	78		15
9. Noel	1791	476	60	6	901	29	200		93
10. Nine Mile River	1920	207	209	63	1122	74	183		40
11. Maitland	1967	437	177	1	948	64	330		10
12. Chester Road	535	236	15		6	165	88	14	
	17460	3456	1231	117	5065	2905	3946	14	303

BY RELIGION...1860-61.

VICTORIA.

Congregationalists.	Ref'md Presbyterians.	Lutherans.	Universalists.	Quakers.	Sandemanians.	Bible Christians.	Campbellites.	Evangelical Union.	Swedenborgians.	Mormons.	Deists.	Other Creeds not classed.	No Creed given.
18													
15													
33													

CAPE BRETON.

Congregationalists.	Ref'md Presbyterians.	Lutherans.	Universalists.	Quakers.	Sandemanians.	Bible Christians.	Campbellites.	Evangelical Union.	Swedenborgians.	Mormons.	Deists.	Other Creeds not classed.	No Creed given.
												30	
7													49
													4
			1									3	
													7
7			1									33	60

HANTS.

Congregationalists.	Ref'md Presbyterians.	Lutherans.	Universalists.	Quakers.	Sandemanians.	Bible Christians.	Campbellites.	Evangelical Union.	Swedenborgians.	Mormons.	Deists.	Other Creeds not classed.	No Creed given.
1			3								1		5
1			10										17
												7	21
	1		4									13	29
75			21			16						29	21
4	2		2										28
						21							17
			15				2					5	18
			1									14	8
				1								10	
81	3		56	1		21	18				1	78	164

16

No. 3—PERSONAL CENSUS

COUNTY OF

POLLING DISTRICTS.	Total Population.	Church of England.	Church of Rome.	Church of Scotland.	Presbyterian Church of L. P.	Baptists.	Wesleyan Methodists.	Free Will and Free Christian Baptists	Christians, Disciples, & Reformed Baptists.
1. Canning	2256	98	162	1	309	789	461	281	34
2. Canard	1342	213	399		203	541	165	2	68
3. Centreville	2948	367	258	14	247	992	162	183	37
4. Lakeville	1599	81	136	9	187	826	342	25	26
5. Somerset	2286	98	379		356	1079	429	58	
6. Kentville	1483	254	375	6	152	676	115	4	18
7. Gaspereaux	1069	41	55		76	814	50	1	
8. Wolfville	1577	324	117		138	733	262	28	7
9. Lower Horton	1335	56	41		120	528	590	7	
10. Aylesford	1361	202	23		51	870	278	6	
11. West Sherbrooke	197	69	58			67			
12. Aylesford	1342	328	177		31	456	295		13
13. Berwick	872	51	7		76	533	158	10	4
	18731	1677	1484	20	1758	8813	3130	675	207

COUNTY OF

1. Wilmot	1836	135	28		109	1143	385		
2. Wilmot, Middleton Corner	1474	159	14	4	41	906	214		
3. Clarence, Wilmot	1434	82	2		25	1098	222		
4. Bridgetown	1404	267	55	6	34	837	189		
5. Bellisle	1153	473	71		32	284	329	2	
6. New Caledonia	1252	277	21	3	16	669	239	5	
7. Broad Cove	898	258	26		21	546	43		
8. Clementsport	1319	276	46		7	594	351		5
9. Hessian Line	941	149	14		3	543	227		
10. Annapolis Royal	1803	1123	137	4	100	202	228		
11. Carleton's Corner	707	59	9		11	429	156	15	
12. Nictaux	1238	94	8		27	758	294		
13. Dalhousie	561	58	32		9	378	50		
14. Maitland	369	19	9			347	25		
15. Morse Road	362	151	14		11	138	42		
	16753	3580	439	17	454	8827	3104	22	5

COUNTY OF

1. Hillsburg	1191	125	41	12	19	674	254		
2. Head St. Mary's Bay	954	281	199	1	11	375	81		
3. Digby	1851	797	146	28	70	591	261	15	8
4. Sandy Cove	1184	132	129		1	661	227	3	7
5. Long Island	954	28	46		11	793	22	29	17
6. Westport	678	85	3		8	475	19	42	16
7. On St. Mary's Bay	1466	173	678		13	477	115		
8. Weymouth	1308	404	370	6	10	403	34	36	9
9. Bellivoo Cove	1116	65	734		8	309			
10. Session House, Clare	1586	6	1574			6			
11. Montegan	1531	7	1505		8	7	1		
12. Salmon River	929	12	589			248		74	
	14751	2115	6014	47	159	4944	1014	199	57

BY RELIGION...1860—61.

KING'S.

Congregationalists.	Ref'med Presbyterians	Lutherans.	Universalists.	Quakers.	Sandemonians.	Bible Christians.	Campbellites.	Evangelical Union.	Swedenborgians.	Mormons.	Deists.	Other Creeds not classed.	No Creed given.
182			1									38	105
1	19		1					4				7	10
			15	2						1		15	23
	2	1	2									14	76
2			2	1								28	65
		3	13		7							30	41
	2		17	1		18						2	3
2	11	3	30									22	
2				10								56	
	15		5										3
		1	2										
3	6		1									2	28
1	10		3									16	
195	65	8	92	14	7	18	4			1		208	352

ANNAPOLIS.

1	20		3	2									1
7			11	17									1
			3	1									
7	6		1										4
			1	23									
1				2								9	10
3													1
			2	6								31	4
		5		1									3
				9								5	
7		4	1	20	4			4				5	13
		30		4									
				1									
		1											
26	26	40	47	65				4				50	37

DIGBY.

			9	2								55	
				6									
4			1	8								2	
			7										14
				6								2	
												2	28
1												3	9
2			2	1								20	9
													3
				1									5
7			19	24								84	68

No. 3.—PERSONAL CENSUS

COUNTY OF

POLLING DISTRICTS.	Total Population.	Church of England.	Church of Rome.	Church of Scotland.	Presbyterian Church of L. P.	Baptists.	Wesleyan Methodists.	Free Will and Free Christian Baptists.	Christians, Disciples, & Ref'md Baptists.
1. Ohio	2294	1	3	6	21	1667	21	502	
2. Yarmouth	4152	483	323		252	1802	746	297	
3. Chebogue	1687	77	92		108	823	90	248	
4. Carleton	716	13			81	360		246	
5. Plymouth	1098	37	764			57	2	224	
6. Tusket	2255	104	1691	4	26	276	2	124	
7. Argyle	1120	11	254		6	723	4	116	
8. Pubnico	1503	43	743		4	309	4	383	
9. Kempt	309	18				22		227	
10. West side Tusket River	312	62				139	4	107	
	15446	849	3870	10	498	6178	873	2474	

COUNTY OF

POLLING DISTRICTS.	Total Population.	Church of England.	Church of Rome.	Church of Scotland.	Presbyterian Church of L. P.	Baptists.	Wesleyan Methodists.	Free Will and Free Christian Baptists.	Christians, Disciples, & Ref'md Baptists.
1. Carleton Village	869	32		7	168	21	641		
2. Shelburne	2300	1235	43	5	410	280	316	3	
3. Ragged Islands	1247	318	36		168	588	124		
4. Louis Head	872	59	7		16	361	375	22	5
5. Shag Harbor	1179	29	21			411	48	636	
6. Cape Sable Island	1412	37	2	15	38	153	121	151	
7. Barrington	1508	59	19		45	88	507	785	
8. Port LaTour	1281	47	2		90	135	962	45	
	10668	1816	130	27	935	2040	2985	2642	5

COUNTY OF

POLLING DISTRICTS.	Total Population.	Church of England.	Church of Rome.	Church of Scotland.	Presbyterian Church of L. P.	Baptists.	Wesleyan Methodists.	Free Will and Free Christian Baptists.	Christians, Disciples, & Ref'md Baptists.
1. Liverpool	2936	699	248	3	22	555	964	16	92
2. Bristol	1865	449	9		15	509	161	13	147
3. Port Medway	1833	431	116	3	11	527	443	255	
4. Port Mouton	743	73	1		7	101	416	124	11
5. Brookfield	616	55	21		7	340	15	87	6
6. Caledonia	1029	68	304	3	13	328	50	134	35
7. Greenfield	343	47	10		5	234	10		
	9365	1822	712	9	80	2594	2089	629	291

COUNTY OF

POLLING DISTRICTS.	Total Population.	Church of England.	Church of Rome.	Church of Scotland.	Presbyterian Church of L. P.	Baptists.	Wesleyan Methodists.	Free Will and Free Christian Baptists.	Christians, Disciples, & Ref'md Baptists.
1. Lunenburg	3048	1005	47		601	137	304		
2. Ritsey's Cove	1415	87	2	1	429	22	332		
3. Mahone Bay	2699	1187	5	2	452	298	158		
4. LaHave	967	302	16		125	131	61	6	
5. New Germany	2131	551	1		167	422	199		
6. Chester	2639	1429	105		49	968	42		
7. Sherbrooke	912	470	217		6	205			
8. Petite Riviere	2903	1132	47		288	375	781		
9. Bridgewater	2029	353	98		252	393	100	9	
10. Tancook Island	379	43			11	262	61		
11. Mill Cove, St. Margaret's Bay	510	481			1	27			
	19632	7040	538	3	2381	3240	2038	15	

BY RELIGION...1860—61.

YARMOUTH.

Congregationalists.	Ref'md Presbyterians.	Lutherans.	Universalists.	Quakers.	Sandemanians.	Bible Christians.	Campbellites.	Evangelical Union.	Swedenborgians.	Mormons.	Deists.	Other Creeds not classed.	No Creed given.
3			14									5	65
146												9	80
205												12	32
9				7									
													14
1													27
										1		1	4
				1						5			11
													42
364			14	8								27	275

SHELBURNE.

3			10	1								7	
22			1										1
				1								16	17
												4	
2		3											
27		3	11	2								27	18

QUEEN'S.

314		3	7				1					11	1
538		7					3					12	2
6		24	4									13	
6												3	1
38		4	9									1	
24		2	10									11	47
													37
926		40	30				4					51	88

LUNENBURG.

		952	1									1	
		542											
		559	5										33
		318	6	1									1
		778	6	7									
		37	9										
		2										1	11
10		251											19
7		764	8					1				2	42
		2											
		1											
17		4206	35	8				1				4	106

GENERAL ABSTRACT.

COUNTIES	Total Population	Church of England	Church of Rome	Church of Scotland	Presbyterian Church of L.C.	Baptists	Methodists	Free Will and Free Christian Baptists	Universalists, Christians & Spiritual Baptists	Congregationalists	Second Presbyterians
1. Halifax (City)	25025	5858	11049	955	1955	1505	1979		7	37	
" (Outside City)	23995	8054	6212	570	4597	2856	1921			83	
Total in County	49021	14132	17861	1528	6550	4361	3900		7	120	
2. Colchester	20045	1151	448	1389	12014	3097	1496	3	17	32	4
3. Cumberland	16032	2261	1457	1438	3232	4406	6347	16		23	137
4. Pictou	28785	1242	2846	10671	13444	297	493	3	15	9	1
5. Sydney	14871	389	12432	220	1477	283	53				
6. Guysborough	12713	3249	4603	81	1425	2062	1712			103	
7. Inverness	19867	991	15997	997	6239	461	248			203	
8. Richmond	12867	620	8900	777	2089	90	172			11	
9. Victoria	9643	247	2250	1074	5726	99	193	9		33	
10. Cape Breton	20666	2089	10609	484	5928	795	861	1		7	
11. Hants	17460	3456	1251	117	6465	2966	2946	14	308	81	3
12. King's	18731	1677	1484	29	1755	8813	3130	675	202	195	65
13. Annapolis	16735	2980	439	17	454	8527	3104	22	5	26	26
14. Digby	14751	2115	6054	47	150	4944	1004	189	37	7	
15. Yarmouth	15446	649	3300	10	498	6178	873	2474		364	
16. Shelburne	10668	1816	180	27	935	3040	2965	2043	5	27	
17. Queen's	9365	1892	712	9	80	2294	2969	629	201	226	
18. Lunenburg	19632	7080	558	3	2381	3240	2698	15		17	
	32667	47744	88385	19003	69456	55335	38055	4708	902	2163	234

GENERAL ABSTRACT, · · · · · · · Continued.

COUNTIES.					Bible Christians		Evangelical Union				Other Creeds not classed	Not classed given
1. { Halifax (City)	34	255	1	25	56			6	3	1	94	296
{ " (Outside City)	10	147		14	7			1	1		10	145
Total in County	44	393	1	30	63			7	4	1	104	541
2. Colchester	3	19	1		8		35	6	16	1	27	322
3. Cumberland	33	158	5		2	1					12	178
4. Pictou		1	29				108				74	22
5. Sydney											15	30
6. Guysborough		4									11	34
7. Inverness		2									17	12
8. Richmond												7
9. Victoria												
10. Cape Breton		1									33	60
11. Hants		56			21	18				5	78	164
12. King's	8	22	14		18	4			1		268	322
13. Annapolis	40	47	65	7		4					50	37
14. Digby		19	24								84	68
15. Yarmouth		14	5						6		27	275
16. Shelburne	3	11	2								27	18
17. Queen's	40	30				4					51	68
18. Lunenburg	4205	33	8			1					4	106
	4382	845	158	45	112	33	183	13	27	8	822	2344

PERSONAL CENSUS.

DEATHS, AND CAUSES OF DEATHS.

No. 4.—PERSONAL CENSUS...DEATHS,

COUNTY OF

Epidemic, Endemic, and

POLLING DISTRICTS.	Cholera.	Cramp.	Intermittent Fever.	Dyptheria.	Dysentery.	Typhus Fever.	Hooping Cough.	Influenza.
1. Ward 1, (City)				1			3	
2. do. 2, do.								1
3. do. 3, do.				1			5	
4. do. 4, do.			1	3			1	
5. do. 5, do. { 1st Section				2			3	
5. do. 5, do. { 2nd do.			1	2			1	
6. do. 6, do.								
Total in City			2	9			13	1
7. Ferguson's Cove								
8. Portuguese Cove								
9. Sambro								
10. Prospect								
11. Hagget's Cove								
12. French Village								
13. Drysdale's							1	
14. North West Arm							2	
15. Piers' Mill				2				
16. Hammond's Plains						2		
17. Windsor Road						1		
18. Truro Road								
19. Gay's River								
20. Wise's Corner				2				
21. Middle Musquodoboit				16		1		
22. Upper Musquodoboit				3				
23. Caledonia								
24. Salmon River								
25. Sheet Harbor								
26. Pope's Harbor	1			13				
27. Jeddore	1			2			1	
28. Chezetcook				3			1	
29. Lawrencetown								
30. Preston				9				
31. Dartmouth				2				
32. Black Point				5				
33. Eastern Passage	1							
	3		2	66		4	18	

COUNTY OF

1. Truro				2		1	2	
2. Old Barns								
3. Lower Stewiacke						1		
4. Upper Stewiacke				7				
5. Upper Onslow and Kemptown						1		1
6. Onslow				9				
7. Earltown								
8. New Annan								
9. Waugh's River								
10. Tatamagouche				2				
11. Upper Londonderry				4				
12. Lower Londonderry				2	8			
13. Economy and Five Islands				3				
			2	28		3	2	1

AND CAUSES OF DEATHS...1860--61.

HALIFAX.

	Contagious Diseases.						Diseases of the Nervous System.							
	Measles	Mumps	Scarlet Fever	Small Pox	Hives	Total	Apoplexy	Brain Fever	Disease of Brain	Epilepsy	Paralysis	Insanity	Convulsions	Total
			1	1		6	1		1	1			1	4
	2					3		2		2			1	2
				2		8		1	2	1			1	5
	2			2		9		1				1	2	4
	1			2		8	1		1		1		1	4
			1			5		1		1			1	3
				1		1	2	1	2				2	8
	5		2	8		46	4	6	6	2	3		9	30
													2	2
								1						1
				1		1								
			1			1							1	1
						1								1
						2			1				1	1
	1		3	1		7							2	2
						1						1		1
	1					1								
			1			3		1						1
						17	2		1				1	4
						3								
			1			1			1					1
				1		15								
	1					5								
				16		20								
	2					11			1					1
						2			2					2
						5							1	1
	3					4		1						1
	13		8	27		142	6	9	12	2	4		17	30

COLCHESTER.

			1			6		1	1					3
			3			3			1					1
	2					3			1					1
			3			10	1	1	3					5
	1			2		5								
			2			4		1	1					2
	1		2			3				1				1
	1					1								
	1					1								
						2								
			6			10						1		1
			1			11								
	1					4								
	7		17	3		63	1	3	7		2			13

No. 4.—PERSONAL CENSUS...DEATHS,

COUNTY OF

POLLING DISTRICTS.	Asthma.	Bronchitis.	Consumption.	Croup.	Cough.	Disease of Lungs.	Disease of Heart.	Inflammation of Lungs.
			Diseases of the Respiratory					
1. Ward 1, (City)	1		5	1				
2. do. 2, do.			10				2	
3. do. 3, do.	1		12			1	3	
4. do. 4, do.	1		4	1		1		
5. do. 5, do. { 1st Section			6			1		
2nd do.		1	9				2	2
6. do. 6, do.	1		11					2
Total in City	4	1	57	2		3	7	4
7. Ferguson's Cove								
8. Portuguese Cove							1	1
9. Sambro			3					1
10. Prospect						3	1	
11. Hagget's Cove						3		
12. French Village			1					
13. Drysdale's								
14. North West Arm			2					
15. Piers' Mill								
16. Hammond's Plains			1	1				
17. Windsor Road			2				1	1
18. Truro Road			4					
19. Gay's River								
20. Wise's Corner			3					1
21. Middle Musquodoboit			2	1				3
22. Upper Musquodoboit			6	1				
23. Caledonia								
24. Salmon River			3					1
25. Sheet Harbor			1					
26. Pope's Harbor								
27. Jeddore			4	2				
28. Chezetcook			4	2				
29. Lawrencetown			3					
30. Preston	1		3					
31. Dartmouth		1	2					
32. Black Point			1					
33. Eastern Passage			2					
	5	2	107	17		3	10	12

COUNTY OF

1. Truro	1		3	1				2
2. Old Barns			1				1	
3. Lower Stewiacke			1					2
4. Upper Stewiacke				1				1
5. Upper Onslow and Kemptown			8	1				3
6. Onslow			6				1	
7. Earltown			1				1	1
8. New Annan		1	4	2				
9. Waugh's River			3					2
10. Tatamagouche			2					2
11. Upper Londonderry			8				1	1
12. Lower Londonderry			3	1			1	
13. Economy and Five Islands			3					2
		2	45	5	1	2	4	14

AND CAUSES OF DEATHS...1860—61.

HALIFAX, Continued.

and Circulating Organs.						Diseases of the Digestive Organs.					
Inflammation of Chest.	Inflammation of Heart.	Pleurisy.	Quinsy.	Sore Throat.	Total.	Bilious Fever.	Disease of Liver.	Disease of Stomach.	Indigestion.	Debility.	Jaundice.
.....	.....	.....	.....	3	10	1	2	.....	.....	1	.....
.....	.....	.....	.....	.....	12	.....	.....	.....	.....	.....	1
.....	.....	.....	.....	.....	17	.....	.....	.....	.....	.....	.....
.....	.....	1	.....	1	9	.....	1	.....	.....	1	.....
.....	.....	.....	.....	.....	7	.....	1	.....	.....	1	.....
.....	.....	.....	.....	.....	14	.....	1	.....	.....	1	.....
.....	.....	.....	.....	.....	14	.....	.....	.....	.....	.....	.....
.....	.....	1	.....	4	83.	1	5	.....	.....	4	1
.....	.....	.....	.....	.....		.....	.....	.....	.....	.....	.....
.....	.....	.....	.....	.....	2	.....	.....	.....	.....	.....	.....
.....	.....	.....	.....	.....	4	.....	.....	.....	.....	.....	.....
.....	.....	.....	.....	.....	4	.....	.....	.....	.....	.....	.....
.....	.....	.....	.....	1	4	.....	.....	.....	.....	.....	.....
.....	.....	.....	.....	.....	1	.....	.....	.....	.....	.....	.....
.....	.....	.....	.....	.....	2	.....	1	.....	.....	.....	.....
1	.....	.....	.....	4	13	.....	.....	.....	.....	.....	.....
.....	.....	.....	.....	.....	4	.....	.....	.....	.....	.....	.....
.....	.....	2	.....	.....	6	.....	.....	.....	.....	.....	.....
.....	.....	.....	.....	1	5	.....	.....	.....	.....	.....	.....
.....	.....	.....	.....	9	13	.....	.....	.....	.....	.....	.....
.....	.....	.....	.....	2	8	.....	.....	.....	.....	.....	.....
.....	.....	1	.....	1	6	.....	1	.....	.....	.....	.....
.....	.....	.....	.....	.....	1	.....	.....	.....	.....	.....	.....
.....	.....	.....	.....	.....		1	.....	.....	.....	.....	4
.....	.....	.....	.....	.....	6	1.	.....	.....	.....	.....	.....
.....	.....	.....	.....	.....	6	.....	1	.....	.....	.....	.....
.....	.....	.....	.....	1	5	.....	.....	.....	.....	.....	.....
.....	.....	.....	.....	.....	4	.....	.....	.....	.....	.....	.....
.....	.....	.....	.....	.....	3	.....	.....	.....	.....	.....	.....
.....	.....	.....	.....	.....	1	.....	.....	.....	.....	.....	.....
.....	.....	.....	.....	1	5	.....	.....	.....	.....	.....	.....
1	.....	4	1	22	184	3	8	.....	.....	4	5

COLCHESTER, Continued.

.....	.....	.....	.....	1	8	1	1	1	.....	.....	.....
.....	.....	.....	.....	.....	2	.....	.....	.....	.....	.....	.....
.....	.....	.....	.....	.....	4	.....	.....	.....	.....	.....	.....
.....	.....	.....	.....	2	12	.....	.....	.....	.....	.....	.....
.....	.....	.....	.....	.....	16	.....	.....	.....	.....	.....	.....
.....	.....	1	.....	.....	7	.....	.....	.....	.....	.....	.....
.....	.....	.....	.....	.....		.....	.....	.....	1	.....	.....
.....	.....	.....	.....	2	9	.....	.....	.....	.....	.....	.....
.....	.....	.....	.....	4	8	.....	.....	.....	.....	.....	1
.....	.....	.....	.....	.....	4	.....	.....	.....	.....	.....	.....
.....	.....	.....	.....	4	13	.....	.....	.....	1	.....	.....
.....	.....	.....	.....	.....	5	.....	.....	.....	.....	.....	.....
.....	.....	.....	.....	4	9	.....	.....	.....	.....	.....	.....
.....	.....	1	.....	17	91	1	1	3	.....	.....	1

No. 4.—PERSONAL CENSUS. DEATHS,

COUNTY OF

Diseases of the Digestive Organs—*Continued*

POLLING DISTRICTS.	Inflammation of Bowels.	Inflammation of Stomach.	Disease of Bowels.	Worms.	Teething.	Total
1. Ward 1, (City)				1		6
2. do. 2, do	3		2			6
3. do. 3, do	1					1
4. do. 4, do						2
5. do. 5, do { 1st Section			3			3
{ 2nd do.	3	1	1			7
6. do. 6, do					3	3
Total in City	7	1	6	1	3	28
7. Ferguson's Cove						
8. Portuguese Cove						
9. Sambro						
10. Prospect						
11. Hagget's Cove						
12. French Village	1					1
13. Drysdale's						
14. North West Arm						1
15. Piers' Mill						
16. Hammond's Plains						
17. Windsor Road						
18. Truro Road				2		2
19. Gay's River						
20. Wise's Corner						
21. Middle Musquodoboit	2					2
22. Upper Musquodoboit	1					1
23. Caledonia						
24. Salmon River						1
25. Sheet Harbor						
26. Pope's Harbor						5
27. Jeddore	2			1		4
28. Chezetcook	2			1		4
29. Lawrencetown						
30. Preston						
31. Dartmouth	3				1	4
32. Black Point	1					1
33. Eastern Passage				1		1
	19	1	5	6	4	55

COUNTY OF

1. Truro	2					5
2. Old Barns						
3. Lower Stewiacke	1					1
4. Upper Stewiacke						
5. Upper Onslow and Kemptown						
6. Onslow						
7. Earltown					1	2
8. New Annan						
9. Waugh's River			2			3
10. Tatamagouche						
11. Upper Londonderry				1		2
12. Lower Londonderry	2					2
13. Economy and Five Islands						
	5		2	1	1	15

AND CAUSES OF DEATHS. 1860—61.

HALIFAX. Continued.

	Diseases of Urinary and Generative Organs.					Diseases of Uncertain Seat.					
Disease of Bladder.	Diabetes.	Inflammation of Kidneys.	Puerperal Fever.	Child-bed.	Total.	Abscess.	Cancer.	Colds.	Scrofula.	After Amputation.	Mortification.
				1	1						
				1	1	1		1			
1					1		1	1			
							2				
							1				
1				2	3	1	4	2			
	1				1						
							1				
		1			1		1				
1					1						
				2	2				1		
2	1	1		4	8	1	6	3			

COLCHESTER. Continued.

									1		
				1	1		2	1			
								1	1		
1					1						
		1			1						
											1
1		1		1	3		2	2	2		1

No. 4.—PERSONAL CENSUS...DEATHS,

COUNTY OF

POLLING DISTRICTS.		Diseases of Uncertain Seat—*Continued.*							
	Dropsy.	Old Age.	Erysipelas.	Intemperance.	Rheumatism.	Rickets.	Tumor.	Carbuncle.	Total.
1. Ward 1, (City)	1	4							5
2. do. 2, do	1								1
3. do. 3, do		4					1		5
4. do. 4, do	1	2	1						6
5. do. 5, do { 1st Section		2							4
{ 2nd do	1	3	1		1				8
6. do. 6, do		3	2						6
Total in City	4	18	4		1		1		35
7. Ferguson's Cove									
8. Portuguese Cove									
9. Sambro									
10. Prospect	1	9							10
11. Hagget's Cove			1						1
12. French Village									
13. Drysdale's									
14. North West Arm									
15. Piers' Mill		1							1
16. Hammond's Plains		1							1
17. Windsor Road	1								1
18. Truro Road	1								1
19. Gay's River		2							2
20. Wise's Corner		1							1
21. Middle Musquodoboit		1	1						3
22. Upper Musquodoboit		1			1				2
23. Caledonia									
24. Salmon River									
25. Sheet Harbor									
26. Pope's Harbor									1
27. Jeddore		2							2
28. Chezetcook		2							3
29. Lawrencetown		1							1
30. Preston		1							1
31. Dartmouth									
32. Black Point									
33. Eastern Passage	2	1							3
	9	41	6		2		1		69

COUNTY OF

POLLING DISTRICTS.	Dropsy.	Old Age.	Erysipelas.	Intemperance.	Rheumatism.	Rickets.	Tumor.	Carbuncle.	Total.
1. Truro	1	3	1						5
2. Old Barns		1							1
3. Lower Stewiacke	2								3
4. Upper Stewiacke	1								4
5 Upper Onslow and Kemptown		2							4
6. Onslow									
7. Earltown		1							1
8. New Annan									
9. Waugh's River	1								1
10. Tatamagouche			1						1
11. Upper Londonderry	1	2			1				4
12. Lower Londonderry				1					2
13. Economy and Five Islands									
	6	9	2	1	1				26

AND CAUSES OF DEATHS...1860—61.

HALIFAX, Continued.

Burns and Scalds.	Frozen.	Drowned.	Murdered.	Poisoned.	Other Accidents.	Total.	Disease of Eye.	Disease of Ear.	Total.	Causes not specified.	Total of Deaths.
		2				2				4	37
		2			1	3				1	29
		1				1				4	41
										1	32
		1				1				5	33
	1	2			1	4				11	52
											32
	1	8			2	11				26	256
						Poors' Asylum...				68	68
											5
										1	5
		3				3					18
		1				1				3	11
				1		1				1	4
											1
		1				1				1	8
											4
										2	26
										1	7
				1		1					11
1						1					4
										1	11
1						1				1	43
1						1				1	16
										2	2
										2	11
		1				1				1	4
		5				5				3	29
				1	2	3					21
				2	2					4	41
										2	6
										2	19
										1	12
										1	9
											12
3	1	19		1	8	32				124	664

COLCHESTER, Continued.

Burns and Scalds.	Frozen.	Drowned.	Murdered.	Poisoned.	Other Accidents.	Total.	Disease of Eye.	Disease of Ear.	Total.	Causes not specified.	Total of Deaths.
					2	2		1	1	1	30
											7
					1	1				3	16
					1	1				4	37
							1		1	1	21
											13
											7
1		1				2				5	17
										2	15
					2	2				4	14
											31
		1			3	4				8	32
		1				1				2	16
1		3			9	13	1	1	2	30	256

18

No. 4.—PERSONAL CENSUS...DEATHS,

COUNTY OF

POLLING DISTRICTS.	Epidemic, Endemic, and							
	Cholera.	Cramp.	Intermitting Fever.	Diphtheria.	Dysentery.	Typhus Fever.	Hooping Cough.	Influenza.
1. Amherst				1		1		
2. Westchester				4		3		
3. Head of Amherst								
4. River Philip								
5. River Hebert				3				
6. Maccan				14		2		
7. Pugwash				6		4		
8. Wallace				30				
9. Wentworth				14				
10. Advocate Harbor								
11. Mill Village				24				
				96		10		

COUNTY OF

POLLING DISTRICTS.	Cholera.	Cramp.	Intermitting Fever.	Diphtheria.	Dysentery.	Typhus Fever.	Hooping Cough.	Influenza.
1. Pictou			2			2		
2. Carriboo				6				
3. Cape John	1		1					
4. West side River John						2		
5. West branch River John				2				
6. Rogers Hill				2				
7. Hardwood Hill				2				
8. Green Hill, West River				4				
9. Mount Thom								
10. Gairloch								
11. New Lairg								
12. Albion Mines						2	1	
13. New Glasgow					1			3
14. Little Harbor								
15. McLellan's Mountain	1							
16. East branch East River								
17. Hopewell, W. branch E. River						1		
18. Middle River								
19. Gulf Shore				4				
20. Barney's River				2				
21. Merrigomish						4		
22. Blue Mountain, St. Mary's, &c.				4				
	2		3	26	1	11	1	3

COUNTY OF

POLLING DISTRICTS.	Cholera.	Cramp.	Intermitting Fever.	Diphtheria.	Dysentery.	Typhus Fever.	Hooping Cough.	Influenza.
1. Arisaig								
2. Cape George				9				
3. Morristown								
4. Antigonish				2			1	
5. Lochaber		1		2				
6. Upper South River				1				
7. St. Andrew's	1			2			2	
8. Tracadie				6			1	
9. Harbor Bouche				14			3	
	1	1		36			7	

AND CAUSES OF DEATHS...1860—61.

CUMBERLAND.

| | Contagious Diseases. | | | | | | Diseases of the Nervous System. | | | | | | | |
Measles.	Mumps.	Scarlet Fever.	Small Pox.	Hives.	Total.	Apoplexy.	Brain Fever.	Disease of Brain.	Epilepsy.	Paralysis.	Insanity.	Convulsions.	Total.
1		12			15		1					3	4
1					8								
		1			1			1				1	2
1					1			2					3
1		5			9		2						3
		1			17			1					1
1		3			14								
10					40			1		1			2
		3			17								
		1			1							1	1
		1	2		27			1				1	2
15		27	2		150		3	6		1		6	16

PICTOU.

Measles.	Mumps.	Scarlet Fever.	Small Pox.	Hives.	Total.	Apoplexy.	Brain Fever.	Disease of Brain.	Epilepsy.	Paralysis.	Insanity.	Convulsions.	Total.
		1			5	1	1						2
			1		7				1				1
1					3								
1		3			6	1			1	1			3
		2	1		5								
		2			4								
					2			1					1
					4	1							1
					3			1		1			2
					4	2	1			1	1		5
										2			2
		1			2				1				1
					1		1						1
		5			9								
		2			4				1				1
		1			5								
					4								
2		17	2		68	5	2	3		8	2		20

SYDNEY.

Measles.	Mumps.	Scarlet Fever.	Small Pox.	Hives.	Total.	Apoplexy.	Brain Fever.	Disease of Brain.	Epilepsy.	Paralysis.	Insanity.	Convulsions.	Total.
1					1					1			1
		1			10	7				1			2
1					1								
		2	2		7		1						1
1		4			8						1		1
		4			5		1						1
1		3	1		10				1				1
1		1			9	1						1	2
					17								
5		15	3		68	2	2		1	2		2	9

No. 4.—PERSONAL CENSUS...DEATHS,

COUNTY OF

POLLING DISTRICTS.	Asthma.	Bronchitis.	Consumption.	Croup.	Cough.	Disease of Lungs.	Disease of Heart.	Inflammation of Lungs.
1. Amherst			7	2			3	4
2. Westchester			3	1				
3. Head of Amherst			2					2
4. River Philip			10					
5. River Hebert			1					
6. Maccan			2	1			1	
7. Pugwash	1		9					2
8. Wallace	1		4	1				6
9. Wentworth			1	2				
10. Advocate Harbor			1					
11. Mill Village			7	2				
	2		47	9			4	14

COUNTY OF

	Asthma.	Bronchitis.	Consumption.	Croup.	Cough.	Disease of Lungs.	Disease of Heart.	Inflammation of Lungs.
1. Pictou			12	1			2	4
2. Carriboo			2	1				
3. Cape John			2	2				
4. West side River John			3					1
5. West branch River John				3				
6. Rogers Hill			1			2		
7. Hardwood Hill		1	3					
8. Green Hill, West River		3	1					
9. Mount Thom			2				1	
10. Gairloch							1	
11. New Lairg			1					
12. Albion Mines			4					1
13. New Glasgow			6	2			2	3
14. Little Harbor			2					
15. McLellan's Mountain			1					
16. East branch East River			2					
17. Hopewell, W. branch E. River								
18. Middle River	1		3					
19. Gulf Shore			1					
20. Barney's River			2	1				
21. Merrigomish			2					1
22. Blue Mountain, St. Mary's, &c				2				
	1	4	50	12		3	5	10

COUNTY OF

	Asthma.	Bronchitis.	Consumption.	Croup.	Cough.	Disease of Lungs.	Disease of Heart.	Inflammation of Lungs.
1. Arisaig			3					
2. Cape George			2					
3. Morristown			2					
4. Antigonish			10	1			2	4
5. Lochaber			7				1	
6. Upper South River			1					1
7. St. Andrew's			1			1		
8. Tracadie			12				2	
9. Harbor Bouche			2	1				
			40	2		1	5	5

AND CAUSES OF DEATHS...1860—61.

CUMBERLAND, Continued.

and Circulating Organs.						Diseases of the Digestive Organs.					
Inflammation of Chest.	Inflammation of Heart.	Pleurisy.	Quinsy.	Sore Throat.	Total.	Bilious Fever.	Disease of Liver.	Disease of Stomach.	Indigestion.	Debility.	Jaundice.
				5	26	1					
					4						
					4						
					10						
					1						
					4	1			1		
				1	13		1		1		
					12		1		1		
					3						
					1		1				
					9					1	
				6	82	2	2	1	2	1	

PICTOU, Continued.

					19		1	2		1	
				3	6					2	
		3			7						
		1			4						
					4						
					3		2			1	
					4		1				
					4					1	
					3						
					1				1		
					1					1	
					5	2	1				
					13		1				
					2						
					1						
					2						
						3	1				
		1			4		2				
					2						
					3						
				1	4						
		1			3						
		5	1	4	95	5	9	2	1	6	

SYDNEY, Continued.

			4	5	12		1				
			1		3						
			1		4					1	
				6	23		1				
				2	10		1				
			2	2	6					2	
			2	8	12		2				1
			4	2/9	20						
			2	2	7	1					
			16	2/35	106	1	5			3	1

No. 4.—PERSONAL CENSUS...DEATHS,

COUNTY OF

Diseases of the Digestive Organs—*Continued.*

TOLLING DISTRICTS.	Inflammation of Bowels.	Inflammation of Stomach.	Disease of Bowels.	Worms.	Teething.	Total.
1. Amherst						1
2. Westchester	1					1
3. Head of Amherst						
4. River Philip	1			1		2
5. River Hebert				1		1
6. Maccan						2
7. Pugwash	2			3		6
8. Wallace				6		8
9. Wentworth				1		1
10. Advocate Harbor						1
11. Mill Village						1
	4			12		24

COUNTY OF

	Inflammation of Bowels.	Inflammation of Stomach.	Disease of Bowels.	Worms.	Teething.	Total.
1. Pictou	3		1			8
2. Carriboo						2
3. Cape John						
4. West side River John	1					1
5. West branch River John						
6. Rogers Hill	1	2				6
7. Hardwood Hill		2	2			5
8. Green Hill and West River						1
9. Mount Thom		2				2
10. Gairloch						1
11. New Lairg				1		2
12. Albion Mines				1		4
13. New Glasgow	1					2
14. Little Harbor						
15. McLellan's Mountain						
16. East branch East River						
17. Hopewell, West branch East River	1		1			6
18. Middle River		2				2
19. Gulf Shore						2
20. Barney's River						
21. Merrigomish	1	1			.	2
22. Blue Mountain, St. Mary's, &c.	1					1
	9	9	6			47

COUNTY OF

	Inflammation of Bowels.	Inflammation of Stomach.	Disease of Bowels.	Worms.	Teething.	Total.
1. Arisaig						1
2. Cape George						
3. Morristown						1
4. Antigonish						1
5. Lochaber	1					2
6. Upper South River						2
7. St. Andrew's	1					4
8. Tracadie		1	1			2
9. Harbor Bouche			1			2
	2	1	2			15

AND CAUSES OF DEATHS 1860—61.

CUMBERLAND, Continued.

		Diseases of Urinary and Generative Organs.					Diseases of Uncertain Seat.					
Disease of Bladder.	Diabetes.	Inflammation of Kidneys.	Puerperal Fever.	Child-bed.	Total.	Abscess.	Cancer.	Colds.	Scrofula.	After Amputation.	Mortification.	
				2	2		1					
							1					
								2				
							1					
				2	2		3	2				

PICTOU, Continued.

1					1							
			1		1							
								1			1	
				1	1							
								1				
1			1	1	2							
					1							
1			2	2	5	1		2			1	

SYDNEY, Continued.

1					1							
						1						
1					1							
1			1	2				1				
								2	1			
				1	1							
3				3	5		1	3	1			

No. 4.—PERSONAL CENSUS...DEATHS,

COUNTY OF

POLLING DISTRICTS.	Dropsy.	Old Age.	Erysipelas.	Intemperance.	Rheumatism.	Rickets.	Tumor.	Carbuncle.	Total.
1. Amherst	1	2							4
2. Westchester		2							2
3. Head of Amherst	1								2
4. River Philip	1								3
5. River Hebert			1						1
6. Maccan	2			2	1		1		6
7. Pugwash		1							1
8. Wallace	1	3			4				8
9. Wentworth		1							1
10. Advocate Harbor									
11. Mill Village		1							2
	6	10	3		5		1		30

COUNTY OF

POLLING DISTRICTS.	Dropsy.	Old Age.	Erysipelas.	Intemperance.	Rheumatism.	Rickets.	Tumor.	Carbuncle.	Total.
1. Pictou									
2. Carriboo		2							2
3. Cape John									
4. West side River John		1							1
5. West branch River John									
6. Rogers Hill		1							1
7. Hardwood Hill		1							1
8. Green Hill and West River									
9. Mount Thom		3					1		4
10. Gairloch		2							4
11. New Lairg		1							1
12. Albion Mines		1							1
13. New Glasgow								1	1
14. Little Harbor									
15. McLellan's Mountain									1
16. East branch East River									
17. Hopewell, W. branch E. River	1		1						2
18. Middle River	1								1
19. Gulf Shore	1	1			1				3
20. Barney's River		2							2
21. Merrigomish									
22. Blue Mountain, St. Mary's, &c.		1							2
	3	16	1		1		1	1	27

COUNTY OF

POLLING DISTRICTS.	Dropsy.	Old Age.	Erysipelas.	Intemperance.	Rheumatism.	Rickets.	Tumor.	Carbuncle.	Total.
1. Arisaig					1				1
2. Cape George									1
3. Morristown									
4. Antigonish							2		2
5. Lochaber					1				2
6. Upper South River									3
7. St. Andrew's		2			1				3
8. Tracadie	1	1			1				3
9. Harbor Bouche		1							1
	1	4			4		2		16

AND CAUSES OF DEATHS...1860—61.

CUMBERLAND. Continued.

Burns and Scalds.	Frozen.	Drowned.	Murdered.	Poisoned.	Other Accidents.	Total.	Disease of Eye.	Disease of Ear.	Total.	Causes not specified.	Total of Deaths.
										6	53
										2	15
										2	11
										1	19
										2	16
										1	31
1					1	2				8	44
		1				1					71
1						1				1	23
					2	1					5
					2	2				7	50
2		1			3	6				28	338

PICTOU, Continued.

Burns and Scalds.	Frozen.	Drowned.	Murdered.	Poisoned.	Other Accidents.	Total.	Disease of Eye.	Disease of Ear.	Total.	Causes not specified.	Total of Deaths.
		2			1	3				2	30
		2			1	3				1	22
										3	13
										1	16
										2	11
										1	15
			2		2					2	18
							1		1	1	13
										3	12
										3	9
										2	6
		1			1	2				1	18
										1	27
					1	1					5
										2	7
										2	6
					1	1				4	15
					1	1					8
					1	1				2	19
											10
1						1				4	16
										4	14
1		5			9	15		1	1	41	319

SYDNEY, Continued.

Burns and Scalds.	Frozen.	Drowned.	Murdered.	Poisoned.	Other Accidents.	Total.	Disease of Eye.	Disease of Ear.	Total.	Causes not specified.	Total of Deaths.
						1				1	18
		1				1					17
		2				2				1	9
										5	40
											25
					1	1				1	19
										5	35
		1				2				7	55
1		1				2				4	33
1		5	1		1	8				24	251

19

No. 4.—PERSONAL CENSUS...DEATHS,

COUNTY OF

POLLING DISTRICTS.	Cholera.	Cramp.	Intermittent Fever.	Dyphtheria.	Dysentery.	Typhus Fever.	Hooping Cough.	Influenza.
1. Guysborough				10			3	
2. Intervale				10				
3. Manchester				4			2	
4. Melford				5			6	
5. Crow Harbor				5			2	
6. Cape Canso				3				
7. Country Harbor				7				
8. Sherbrooke				3				
9. Marie Joseph								
10. Forks, St. Mary's			1	5				
11. Molasses Harbor								
			1	52			13	

COUNTY OF

POLLING DISTRICTS.	Cholera.	Cramp.	Intermittent Fever.	Dyphtheria.	Dysentery.	Typhus Fever.	Hooping Cough.	Influenza.
1. Plaster Cove				3			2	
2. Judique								
3. River Inhabitants								
4. Port Hood								
5. Mabou			2			2	2	
6. Broad Cove (Intervale)			1				1	
7. Broad Cove								
8. Margaree				4				
9. Young's Bridge		1		4				
10. Friar's Head			1	4		1		
11. Cheticamp				15				
12. Whycocomagh	1							
13. Lake Ainslie								
14. River Dennis								
15. North-east Margaree				3				
	1	1	4	33		3	5	

COUNTY OF

POLLING DISTRICTS.	Cholera.	Cramp.	Intermittent Fever.	Dyphtheria.	Dysentery.	Typhus Fever.	Hooping Cough.	Influenza.
1. Arichat				8		2		
2. Petit Degrat				38		3	1	
3. D'Escouse				60		4		
4. Black River								
5. River Bourgeoise							1	
6. St. Peter's				4				
7. L'Ardoise			2				1	
8. Grand River								
9. Red Islands								
10. River Inhabitants								
11. Little Arichat				41		5		
12. Loch Lomond								
13. Flamboise		1						
		1	2	151		14	3	

AND CAUSES OF DEATHS...1860—61.

GUYSBOROUGH.

Contagious Diseases.						Diseases of the Nervous System.							
Measles.	Mumps.	Scarlet Fever.	Small Pox.	Hives.	Total.	Apoplexy.	Brain Fever.	Disease of Brain.	Epilepsy.	Paralysis.	Insanity.	Convulsions.	Total.
		5			18		1	3				1	5
		7			17		1	1					2
		4			10			1					1
		3			14								
		3			10								
		2			5					1			1
1			1		9			1					1
		6			9								
						1							1
		3	2		11					1			1
1		33	3		103		3	6		2		1	12

INVERNESS.

Measles.	Mumps.	Scarlet Fever.	Small Pox.	Hives.	Total.	Apoplexy.	Brain Fever.	Disease of Brain.	Epilepsy.	Paralysis.	Insanity.	Convulsions.	Total.
		1			6								
1					1								
1					1								
1		2			9					1			1
		3			5				1				1
					4								
		1			6								
2					8								
					15								
1					2			1					1
							1						1
		1			4					1			1
6		8			61	1	1			2	1		5

RICHMOND.

Measles.	Mumps.	Scarlet Fever.	Small Pox.	Hives.	Total.	Apoplexy.	Brain Fever.	Disease of Brain.	Epilepsy.	Paralysis.	Insanity.	Convulsions.	Total.
					10			1				3	4
		1			43								
					64								
		17			18								
		5			9								
1		12			16		1						1
			1		1								
1		3			4								
1		1			2								
1		1			48								
		1			1								
		1			1								
4		41	1		217		1	1				3	5

No: 4.—PERSONAL CENSUS...DEATHS,

COUNTY OF

POLLING DISTRICTS.	Diseases of the Respiratory							
	Asthma.	Bronchitis.	Consumption.	Croup.	Cough.	Disease of Lungs.	Disease of Heart.	Inflammation of Lungs.
1. Guysborough			3	1				
2. Intervale			5					
3. Manchester			5				3	
4. Melford			3					1
5. Crow Harbor			1					
6. Cape Canso			1	2				
7. Country Harbor								
8. Sherbrooke								
9. Marie Joseph				1				
10. Forks, St. Mary's			1					1
11. Molasses Harbor								
			19	4			3	2

COUNTY OF

1. Plaster Cove			5					
2. Judique			5				1	
3. River Inhabitants			4				1	
4. Port Hood			3					
5. Mabon			8	1				
6. Broad Cove (Intervale)			1				1	
7. Broad Cove								
8. Margaree			1					
9. Young's Bridge			1					
10. Friar's Head			4	3				
11. Cheticamp			7					
12. Whycocomagh			2	1				1
13. Lake Ainslie			1					
14. River Dennis			2					
15. North-east Margaree								
			44	5			3	1

COUNTY OF

1. Arichat			1					
2. Petit Degrat	1		5	1			1	
3. D'Escouse			6					
4. Black River			4	1				
5. River Bourgeoise			1					
6. St. Peter's			1					
7. L'Ardoise			4					
8. Grand River			3					
9. Red Islands			2					
10. River Inhabitants			1					
11. Little Arichat								
12. Loch Lomond								
13. Flamboise			3					
	1		31	2			1	

AND CAUSES OF DEATHS...1860—61.

GUYSBOROUGH, Continued.

	and Circulating Organs						Diseases of the Digestive Organs.					
Inflammation of Chest.	Inflammation of Heart.	Pleurisy.	Quinsy.	Sore Throat.	Total.	Bilious Fever.	Disease of Liver.	Disease of Stomach.	Indigestion.	Debility.	Jaundice.	
					4		1					
				1	6							
		2			10				1			
				4	8	1						
					1	1						
					3							
				1	1						1	
		1			1		1					
					1							
					2							
				1	1							
		3		7	38	2	2		1		1	

INVERNESS, Continued.

Inflammation of Chest.	Inflammation of Heart.	Pleurisy.	Quinsy.	Sore Throat.	Total.	Bilious Fever.	Disease of Liver.	Disease of Stomach.	Indigestion.	Debility.	Jaundice.
		1			6						1
		1		1	8						
				1	6						
				2	5						
		3			12	1				2	
		2		1	5	1			1		
					1						
					1						
					7	1					
					7	3				1	
		3			7						
					1						
		1			3						
					4						
		11		5	69	10			1	3	1

RICHMOND, Continued.

Inflammation of Chest.	Inflammation of Heart.	Pleurisy.	Quinsy.	Sore Throat.	Total.	Bilious Fever.	Disease of Liver.	Disease of Stomach.	Indigestion.	Debility.	Jaundice.
				1	2		1				1
		1			9	3					
					6	4					
					5						
				1	2						
					1		1				
		1			5	3					
		1			4						
		2	1		5						
				1	2						
			1	6	7						
					3						
		5	3	8	51	10	2				1

No. 4.—PERSONAL CENSUS...DEATHS,

COUNTY OF

POLLING DISTRICTS.	Diseases of the Digestive Organs—Continued.					
	Inflammation of Bowels.	Inflammation of Stomach.	Disease of Bowels.	Worms.	Teething.	Total.
1. Guysborough	1					2
2. Intervale		1				1
3. Manchester						1
4. Melford						1
5. Crow Harbor						1
6. Cape Canso						
7. Country Harbor						1
8. Sherbrooke			3			4
9. Marie Joseph						
10. Forks, St. Mary's						
11. Molasses Harbor						
	1	1	3			11

COUNTY OF

1. Planter Cove						1
2. Judique		1				1
3. River Inhabitants	1					1
4. Port Hood						
5. Mabou						3
6. Broad Cove (Intervale)						2
7. Broad Cove						
8. Margaree						
9. Young's Bridge						
10. Friar's Head		2				3
11. Cheticamp						4
12. Whycocomagh						
13. Lake Ainslie						
14. River Dennis		2				2
15. North-east Margaree						4
	1	5				21

COUNTY OF

1. Arichat			1	1		4
2. Petit Degrat		1				4
3. D'Escouse					2	6
4. Black River						
5. River Bourgeoise						
6. St. Peter's						1
7. L'Ardoise						3
8. Grand River						
9. Red Islands	1					1
10. River Inhabitants	1					1
11. Little Arichat						
12. Loch Lomond						
13. Flamboise						
	3		1	1	2	20

AND CAUSES OF DEATHS...1860—61.

GUYSBOROUGH, Continued.

	Diseases of Urinary and Generative Organs.						Diseases of Uncertain Seat.					
Disease of Bladder.	Diabetes.	Inflammation of Kidneys.	Puerperal Fever.	Child-bed.	Total.	Abscess.	Cancer.	Colds.	Scrofula.	After Amputation.	Mortification.
								1			
		1			1			1			
				1	1						
				1	1	1			1		
									1		
				1	1						
				1	1						
		1		4	5	1			4		

INVERNESS, Continued.

				1	1			1			
									1		
							1	1			
									1		
				1	1						
1					1						
								1			
1				2	3	1	3	2			

RICHMOND, Continued.

1				1	2					1	
				2	2						
1					1						
2				3	5					1	

No. 4.—PERSONAL CENSUS...DEATHS,

COUNTY OF

Diseases of Uncertain Seat—*Continued.*

POLLING DISTRICTS.	Dropsy.	Old Age.	Erysipelas.	Intemperance.	Rheumatism.	Rickets.	Tumor.	Carbuncle.	Total.
1. Guysborough	1								2
2. Intervale									1
3. Manchester		2			1				3
4. Melford	1	1							2
5. Crow Harbor		1							3
6. Cape Canso									
7. Country Harbor									1
8. Sherbrooke					2				2
9. Marie Joseph									
10. Forks, St. Mary's	1	1							2
11. Molasses Harbor		1							1
	3	6			3				17

COUNTY OF

POLLING DISTRICTS.	Dropsy.	Old Age.	Erysipelas.	Intemperance.	Rheumatism.	Rickets.	Tumor.	Carbuncle.	Total.
1. Plaster Cove		2							2
2. Judique									1
3. River Inhabitants							1		2
4. Port Hood		3							3
5. Mabou		1			1				4
6. Broad Cove (Intervale)		2							2
7. Broad Cove									
8. Margaree									
9. Young's Bridge									
10. Friar's Head					1				2
11. Cheticamp									
12. Whycocomagh									
13. Lake Ainslie	1								1
14. River Dennis		1							2
15. North-east Margaree		1							1
	1	10			2		1		20

COUNTY OF

POLLING DISTRICTS.	Dropsy.	Old Age.	Erysipelas.	Intemperance.	Rheumatism.	Rickets.	Tumor.	Carbuncle.	Total.
1. Arichat									
2. Petit Degrat		1			2				4
3. D'Escouse					1				1
4. Black River									
5. River Bourgeoise									
6. St. Peter's									
7. L'Ardoise									
8. Grand River									
9. Red Islands	1								1
10. River Inhabitants			1						1
11. Little Arichat									
12. Loch Lomond									
13. Flamboise									
	1	1	1		3				7

AND CAUSES OF DEATHS...1860—61.

GUYSBOROUGH, Continued.

	Violent and Accidental Deaths.						Diseases of Organs of Sight & Hearing.				
Burns and Scalds.	Frozen.	Drowned.	Murdered.	Poisoned.	Other Accidents.	Total.	Disease of Eye.	Disease of Ear.	Total.	Causes not specified.	Total of Deaths.
											31
										4	32
										1	26
1						1					27
											16
		2		1		3				1	13
											13
		2				2					19
		1				1				2	5
1						1					18
				1		1					3
2		5		2		9				8	203

INVERNESS, Continued.

										3	18
											13
										1	10
										3	12
			1	1						5	35
										3	18
										2	2
											5
										1	8
		2			2					2	21
										5	32
4		1			1					2	13
1					1					3	8
										4	11
											10
1		3		1	5					34	218

RICHMOND, Continued.

										4	24
		3			3					2	67
										5	82
		1			1						6
		1			1						23
1		1			2					1	15
											25
				1	1					1	7
										1	12
		1			1					2	9
		1			1					2	58
1					1						2
											4
2		8		1	11					18	334

No. 4.—PERSONAL CENSUS...DEATHS,

COUNTY OF

POLLING DISTRICTS.	Epidemic, Endemic, and							
	Cholera.	Cramp.	Intermittent Fever.	Dyptheria.	Dysentery.	Typhus Fever.	Hooping Cough.	Influenza.
1. Washabok								
2. Middle River								
3. Baddeck								
4. Munro's Point, St. Ann's								
5. Englishtown, St. Ann's					1			
6. Boulardrie							1	
7. Ingonish								
8. Cape North								
9. Bay St. Lawrence								
10. Little Narrows								
					1		1	

COUNTY OF

POLLING DISTRICTS.	Cholera.	Cramp.	Intermittent Fever.	Dyptheria.	Dysentery.	Typhus Fever.	Hooping Cough.	Influenza.
1. Sydney				1				
2. Ball's Bridge								
3. Mira Ferry				3				
4. Sydney Mines							2	2
5. Mainadieu								
6. Louisburg				9				
7. Gabarus				1				
8. East Bay		2						
9. Beaver Cove								
10. Howley's Ferry								
11. Lingan Mines							•	
12. Cow Bay								
13. Big Pond				1				
14. Christmas Island		2		2				
		4		17			2	2

COUNTY OF

POLLING DISTRICTS.	Cholera.	Cramp.	Intermittent Fever.	Dyptheria.	Dysentery.	Typhus Fever.	Hooping Cough.	Influenza.
1. Windsor				4			1	
2. St. Croix								
3. Brooklyn				2				
4. Scotch Village				17			1	
5. Falmouth								
6. Kempt				3		1		
7. Rawdon Church							1	
8. South Rawdon								
9. Noel				16		1		
10. Nine Mile River	1							
11. Maitland				4				
12. Chester Road				5		1		
	1			58		3	3	

AND CAUSES OF DEATHS...1860—61.

VICTORIA.

	Contagious Diseases.						Diseases of the Nervous System.							
	Measles.	Mumps.	Scarlet Fever.	Small Pox.	Hives.	Total.	Apoplexy.	Brain Fever.*	Disease of Brain.	Epilepsy.	Paralysis.	Insanity.	Convulsions.	Total.
			3			3							1	1
			1			1								
			5			5								
	2		2			2				1				
	12		2			5					1		1	1
						1						12	12	12
	1					1						12	12	12
	5		11			18					1	1	6	8

CAPE BRETON.

	Measles.	Mumps.	Scarlet Fever.	Small Pox.	Hives.	Total.	Apoplexy.	Brain Fever.*	Disease of Brain.	Epilepsy.	Paralysis.	Insanity.	Convulsions.	Total.
	1		4			6	1		1				2	4
	4			1		5								
	13		1			3								
			1			18	1						1	2
			1			7								
						10								
	2					3		1		1		2	4	
	1					3		1		1			2	
												1	1	
	3			1		4								
								1					1	
						1				1			1	
						4								
	24		13	2		64	2	3		1	3		6	15

HANTS.

No. 4.—PERSONAL CENSUS...DEATHS,

COUNTY OF

POLLING DISTRICTS.	Asthma.	Bronchitis.	Consumption.	Croup.	Cough.	Disease of Lungs.	Disease of Heart.	Inflammation of Lungs.
					Diseases of the Respiratory			
1. Washabok			8					
2. Middle River								
3. Baddeck			1	2				
4. Munro's Point, St. Ann's			2				1	
5. Englishtown, St. Ann's			3					
6. Boularderie			1	1				
7. Ingonish			3					
8. Cape North			3					
9. Bay St. Lawrence			2					
10. Little Narrows								
			23	3			1	

COUNTY OF

1. Sydney			6	3				
2. Ball's Bridge			5	4				
3. Mira Ferry	1		2					
4. Sydney Mines	1		5			1		
5. Mainadieu			3					
6. Louisburg				2				1
7. Gabarus								
8. East Bay			1				1	
9. Beaver Cove								
10. Howley's Ferry			1					
11. Lingan Mines			5					
12. Cow Bay			3					
13. Big Pond			1					
14. Christmas Island			3					
	2		35	9		1	1	1

COUNTY OF

1. Windsor			8				1	
2. St. Croix			4					1
3. Brooklyn			6					
4. Scotch Village			7					
5. Falmouth			2			1		
6. Kempt			3	1				4
7. Rawdon Church	1		1					1
8. South Rawdon			1	1		1		1
9. Noel			6	3	1		1	
10. Nine Mile River			3	1				2
11. Maitland			5					
12. Chester Road								
	1		46	6	1	2	2	9

AND CAUSES OF DEATHS...1860—61.

VICTORIA, Continued.

Inflammation of Chest.	Inflammation of Heart.	Pleurisy.	Quinsy.	Sore Throat.	Total.	Bilious Fever.	Disease of Liver.	Disease of Stomach.	Indigestion.	Debility.	Jaundice.
					8						
				2	2						1
					3	1					
					3						
					3						
		1			3						
				1	4						
					3						
					2						
						1					
		1		3	31	2					1

CAPE BRETON, Continued.

Inflammation of Chest.	Inflammation of Heart.	Pleurisy.	Quinsy.	Sore Throat.	Total.	Bilious Fever.	Disease of Liver.	Disease of Stomach.	Indigestion.	Debility.	Jaundice.
		1		2	12						
		3			12						1
		1			4						
		1			8						
		2			5						
		2			5		1				
		1			1						
		3	1	1	7	1					
		4		1	5						
		1			2						
		3	1		9						
					3						
		1			2						
					3						1
		23	2	4	78	1	1				2

HANTS, Continued.

Inflammation of Chest.	Inflammation of Heart.	Pleurisy.	Quinsy.	Sore Throat.	Total.	Bilious Fever.	Disease of Liver.	Disease of Stomach.	Indigestion.	Debility.	Jaundice.
				2	11		1				
				2	7						
					6						
					7			1			1
				1	4						
				1	9						
					3						
					4						
				4	15						1
		1			7		1				
					5						1
		1		10	78		2	1			3

No. 4.—PERSONAL CENSUS...DEATHS,

COUNTY OF

POLLING DISTRICTS.	Inflammation of Bowels.	Inflammation of Stomach.	Disease of Bowels.	Worms.	Teething.	Total.
			Diseases of the Digestive Organs—*Continued.*			
1. Washabok	1					1
2. Middle River	1					2
3. Baddeck						1
4. Munro's Point, St. Ann's			1		1	2
5. Englishtown, St. Ann's						
6. Boularderie						
7. Ingonish	1					1
8. Cape North						
9. Bay St. Lawrence						
10. Little Narrows						1
	3		1		1	8

COUNTY OF

1. Sydney	2					2
2. Ball's Bridge			1			2
3. Mira Ferry						
4. Sydney Mines	1	1				2
5. Mainadieu	4					4
6. Louisburg						1
7. Gabarus						
8. East Bay						1
9. Beaver Cove			3			3
10. Howley's Ferry						
11. Lingan Mines						
12. Cow Bay						
13. Big Pond						
14. Christmas Island						1
	7	1	4			16

COUNTY OF

1. Windsor			1			2
2. St. Croix		1				1
3. Brooklyn						
4. Scotch Village	1		1	1		5
5. Falmouth	1		1			2
6. Kempt			1			1
7. Rawdon Church						
8. South Rawdon						
9. Noel	1					2
10. Nine Mile River						1
11. Maitland						1
12. Chester Road						
	3	1	4	1		15

AND CAUSES OF DEATHS...1860—61.

VICTORIA, Continued.

		Diseases of Urinary and Generative Organs.						Diseases of Uncertain Seat.				
Disease of Bladder.	Diabetes.	Inflammation of Kidneys.	Puerperal Fever.	Child-bed.	Total.	Abscess.	Cancer.	Colds.	Scrofula.	After Amputation.	Mortification.
				1	1		1				
							1	1			
1					1			1			
				1	1			1			
1				2	3		2	2			

CAPE BRETON, Continued.

											1
							2				
		1		1	2			1			
				2	2		1				
				2	2			1			
		1		5	6		3	3			1

HANTS, Continued.

							2				
									1		
			1		1						
						1					
			1		1	1		2	1		

No. 4.—PERSONAL CENSUS...DEATHS,

COUNTY OF

POLLING DISTRICTS.	\<div\>Diseases of Uncertain Seat—*Continued.*\</div\> Dropsy.	Old Age.	Erysipelas.	Intemperance.	Rheumatism.	Rickets.	Tumor.	Carbuncle.	Total.
1. Washabok									1
2. Middle River	1								3
3. Baddeck					2				2
4. Munro's Point, St. Ann's		2		1					3
5. Englishtown, St. Ann's									
6. Boulardrie						3			3
7. Ingonish			1						1
8. Cape North									1
9. Bay St. Lawrence									1
10. Little Narrows									
	1	3		1	5				15

COUNTY OF

POLLING DISTRICTS.	Dropsy.	Old Age.	Erysipelas.	Intemperance.	Rheumatism.	Rickets.	Tumor.	Carbuncle.	Total.
1. Sydney		1	1						3
2. Ball's Bridge	2	1	1		2				8
3. Mira Ferry									
4. Sydney Mines	1								1
5. Mainadieu		2							2
6. Louisburg		1							2
7. Gabarus		1			1				3
8. East Bay	1	1	1						3
9. Beaver Cove									1
10. Howley's Ferry									
11. Lingan Mines									
12. Cow Bay					2				3
13. Big Pond									
14. Christmas Island		1							1
	4	8	3		5				27

COUNTY OF

POLLING DISTRICTS.	Dropsy.	Old Age.	Erysipelas.	Intemperance.	Rheumatism.	Rickets.	Tumor.	Carbuncle.	Total.
1. Windsor									2
2. St. Croix									
3. Brooklyn			4						4
4. Scotch Village		2	1						4
5. Falmouth									
6. Kempt	1								1
7. Rawdon Church		2							2
8. South Rawdon	1								1
9. Nool	2	2							4
10. Nine Mile River	1	1			1				4
11. Maitland		3							3
12. Chester Road	1								1
	6	10	5		1				26

AND CAUSES OF DEATHS...1860--61.

VICTORIA, Continued.

Burns and Scalds	Frozen	Drowned	Murdered	Poisoned	Other Accidents	Total	Disease of Eye	Disease of Ear	Total	Causes not specified	Total of Deaths
										2	17
		1				1					9
										1	12
		1				1				1	13
										4	14
										5	14
										1	10
			1			1				1	7
											4
										2	3
		2	1			3				17	103

CAPE BRETON, Continued.

Burns and Scalds	Frozen	Drowned	Murdered	Poisoned	Other Accidents	Total	Disease of Eye	Disease of Ear	Total	Causes not specified	Total of Deaths
		1				1				4	32
1						1				1	29
										1	8
		1		1		2				6	39
		1				1				1	20
										2	20
		1				1					14
										5	21
										3	15
			1			1					3
											15
											7
											4
	1					1				4	14
1		5		2		8				27	241

HANTS, Continued.

Burns and Scalds	Frozen	Drowned	Murdered	Poisoned	Other Accidents	Total	Disease of Eye	Disease of Ear	Total	Causes not specified	Total of Deaths
				1		1				1	25
										1	10
										1	23
		1		1		2					43
				1		1					10
		1				1				2	23
										2	8
											6
1						1				3	44
										6	24
										3	19
										1	8
1		2		3		6				20	243

21

No. 4.—PERSONAL CENSUS...DEATHS,

COUNTY OF

POLLING DISTRICTS.	Cholera.	Cramp.	Intermittent Fever.	Dyptheria.	Dysentery.	Typhus Fever.	Hooping Cough.	Influenza.
				Epidemic, Endemic, and				
1. Canning	1			15			2	1	I
2. Canard			1	6					1
3. Centreville				8					
4. Lakeville				5					
5. Somerset				23					1
6. Kentville				10					
7. Gaspereaux				10		1			
8. Wolfville				5					
9. Lower Horton				2					
10. Aylesford				37					
11. West Sherbrooke									
12. Aylesford				13					
13. Berwick				10					
	1		1	144			3	1	3

COUNT OF

1. Wilmot				18			1		
2. Wilmot, Middleton Corner				8			2		
3. Clarence, Wilmot				5					
4. Bridgetown				3					
5. Bellisle				5					
6. New Caledonia	1			10					1
7. Broad Cove				2					
8. Clementsport				6			1		
9. Hessian Line				5					
10. Annapolis Royal									
11. Carleton's Corner				2					
12. Nictaux				2					1
13. Dalhousie				2					
14. Maitland				3					
15. Morse Road			3	6					
	1		3	75			4		2

COUNTY OF

1. Hillsburg				7					
2. Head St. Mary's Bay				1				1	
3. Digby			1	11					
4. Sandy Cove				1					
5. Long Island									
6. Westport									
7. On St. Mary's Bay									
8. Weymouth				1					
9. Belivoe Cove									
10. Session House, Clare									
11. Montegan									
12. Salmon River							1		
			1	24			1	1	

AND CAUSES OF DEATHS...1860—61.

KING'S.

						Diseases of the Nervous System.							
Measles.	Mumps.	Scarlet Fever.	Small Pox.	Hives.	Total.	Apoplexy.	Brain Fever.	Disease of Brain.	Epilepsy.	Paralysis.	Insanity.	Convulsions.	Total.
4					24							1	1
1					9								
			1		9		1	1					2
			1		6								
					24		1	1					2
2					12			1			1		2
					11								
					5		1						1
			1		3					1		1	2
					37			2					2
					13	1					1	1	3
					10	1							1
7			3		163	5	5		1	1		4	16

ANNAPOLIS.

1		2			22			3					3
					10								
					3	1						1	2
					3			3					3
					5							3	3
					12	1							1
					2								
					7		1						1
					5					1			1
											1		1
					2	1	1						2
2		1			6								
					2			1					1
					3								
					9								
3		3			91	2	2	8		1		5	18

DIGBY.

					7								
					2								
					15								
					1							1	1
		1			1							1	1
			1		1								
									1				1
					1	1	1						2
		1			1								
								1					1
3					4	1							1
3		2	1		33	2	2		1		2	7	

No. 4.—PERSONAL CENSUS...DEATHS,

COUNTY OF

POLLING DISTRICTS.	Asthma.	Bronchitis.	Diseases of the Respiratory					
			Consumption.	Croup.	Cough.	Disease of Lungs.	Disease of Heart.	Inflammation of Lungs.
1. Canning			4					1
2. Canard			3					1
3. Centreville			3	2			2	1
4. Lakeville			6				1	
5. Somerset			6				1	1
6. Kentville			5				1	1
7. Gaspereaux			4					2
8. Wolfville			3				1	1
9. Lower Horton			4	1			2	2
10. Aylesford			6				1	2
11. West Sherbrooke								
12. Aylesford			5					1
13. Berwick			3					
			52	3			9	13

COUNTY OF

	Asthma.	Bronchitis.	Consumption.	Croup.	Cough.	Disease of Lungs.	Disease of Heart.	Inflammation of Lungs.
1. Wilmot			14					1
2. Wilmot, Middleton Corner			5	1				
3. Clarence, Wilmot			5	1			1	
4. Bridgetown		1	10	1				1
5. Bellisle			3					
6. New Caledonia			1					
7. Broad Cove			3					
8. Clementsport			3					
9. Hessian Line			1					
10. Annapolis Royal			3					
11. Carleton's Corner			5				1	1
12. Nictaux			7				2	
13. Dalhousie			1					2
14. Maitland								
15. Morse Road			2					
		1	63	3			4	5

COUNTY OF

	Asthma.	Bronchitis.	Consumption.	Croup.	Cough.	Disease of Lungs.	Disease of Heart.	Inflammation of Lungs.
1. Hillsburg			4	1				
2. Head St. Mary's Bay			3				1	
3. Digby		1	4					
4. Sandy Cove			2					
5. Long Island			2					
6. Westport			6					
7. On St. Mary's Bay			1					
8. Weymouth			2					1
9. Belivoe Cove			4					
10. Session House, Clare			3	1				
11. Montegan			1	3				
12. Salmou River			3	1				
		1	35	6			1	1

AND CAUSES OF DEATHS...1860—61.

KING'S, Continued.

	and Circulating Organs.					Diseases of the Digestive Organs.					
Inflammation of Chest.	Inflammation of Heart.	Pleurisy.	Quinsy.	Sore Throat.	Total.	Bilious Fever.	Disease of Liver.	Disease of Stomach.	Indigestion.	Debility.	Jaundice.
					5				1		
					4						
					8	1					1
					7				1		
					8						
				2	9						
1					7						
					5						1
					9						
					9						
					6						
					3						
1				2	80	1			2		2

ANNAPOLIS, Continued.

					15	1	2		2		
				2	8		1				1
				1	8		1				
					13						
					3						
					1						1
					3	2					1
				2	5						
					1						
		1		1	5	2			1		
				1	8		2				
					9	1					
					3						
				1	3	1					
1				8	85	7	6		3		3

DIGBY, Continued.

					5						1
					4						
				2	7	1					
					2						
					2						
					6						
				1	2						
					3						1
					4						
		1	1		6	3				1	
			4		8	3				1	
		1		3	8						2
		2	5	6	57	7				2	4

No. 4.—PERSONAL CENSUS...DEATHS,

COUNTY OF

POLLING DISTRICTS.	Inflammation of Bowels.	Inflammation of Stomach.	Disease of Bowels.	Worms.	Teething.	Total.
1. Canning		3				4
2. Canard						
3. Centreville						2
4. Lakeville						1
5. Somerset	3					3
6. Kentville						
7. Gaspereaux						
8. Wolfville						1
9. Lower Horton						
10. Aylesford						
11. West Sherbrooke	1					1
12. Aylesford						
13. Berwick	2					2
	6	3				14

COUNTY OF

POLLING DISTRICTS.	Inflammation of Bowels.	Inflammation of Stomach.	Disease of Bowels.	Worms.	Teething.	Total.
1. Wilmot						5
2. Wilmot, Middleton Corner	1		2			5
3. Clarence, Wilmot	1					2
4. Bridgetown						
5. Bellisle				1		1
6. New Caledonia						1
7. Broad Cove						3
8. Clementsport						
9. Hessian Line						
10. Annapolis Royal			1			4
11. Carleton's Corner						2
12. Nictaux	2		1			4
13. Dalhousie						
14. Maitland						
15. Morse Road						1
	4		4	1		28

COUNTY OF

POLLING DISTRICTS.	Inflammation of Bowels.	Inflammation of Stomach.	Disease of Bowels.	Worms.	Teething.	Total.
1. Hillsburg				1		2
2. Head St. Mary's Bay						
3. Digby		1	1			3
4. Sandy Cove						
5. Long Island	1					1
6. Westport						
7. On St. Mary's Bay						
8. Weymouth						1
9. Belivos Cove				1		1
10. Session House, Clare						4
11. Montegan						4
12. Salmon River	2					4
	3	1	2	1		20

AND CAUSES OF DEATHS...1860—61.

KING'S, Continued.

	Diseases of Urinary and Generative Organs.						Diseases of Uncertain Seat.					
Disease of Bladder.	Diabetes.	Inflammation of Kidneys.	Puerperal Fever.	Child-bed.	Total.	Abscess.	Cancer.	Colds.	Scrofula.	After Amputation.	Mortification.
										1	
				1	1						
								1			
				1	1				1	1	

ANNAPOLIS, Continued.

							1				
						1					
							1				
		1			1				1		
									1		
		1			1	1	1	3			

DIGBY, Continued.

			1	1							
						1	1				
			1	1							
								1			
			2	2		1	1	1			

No. 4.—PERSONAL CENSUS...DEATHS,

COUNTY OF

POLLING DISTRICTS.	Diseases of Uncertain Seat—*Continued.*								
	Dropsy.	Old Age.	Erysipelas.	Intemperance.	Rheumatism.	Rickets.	Tumor.	Carbuncle.	Total.
1. Canning									
2. Canard		1							1
3. Centreville									
4. Lakeville		1						1	2
5. Somerset		1							1
6. Kentville									1
7. Gaspereaux			1						1
8. Wolfville	1		1						2
9. Lower Horton			1						1
10. Aylesford		1							2
11. West Sherbrooke									
12. Aylesford	1								1
13. Berwick									
	2	4	3					1	12

COUNTY OF

POLLING DISTRICTS.	Dropsy.	Old Age.	Erysipelas.	Intemperance.	Rheumatism.	Rickets.	Tumor.	Carbuncle.	Total.
1. Wilmot		2							3
2. Wilmot, Middleton Corner	1	2	1						4
3. Clarence, Wilmot		1							1
4. Bridgetown		2			1				3
5. Bellisle		1	1						3
6. New Caledonia		2							2
7. Broad Cove									
8. Clementsport	2	1							3
9. Hessian Line	1								2
10. Annapolis Royal	1								1
11. Carleton's Corner									
12. Nictaux									1
13. Dalhousie		1							2
14. Maitland									
15. Morse Road									
	5	12	2		1				25

COUNTY OF

POLLING DISTRICTS.	Dropsy.	Old Age.	Erysipelas.	Intemperance.	Rheumatism.	Rickets.	Tumor.	Carbuncle.	Total.
1. Hillsburg									
2. Head St. Mary's Bay	1	1			2				4
3. Digby			1						3
4. Sandy Cove	1	1			1				3
5. Long Island									
6. Westport		1							1
7. On St. Mary's Bay	1								1
8. Weymouth									
9. Belivoe Cove	1								1
10. Session House, Clare		3			2				6
11. Montegan									
12. Salmon River	1		2						3
	5	6	3		5				22

AND CAUSES OF DEATHS...1860--61.

KING'S, Continued.

Burns and Scalds.	Frozen.	Drowned.	Murdered.	Poisoned.	Other Accidents.	Total.	Disease of Eye.	Disease of Ear.	Total.	Causes not specified.	Total of Deaths.
										1	35
										3	17
											21
										1	17
					1	1				5	44
		3			1	4				1	29
											19
		2				2					16
		1			1	2					18
										1	51
											1
1						1					.24
										1	17
1		6			3	10				13	309

ANNAPOLIS, Continued.

Burns and Scalds.	Frozen.	Drowned.	Murdered.	Poisoned.	Other Accidents.	Total.	Disease of Eye.	Disease of Ear.	Total.	Causes not specified.	Total of Deaths.
		1			1	2				1	51
											27
											16
		1			1					4	27
		1			1						16
										3	20
											8
										2	18
		1			1						5
										2	18
											15
			1		1						21
										1	9
											3
											13
		4			2	6				13	267

DIGBY, Continued.

Burns and Scalds.	Frozen.	Drowned.	Murdered.	Poisoned.	Other Accidents.	Total.	Disease of Eye.	Disease of Ear.	Total.	Causes not specified.	Total of Deaths.
		2			2						16
										1	12
		1			1					2	31
										1	8
		1			1						6
				2	2						10
										1	6
		1			1					1	9
										2	9
						1			1	1	19
										2	14
		1			1					2	23
		6			2	6	1		1	13	163

22

No. 4.—PERSONAL CENSUS...DEATHS,

COUNTY OF

POLLING DISTRICTS.	Epidemic, Endemic, and							
	Cholera.	Cramp.	Intermittent Fever.	Dyptheria.	Dysentery.	Typhus Fever.	Hooping Cough.	Influenza.
1. Ohio				5				
2. Yarmouth			2	2		1		
3. Chebogue				2				
4. Carleton				1		1		
5. Plymouth			1					1
6. Tusket		1		4				
7. Argyle				1				
8. Pubnico				1	1			
9. Kempt								
10. West side Tusket River								
		1	3	16	1	2		1

COUNTY OF

POLLING DISTRICTS.	Cholera.	Cramp.	Intermittent Fever.	Dyptheria.	Dysentery.	Typhus Fever.	Hooping Cough.	Influenza.
1. Carleton Village								
2. Shelburne				16				
3. Ragged Islands				3				
4. Louis Head								
5. Shag Harbor								
6. Cape Sable Island								
7. Barrington				2				
8. Port LaTour							2	
				21		2		

COUNTY OF

POLLING DISTRICTS.	Cholera.	Cramp.	Intermittent Fever.	Dyptheria.	Dysentery.	Typhus Fever.	Hooping Cough.	Influenza.
1. Liverpool			1	14		2		
2. Bristol				6		2		
3. Port Medway				6		1		
4. Port Mouton								
5. Brookfield								
6. Caledonia				13				
7. Greenfield								
			1	39		3		

COUNTY OF

POLLING DISTRICTS.	Cholera.	Cramp.	Intermittent Fever.	Dyptheria.	Dysentery.	Typhus Fever.	Hooping Cough.	Influenza.
1. Lunenburg				21				
2. Ritsey's Cove				10				
3. Mahone Bay				1				
4. LaHave				2				
5. New Germany				15				1
6. Chester				11		1		
7. Sherbrooke								
8. Petite Riviere				25				
9. Bridgewater				31				
10. Tancook Island				2				
11. Mill Cove, St. Margaret's Bay				2				
				120		1		1

AND CAUSES OF DEATHS...1860—61.

YARMOUTH.

	Contagious Diseases.					Diseases of the Nervous System.							
Measles.	Mumps.	Scarlet Fever.	Small Pox.	Hives.	Total.	Apoplexy.	Brain Fever.	Disease of Brain.	Epilepsy.	Paralysis.	Insanity.	Convulsions.	Total.
					5		1	3					4
3		2			10		2	1					3
2					4		1	1					2
					2		1	1					2
3					5							2	2
5					10		1	1				3	5
1					1	1	2			1			4
					3			1				1	2
14		2			40	1	8	8		1		6	24

SHELBURNE.

Measles.	Mumps.	Scarlet Fever.	Small Pox.	Hives.	Total.	Apoplexy.	Brain Fever.	Disease of Brain.	Epilepsy.	Paralysis.	Insanity.	Convulsions.	Total.
4					4								
2					18		1			1			2
2					5			1			1		2
1					1								
1					1		1						1
								1					1
					2	2		1		1		1	5
					2								
10					33	2	3	2		2	1	1	11

QUEEN'S.

Measles.	Mumps.	Scarlet Fever.	Small Pox.	Hives.	Total.	Apoplexy.	Brain Fever.	Disease of Brain.	Epilepsy.	Paralysis.	Insanity.	Convulsions.	Total.
					15	1				1			2
4					12		1	1		1		1	3
					7	1	1			1			2
										1		2	1
													2
					13								
4					47	2	2			3		3	10

LUNENBURG.

Measles.	Mumps.	Scarlet Fever.	Small Pox.	Hives.	Total.	Apoplexy.	Brain Fever.	Disease of Brain.	Epilepsy.	Paralysis.	Insanity.	Convulsions.	Total.
7					28		1		3				4
1					11		1					2	3
3		1			5		1						1
1					3				1				1
					16							2	2
					12	1							1
3					3							3	3
5		3			33						2	5	7
3					34					1		1	2
1					3							1	1
2					4							2	2
26		4			152	1	3			5	2	16	27

No. 4.—PERSONAL CENSUS...DEATHS,

COUNTY OF

POLLING DISTRICTS.	Diseases of the Respiratory							
	Asthma.	Bronchitis.	Consumption.	Croup.	Cough.	Disease of Lungs.	Disease of Heart.	Inflammation of Lungs.
1. Ohio			9				2	2
2. Yarmouth			10	1			3	4
3. Chebogue			8				1	1
4. Carleton			2					
5. Plymouth			3					1
6. Tusket			9	2				2
7. Argyle	1		1					
8. Pubnico			1				1	
9. Kempt								
10. West side Tusket River								
	1		43	3			7	10

COUNTY OF

1. Carleton Village			7	1			2	
2. Shelburne			4					2
3. Ragged Islands			1				1	1
4. Louis Head			3					1
5. Shag Harbor			4	1				
6. Cape Sable Island			7			2		
7. Barrington			5	1			1	1
8. Port LaTour			4	2			1	2
			35	5		2	5	7

COUNTY OF

1. Liverpool			8	3				1
2. Bristol			3	1				4
3. Port Medway			2	1				2
4. Port Monton			2					1
5. Brookfield			1	1				
6. Caledonia								
7. Greenfield								
			16	6				8

COUNTY OF

1. Lunenburg			4	7			1	1
2. Ritsey's Cove			3					
3. Mahone Bay			7	4	1			
4. LaHave			1				1	
5. New Germany	1		2	2				
6. Chester			10					
7. Sherbrooke								
8. Petite Riviere		1	6	6				
9. Bridgewater			3	2				1
10. Tancook Island								
11. Mill Cove, St. Margaret's Bay				1				
	1	1	36	22	1		2	2

AND CAUSES OF DEATHS...1860—61.

YARMOUTH, Continued.

	and Circulating Organs.					Diseases of the Digestive Organs.					
Inflammation of Chest	Inflammation of Heart	Pleurisy	Quinsy	Sore Throat	Total	Bilious Fever	Disease of Liver	Disease of Stomach	Indigestion	Debility	Jaundice
					13						
					18	1	1			1	
					10	1	1				1
					2						
				1	5						
		1			14				1		
					2	2			1		
					2		1				
				1	1						
		1		2	67	4	3		2	1	1

SHELBURNE, Continued.

				1	11						
				1	7						
					3				1		
					4						
		1			6						
					9						
					8						1
					9						
		1		2	57				1		1

QUEEN'S, Continued.

1					13						1
					8	1	1		1		
				2	7	1					
				1	4						
					2						
		1			1						
1				1	3	35	2	1		1	1

LUNENBURG, Continued.

					13						
				3	6						
					12						
		1			3						
				6	11				1		
					10	2			1		
					13						
					6						
					1						
		1		9	75	2			2		

No. 4.—PERSONAL CENSUS...DEATHS,

COUNTY OF

Diseases of the Digestive Organs—*Continued.*

POLLING DISTRICTS.	Inflammation of Bowels.	Inflammation of Stomach.	Disease of Bowels.	Worms.	Teething.	Total.
1. Ohio	5					5
2. Yarmouth	4		1			8
3. Chebogue	2	1	1			7
4. Carleton	1					1
5. Plymouth	2		1			3
6. Tusket						1
7. Argyle						3
8. Pubnico						1
9. Kempt						
10. West side Tusket River						
	14	1	3			29

COUNTY OF

	Inflammation of Bowels.	Inflammation of Stomach.	Disease of Bowels.	Worms.	Teething.	Total.
1. Carleton Village		1				1
2. Shelburne						
3. Ragged Islands						1
4. Louis Head						
5. Shag Harbor			3			3
6. Cape Sable Island						
7. Barrington						1
8. Port LaTour	2					2
	2	1	3			8

COUNTY OF

	Inflammation of Bowels.	Inflammation of Stomach.	Disease of Bowels.	Worms.	Teething.	Total.
1. Liverpool	2	3				6
2. Bristol	1					4
3. Port Medway	1		1			3
4. Port Mouton						
5. Brookfield				1		1
6. Caledonia	1			1		2
7. Greenfield						
	5	3	1	2		16

COUNTY OF

	Inflammation of Bowels.	Inflammation of Stomach.	Disease of Bowels.	Worms.	Teething.	Total.
1. Lunenburg			1			1
2. Ritsoy's Cove						
3. Mahone Bay						
4. LaHave						
5. New Germany						1
6. Chester	1					4
7. Sherbrooke						
8. Petite Riviere						
9. Bridgewater	1					1
10. Tancook Island						
11. Mill Cove, St. Margaret's Bay				1	1	2
	2		1	1	1	9

AND CAUSES OF DEATHS...1860—61.

YARMOUTH, Continued.

		Diseases of Urinary and Generative Organs.				Diseases of Uncertain Seat.					
Diseases of Bladder.	Diabetes.	Inflammation of Kidneys.	Puerperal Fever.	Child-bed.	Total.	Abscess.	Cancer.	Colds.	Scrofula.	After Amputation.	Mortification.
											1
				2	2			1			
				1	1						
									1		
				3	3				2		1

SHELBURNE, Continued.

		Diseases of Urinary and Generative Organs.				Diseases of Uncertain Seat.					
Diseases of Bladder.	Diabetes.	Inflammation of Kidneys.	Puerperal Fever.	Child-bed.	Total.	Abscess.	Cancer.	Colds.	Scrofula.	After Amputation.	Mortification.
					1						
					1						

QUEEN'S, Continued.

		Diseases of Urinary and Generative Organs.				Diseases of Uncertain Seat.					
Diseases of Bladder.	Diabetes.	Inflammation of Kidneys.	Puerperal Fever.	Child-bed.	Total.	Abscess.	Cancer.	Colds.	Scrofula.	After Amputation.	Mortification.
							1				
							1				

LUNENBURG, Continued.

		Diseases of Urinary and Generative Organs.				Diseases of Uncertain Seat.					
Diseases of Bladder.	Diabetes.	Inflammation of Kidneys.	Puerperal Fever.	Child-bed.	Total.	Abscess.	Cancer.	Colds.	Scrofula.	After Amputation.	Mortification.
1				1		1					
			3	3				1			
								1			
	1			1		2					
1		1		3	5		3	2			

No. 4.—PERSONAL CENSUS...DEATHS,

COUNTY OF

Diseases of Uncertain Seat—*Continued.*

POLLING DISTRICTS.	Dropsy.	Old Age.	Erysipelas.	Intemperance.	Rheumatism.	Rickets.	Tumor.	Carbuncle.	Total.
1. Ohio	1								2
2. Yarmouth	1								2
3. Chebogue	1								1
4. Carleton									
5. Plymouth	1		1						2
6. Tusket			1						1
7. Argyle	1								1
8. Pubnico	1				1				2
9. Kempt	2								3
10. West side Tusket River									
	8		2		1				14

COUNTY OF

POLLING DISTRICTS.	Dropsy.	Old Age.	Erysipelas.	Intemperance.	Rheumatism.	Rickets.	Tumor.	Carbuncle.	Total.
1. Carleton Village									
2. Shelburne				1			1		2
3. Ragged Islands	1	1	1						3
4. Louis Head		1							1
5. Shag Harbor									1
6. Cape Sable Island	2	1							3
7. Barrington	1								1
8. Port LaTour		1							1
	4	4	2				1		12

COUNTY OF

POLLING DISTRICTS.	Dropsy.	Old Age.	Erysipelas.	Intemperance.	Rheumatism.	Rickets.	Tumor.	Carbuncle.	Total.
1. Liverpool	2								2
2. Bristol					1				2
3. Port Medway	1								1
4. Port Mouton									
5. Brookfield									
6. Caledonia		1							1
7. Greenfield									
	3	1			1				6

COUNTY OF

POLLING DISTRICTS.	Dropsy.	Old Age.	Erysipelas.	Intemperance.	Rheumatism.	Rickets.	Tumor.	Carbuncle.	Total.
1. Lunenburg		2							3
2. Ritsey's Cove	1								1
3. Mahone Bay									1
4. LaHave		1	1						2
5. New Germany				1					2
6. Chester			1						3
7. Sherbrooke									
8. Petite Riviere	1								1
9. Bridgewater									
10. Tancook Island									
11. Mill Cove, St. Margaret's Bay									
	2	4	2						13

AND CAUSES OF DEATHS...1860—61.

YARMOUTH, Continued.

	Violent and Accidental Deaths.						Diseases of Organs of Sight & Hearing.				
Burns and Scalds.	Frozen.	Drowned.	Murdered.	Poisoned.	Other Accidents.	Total.	Disease of Eye.	Disease of Ear.	Total.	Causes not specified.	Total of Deaths.
1		1				1				2	32
		3		1		4				1	48
		1		1		2				1	27
											7
		1				1				3	21
		1				1				6	39
										1	12
										2	12
					1	1					4
										1	2
		7		3		10				17	204

SHELBURNE, Continued.

3		1				4				1	21
										3	32
		1				1					15
		2				2					8
										2	14
		3				3					16
		1				1					18
				2		2					16
3		8		2		13				6	140

QUEEN'S, Continued.

		1				1				3	42
			1			1				1	31
											20
											5
											5
											17
		1		1		2				4	120

LUNENBURG, Continued.

		3		1		4				4	58
		2				2					23
										1	23
										2	11
				1		1				3	36
											31
										2	8
2						2				2	58
											43
										1	5
1						1					10
3		5		2		10				15	306

23

GENERAL ABSTRACT.

COUNTIES.				Epidemic, Endemic, and Contagious Diseases.													
	Cholera	Croup	Inflammatory Fever	Typhoid	Dysentery	Typhus Fever	Hooping Cough	Influenza	Measles	Mumps	Scarlet Fever	Small Pox	Others	Total
1. { Halifax (City)			2	9			12	1	5		2	8		40
{ " (Outside City)	3			57		4	6		8		6	10		102
Total in County	3		2	66		4	18	1	13		8	37		142
2. Colchester			2	26		3	2	1	7		17	3		62
3. Cumberland				96		10			15		27	2		150
4. Pictou			5	29	1	11	5	8	3		17	1		68
5. Sydney	1	1		39					6		15	2		68
6. Guysborough			1	59			13		1		38	3		103
7. Inverness	1	1	4	33		3	5		6		8			65
8. Richmond		1	2	151		14	3		4		41	1		217
9. Victoria				1					9		11			18
10. Cape Breton		4		17		3	3		24		13	2		64
11. Hants	1			58		3	3		3		9	3		79
12. King's	1		5	144		3	1		7			3		162
13. Annapolis	1			75		3	1	2	3		3			91
14. Digby			1	24		1	1		2		5			33
15. Yarmouth		1	3	16	1	3		1	14		2			40
16. Shelburne				20		3			10					33
17. Queen's		1		29		3			6					47
18. Lunenburg				134		1		1	24		4			153
	12	9	32	2003	2	62	57	12	162		210	49		1593

GENERAL ABSTRACT, Continued.

COUNTIES.			Diseases of the Nervous System.							Diseases of the Respiratory and Circulating Organs.				
	Apoplexy.	Brain Fever.	Disease of Brain	Epilepsy.	Paralysis.	Insanity.	Convulsions.	Total.	Asthma.	Bronchitis.	Consumption.	Croup.	Cough.	
1. { Halifax (City)	4	6	6	2	3		9	30	4	1	57	2		
" (Outside City)	2	3	6		1		8	20	1	1	50	15		
Total in County	6	9	12	2	4		17	50	5	2	107	17		
2. Colchester	1	3	7		2			13		2	45	5	1
3. Cumberland		3	6		1		6	16	2		47	9	
4. Pictou	2	2	3		3	2		20	1	4	50	12	
5. Sydney	2	2		1	2		2	9			40	2	
6. Guysborough		3	6		2		1	13			19	4	
7. Inverness		1	1		2	1		5			44	5	
8. Richmond		1	1				3	6	1		31	2	
9. Victoria					1		1	6			23	3	
10. Cape Breton	2	3		1	3		6	15	2		35	9	
11. Hants		2	8		2		6	18	1		46	6	1
12. King's		5	5		3	1	4	16			52	8	
13. Annapolis	2	2	8		1		5	18		1	53	8	
14. Digby		2	2		1		2	7		1	38	6	
15. Yarmouth	1	8	8		1		6	24	1		43	3	
16. Shelburne	2	3	2		2	1	1	11			35	5	
17. Queen's		2	2		3		3	10			16	6	
18. Lunenburg		1	3		5	2	10	27	1	1	36	22	1
	21	53	74	5	41	7	84	284	14	11	767	122	8

GENERAL ABSTRACT, Continued.

COUNTIES	Disease of Lungs	Disease of Heart	Inflammation of Lungs	Inflammation of Chest	Inflammation of Ribs	Pleurisy	Quinsy	Sore Throat	Total	Bilious Fever	Disease of Liver	Disease of Stomach	Indigestion
1. Halifax (City)	3	7	4			1		4	63	1	5		
" (Outside City)		3	8	1		3	1	18	121	2	3		
Total in County	3	10	12	1		4	1	22	184	3	8		
2. Colchester	2	4	14			1		17	91	1	1	3	
3. Cumberland		4	14					6	82	2	2	1	2
4. Picton	3	5	10			5	1	4	56	5	0	2	1
5. Sydney	1	5	6			16	2	36	106	1	5		
6. Guysborough		3	5			3		7	56	2	2		1
7. Inverness		3	1			11		5	69	10			1
8. Richmond		1				5	3	8	51	10	2		
9. Victoria		1						3	31	2			
10. Cape Breton	1	1	1			23	2	4	78	1	1		
11. Hants	2	2	9			1		10	78		2	1	
12. King's		9	13	1				2	80				2
13. Annapolis		4	5			1		8	85	7	6		
14. Digby		1	1			2	5	6	57	7			2
15. Yarmouth		7	10			1		2	67	4	3		1
16. Shelburne	2	5	7			1		2	57				1
17. Queen's			8	1			1	3	35	2	1		1
18. Lunenburg		3	2		1			9	75	2			2
	14	67	114	3	1	76	15	153	1369	80	42	7	13

GENERAL ABSTRACT, Continued.

COUNTIES.			Diseases of the Digestive Organs—Continued.							Diseases of Urinary and Generative Organs.						
	Teething	Jaundice	Inflammation of Bowels	Inflammation of Stomach	Disease of Bowels	Worms	Teething	Total	Disease of Bladder	Diabetes	Inflammation of Kidneys	Puerperal Fever	Childbed	Total		
1. Halifax (City)	4	1	7	1	5	1	3	28	1				2	3		
" (Outside City)	4		12			5	1	27	1	1	1		2	5		
Total in County	4	5	19	1	5	6	4	55	2	1	1		4	8		
2. Colchester		1	3		2		1	15	1		1		1	3		
3. Cumberland	1		4			12		24					2	2		
4. Pictou	6		9	2	5			47	1			2	2	2		
5. Sydney	3	1	2	2	2			15	3				2	5		
6. Guysborough		1	1	1	3			11			1		4	5		
7. Inverness	3	1	1	5				21	1				2	3		
8. Richmond		1	3		1	1	2	20	2				3	5		
9. Victoria		1	3		1			8	1				2	3		
10. Cape Breton	2		7	1	4			16			3		3	3		
11. Hants		3	3	1	4	1		15				1		1		
12. King's		2	6	3				14					1	1		
13. Annapolis	3	3	4		4	1		20			1			1		
14. Digby	2	4	3		2	1		20					2	2		
15. Yarmouth	1	1	16	1	3			29					3	3		
16. Shelburne		1	2	1	3			8								
17. Queen's		1	5	3	1	2		16								
18. Lunenburg			2		1	1	1	9	1		1		3	5		
	25	26	33	28	43	26	9	371	12	1	6	3	36	59		

No. 4.—PERSONAL CENSUS...DEATHS, AND CAUSES OF DEATHS...1860—61.

GENERAL ABSTRACT, Continued.

COUNTIES.								Disease of Uncertain Seat.								Total
1. { Halifax (City)	1	4	2					4	15	4			1		1		35
{ " (Outside City)		2	1					5	29	2			1				34
Total in County	1	6	3					9	41	6			2		1		69
2. Colchester		2	2	2		1		6	9	2	1		1				26
3. Cumberland		3	2					6	10	3			5		1		30
4. Pictou	1		2			1		3	16	1			1		1	1	27
5. Sydney		1	2	1				1	4				4		2		16
6. Guysborough			4					1	4				3				17
7. Inverness	1	3	2					1	10				2		1		20
8. Richmond						1		1	1	1			2				7
9. Victoria		2	3					1	3		1		5				15
10. Cape Breton		3	3			1		5	8				6				27
11. Hants	1		1					6	10	5			1				28
12. King's			2	1				2	4	2					1		12
13. Annapolis	1	1	3					5	12	2			1				23
14. Digby	1	1	1					3	6	2			5				22
15. Yarmouth			2			1		3		2			1				14
16. Shelburne	1							4	4	2					1		13
17. Queen's								3	1				1				6
18. Lunenburg		1	2					2	4	2							13
	8	20	35	5	1	4		70	169	35	3		40		8	1	384

GENERAL ABSTRACT, Continued.

COUNTIES.	Burns and Scalds	Poison	Drowned	Murdered	Poisoned	Other Accidents	Total	Disease of Eye	Disease of Ear	Total	Causes not specified	Total of Deaths
1. { Halifax (City)		1	8			2	11				54	324
" (Outside City)	3		11		1	6	21				30	340
Total in County	3	1	19		1	8	32				124	664
2. Colchester	1		3			9	13	1	1	2	30	256
3. Cumberland	2		1			3	6				29	338
4. Pictou	1		5			9	15			1	41	319
5. Sydney	1		5	1		1	8		1	1	24	251
6. Guysborough	2		5			2	9				8	203
7. Inverness	2		3			1	5				34	218
8. Richmond			8			1	11				18	334
9. Victoria			2		1		3				17	103
10. Cape Breton	1		5			2	8				27	341
11. Hants	1		2			3	6				20	243
12. King's	1		6			3	10				13	309
13. Annapolis			4			2	6				13	263
14. Digby			6			2	8	1		1	13	163
15. Yarmouth			7			3	10				17	204
16. Shelburne	3		8			2	13				6	140
17. Queen's			1		1		2				4	120
18. Lunenburg	3		5			2	10				15	390
	22	1	95	1	3	53	175	2	2	4	452	4070

PERSONAL CENSUS.

PROFESSIONS, TRADES, AND OCCUPATIONS.

No. 5.—PERSONAL CENSUS. PROFESSIONS, TRADES, AND OCCUPATIONS.—1860—61.

PUBLIC, JUDICIAL, AND MUNICIPAL OFFICERS.

COUNTIES.	Archbishops Roman Catholic	Bishops, Protestant.	Bishops, R. Catholic	Archdeacons	Chief Justice	Judges	Presiding Attorney	Attorney General	Solicitor General	Receiver General	Financial Secretary	Railway Commr's	Commr's. Crown Lands	Postmaster General	Collectors and Controllers of Customs	Mayors	Sheriffs
1. Halifax	1	1	....	1	1	2	1	1	1	1	1	1	1	1	22	1	1
2. Colchester																	
3. Cumberland																	
4. Pictou																	
5. Sydney			1														
6. Guysborough																	
7. Inverness																	
8. Richmond																	
9. Victoria																	
10. Cape Breton																	
11. Hants						1											
12. King's																	
13. Annapolis																	
14. Digby																	
15. Yarmouth																	
16. Shelburne																	
17. Queen's																	
18. Lunenburg																	
	1	1	1	1	1	4	1	1	1	1	1	1	1	1	61	1	18

PUBLIC, JUDICIAL, AND MUNICIPAL OFFICERS, · · · · · · Continued.

COUNTIES.	Attorneys	Registrars	County Treasurers	Sheriffs	Coroners	Prothonotaries and Clerks of the Crown	City Clerk	Clerks of the Peace	Judges of Probate	Registrars of Probate	Registrars of Deeds	City Marshal	Police Constables	Deputy Postmasters	Stipendiary Magistrates	Keeper of Provincial Penitentiary	Queen's Printer
1. Halifax	18	77	1	1	4	1	1	1	1	1	1	1	12	3	1	1	1
2. Colchester		73	1		6	1		1	1	1	2			5			
3. Cumberland		103	2		7	1		1	1	1	2			5			
4. Pictou		106	1		6	1		1	1	1	1			5			
5. Sydney		47	1		2	1		1	1	1	1			1			
6. Guysborough		69	1		4	1		2	2	2	2			5			
7. Inverness		47	1		5	1		1	1	1	1			6			
8. Richmond		50	1		2	1		1	1	1	1			2			
9. Victoria		36	1		3	1		1	1	1	1			3			
10. Cape Breton		63	1		3	1		1	1	1	1			3			
11. Hants		80	1		6	1		2	1	1	3			6			
12. King's		103	1		3	1		1	1	1	1			5			
13. Annapolis		69	1		11	1		1	1	1	1			5			
14. Digby		71	1		6	1		1	1	1	1			3			
15. Yarmouth		64	1		3	1		2	1	1	1			3			
16. Shelburne		34	1		3	1		2	1	1	1			3			
17. Queen's		47	1		2	1		1	1	1	1			4			
18. Lunenburg		56	1		7	1		1	1	1	1			6			
	18	1200	18	1	84	18	1	22	18	19	20	1	12	71	1	1	1

No. 5.—PERSONAL CENSUS. PROFESSIONS, TRADES, AND OCCUPATIONS. 1860—61.

COUNTIES.																		
1 { Halifax (City)	16	6	34	2	4	8	108	10	95	4	10	12	69	10	13	16	11	1
" (Outside City)	1		2				81		10		2		3	4	1		1	56
Total in County	17	6	36	2	5	8	189	10	105	4	12	12	72	14	14	16	12	57
2. Colchester					3		148		3	3				3		1		
3. Cumberland				1	2		131		3		3							9
4. Pictou			1				227		6		10		8	3	1			2
5. Sydney							60											
6. Guysborough							32			3								
7. Inverness							67											
8. Richmond							16		2									
9. Victoria							26											
10. Cape Breton			2				78		3				1					
11. Hants	1		2				120		6		2			1	1			13
12. King's				1			104		1				3					3
13. Annapolis							74				3							6
14. Digby							62		2		3							2
15. Yarmouth							42				7		3					1
16. Shelburne							36				2							
17. Queen's			2	2			17		4		1		3					
18. Lunenburg							74		10		1		1		1			2
	18	6	46	11	5	8	1316	10	147	7	47	13	90	24	18	17	12	95

COUNTIES.																			
1. { Halifax (City)	9	5	50	3	1	2	78	408	170	10	312	20	26	10	35	5	12	19
" (Outside City)		15	7	1	1		6	225	227	3	26		1	1	22	6	2	1
Total in County	9	20	57	4	2	2	84	633	397	13	338	20	26	11	57	11	14	20
2. Colchester	1	3	6	2	1		4	379	13	32	14			4	22	2		
3. Cumberland		1	19				6	209	25	17	23		3	5	19			
4. Pictou	3		11				10	442	35	21	10		3		29		1	
5. Sydney			4					194	46	13	8				33			1
6. Guysborough		3	3				2	108	100	6	9				15	1		
7. Inverness		1	2					347	53	10	11				13			
8. Richmond			4					91	46	1	15				5			3
9. Victoria			1					69	12	1	9			1	5			
10. Cape Breton		2	6	1	3	2		166	23		20				14			
11. Hants		1	4				5	351	6	6	2		4	1	26			
12. King's		2	7				4	350	13	8	7		2		32	4		
13. Annapolis			7				12	312	36	11	4		3		22			
14. Digby		1	3				2	208	20	3	7				14			
15. Yarmouth		7	4		3		4	256	45	4					20			
16. Shelburne		16	2					139	63	2					17			
17. Queen's		6	4				4	95	29	1	6		1		20	4		
18. Lunenburg		6	7				5	163	182	1	5				19			
	17	71	147	6	7	6	147	4463	1145	163	494	20	47	23	385	15	15	22

No. 5.—PERSONAL CENSUS...PROFESSIONS, TRADES, AND OCCUPATIONS...1860—61.

COUNTIES.	Medical Doctors		Clergymen	Lawyers	Coroners and Printers	Chemists Manufac'rs	Millers	Engineers, Surveyors, Architects	Dyers	Dentists	Stone Makers	Engineers	Surgeons	Landowners Brokers	Surveyors	Fishers	Farm Laborers	Paupers
1. { Halifax (City)	5	2	2	2			3	6	1	3	134	15	1	6		166	29	69
{ " (Outside City)			6		1	2	1				10	9				2130	496	1668
Total in County	5	2	8	2	1	2	4	6	1	3	144	24	1	6		2306	525	1737
2. Colchester			8		6		2	6			17	3				3082	784	20
3. Cumberland			6		1					1	8	2			5	2003	771	9
4. Pictou			8				1	7			9	20				3719	799	14
5. Sydney			3					1								2011	836	110
6. Guysborough			2				1	1			3					1433	103	820
7. Inverness			2					5							1	2708	1107	279
8. Richmond			2												2	932	304	1000
9. Victoria			1													1208	483	185
10. Cape Breton			8								2	8				2407	981	454
11. Hants			8				1				1	9			1	2164	666	7
12. King's			4		6		2				9	1				2698	234	14
13. Annapolis			2				2				7				1	2613	403	93
14. Digby			5									1				1714	361	280
15. Yarmouth			5		1						2		1			1661	271	343
16. Shelburne							2				4				2	1043	38	1035
17. Queen's			6	2							4	2				899	73	262
18. Lunenburg			6								2				1	2450	416	890
	5	2	76	4	17	2	5	16	21	5	206	64	2	6	15	37367	9300	7529

COUNTIES.	Farriers	Fishing Tackle Man'ufacturers.	Gardeners	Grocers	Gunsmiths	Hat Makers	Grindstone Makers	Metal & Iron Keepers	Saddlers	Sawers	Iron Founders	Iron Puddlers	Ice Dealers	Jewellers	Lamplighters	Labourers	Lime Burners	Leather Dealers
1. Halifax (City)	8	1	28	185	4	13		17	5	4	8			11		1072	2	4
" (Outside City)			1	14	1			19			3		1		68	355		
Total in County	8	1	29	199	5	13		36	5	4	11		1	11	68	1427	1	4
2. Colchester			8	2				6			2				6	168		
3. Cumberland			5	1			56	13		1	2	2			107	461	2	
4. Picton	3		1	4		1		16			3				4	166		
5. Sydney				1				4								25		
6. Guysborough								1							23	82		
7. Inverness								4							1	50		
8. Richmond			4					3							1	117		
9. Victoria								1								4		
10. Cape Breton				1				9							1	169	1	
11. Hants	1		4		1			6							6	97	1	
12. King's			3					11		1					5	156		
13. Annapolis								6							14	71		
14. Digby			2	1				6							13	193		
15. Yarmouth								4							10	60		
16. Shelburne								3							12	63		
17. Queen's								2		2					103	256		
18. Lunenburg				4				9							54	206	1	
	13	1	46	213	6	14	76	159	5	8	15	7	1	11	507	2009	6	4

COUNTIES.																	
1. { Halifax (City)	5	2	7		5	291	465	172	16	19	1	14	37	1	7	2	4	19
" (Outside City)	2			2		41	277	28		2		1	9	1		26	3	
Total in County	7	2	7	2	5	332	742	200	16	21	1	15	46	2	7	28	7	19
2. Colchester						95	148	47				15	1	5		7		1
3. Cumberland				2		98	173	35		1		40	2	3	7	17		1
4. Pictou	2			2		186	137	90	16	5		303		6		28		
5. Sydney				1		35	173	23					1	7				
6. Guysborough				3		31	188	9				1				6		
7. Inverness						75	106	32					2					
8. Richmond				1		46	632	7				107				5		
9. Victoria						31	33					13						
20. Cape Breton	1			2		55	237	20				200				5		
11. Hants				1		69	452	29		3		31	2			4		
12. King's				2		98	302	40		1					2	4		
13. Annapolis				2	1	69	306	33		7			2	5		10		
14. Digby				2		45	429	16						1		2		2
15. Yarmouth				1		65	543	22	4			2				2		
16. Shelburne				1		74	292	17								2		
17. Queen's				2		84	219	13					1			6		1
18. Lunenburg				1		76	195	20				1	2			4		
	10	2	7	20	3	1872	5242	630	36	35	1	665	27	76	2	10	134	7	26

COUNTIES.									Physicians & Surgeons		Professors of Music					Free Press Handbills	Paper Makers		
1. { Halifax (City)						105	84	10	25	20	1	13	1	1	7	5		20
" (Outside City)	40	8	2			12	3	1	11			3		24	1		13	1
Total in County	40	8	2			117	87	11	33	20	1	13	1	25	8	5	13	21
2. Colchester	70			1	1	6		3	11			2						3
3. Cumberland	60					4		1	15			1		3			10	
4. Pictou	80				1	7	10	20	13	2		2		13			5	1
5. Sydney	48				1	4	1		3									
6. Guysborough	26					3		2	2									4
7. Inverness	53					4		1	2									1
8. Richmond	8							2										
9. Victoria	25					1		2	2									
10. Cape Breton	27					3	3	1	3					20				3
11. Hants	42					7		6	12					1			22	
12. King's	35					7		1	18				4					
13. Annapolis	23					10			15				2	1	1			
14. Digby	13					5	1		10									1
15. Yarmouth	4					12	9		10									2
16. Shelburne	3					3		2	6									
17. Queen's	4					10	2	1	5					1				1
18. Lunenburg	33					5			12			1						1
	592	3	2	1	3	208	118	58	170	22	1	16	6	63	9	5	50	38

COUNTIES																				
1 { Halifax (City)	3			80	58	12	51	34	2	55	367	3	1			16	2	3
{ " (Outside City)		1	8	3	1		5	6	2	72	95				2	5	1	
Total in County	3	1	8	83	59	12	56	40	4	127	462	3	1		3	15	3	3
2. Colchester				10		1		15	4		78	110		1		12	6	
3. Cumberland				4	5	1	2	9	10		146	103				8	3	
4. Picton	1			22	2	10	1	33	6		183	240				16	6	
5. Sydney					1			8			12	80				1		
6. Guysborough						1		5			36	50						
7. Inverness					3		4	5			9	55						2
8. Richmond					8	4	1	3			8	31				5	2	
9. Victoria								3			4	26				3	2	
10. Cape Breton				2	3	4		6	1		42	66				1		
11. Hants				1	1	4		12	1		58	107				1	4	
12. King's				5				9	6		53	148				26		
13. Annapolis		1		2	1			6	5		76	129				7	1	
14. Digby				10		4		8	8		61	70				1	4	
15. Yarmouth				4		12		5			46	106				2	1	1
16. Shelburne					1		5		1		44	53					1	
17. Queen's						6			2		36	61				1		
18. Lunenburg			2		10						79	116						
	6	3	68	107	121	20	107	93	4	1129	1976	3	3	1	3	95	25	6

COUNTIES.	Shoe Colours	School Teachers	Servants	Traders	Tanners and Curriers	Theatchers	Tinsmiths	Turners	Truck Makers	Tailors	Tallowmen	Teachers of Deaf and Dumb	Wheelmen	Telegraph Operators	Upholsterers	Washington	Watch and Clock Makers	Wine and Spirit Dealers	Weavers
1. Halifax (City)	51	85	215	26	15	50	14	6	2	136	51	2	126	2	2	19	25	8	5
" (Outside City)	4	57	23	17	18	8	1	1		20		1	10			16	1		7
Total in County	55	130	238	43	33	58	15	7	2	156	51	2	136	2	2	35	26	8	12
2. Colchester	2	70		6	22	9		5		35	6			2		19	1		20
3. Cumberland	11	58	134	2	35	5				32	1					19	6		2
4. Pictou	6	85	11	14	57	12	1	7		89			3	3		10	8		63
5. Sydney	2	43	14	21	20	2		2		53				1		1	1		11
6. Guysborough	1	25		24	10	1				17	1			2			1		10
7. Inverness	1	56	63	18	10	1		7		56	1			3		14	1		29
8. Richmond		18	4	10	7					18			2	1					7
9. Victoria		23	1	4	1		6			22				3		1			2
10. Cape Breton	2	53		13	19	3	2	1		43						7			17
11. Hants	1	62	12	26	19	5				26	6		6	1		10	2		2
12. King's		59		24	20	6				21	3			2		6	8		2
13. Annapolis	1	45		43	16	3				24	2		2	3		6	6		2
14. Digby		29		31	16	2				6	1			1		2	3		
15. Yarmouth		28		29	18	5				23	6					2	3		
16. Shelburne		20		26	7	4				9	3					3	2		
17. Queen's		16		15	13	9				14	1		2			0	2		
18. Lunenburg		37		11	23	4				14	1			3		23			2
	82	804	474	368	353	133	18	34	2	670	94	2	160	21	2	173	71	8	186

APPENDIX NO. 6.

RETURN

AGRICULTURAL PRODUCE, STOCK, FISHERIES, &c.

No. 6.—RETURN OF AGRICULTURAL PRODUCE,

COUNTY OF

	Lands—Acres					
POLLING DISTRICTS.	Dyke Marsh.		Salt Marsh.		Cultivated Intervale.	
	Acres.	Value in Dollars.	Acres.	Value in Dollars.	Acres.	Value in Dollars.
1. Ward 1, (City)					18	9000
2. do. 2, do.						
3. do. 3, do.						
4. do. 4, do.					10	300
5. do. 5, do. { 1st Section						
{ 2nd do.						
6. do. 6, do.						
Total in City					28	9300
7. Ferguson's Cove						
8. Portuguese Cove					14	700
9. Sambro						
10. Prospect			5	115	169	8825
11. Hagget's Cove					13	2230
12. French Village			3	50		
13. Drysdale's	10	40			46	320
14. North West Arm						
15. Piers' Mill						
16. Hammond's Plains					22	742
17. Windsor Road	17	200			154	2032
18. Truro Road					2	24
19. Gay's River			2	200	489	23058
20. Wise's Corner			5	100	578	11590
21. Middle Musquodoboit					1253	30070
22. Upper Musquodoboit					385	8054
23. Caledonia					238	3752
24. Salmon River			37	980	48	1920
25. Sheet Harbor			9	155	30	120
26. Pope's Harbor					25	436
27. Jeddore			166	3016	124	2972
28. Chezetcook	83	1862	241	5043	66	2566
29. Lawrencetown	375	9826	59	1688	40	1061
30. Preston			162	636		
31. Dartmouth	4	64	37	788	28	2800
32. Black Point					3	26
33. Eastern Passage						
	489	11992	726	12771	3755	112598

COUNTY OF

1. Truro	891	57769	48	2500	1722	76981
2. Old Barns	232	12222	77	2306	187	5278
3. Lower Stewiacke	520	44273	92	8592	1416	57054
4. Upper Stewiacke	23	1800	3	120	4269	126641
5. Upper Onslow and Kemptown	161	14956	28	1418	1084	47984
6. Onslow	732	56632	119	4510	400	12130
7. Earltown					128	2774
8. New Annan					218	3409
9. Waugh's River			114	1290	96	2238
10. Tatamagouche			111	1528	369	6425
11. Upper Londonderry	1035	63768	398	9647	306	11374
12. Lower Londonderry	347	20472	481	15229	409	10161
13. Economy and Five Islands	28	1220	363	12518	242	8224
	3969	273112	1834	59658	10846	370673

STOCK, FISHERIES, &c....1860—61.

HALIFAX.

| Occupied. | | | Grain, &p., raised in 1860. | | | | | | |
| Cultivated Upland. | | Tons of Hay cut in 1860. | Bushels Wheat. | Bushels Barley. | Bushels Rye. | Bushels Oats. | Bushels Buck- wheat. | Bushels Indian Corn. | Bushels Peas and Beans. |
Acres.	Value in Dollars.								
367	145520	391	81	100	90	885			4
165	45300	125	35			230			26
150	10900					30			
107	1080	107		20		60	12		
82	16800	43				60			5
414	13920	118	16	40		291			4
445	127640	474	45	142	10	2276		1	22
1730	361160	1258	177	302	100	3832	12	1	61
98	5726	64				68			
490	5995	93		19		3			
158	3618	271	35	630	6	359			30
291	14112	293	86	575	6	178			3
409	19207	359	7	827		218			11
317	6291	292				375			
167	14460	120				163			10
168	13467	112				217			18
942	20784	529		10		577			16
1331	26555	911	48	285		1952	53	1	31
890	12890	543	82	12		909	217		17
2403	36456	1519	719	211	291	6629	973	7	88
1550	27656	1489	81	386	10	4135	1679	1	6
4335	53348	3319	351	803		16154	2965	9	25
1956	35934	1949	52	1271	33	11553	2041	1	12
323	3130	460	184	161		2527	220		4
486	17940	697	11	11		592			
483	13673	458		28	30	522	36		2
602	12231	411	2		1	148			2
1191	16985	1306	64	437		1309	70		11
914	30484	1198	47	1564	2	2750	8		1
412	10503	735	113	1450	34	1299			29
528	12026	324	165	208		528	2		10
1166	88504	1211	101	1338	10	2110	44	23	89
314	17566	251	32	634	3	166	3		2
651	24318	700	56	1007		1432	36		2
24305	905019	20972	2413	12160	526	60705	8353	42	480

COLCHESTER.

4394	139430	4154	2027	1185	259	20069	3583	22	189
1833	40976	1362	1322	187		8333	857		15
5118	82910	4000	957	1189	278	20948	2115	66	100
9145	110099	5410	756	1170	301	28369	3784	22	240
5693	93657	3136	1383	493	957	16575	4656	35	99
2448	93725	2086	1508	327	380	7279	2104	10	91
6627	87566	1229	572	874	460	21586	3123	11	55
3636	38272	1177	3000	638	224	12581	3088	11	437
3429	52754	861	5603	610	75	10362	2157	10	561
2437	41320	928	3522	749	13	8683	2410	4	462
4503	118794	3356	2679	743	328	14730	3562	1	45
5332	61027	2774	1517	507	118	13113	4096		56
6989	107687	2538	2514	236	115	10348	2976	6	81
61583	1068217	33101	27360	8968	3508	192976	38511	198	2431

No. 6.—RETURN OF AGRICULTURAL PRODUCE,

COUNTY OF

Grain, &c., raised in 1860—*Continued.*

POLLING DISTRICTS.	Bushels Timothy Seed.	Bushels Potatoes.	Bushels Turnips.	Bushels other Roots.	Bushels Apples.	Bushels Plums.
1. Ward 1, (City.)	3	911	1813	1098	122	9
2. do. 2, do		440	1405	760	105	
3. do. 3, do		40	60			3
4. do. 4, do		20				
5. do. 5, do. { 1st Section		125	70	40	12	2
{ 2nd do.......		347	1052	574	20	
6. do. 6. do	1	1951	4149	4692	231	30
Total in City.....	4	3834	8549	7164	490	44
7. Ferguson's Cove						
8. Portuguese Cove....................		143				
9. Sambro		1253	41	49		
10. Prospect....................		6172	1041	242	6	
11. Hagget's Cove....................	1	4016	515	287	144	
12. French Village		3327	642	459	396	
13. Drysdale's....................		1552	391	58	27	
14. North West Arm		560	381	95	44	
15. Piers' Mill		814	248	51	73	
16. Hammond's Plains		2738	640	35	123	
17. Windsor Road....................	9	4889	2324	112	366	
18. Truro Road....................		3255	750	69	162	
19. Gay's River....................	25	5945	2505	331	272	
20. Wise's Corner	9	5656	1021	136	278	
21. Middle Musquodoboit....................	57	12022	3090	1293	296	
22. Upper Musquodoboit	60	7835	1846	1085	190	
23. Caledonia....................	18	2440	110		29	
24. Salmon River	1	5057	646		9	
25. Sheet Harbor		2138	401	53	20	
26. Pope's Harbor....................		1972	201	18		
27. Jeddore		5868	2825	94	107	
28. Chezetcook		6579	3810	14	36	
29. Lawrencetown....................		5713	665	15	61	
30. Preston		2107	467	15	205	
31. Dartmouth....................		8435	7280	1307	93	
32. Black Point....................	1	4756	727	170	72	
33. Eastern Passage		2535	3546	1084		
	185	111611	44674	14236	3499	44

COUNTY OF

1. Truro....................	80	53681	8791	2320	461	2
2. Old Barns	27	17628	1556	99	471	19
3. Lower Stewiacke	67	18908	7305	1217	297	1
4. Upper Stewiacke....................	79	27058	5467	1330	493	2
5. Upper Onslow and Kemptown.	86	32931	3657	247	217	
6. Onslow	38	29942	4604	705	95	
7. Earltown	135	13958	471	3	235	2
8. New Annan....................	52	15278	2578	70	660	
9. Waugh's River....................	101	11819	3932	20	128	2
10. Tatamagouche....................	93	12884	1920	84	410	1
11. Upper Londonderry....................	39	51112	2491	202	353	
12. Lower Londonderry....................	29	32690	3195	1076	206	2
13. Economy and Five Islands	74	40106	2343	180	292	8
	900	358001	48310	7652	4318	39

STOCK, FISHERIES, &c....1860—61.

HALIFAX, Continued.

	Cattle.				Hand Looms.	Fulled Cloth, y'ds made in 1860.	Not Fulled, yards made in 1860.	Butter, lbs. made in 1860.
Neat Cattle, exclusive of Cows.	Milch Cows.	Horses.	Sheep.	Pigs.				
18	138	111	35	40	....	19	40	1965
11	77	90	11	3	....	....	....	340
....	15	32	....	2	....	24	....	20
....	9	37	....	....	....	20	....	....
1	27	90	....	....	....	....	....	....
3	61	84	5	61	1	40	....	301
32	118	84	14	53	1	....	50	1692
65	445	527	65	169	2	103	90	4318
3	42	20	....	....	....	....	....	....
51	70	19	....	74	....	....	....	3360
20	62	4	346	118	11	149	560	3588
92	112	7	464	179	3	....	....	752
168	133	13	327	160	3	35	673	3504
194	132	18	409	128	18	40	1848	4251
81	164	43	76	24	2	27	....	9447
24	56	34	5	8	....	....	....	908
22	60	42	19	52	....	....	....	3348
87	141	103	55	28	....	....	252	10209
190	284	146	346	110	8	510	2220	12186
139	165	61	141	30	2	55	183	7195
346	348	124	1045	96	36	516	4007	20150
507	355	114	935	82	34	86	4782	12575
1201	883	280	2522	207	112	641	12039	37379
836	625	203	1625	96	82	678	11694	26715
173	138	55	359	51	19	344	1455	4760
370	253	19	864	112	21	....	2287	8416
190	152	34	411	55	5	43	873	6967
298	192	24	1019	204	23	186	2925	2238
773	465	60	1466	223	55	93	4180	8274
870	361	74	1160	334	41	295	1998	6343
281	194	71	535	97	8	200	1025	5711
168	135	53	132	21	5	130	722	2728
241	439	180	333	137	3	....	722	11505
128	106	12	60	134	5	345	80	2274
223	133	52	994	103	2	....	350	1494
7741	6645	2392	15720	3022	500	4476	55865	220595

COLCHESTER, Continued.

1196	959	539	2852	443	105	1329	10981	45096
494	308	161	1400	140	50	316	6430	14714
1477	875	317	2716	289	83	850	12057	41651
2317	1405	486	4836	438	185	1518	24533	69071
1080	779	313	2242	219	88	1179	9400	33851
716	361	199	1235	257	65	289	5209	23005
761	688	260	2077	440	111	1935	6604	17777
540	545	248	1083	186	73	1516	5229	33914
512	388	170	912	257	31	771	4504	15258
477	441	184	887	197	38	1514	3202	15713
1118	616	348	2462	268	151	1269	10812	27392
917	727	381	2424	304	137	1477	7265	27271
980	697	317	2368	319	110	1002	8619	33516
12585	8789	3923	27494	3757	1227	14965	114845	398229

No. 6.—RETURN OF AGRICULTURAL PRODUCE,

COUNTY OF

POLLING DISTRICTS.	Cheese. lbs. made in 1860.	Maple Sugar, lbs. made in 1860.	Bricks made in 1860.		Grindstones made in 1860.	
			M.	Value in Dollars.	No.	Value in Dollars.
1. Ward 1, (City.)	40					
2. do. 2, do						
3. do. 3, do						
4. do. 4, do						
5. do. 5, do. { 1st Section						
{ 2nd do						
6. do. 6. do						
Total in City	40					
7. Ferguson's Cove						
8. Portuguese Cove						
9. Sambro						
10. Prospect						
11. Hagget's Cove	80					
12. French Village						
13. Drysdale's						
14. North West Arm						
15. Piers' Mill						
16. Hammond's Plains						
17. Windsor Road	80					
18. Truro Road		12			1	2
19. Gay's River	378	80				
20. Wise's Corner	339	180				
21. Middle Musquodoboit	869	677			15	12
22. Upper Musquodoboit	460	2175	1	12		
23. Caledonia	170	330	5	50		
24. Salmon River	80					
25. Sheet Harbor		10				
26. Pope's Harbor						
27. Jeddore	54					
28. Chezetcook	40		936	6982		
29. Lawrencetown						
30. Preston	50					
31. Dartmouth			150	90·		
32. Black Point						
33. Eastern Passage	50					
	2690	3464	1092	7944	16	14

COUNTY OF

	Cheese.	Maple Sugar.	Bricks M.	Bricks Value	Grindstones No.	Grindstones Value
1. Truro	2657	350	505	3230		
2. Old Barns	431	70				
3. Lower Stewiacke	4215	467			50	82
4. Upper Stewiacke	2627	2096				
5. Upper Onslow and Kemptown	2087	2532	45	225		
6. Onslow	3280	367	110	800		
7. Earltown	2102	5034				
8. New Annan	1087	4267			40	
9. Waugh's River	292	90			16	26
10. Tatamagouche	226	20			500	500
11. Upper Londonderry	228	2290				
12. Lower Londonderry	454	3494	100	650		
13. Economy and Five Islands	1070	5501				
	20756	26578	760	4905	606	608

STOCK, FISHERIES, &c....1860—61.

HALIFAX, Continued.

Gypsum quarried in 1860.		Vessels employed in the Fisheries.		Boats engaged in the Fisheries.		No. Nets and Seines.	Fish Cured in 1860.		
Tons.	Value in Dollars.	No.	Men.	No.	Men.		Quintals Dry.	Barrels Mackerel.	Barrels Shad.
		6	54	5		12	100		
		9	72	27	66	38	50	5	15
		5	36	8		35	880	20	
		1	10	1		10	425	10	
		4	28	13	39	26			
		1	5	6	1	15	140	137	
		26	205	60	106	136	1595	172	15
		17	93	28	44	346	2780		
		2		177	39	1210	1745	262	40
		2	9	122	69	602	4226	614	22
		21	77	417	367	2779	9514	2432	91
		12	45	241	79	1523	2743	2657	164
		5	21	177	59	783	278	2486	106
				4	5	5	75		
				6	4	17	10	19	
						2		10	
						1			
25	20								
33	33								
		9	55	44	71	·347	2618	436	
		8	43	40	56	363	2346	210	
		24	81	161	69	1965	3755	2569	12
		26	160	163	179	624	9078	839	6
		12	60	117	226	577	3197	562	
		2	5	26	14	197	153	392	
				2		15		20	
		7	33	120	91	375	36	1451	
				27	1	139	456	6	
58	53	175	887	1932	1479	12006	44645	15137	456

COLCHESTER, Continued.

55	40			3	2	6			15
5940	5368			15	14	29	1	8	162
8	8			3	2	16			9
21									
				1	2	1			10
				3		8	9		
2	1			26	37	25	3		616
				42	71	39	11		1438
				25	35	31	32	48	1441
6026	5417			118	163	155	56	56	3691

No. 6.—RETURN OF AGRICULTURAL PRODUCE,

COUNTY OF

POLLING DISTRICTS.	Fish Cured in 1860—*Continued.*					Gallons Fish Oil in 1860.
	Barrels Herring.	Barrels Alewives.	Barrels Salmon.	No. Smoked Salmon.	Boxes Herring.	
1. Ward 1, (City.)	150		70			9120
2. do. 2, do.	500					28
3. do. 3, do.	718		66			848
4. do. 4, do.	15					128
5. do. 5, do. { 1st Section	7000					
{ 2nd do.	517	33				30
6. do. 6, do.						
Total in City	8900	33	130			10154
7. Ferguson's Cove	853					
8. Portuguese Cove	942		3			863
9. Sambro	437	62			29	1710
10. Prospect	7360	234	144		261	6351
11. Hagget's Cove	6831	12	8	20		1002
12. French Village	2591	74	6	27		373
13. Drysdale's	14	5	1			
14. North West Arm						
15. Piers' Mill	10					
16. Hammond's Plains	8					
17. Windsor Road						
18. Truro Road		28				
19. Gay's River		17				
20. Wise's Corner						
21. Middle Musquodoboit		2				
22. Upper Musquodoboit						
23. Caledonia						
24. Salmon River	1928	23	23	33		985
25. Sheet Harbor	3505	8	4	644		971
26. Pope's Harbor	5222	63	4	1		1542
27. Jeddore	1144	100	13	12	10	3975
28. Chezetcook	1415	122	6		6	1882
29. Lawrencetown	401	59				207
30. Preston						
31. Dartmouth	25					8
32. Black Point	1770	54	2	26		2
33. Eastern Passage	159					945
	44199	968	360	758	307	30070

COUNTY OF

1. Truro		12				
2. Old Barns	1	21	2	4		2
3. Lower Stewiacke	2	23	3			
4. Upper Stewiacke						
5. Upper Onslow and Kemptown						
6. Onslow	6					
7. Earltown						
8. New Annan						
9. Waugh's River	3		2			7
10. Tatamagouche			1	30		
11. Upper Londonderry	2		15	40		5
12. Lower Londonderry	30	379	8		7	30
13. Economy and Five Islands	343	2	2		36	44
	387	437	33	74	43	88

STOCK, FISHERIES, &c....1860—61.

HALIFAX, Continued.

Value of Leather manufact'd in 1860.	Carriages made in 1860.	Bush. Lime burnt in 1860.	Gallons Malt Liquor made in 1860.	Boats built in 1860.	Lumber manufactured in 1860.				
					M. feet Deals, Superficial.	M. feet Pine Boards.	M. feet Spruce & Hemlock Boards.	Tons Square Timber.	M. Staves.
1000	14	600				50			130
			91000						
	3		18000						1
	6			1					8
15000				2					
16000	23	600	109000	3		50			130
				7					
				32					
				48					
				16					
	1			2	4	21	75		25
									41
				1		5	220		43
						177	269		1564
	3				179	86	308	603	
	1					28	84	229	44
63						81	167	55	
						73	157	10	22
2701	25	250			4	53	108	4	
80	4	200			2	205	183	5	
	1					17	45	1620	
				11		27			
				10	50	211	1089		
				32		1			70
				67	17	85	210	6	901
				15	1	17	30		
	2			11	3	1	34		205
					30	49	35		45
19500	12	25000		20				5	3
		2		17	25	75	119		134
38344	74	26050	109000	293	315	1262	3138	2532	3236

COLCHESTER, Continued.

Value of Leather	Carriages	Bush. Lime	Gallons Malt Liquor	Boats built	M. feet Deals, Superficial.	M. feet Pine Boards.	M. feet Spruce & Hemlock Boards.	Tons Square Timber.	M. Staves.
4396	178	2195			147	49	388	446	
	6	560		2	44	21	142	36	
1387	8	140			3	174	299	238	45
1285	57	162				230	253	39	
1221		1200			222	78	454	109	
240	16				15	26	75	35	10
800	64				4	13	192	893	
380	1				149	48	152	718	
	6	3		4	40	5	223	6	7
2000	26			1	194	46	758	332	
234	57			5	167	16	89	282	
4018	21	400		5	9	40	92	9	20
273	49	200		9	63	13	382	172	41
16234	489	4860		26	1057	759	3199	3315	123

No. 6.—RETURN OF AGRICULTURAL PRODUCE,

COUNTY OF

					Lands—Acres	
POLLING DISTRICTS.	Dyke Marsh.		Salt Marsh.		Cultivated Intervals.	
	Acres.	Value in Dollars.	Acres.	Value in Dollars.	Acres.	Value in Dollars.
1. Amherst	7179	302838	714	18775	485	34606
2. Westchester	6	160			155	2255
3. Head of Amherst	501	20563	227	5275	185	2691
4. River Philip	6	220	49	1070	1263	27622
5. River Hebert	2821	118437	561	11404	53	1400
6. Maccan	572	30374	69	2088	1218	39660
7. Pugwash			1085	15136	104	2611
8. Wallace			645	9585	38	672
9. Wentworth			6	120	671	12788
10. Advocate Harbor	397	18140	317	4259	6	96
11. Mill Village	126	6808	137	2882	870	21799
	11608	497540	3810	70594	5048	146200

COUNTY OF

1. Pictou	26	1400	47	556	71	920
2. Carriboo	25	680	42	1014	86	2422
3. Cape John			89	864	121	2022
4. West side River John	1	120	82	929	78	1454
5. West branch River John					118	2104
6. Rogers Hill					280	4328
7. Hardwood Hill			11	280	99	2628
8. Green Hill and West River					484	10413
9. Mount Thom					449	11459
10. Gairloch					147	2910
11. New Lairg					18	144
12. Albion Mines			40	218	186	4660
13. New Glasgow			23	506	143	3186
14. Little Harbor			17	198	35	353
15. McLellan's Mountain					241	5014
16. East branch East River	600	1640			953	25960
17. Hopewell, W. branch E. River	1	40	4	10	388	5392
18. Middle River					324	5123
19. Gulf Shore			227	2306	158	3463
20. Barney's River			77	906	313	5018
21. Merrigomish			68	902	224	3275
22. Blue Mountain, St. Mary's, &c.					469	4882
	653	3880	727	8689	5445	107130

COUNTY OF

1. Arisaig					162	2770
2. Cape George			2	50	51	804
3. Morristown	6	40	24	456	282	8658
4. Antigonish	171	1752	51	1094	2505	58671
5. Lochaber	100	600			1014	13452
6. Upper South River	4	160			1049	24591
7. St. Andrew's			84	1449	965	29897
8. Tracadie	5	66	88	1368	359	5828
9. Harbor Bouche	180	410	13	68	71	717
	466	3036	262	4485	6458	145388

STOCK, FISHERIES, &c....1860—61.

CUMBERLAND.

Occupied.			Grain, &c., raised in 1860.						
Cultivated Acres.	Upland. Value in Dollars.	Tons of Hay cut in 1860.	Bushels Wheat.	Bushels Barley.	Bushels Rye.	Bushels Oats.	Bushels Buckwheat.	Bushels Indian Corn.	Bushels Peas and Beans.
9775	329216	8988	6717	4411	773	28213	10345	16	151
3636	28821	1033	592	61	4	6474	6287	....	32
9414	173511	2701	6997	1067	443	15276	12848	27	156
6926	74206	2886	3531	1113	1010	16749	13615	14	180
2803	84818	3019	1801	2054	386	9758	1926	12	111
5214	55752	2079	876	1063	1450	7609	2790	4	60
18844	216364	3718	16960	1759	2	14343	11837	76	459
10358	169264	2686	13838	1256	11	12469	9243	46	550
2048	21428	1138	1716	312	50	5325	3441	14	94
2516	25561	875	347	40	30	3310	1539	12	16
8896	140210	2459	1037	383	658	14829	5142	8	93
80430	1319151	31582	54412	13519	4817	134355	79013	229	1902

PICTOU.

6210	113200	946	5091	813	128	9864	174	2	85
5254	82897	885	5418	1217	20	16204	359	2	138
4933	74302	1410	10658	555	54	15907	1097	12	197
4018	86350	1120	6203	308	50	10260	1129	14	325
3253	27344	758	1292	460	1	12211	973	2	98
6347	65350	1927	3663	757	....	24683	1329	....	112
4124	94993	1159	3654	582	255	19260	433	1	224
4685	69881	1657	4307	1117	10	24957	587	16	411
5024	60883	1490	1718	598	90	26321	2348	....	165
5441	70643	1528	2613	694	....	26011	1237	10	124
3581	18966	796	553	462	16	14538	962	3	28
2455	39244	556	2025	268	....	7138	41	1	210
5874	109311	1548	5423	1502	241	18346	472	29	689
3221	38060	777	4812	761	....	11448	9	3	124
4793	54051	1298	3447	1177	....	19767	550	12	303
6279	83616	1788	1377	2763	250	21447	1417	51	339
6700	50107	1618	2834	1413	277	21692	1158	28	647
5091	50354	1417	2499	1395	204	22243	1726	13	237
7161	112330	1604	7029	1296	38	11750	73	2	192
5702	46917	1032	2146	1283	91	14860	524	....	84
7811	89260	1475	6488	1341	63	22296	153	2	245
1794	10796	705	217	941	4	11510	925	....	8
109751	1448855	27494	83467	21703	1792	382713	17676	203	4985

SYDNEY.

7373	106315	2086	8698	1985	175	16313	100	....	71
5348	54657	1735	5886	1674	60	10920	6	....	14
6343	55687	1866	4239	788	206	14188	104	7	43
17223	174819	5355	9132	1172	107	35725	559	10	197
11820	83255	2651	1669	733	367	27714	2164	12	56
7803	70154	2220	2328	779	2	24434	834	....	27
12691	119482	3780	6181	1685	14	28827	421	49	192
7073	63734	2368	3407	1880	158	17567	227	23	485
6460	42578	1474	2325	1496	85	8285	16	30	300
82078	770681	23535	43865	12192	1174	183973	4431	131	1385

No. 6.—RETURN OF AGRICULTURAL PRODUCE,

COUNTY OF

Grain, &c., raised in 1860—*Continued.*

POLLING DISTRICTS.	Bushels Timothy Seed.	Bushels Potatoes.	Bushels Turnips.	Bushels other Roots.	Bushels Apples.	Bushels Plums.
1. Amherst	266	38694	17478	986	1514	
2. Westchester	35	9715	1687	58	453	
3. Head of Amherst	137	46353	6302	207	1172	1
4. River Philip	157	31993	3746	302	1025	
5. River Hebert	66	39598	3544	207	338	1
6. Maccan	64	32565	691	159	402	
7. Pugwash	423	37049	8962	307	683	9
8. Wallace	401	23631	6173	348	597	14
9. Wentworth	98	10304	3661	108	404	
10. Advocate Harbor	16	18495	353	15	48	
11. Mill Village	106	48480	3218	192	856	7
	1709	336877	55815	2889	7492	32

COUNTY OF

1. Pictou	55	12177	8850	293	524	35
2. Carriboo	93	13250	4303	62	257	16
3. Cape John	152	11965	2873	58	279	31
4. West side River John	122	11065	2025	126	438	33
5. West branch River John	78	8924	225	8	381	
6. Rogers Hill	106	17641	1653	24	898	6
7. Hardwood Hill	128	17136	3220	324	543	4
8. Green Hill and West River	144	11564	2184	370	1365	29
9. Mount Thom	108	16821	1720	38	1502	1
10. Gairloch	204	13567	753	250	905	5
11. New Lairg	68	8789	523	3	180	
12. Albion Mines	15	5836	2167	76	245	16
13. New Glasgow	193	12891	4854	65	264	49
14. Little Harbor	28	9357	2567	7	156	42
15. McLellan's Mountain	128	11705	864	46	335	4
16. East branch East River	212	16002	1115	54	150	6
17. Hopewell, W. branch E. River	96	12672	2433	30	239	12
18. Middle River	141	13605	2042	16	458	7
19. Gulf Shore	131	16914	2190	55	123	106
20. Barney's River	106	16696	2176	19	229	61
21. Merrigomish	139	20244	2358	43	288	299
22. Blue Mountain, St. Mary's, &c	44	9288	435	6	68	
	2485	288109	51530	1973	9827	762

COUNTY OF

1. Arisaig	112	20915	400	14	121	25
2. Cape George	58	14404	858	7	65	26
3. Morristown	50	12661	612	17	167	100
4. Antigonish	141	27888	5184	221	627	263
5. Lochaber	71	16950	965	5	296	13
6. Upper South River	65	12501	1139		97	27
7. St. Andrew's	104	16913	1131	22	225	290
8. Tracadie	37	12727	1436	78	163	197
9. Harbor Bouche	13	11247	1155	23	243	69
	651	146206	12880	387	2004	1010

STOCK, FISHERIES, &c....1860—61.

CUMBERLAND, Continued.

Cattle.					Hand Looms.	Fulled Cloth, y'ds made in 1860.	Not Fulled, yards made in 1860.	Butter, lbs. made in 1860.
Neat Cattle, exclusive of Cows.	Milch Cows.	Horses.	Sheep.	Pigs.				
2653	1279	786	3407	747	166	2291	11778	85829
405	264	146	863	84	57	375	4733	12232
1152	624	381	2137	443	116	1714	10823	41125
1244	630	373	2569	414	103	1157	13499	37576
997	501	317	1640	337	68	948	6204	29527
798	448	202	1363	326	84	1014	6411	30081
1788	1119	528	3528	599	166	2473	14639	48789
1396	852	454	2835	436	131	2255	12433	36236
475	286	117	790	141	57	761	4212	13016
400	277	88	813	201	41	113	2826	9843
1206	794	361	2177	537	84	342	8414	39700
12514	7074	3753	22122	4265	1073	13443	95972	383954

PICTOU, Continued.

310	436	216	899	227	18	1634	3035	11200
609	593	303	1601	335	50	1755	4230	15903
831	586	238	1577	273	85	1563	6715	18293
579	394	187	889	158	51	664	4446	15608
473	470	207	1167	231	68	1414	5253	13314
647	605	316	1745	218	84	2629	6116	21472
623	627	298	2177	158	56	1578	5362	24630
656	637	294	1668	93	62	2064	6600	34285
710	724	306	1731	203	66	2139	7205	31756
543	656	283	1712	176	79	2203	5329	32582
379	392	179	951	61	59	1311	4401	11939
214	372	220	836	83	23	1268	2740	11791
667	790	366	2002	193	54	2678	5191	24738
534	513	222	1610	227	51	1787	3626	14098
685	681	292	1545	218	69	1583	5580	23159
906	916	421	2526	362	110	3268	6827	28709
697	818	399	2115	200	84	2720	5759	24330
628	649	324	1762	187	113	3041	6424	23647
1021	713	262	2315	456	86	3683	6007	24544
760	645	279	1875	388	52	2228	5673	24728
1040	848	366	2656	352	90	3263	8781	29577
493	435	185	1094	220	41	653	3758	11155
14005	13590	6163	36453	5079	1463	45126	119058	471486

SYDNEY, Continued.

1467	896	273	3200	644	96	7473	8600	35936
1217	762	201	2277	405	80	3252	6106	25105
1010	652	185	2116	214	59	2646	5132	30555
2527	1679	644	5303	808	155	7696	13743	73273
1534	1058	364	2696	614	113	3243	8852	39348
1294	867	256	2699	455	96	3043	7482	31739
2165	1390	352	4269	663	184	6445	10252	62170
1392	891	240	2569	393	70	2444	7009	42460
897	564	180	1984	335	95	1544	5365	17210
13503	8759	2695	27113	4531	948	37786	72541	357856

No. 6.—RETURN OF AGRICULTURAL PRODUCE,

COUNTY OF

POLLING DISTRICTS.	Cheese, lbs. made in 1860.	Maple Sugar, lbs. made in 1860.	Bricks made in 1860.		Grindstones made in 1860.	
			M.	Value in Dollars.	No.	Value in Dollars.
1. Amherst	5821	22913				
2. Westchester	72	15790			1	
3. Head of Amherst	1420	1695			3	1
4. River Philip	1307	12235			300	150
5. River Hebert	1659	6250	25	130	41475	39384
6. Maccan	2101	46903				
7. Pugwash	2923	3544	310	2335	220	180
8. Wallace	1027	1380			42	19
9. Wentworth	481	8871				
10. Advocate Harbor	9					
11. Mill Village	1049	1062			665	432
	17869	130210	335	2465	42706	40166

COUNTY OF

1. Pictou	1001		400	3200	24	30
2. Carriboo	2245	260			1	1
3. Cape John	706	50			5	5
4. West side River John	756	205			303	150
5. West branch River John	1231	1015				
6. Rogers Hill	4939	425				
7. Hardwood Hill	2497	70				
8. Green Hill and West River	4015	140			2	1
9. Mount Thom	2506	1891				
10. Gairloch	2513	1490	1	6		
11. New Lairg	1707	2390				
12. Albion Mines	708	12				
13. New Glasgow	5634	670				
14. Little Harbor	1849	20			493	404
15. McLellan's Mountain	6000	1626				
16. East branch East River	5769	5690			16	14
17. Hopewell, W. branch E. River	3273	2801				
18. Middle River	2015	1325				
19. Gulf Shore	17164	490			247	165
20. Barney's River	2422	4453				
21. Merrigonish	3418	866			202	220
22. Blue Mountain, St. Mary's, &c.	1541	4816	10	80		
	73918	30707	411	3286	1203	990

COUNTY OF

1. Arisaig	30302	2082	90	500		
2. Cape George	16175	40			21	21
3. Morristown	11732	226			6	3
4. Antigonish	28497	352	89	800		
5. Lochaber	14376	4396			3	5
6. Upper South River	18814	6705			2	2
7. St. Andrew's	37981	1299	1	9	7	7
8. Tracadie	7826	767			2	4
9. Harbor Bouche	1060	152			8	7
	166763	16019	180	1309	49	49

STOCK, FISHERIES, &c....1860—61.

CUMBERLAND, Continued.

Gypsum quarried in 1860.		Vessels employed in the Fisheries.		Boats engaged in the Fisheries.		No. Nets and Seines.	Fish Cured in 1860.		
Tons.	Value in Dollars.	No.	Men.	No.	Men.		Quintals Dry.	Barrels Mackerel.	Barrels Shad.
121	65	1	3	......	......	81	9	3	301
......	......	......	......	20	14	102	40	3	9
54	52	......	......	1	1	17	......	......	......
......	1	1	2	19	33	135	5	......	321
6	1	......	......	......	......	......	......	......	......
18	14	......	......	21	19	71	3	20	......
60	74	2	8	16	11	62	23	6	1
......	......	......	......	6	1	10	77	12	......
......	......	......	......	6	6	17	101	......	20
259	206	4	13	89	85	495	260	44	652

PICTOU, Continued.

Gypsum quarried in 1860.		Vessels employed in the Fisheries.		Boats engaged in the Fisheries.		No. Nets and Seines.	Fish Cured in 1860.		
Tons.	Value in Dollars.	No.	Men.	No.	Men.		Quintals Dry.	Barrels Mackerel.	Barrels Shad.
......	......	2	17	19	10	53	495	239	......
......	......	......	......	27	......	106	103	3	......
......	......	......	......	19	2	98	61	......	......
......	......	......	......	3	......	8	2	......	......
......	......	......	......	......	......	......	......	......	......
......	......	......	......	......	......	3	1	......	......
......	......	......	......	......	......	......	......	......	......
......	......	......	......	1	2	11	7	......	......
30	30	......	......	3	......	13	2	......	......
......	......	......	......	......	......	......	......	......	......
40	16	......	......	......	......	2	......	......	......
......	......	......	......	6	3	109	65	26	......
......	......	......	......	3	......	19	21	......	......
70	46	2	17	81	17	422	757	268	......

SYDNEY, Continued.

Gypsum quarried in 1860.		Vessels employed in the Fisheries.		Boats engaged in the Fisheries.		No. Nets and Seines.	Fish Cured in 1860.		
Tons.	Value in Dollars.	No.	Men.	No.	Men.		Quintals Dry.	Barrels Mackerel.	Barrels Shad.
......	......	......	3	45	53	176	183	14	......
......	......	1	3	37	24	242	444	83	6
......	......	1	8	22	14	56	155	212	3
......	......	......	......	2	......	6	7	......	......
......	......	......	......	1	......	12	7	......	......
10	10	......	......	......	......	......	......	......	......
......	......	......	......	12	16	45	144	11	......
......	......	......	......	10	5	74	63	18	......
......	......	1	6	84	168	379	379	319	......
10	10	3	17	213	280	990	1382	657	9

No. 6.—RETURN OF AGRICULTURAL PRODUCE,

COUNTY OF

POLLING DISTRICTS.	Fish Cured in 1860—*Continued.*					Gallons Fish Oil in 1860.
	Barrels Herring.	Barrels Alewives.	Barrels Salmon.	No. Smoked Salmon.	Boxes Herring.	
1. Amherst	15	4	2			10
2. Westchester						
3. Head of Amherst	259	304	2			48
4. River Philip		88	16	20		
5. River Hebert		39	2			6
6. Maccan						
7. Pugwash	186	688	3		20	5
8. Wallace	75	117	2		16	29
9. Wentworth						
10. Advocate Harbor	106					72
11. Mill Village	111		6	1	13	38
	752	1240	33	21	49	208

COUNTY OF

1. Pictou	549	33	20		25	280
2. Carriboo	274					52
3. Cape John	374	6	1			52
4. West side River John	305	17				
5. West branch River John						
6. Rogers Hill						
7. Hardwood Hill	2					
8. Green Hill and West River						
9. Mount Thom						
10. Gairloch						
11. New Lairg						
12. Albion Mines			1	14		4
13. New Glasgow						
14. Little Harbor	3					2
15. McLellan's Mountain						
16. East branch East River						
17. Hopewell, W. branch E. River		1				
18. Middle River						
19. Gulf Shore	23		121	40		10
20. Barney's River						
21. Merrigomish	20		6	20		10
22. Blue Mountain, St. Mary's, &c.		1				
	1550	58	149	74	25	410

COUNTY OF

1. Arisaig	247		27			103
2. Cape George	379	56	45	85		307
3. Morristown	37	15	24			64
4. Antigonish	4		2			3
5. Lochaber	44					6
6. Upper South River						
7. St. Andrew's	35	11	21			80
8. Tracadie	31	17	12		4	55
9. Harbor Bouche	836	53	24			592
	1613	152	155	85	4	1210

STOCK, FISHERIES, &c...1860—61.

CUMBERLAND, Continued.

Value of Leather manufact'd in 1860.	Carriages made in 1860.	Bush. Lime burnt in 1860.	Gallons Malt Liquor made in 1860.	Boats built in 1860.	Lumber manufactured in 1860.				
					M. feet Deals, Superficial.	M. feet Pine Boards	M. feet Spruce & Hemlock Boards.	Tons Square Timber.	M. Staves.
3544	106	3950	....	....	952	50	279	68	33
12	......	......	......	......	1534	113	221	......	......
28	17	......	......	4	2708	196	358	21	37
499	24	......	......	1	4946	190	312	131	......
4	......	50	......	8	2272	6	201	......	1
124	25	730	......	......	1116	140	280	20	......
327	66	1000	......	21	813	112	200	394	51
1350	1	135	......	11	80	52	189	136	13
134	......	......	......	......	701	34	207	50	22
......	......	2800	......	4	1330	36	119	15	......
817	26	1970	......	2	1240	104	374	325	2
6839	265	10635	......	51	17794	963	2740	1160	159

PICTOU, Continued.

6200	8	800	......	30	......	......	1	......	......
......	......	20	......	6	......	6	2	157	14
520	2	600	......	3	40	20	173	28	7
......	7	1000	......	......	5	24	411	......	5
300	......	......	......	......	17	8	289	70	3
70	13	......	......	......	22	8	177	182	......
14400	1	......	......	1	......	5	187	59	16
600	18	......	......	......	......	5	163	13	......
2600	1	40	......	......	30	10	188	896	......
2014	3	500	......	......	2	2	95	62	......
......	......	1100	......	......	23	8	33	471	......
4800	......	700	......	1	10	2	126	110	......
3700	27	5590	......	2	......	45	80	166	7
400	......	......	......	......	......	......	......	......	......
......	......	7900	100	......	6	109	104	194	4
400	11	4550	......	......	2	82	172	279	......
2900	10	8290	......	......	4	58	213	215	......
2000	3	4900	......	......	16	76	412	137	2
175	5	......	......	4	21	2	41	174	......
812	3	......	......	......	9	7	195	922	......
20	2	......	......	1	6	154	146	473	......
22	3	......	......	......	......	35	19	542	......
41933	117	35990	100	48	213	666	3227	5159	58

SYDNEY, Continued.

445	15	20	......	1	......	8	169	441	1
342	3	134	......	7	1	17	27	12	5
108	3	355	......	3	6	17	117	17	5
6787	45	1050	......	......	3	70	499	1310	13
410	7	1100	......	......	7	105	218	15	4
301	3	186	......	......	8	59	118	13	......
615	25	97	......	7	5	21	120	2	2
430	6	290	......	1	30	26	162	88	48
9	1	......	......	20	......	17	30	12	48
9447	108	3232	......	39	60	340	1460	1910	126

No. 6.—RETURN OF AGRICULTURAL PRODUCE,

COUNTY OF

POLLING DISTRICTS.	Dyke Marsh.		Salt Marsh.		Cultivated Intervale.	
	Acres.	Value in Dollars.	Acres.	Value in Dollars.	Acres.	Value in Dollars.
1. Guysborough			14	240	109	1532
2. Intervale			26	300	402	8504
3. Manchester			11	170	15	148
4. Melford	75	160			50	359
5. Crow Harbor						
6. Cape Canso						
7. Country Harbor			24	618	228	2327
8. Sherbrooke			16	152	353	12381
9. Marie Joseph			4	15		
10. Forks, St. Mary's	9	260	3	24	1487	33139
11. Molasses Harbor			29	183	22	188
	84	420	127	1702	2666	58578

COUNTY OF

	Dyke Marsh.		Salt Marsh.		Cultivated Intervale.	
1. Plaster Cove					45	282
2. Judique	500	2100	92	1174	365	7638
3. River Inhabitants	60	204			1231	10032
4. Port Hood	16	136	100	1982	326	5749
5. Mabou	125	970	92	3038	731	15394
6. Broad Cove (Intervale)	4	80	21	80	382	9518
7. Broad Cove			27	1252	317	6074
8. Margaree			24	424	62	5256
9. Young's Bridge			12	120	987	21126
10. Friar's Head	2	60	30	1056	113	5500
11. Cheticamp	124	456	164	2468	174	2652
12. Whycocomagh	74	1300	15	170	339	3810
13. Lake Ainslie					101	1648
14. River Dennis			15	146	989	13010
15. North-east Margaree	5	120			977	10444
	910	5426	592	11910	7139	118133

COUNTY OF

	Dyke Marsh.		Salt Marsh.		Cultivated Intervale.	
1. Arichat	100	700	2	400	60	4011
2. Petit Degrate	15	285				
3. D'Escouse	10	100			27	1500
4. Black River	312	1030	12	82	217	1148
5. River Bourgeoise			4	48	338	4601
6. St. Peter's	400	460	8	200	293	1230
7. L'Ardoise			31	187	29	151
8. Grand River	301	420	21	174	107	750
9. Red Islands			3	16	44	275
10. River Inhabitants			17	44	33	980
11. Little Arichat			6	36		
12. Loch Lomond					38	195
13. Flamboise						
	1138	2995	104	1187	1186	14841

STOCK, FISHERIES, &c....1860—61.

GUYSBOROUGH.

Occupied.			Grain, &c., raised in 1860.						
Cultivated Upland.		Tons of Hay cut in 1860.	Bushels Wheat.	Bushels Barley.	Bushels Rye.	Bushels Oats.	Bushels Buckwheat.	Bushels Indian Corn.	Bushels Peas and Beans.
Acres.	Value in Dollars.								
2885	44659	1732	258	192	....	12356	716	8	61
1649	31200	1098	287	573	....	7785	482	10	47
2734	32061	1714	244	575	5	9613	574	6	46
1631	20125	802	20	148	....	1558	4	2	7
182	3152	182	10	2	....	424	.....	.....	1
178	5142	111	....	....	....	172	4	.....	4
589	5676	423	38	10	5	1064	334	....	8
507	11652	765	137	314	31	3416	565	....	3
266	7321	330	....	....	....	372	.....	.....	6
2073	26313	2251	1416	1146	....	14968	3105	6	38
198	2349	209	7	4	3	152	.....	.....	.....
12802	192659	9617	2417	2961	44	51880	5781	32	221

INVERNESS.

4962	110162	1076	676	1338	....	11508	.....	.....	52
10425	67764	1941	1064	4617	....	26417	15	7	173
4651	23052	1785	152	1846	426	19409	.....	.....	1
4623	37647	1141	1412	2517	120	12828	10	....	34
18287	139015	3797	3752	4658	358	41115	1951	6	43
6089	57866	1653	1321	3192	....	19728	18	.....	17
5454	43382	1198	835	2151	40	15530	.....	.....	16
1783	15500	477	1122	369	....	4514	.....	.....	6
3632	25195	1676	37	779	....	13739	5	.....	46
1489	28616	691	873	644	30	4125	....	14	96
1758	19442	1248	1782	1284	30	4388	....	62	271
10413	74378	1444	316	3325	124	29532	384	12	14
4190	36633	720	335	1022	100	13055	28	.....	8
5157	38504	1335	237	2083	76	19918	3	.....	31
3955	25084	1797	60	1178	....	19118	.....	.....	111
86868	742240	21982	14554	31024	1304	258000	2414	101	919

RICHMOND.

140	28590	258	....	10	....	425	.....	....	4
3377	68356	385	....	13	....	783	.....	....	3
633	11957	319	......	78	....	1441	4	1	50
3675	18929	640	726	728	....	9017	8	.....	.....
1188	12746	460	....	18	....	2690	.....	.....	12
2160	8763	482	28	318	....	3473	.....	.....	6
1463	8506	540	....	22	....	3343	.....	.....	1
2644	12965	300	2	47	....	11289	.....	.....	.....
2792	11784	334	416	1193	....	6841	.....	.....	3
1302	10935	366	1	30	3	1569	.....	.....	4
516	26247	370	....	11	4	227	.....	.....	1
1151	8115	205	8	214	50	4536	2	.....	.....
611	3434	168	....	35	....	3119	2	.....	.....
21952	231297	4827	1181	2714	57	48753	16	1	84

No. 6.—RETURN OF AGRICULTURAL PRODUCE,

COUNTY OF

POLLING DISTRICTS.	Grain, &c., raised in 1860—*Continued.*					
	Bushels Timothy Seed.	Bushels Potatoes.	Bushels Turnips.	Bushels other Roots.	Bushels Apples.	Bushels Plums.
1. Guysborough	59	18375	2426	175	425	50.
2. Intervale	7	7746	773	8	112	20
3. Manchester	12	13171	1974	70	813	20
4. Melford		7374	500	42	412	3
5. Crow Harbor		1905	256	5	33	3
6. Cape Canso		1089	30	15		
7. Country Harbor		3925	517	83	146	1
8. Sherbrooke	4	5751	703	74	197	6
9. Marie Joseph	5	3643	885	51	5	
10. Forks, St. Mary's	84	16032	958	14	192	2
11. Molasses Harbor	1	1642	183	26		
	172	80653	9205	563	2335	105

COUNTY OF

1. Plaster Cove	1	10011	261	31	178	50
2. Judique	106	22126	523	10	63	1
3. River Inhabitants	56	12599	407	1	161	
4. Port Hood	50	11611	2131	56	13	9
5. Mabou	164	33180	2175	438	766	4
6. Broad Cove (Intervale)	49	13205	131	28	43	
7. Broad Cove	39	7392	156	5	30	
8. Margaree	1	4514	25			
9. Young's Bridge	44	12493	88	3	47	47
10. Friar's Head		16586	283	10	32	55
11. Cheticamp		38474	314		58	73
12. Whycocomagh	141	22359	616	45	243	1
13. Lake Ainslie	48	7767	130	6	30	
14. River Dennis	52	10417	443	2	195	
15. North-east Margaree	9	19717	166	18	363	60
	760	242451	7849	653	2222	300

COUNTY OF

1. Arichat		820	529	35	1	
2. Petit Degrate		6313	680	112		
3. D'Escouse	1	6300	1071	75	44	9
4. Black River	26	5633	395	9	78	1
5. River Bourgeoise	5	5296	215	18	55	
6. St. Peter's	7	4410	304	6	66	1
7. L'Ardoise		12039	198	3	15	
8. Grand River		7094	127	3		
9. Red Islands	15	5503	245		96	
10. River Inhabitants	1	1859	17	9	90	23
11. Little Arichat		617	73	8	34	4
12. Loch Lomond		3505	304		12	
13. Flamboise		4576	380			
	55	64055	4538	278	491	38

STOCK, FISHERIES, &c....1860—61.

GUYSBOROUGH, Continued.

Neat Cattle, exclusive of Cows.	Cattle.				Hand Looms.	Fulled Cloth, y'ds made in 1860.	Not Fulled, yards made in 1860.	Butter, lbs. made in 1860.
	Milch Cows.	Horses.	Sheep.	Pigs.				
901	732	213	2203	395	51	1545	6841	39158
668	470	109	1467	209	54	935	4450	20730
881	596	206	2140	307	39	900	6134	26737
425	336	61	634	210	22	299	2507	10965
129	112	7	584	144	12	180	701	900
53	95	8	94	109	5	40	280	6305
247	212	26	665	100	14	32	2040	6480
325	372	110	962	154	27	283	3073	10848
206	161	5	576	107	14	45	873	3868
1117	722	295	1722	408	76	1065	8726	26692
134	111	8	679	127	14	239	1251	1465
5086	3919	1048	11756	2270	328	5573	37476	154148

INVERNESS, Continued.

730	697	203	2046	313	81	2285	2805	22289
1236	1145	381	3594	501	115	5430	6023	43647
1098	911	249	2293	313	102	2890	4148	26456
658	648	264	1965	345	53	2302	4058	20791
1872	2135	793	5268	1174	199	6125	10807	99667
989	945	417	2765	547	108	3110	3874	36296
686	580	242	1807	399	45	2106	2875	23785
307	259	109	914	122	30	845	1835	9275
878	591	230	1877	421	54	1691	3999	32280
382	277	129	1721	365	77	1255	3674	9391
784	424	149	2909	572	109	823	9337	14704
1119	1133	483	3261	405	159	3569	7229	36712
453	517	214	1354	273	62	1790	2314	19972
891	780	257	2375	250	108	2400	4467	22220
745	863	266	1995	483	67	2259	6406	49687
12828	11905	4386	36143	6483	1369	38880	73851	467172

RICHMOND, Continued.

74	127	60	290	26	6	80	375	2917
113	334	68	1882	134	91	100	5786	3906
191	187	56	766	77	83	3679	414	6566
426	454	141	1451	110	58	1620	2829	12330
230	246	66	1071	85	53	637	4243	8806
299	271	94	815	96	35	303	2119	6575
603	318	116	2400	239	95	2738	3872	4812
365	416	143	1274	80	63	1963	1401	9551
287	305	109	957	131	57	780	2219	8184
278	229	51	694	135	39	649	1662	5328
139	149	62	663	15	53	190	2715	2686
193	231	91	784	111	37	585	1420	6552
230	170	54	746	68	19	265	1279	4336
3428	3437	1111	13793	1307	689	13589	30334	82449

No. 6.—RETURN OF AGRICULTURAL PRODUCE,

COUNTY OF

POLLING DISTRICTS.	Cheese, lbs. made in 1860.	Maple Sugar, lbs. made in 1860.	Bricks made in 1860.		Grindstones made in 1860.	
			M.	Value in Dollars.	No.	Value in Dollars.
1. Guysborough	1105	794			2	4
2. Intervale	700	665	15	120		
3. Manchester	716	170				
4. Melford	30	30				
5. Crow Harbor						
6. Cape Canso	40					
7. Country Harbor	20					
8. Sherbrooke	20	542	120	940		
9. Marie Joseph	50					
10. Forks, St. Mary's	2092	985	15	152	701	1102
11. Molasses Harbor						
	4773	3186	150	1212	703	1106

COUNTY OF

1. Plaster Cove	4639	94			6	8
2. Judique	26687	1742			26	45
3. River Inhabitants	12262	512	5	25		
4. Port Hood	9017	51			1	1
5. Mabou	24249	1765	40	200	24	50
6. Broad Cove (Intervale)	12234	529			11	15
7. Broad Cove	12250	110			11	19
8. Margaree	3978					
9. Young's Bridge	4626	156				
10. Friar's Head	300	50			23	23
11. Cheticamp	15	562			13	13
12. Whycocomagh	3834	1874	2	12	5	5
13. Lake Ainslie	3854	1024			4	4
14. River Dennis	5400	1290			4	5
15. North-east Margaree	494	177				
	123839	9936	47	237	128	188

COUNTY OF

1. Arichat						
2. Petit Degrate						
3. D'Escouse	40					
4. Black River	1451	20			1	1
5. River Bourgeoise	40				2	3
6. St. Peter's	329	59				
7. L'Ardoise	130				1	2
8. Grand River	806					
9. Red Islands	1170	95				
10. River Inhabitants	135					
11. Little Arichat	20					
12. Loch Lomond	268	115				
13. Flamboise	52	6				
	4441	295			4	6

STOCK, FISHERIES, &c....1860—61.

GUYSBOROUGH, Continued.

Gypsum quarried in 1860.		Vessels employed in the Fisheries.		Boats engaged in the Fisheries.		No. Nets and Seines.	Fish Cured in 1860.		
Tons.	Value in Dollars.	No.	Men.	No.	Men.		Quintals Dry.	Barrels Mackerel.	Barrels Shad.
....	....	12	43	110	131	1100	5285	3542	14
....	....	·11		6	56	110	38	....	
....	....	1	.....	78	44	772	367	677	13
....	....	11	38	142	137	985	558	3775	8
....	....	1	7	120	25	709	1251	1112	2
....	....	19	118	126	70	1330	6190	1403	....
....	....	10	37	122	16	613	4013	209	....
....	....	11	53	100	93	695	1943	42	31
....	....	9	35	102	45	315	4315	172	....
250	190	.....	.....	2	....	14	1	....	3
....	....	11	3	167	64	1411	5671	1549	10
250	190	85	340	1080	631	7391	29734	12519	81

INVERNESS, Continued.

Gypsum quarried in 1860.		Vessels employed in the Fisheries.		Boats engaged in the Fisheries.		No. Nets and Seines.	Fish Cured in 1860.		
Tons.	Value in Dollars.	No.	Men.	No.	Men.		Quintals Dry.	Barrels Mackerel.	Barrels Shad.
..	....	11	57	50	81	142	2314	215	....
....	....	....	....	55	109	237	364	133	....
...	....	....	....	32	....	71	40	60	.
....	....	....	....	52	70	126	1707	59	....
3	12	1	....	28	43	52	139	2	.
2	4	....	....	16	22	32	539	53	..
...	....	....	....	15	31	27	134	89	...
....	....	3	27	9	26	126	338	4	...
....	....	....	....	4	10	6	49	12	.
....	....	8	39	44	94	74	3366	....	.
1	1	15	92	86	208	270	14317	90	....
6	4	....	....	13	13	24	27	....	...
....	....	....	....	3	....	17	....	....	...
....	....	....	....	17	9	63	32	1	...
12	21	38	215	424	716	1267	23366	718	....

RICHMOND, Continued.

Gypsum quarried in 1860.		Vessels employed in the Fisheries.		Boats engaged in the Fisheries.		No. Nets and Seines.	Fish Cured in 1860.		
Tons.	Value in Dollars.	No.	Men.	No.	Men.		Quintals Dry.	Barrels Mackerel.	Barrels Shad.
400	400	3	12	21	40	321	442	416	....
....	....	27	148	156	289	1210	20155	1600	....
1070	826	17	113	25	37	185	7893	161	....
....	....	....	....	23	6	110	65	19	....
..	....	30	163	27	45	297	5813	429	....
...	....	1	4	35	12	176	415	734	....
...	....	5	27	230	339	1211	12134	2450	....
...	....	3	12	50	103	392	515	459	....
...	....	1	3	24	46	19	54	6	....
...	....	12	38	130	160	905	919	720	....
.	....	3	14	128	5	471	2986	214	....
...	....	2	6	2	2	14	65	11	....
...	....	5	47	33	36	113	2449	165	....
1470	1226	109	587	884	1120	5421	53905	7384	....

No. 6.—RETURN OF AGRICULTURAL PRODUCE,

COUNTY OF

POLLING DISTRICTS.	Fish Cured in 1860—*Continued.*					Gallons Fish Oil in 1860.
	Barrels Herring.	Barrels Alewives.	Barrels Salmon.	No. Smoked Salmon.	Boxes Herring.	
1. Guysborough	4712	128	31	8		1362
2. Intervale	169	4				60
3. Manchester	1851	77	11		10	603
4. Melford	10979	687	4	10		706
5. Crow Harbor	538	5	8			1537
6. Cape Canso	8940	22	12			7916
7. Country Harbor	3837	2	12		10	2146
8. Sherbrooke	2597	101	706	2		1985
9. Marie Joseph	1051	1365		10		1539
10. Forks, St. Mary's	74		9			13
11. Molasses Harbor	2211	309	36		24	2503
	36869	2700	829	30	44	20370

COUNTY OF

1. Plaster Cove	3980	130			4	208
2. Judique	880	16	2		5	1382
3. River Inhabitants	276		1		3	39
4. Port Hood	524					705
5. Mabou	38	32	14			93
6. Broad Cove (Intervale)	40	27	16			454
7. Broad Cove	50	170				139
8. Margaree	29	416	14			327
9. Young's Bridge	2	658	4			14
10. Friar's Head	285	35	49	3		2249
11. Cheticamp	1278	18	51			17556
12. Whycocomagh	31	13	1		12	38
13. Lake Ainslie	10	83				
14. River Dennis	175	4			7	20
15. North-east Margaree		69	1	20		
	7617	1671	147	23	31	23224

COUNTY OF

1. Arichat	515	3				12
2. Petit Degrate	1232	22	12			3302
3. D'Escouse	330	1		4		2615
4. Black River	208	3	3			24
5. River Bourgeoise	525	67				3291
6. St. Peter's	126	28	3		20	136
7. L'Ardoise	749	5	4		3	3108
8. Grand River	185	26	1			292
9. Red Islands	17	1				22
10. River Inhabitants	3941	172	3		10	667
11. Little Arichat	942	87				343
12. Loch Lomond	12					19
13. Flamboise	380					791
	9261	415	26	4	33	14622

STOCK, FISHERIES, &c....1860—61.

GUYSBOROUGH, Continued.

Value of Leather manufact'd in 1860.	Carriages made in 1860.	Bush. Lime burnt in 1860.	Gallons Malt Liquor made in 1860.	Boats built in 1860.	Lumber manufactured in 1860.				
					M. feet Deals, Superficial.	M. feet Pine Boards.	M. feet Spruce & Hemlock Boards.	Tons Square Timber.	M. Staves.
1616	4	300	100	28	1	73	61	408	62
40		20		1	20	12	45		29
12	1			15		15	12		333
42				59	1	20	20		108
12				5					1
				30			1		1
	5			43		10	110		121
1320	26			38	700	201	600	467	43
				32		26			186
1580	43				100	176	285	982	115
39				14					12
4661	79	320	100	265	829	542	1134	1857	1011

INVERNESS, Continued.

4204		108		20	10	39	50		56
775	6	347		11	2	28	42	226	16
437	6	97		1	12	54	75	1263	35
397	12	1112		8		13	13	6	1
3449	86	3266	30	2	4	23	143	32	27
281	12	210		1	8	11	106	17	12
241	2	640		4	21	6	46	28	5
50					7	6	26		1
185				5	18	3	49	31	10
3				10			43	117	4
35	12	12		20		4	46	3	
284	27	499		11	47	72	107	19	4
89	4	20			5	5	19		3
302	1	175		3	4	52	38	27	
96					1	9	18	30	12
10828	168	6486	30	96	139	325	815	1799	186

RICHMOND, Continued.

				8					
		20		3					
227	7	65		5	2	11	31	17	32
26	2			23	3	25	6	264	6
63	1	40		16		13	2	11	114
				79		2	1	2	1
				1		2			
4				2		12	6		5
629	4	166		53		17		400	29
114				17					
820		105				2	1		
				7		10			4
1883	14	406		214	11	94	47	694	191

No. 6.—RETURN OF AGRICULTURAL PRODUCE,

COUNTY OF

| | | | | | Lands—Acres |
POLLING DISTRICTS.	Dyke Marsh.		Salt Marsh.		Cultivated Intervale.	
	Acres.	Value in Dollars.	Acres.	Value in Dollars.	Acres.	Value in Dollars.
1. Washabok					166	2480
2. Middle River					722	11806
3. Baddeck			9	80	641	11048
4. Munro's Point, St. Ann's			9	180	115	1258
5. Englishtown, St. Ann's					18	40
6. Boularderie						
7. Ingonish	5	20	18	168	40	404
8. Cape North			94	623	265	1777
9. Bay St. Lawrence						
10. Little Narrows					19	180
	5	20	130	1051	1986	28993

COUNTY OF

1. Sydney			15	198	118	1486
2. Ball's Bridge	57	280	3	22	402	3691
3. Mira Ferry			2	20		
4. Sydney Mines	115	305	73	414	39	470
5. Mainadieu						
6. Louisburg			2	12		
7. Gabarus					30	292
8. East Bay	1	30	19	190	163	2438
9. Beaver Cove					3	24
10. Howley's Ferry						
11. Lingan Mines			62	252	56	429
12. Cow Bay	7	86	41	491	109	698
13. Big Pond			12	240	2	40
14. Christmas Island			9	97	176	1138
	180	701	238	1936	1098	10706

COUNTY OF

1. Windsor	1245	168454	73	2500	331	15010
2. St. Croix	626	51180	48	2425	34	1290
3. Brooklyn	299	32620	104	12500	204	6930
4. Scotch Village	948	86163	528	20636	129	4680
5. Falmouth	959	68463	181	6417	196	9482
6. Kempt	8	700	174	5593	51	350
7. Rawdon Church	12	1600			77	1290
8. South Rawdon			6	240	32	452
9. Noel	66	4412	570	12624	984	17775
10. Nine Mile River	129	12080	7	492	1528	60841
11. Maitland	222	15736	337	14824	200	7844
12. Chester Road	498	47308	107	3980	30	1012
	5012	489616	2135	82031	3902	126886

STOCK, FISHERIES, &c....1860—61.

VICTORIA.

| Occupied | | Grain, &c., raised in 1860. | | | | | | | |
| Cultivated Upland. | | Tons of Hay cut in 1860. | Bushels Wheat. | Bushels Barley. | Bushels Rye. | Bushels Oats. | Bushels Buckwheat. | Bushels Indian Corn. | Bushels Peas and Beans. |
Acres.	Value in Dollars.								
5303	35067	755	132	2890	....	22670	......	......	......
2024	14107	1564	88	832	....	13177	......	......	7
4266	35530	1956	178	1321	....	17392	30	......	16
6127	55949	1088	249	1401	15	18393	42	......	......
3512	23941	494	208	1840	....	11957	120	20	2
3463	38631	403	243	1845	....	20814	......	......	11
576	3864	162	46	19	....	146	......	......	......
1464	4583	191	592	702	135	1084	......	......	......
626	2928	221	272	159	44	486	......	......	......
2314	14288	449	337	772	140	10066	43	......	......
29675	228858	7583	2345	11781	334	117685	235	20	36

CAPE BRETON.

4365	51685	1340	827	1259	126	17739	26	13	51
5245	60079	1320	1895	2034	44	20927	91	6	24
2103	12029	355	110	203	....	7305	67	......	5
1873	34555	453	599	318	....	9160	......	20	29
1191	17106	429	26	296	70	5208	......	......	......
1884	17700	438	15	307	80	8875	......	......	......
4771	21552	666	61	382	....	11208	20	......	......
8424	55831	1357	1170	5149	130	19884	54	4	20
3030	10584	224	372	1456	30	10892	......	......	......
2135	24134	480	409	1044	15	18539	......	5	4
2615	26635	426	1252	2374	1	14265	......	......	10
1775	15508	269	402	602	132	4804	58	......	5
1085	11544	369	607	1421	....	6465	......	......	......
5053	18469	549	427	2910	....	20910	3	......	......
45549	377206	8675	8172	19755	628	176181	319	48	148

HANTS.

2857	145520	2061	1829	828	....	7336	103	25	98
2436	73340	1541	1360	443	406	6910	272	24	53
3155	59730	1826	2390	596	38	20176	86	25	92
8449	128060	3970	3245	759	109	11869	150	77	168
2798	80780	2051	1574	318	345	9439	107	100	96
3940	49357	1653	1913	1119	- 163	4643	60	41	83
4944	38182	1301	695	884	10	10720	1270	5	57
3510	29981	876	426	419	100	5820	377	......	26
8888	90751	3504	3655	1237	157	18115	1912	28	102
8506	92177	3838	1241	1653	21	20337	2629	4	90
3379	64446	2203	2740	595	142	9273	1132	6	49
907	30766	1056	1149	249	35	4286	81	27	29
53769	883096	25880	22217	9100	1526	128924	8179	362	943

No. 6.—RETURN OF AGRICULTURAL PRODUCE,

COUNTY OF

POLLING DISTRICTS.	Bushels Timothy Seed.	Bushels Potatoes.	Bushels Turnips.	Bushels other Roots.	Bushels Apples.	Bushels Plums.
1. Washabok	51	8809	684	8	159	1
2. Middle River	16	7498	426		80	1
3. Baddeck	12	11954	1123	68	569	18
4. Munro's Point, St. Ann's	12	7984	761	22	50	1
5. Englishtown, St. Ann's	4	8668	236	10	57	9
6. Boularderie	28	8607	504	8	86	17
7. Ingonish		5179	106		13	2
8. Cape North		5391	126			
9. Bay St. Lawrence		3900	7			
10. Little Narrows	11	4857	57	4	87	2
	134	72847	4030	120	1101	51

COUNTY OF

	Bushels Timothy Seed.	Bushels Potatoes.	Bushels Turnips.	Bushels other Roots.	Bushels Apples.	Bushels Plums.
1. Sydney	28	19121	3642	326	322	99
2. Ball's Bridge	50	27665	2540	191	1165	314
3. Mira Ferry	1	8191	351	11	88	11
4. Sydney Mines	39	14202	2781	150	175	59
5. Mainadieu		5947	361	4	19	
6. Louisburg	2	9177	252	2	20	
7. Gabarus	4	10682	1391	10	14	
8. East Bay	153	23745	1115	17	296	26
9. Beaver Cove	7	9842	220		7	
10. Howley's Ferry	34	10453	1342	7	108	39
11. Lingan Mines	23	11629	1672		73	18
12. Cow Bay	2	4858	517	7	34	
13. Big Pond	12	6298	48	10	31	
14. Christmas Island	13	6962	202	100	60	
	368	168772	16434	835	2412	566

COUNTY OF

	Bushels Timothy Seed.	Bushels Potatoes.	Bushels Turnips.	Bushels other Roots.	Bushels Apples.	Bushels Plums.
1. Windsor	17	9811	6182	1038	2475	38
2. St. Croix	13	8919	2880	177	500	5
3. Brooklyn	39	13854	1597	167	879	12
4. Scotch Village	33	19754	2597	351	1006	15
5. Falmouth	46	22576	3320	387	2657	42
6. Kempt	42	13367	1825	123	253	9
7. Rawdon Church	90	8424	2859	238	673	
8. South Rawdon	16	4791	1965	121	563	4
9. Noel	339	24921	5531	187	717	4
10. Nine Mile River	218	15766	4559	656	409	
11. Maitland	107	18293	2677	185	888	19
12. Chester Road	62	5909	2926	455	936	11
	1022	166384	38927	4087	11956	159

STOCK, FISHERIES, &c...1860—61.

VICTORIA, Continued.

Neat Cattle, exclusive of Cows.	Milch Cows.	Cattle. Horses.	Sheep.	Pigs.	Hand Looms.	Fulled Cloth, y'ds made in 1860.	Not Fulled yards made in 1860.	Butter, made in 1860.
611	413	146	1753	238	93	4169	2852	12102
805	674	180	1962	247	62	2568	3289	31850
863	884	274	2258	254	72	3597	4718	38481
693	728	208	2120	187	82	3121	2878	26925
511	561	122	1736	195	86	1798	3608	21059
508	582	235	1517	202	50	845	4273	21731
137	121	10	304	106	5	100	716	2479
312	314	48	869	132	29	672	1650	18854
158	122	18	341	55	26	120	1119	3414
303	298	96	1156	143	39	531	2953	9284
5051	4697	1337	14025	1849	544	17524	28656	186179

CAPE BRETON, Continued.

673	768	362	1686	490	91	1339	4109	25345
696	811	510	1579	399	93	3084	4872	34435
322	366	142	1113	72	28	1005	1851	9450
158	344	267	391	331	18	774	400	10860
259	375	147	1365	200	45	64	2580	7994
482	462	173	1581	131	56	183	3883	13846
534	513	223	2383	157	76	1295	3139	11768
854	788	324	2802	499	118	3567	4858	31624
394	326	137	1139	175	80	1960	1083	5251
386	528	201	997	314	51	1619	1765	18417
322	418	223	1028	536	28	1501	1121	11860
211	240	96	1035	207	36	842	2466	8235
264	316	128	1153	178	57	1283	1683	10175
610	507	154	1928	386	96	1770	5675	11127
6165	6762	3087	20170	4075	873	20286	39485	210387

HANTS, Continued.

390	360	308	739	189	5	523	1422	13960
396	350	279	1164	150	13	670	4608	13800
641	444	288	1694	163	29	119	4688	16257
1220	743	321	3099	326	54	528	8262	30900
645	346	217	1076	212	16	197	2297	17041
601	449	95	1653	187	50	253	5756	18434
462	441	206	1308	149	38	675	5186	23215
292	308	124	817	62	25	.....	2505	11705
1374	898	351	2912	285	102	935	11615	39136
1172	933	369	2710	251	78	1081	9558	39577
671	511	251	1853	196	56	841	7486	26471
416	191	112	630	130	19	30	1795	7739
8280	5974	2919	19655	2300	485	5852	65179	258835

No. 6.—RETURN OF AGRICULTURAL PRODUCE,

COUNTY OF

POLLING DISTRICTS.	Cheese, lbs. made in 1860.	Maple Sugar, lbs. made in 1860.	Bricks made in 1860.		Grindstones made in 1860.	
			M.	Value in Dollars.	No.	Value in Dollars.
1. Washabok	1257	102			5	14
2. Middle River	1537	175			2	5
3. Baddeck	1480	159			4	5
4. Munro's Point, St. Ann's	1852	139			3	4
5. Englishtown, St. Ann's	474	6			22	44
6. Boularderie	3079	76			5	6
7. Ingonish	45	90				
8. Cape North	35	27				
9. Bay St. Lawrence	132		6	30		
10. Little Narrows	293	30			4	7
	10188	804	6	30	45	85

COUNTY OF

1. Sydney	603	251			5	5
2. Ball's Bridge	1078	24	4	24	25	23
3. Mira Ferry	65	9				
4. Sydney Mines	412					
5. Mainadieu	75					
6. Louisburg		33				
7. Gabarus	473	20				
8. East Bay	5993	563	1	6	7	10
9. Beaver Cove	470	47				
10. Howley's Ferry	1335	27			5	11
11. Lingan Mines	40					
12. Cow Bay	479				5	9
13. Big Pond	900	100				
14. Christmas Island	1060	257				
	12992	1331	5	30	47	58

COUNTY OF

1. Windsor	2487				250	250
2. St. Croix	1770	150				
3. Brooklyn	743	630				
4. Scotch Village	1954	225			35	154
5. Falmouth	4710	150			563	384
6. Kempt	310	200	50	300		
7. Rawdon Church	273	585			2	6
8. South Rawdon	387	40				
9. Noel	1415	3162			40	18
10. Nine Mile River	1995	855	1500	13250		
11. Maitland	220	3032				
12. Chester Road	1960	210	5	40	3	6
	18224	9239	1555	13590	893	818

STOCK, FISHERIES, &c....1860—61.

VICTORIA, Continued.

Gypsum quarried in 1860.		Vessels employed in the Fisheries.		Boats engaged in the Fisheries.		No. Nets and Seines.	Fish Cured in 1860.		
Tons.	Value in Dollars.	No.	Men.	No.	Men.		Quintals Dry.	Barrels Mackerel.	Barrels Shad.
				40	84	44	172	1	
				1			10		
				69	37	129	517	125	
		2	13	154	47	549	2158	1642	
				32	53	76	485	59	
		1		96	16	327	2670	1861	
				40	59	153	543	69	
				23	15	118	921	117	
				5	7	8	37		
		3	13	413	326	1398	7513	3874	

CAPE BRETON, Continued.

		1	4	31	19	189	1404	81	
30	24	2	12	47	10	169	58	23	
				2		31	12		
		4	60	81	152	519	3022	1272	
				197	178	1137	8035	1915	
		5	17	69	33	297	4785	425	
		6	13	124	92	517	5241	635	
				2	2	48	182		
							2		
		3	31	11	12	77	730	11	
				46	16	120	387		
		2		66	78	301	2157	31	
				3	6	17	24		
						1	390		
30	24	23	137	679	598	3423	26429	4393	

HANTS, Continued.

17564	15735			3	1	6			59
38651	31055								
700	375								
10524	6917			7	11	2			15
				3		3	1		42
24330	14174	1	4	13	4	19	18	30	124
1572	1177			15	19	15	4		461
1206	984			8		18			2
23668	7466			32	40	117			375
						2			
118215	77883	1	4	81	75	182	23	30	1078

No. 6.—RETURN OF AGRICULTURAL PRODUCE,

COUNTY OF

POLLING DISTRICTS.	Fish Cured in 1860—Continued.					Gallons Fish Oil in 1860.
	Barrels Herring.	Barrels Alewives.	Barrels Salmon.	No. Smoked Salmon.	Boxes Herring.	
1. Washabok	103	2				302
2. Middle River						
3. Baddeck	2	4	2	12		21
4. Munro's Point, St. Ann's	279	13				341
5. Englishtown, St. Ann's	1195		35			1484
6. Boularderie	111					346
7. Ingonish	523		124			1917
8. Cape North	88	7	35			349
9. Bay St. Lawrence	40		17			23
10. Little Narrows	11	3				51
	2352	29	213	12		4834

COUNTY OF

1. Sydney	488	37	43	10		1400
2. Ball's Bridge	681	25	1		22	23
3. Mira Ferry		43	5			6
4. Sydney Mines	654	40	117			1707
5. Mainadieu	635	66	162			4924
6. Louisburg	200	28	7	2		985
7. Gabarus	516	73	5	127	22	1856
8. East Bay	182	22	1			87
9. Beaver Cove						
10. Howley's Ferry	290		3			352
11. Lingan Mines	392	30	10			546
12. Cow Bay	92	6	54		1	3632
13. Big Pond	27					19
14. Christmas Island		4				6
	4157	308	408	139	45	15904

COUNTY OF

1. Windsor						
2. St. Croix						
3. Brooklyn						
4. Scotch Village	3	2				
5. Falmouth						
6. Kempt	82				70	10
7. Rawdon Church						
8. South Rawdon						
9. Noel	3		2			45
10. Nine Mile River		122				
11. Maitland		27	1			
12. Chester Road						
	86	151	3		70	55

STOCK, FISHERIES, &c....1860—61.

VICTORIA, Continued.

Value of Leather manufact'd in 1860.	Carriages made in 1860.	Bush. Lime burnt in 1860.	Gallons Malt Liquor made in 1860.	Boats built in 1860.	Lumber manufactured in 1860.				
					M. feet Deals, Superficial.	M. feet Pine Boards	M. feet Spruce & Hemlock Boards.	Tons Square Timber.	M. Staves.
107	1	630	....	9	29	36	17	5	1
59	2	1254	....		4	34	23	.....	.....
2127	16	1300	....	1	3	35	5	.....	.....
108	7	236	....	3	13	75	39	.....	.....
141	6	75	....	30	5	29	4	.....	2
152	1	1200	....	10	3	27	38	17	.....
15	....		10	38	....	49	1	4	32
130	6	....		7	....	27	15	35	22
....	....	....		5	....		1	.....	3
14	....	18	2	2	29	16	62	19	11
2853	39	4703	12	114	77	328	207	80	71

CAPE BRETON, Continued.

422	10	5000	....	4	2	87	63	2	.....
4820	10	7100	80	9	30	91	214	166	12
11	....	....		9	....	47	56	20	5
3100	5	2709		10	....		20	27	.....
....	....	....		14	....	5	....		4
....	....	....	15	6	....	16	9	6	.....
32	....	110		31	2	46	56	....	13
185	16	135	....	4	32	86	283	139	3
15	1	....		....	....	14	109	88	2
12	1	4950		3	....	1	3	.....	.....
12	1	....		13	1	10	5	9	.....
33	....	6		32	2	5	5	.....	7
29	....	112		1	1	9	7	.....	5
4	1	....		2	....	1	1	60	.....
8675	45	20092	95	140	70	417	891	515	51

HANTS, Continued.

1600	62	300	....		200	250	25	54	.....
400	1	....			3	74	173	15	1
1200	27	....				70	354	.....	.....
310	13	....		1	....	5	16	30	.....
82	4	150	....	12	200	55	26	.....	.....
....	1	21	....	1	316	20	394	.....	2
335	13	3	....		60	97	182	26	.....
....	2	....			17	35	57	174	.....
800	5	....		2	63	67	196	116	2
293	28	200	....		54	65	196	104	.....
880	3	16800	....	5	32	34	107	238	.....
....	....	....				132	456	5	11
5900	155	17474	....	21	945	902	2175	742	16

No. 6.—RETURN OF AGRICULTURAL PRODUCE,

COUNTY OF

POLLING DISTRICTS.	Lands—Acres					
	Dyke Marsh.		Salt Marsh.		Cultivated Intervals.	
	Acres.	Value in Dollars.	Acres.	Value in Dollars.	Acres.	Value in Dollars.
1. Canning	446	53190	398	12401	369	17465
2. Canard	1780	168706	398	12844	88	3880
3. Centreville	636	89112	21	810	700	41656
4. Lakeville					719	34227
5. Somerset					752	43021
6. Kentville	380	46250	115	8126	529	24046
7. Gaspereaux	130	14628	86	2272	2908	46116
8. Wolfville	2074	216309	430	10893	240	12900
9. Lower Horton	1424	110288	281	5599	76	3344
10. Aylesford					1006	35071
11. West Sherbrooke					11	160
12. Aylesford	25	2600	5	120	1234	41364
13. Berwick					614	41027
	6895	701083	1734	53065	9246	344277

COUNTY OF

POLLING DISTRICTS.	Dyke Marsh.		Salt Marsh.		Cultivated Intervals.	
1. Wilmot			8	800	1115	37958
2. Wilmot, Middleton Corner	11	808	3	82	943	31040
3. Clarence, Wilmot	41	3280	18	2100	1946	57443
4. Bridgetown	215	22895	74	6330	497	18002
5. Bellisle	717	50222	369	24040	306	11693
6. New Caledonia	220	14074	613	36982	366	6720
7. Broad Cove			220	10506	139	3302
8. Clementsport	59	4200	33	2070	206	6758
9. Hessian Line			6	300	234	3320
10. Annapolis Royal	658	40290	516	22341	356	9337
11. Carleton's Corner	450	33768	246	18514	580	20728
12. Nictaux	4	360	3	460	1595	47049
13. Dalhousie					13	184
14. Maitland					118	968
15. Morse Road					138	2080
	2375	169397	2109	124525	8542	256582

COUNTY OF

POLLING DISTRICTS.	Dyke Marsh.		Salt Marsh.		Cultivated Intervals.	
1. Hillsburg			38	2000	514	5130
2. Head St. Mary's Bay			152	4576	44	845
3. Digby			139	2632	133	2005
4. Sandy Cove					14	219
5. Long Island					8	320
6. Westport					33	3595
7. On St. Mary's Bay			19	600	37	631
8. Weymouth			49	1656	167	873
9. Belivoo Cove	4	110			37	316
10. Session House, Clare			22	413	171	3272
11. Montegan	34	498	8	131	70	1212
12. Salmon River	46	466	93	2154	150	1493
	84	1074	519	14162	1378	19911

STOCK, FISHERIES, &c....1860—61.

KING'S.

Occupied.			Grain, &c., raised in 1860.							
Cultivated Upland.		Tons of Hay cut in 1860.	Bushels Wheat.	Bushels Barley.	Bushels Rye.	Bushels Oats.	Bushels Buckwheat.	Bushels Indian Corn.	Bushels Peas and Beans.	
Acres.	Value in Dollars.									
7950	221154	2965	3484	621	676	8195	741	204	148	
4584	174690	3156	943	225	1214	12737	869	317	106	
11459	136031	3487	1798	576	1929	12610	755	386	123	
10478	165889	2499	2571	788	1812	10267	429	202	137	
9926	162963	3287	3524	1088	1550	16052	966	394	154	
9724	149758	3033	2321	224	1654	7928	734	668	181	
6883	34730	2431	1725	373	618	7876	122	60	92	
3293	215109	3070	1925	848	385	18411	273	281	233	
3834	144100	2478	1785	487	525	17850	304	200	136	
8419	106371	2413	2052	462	4576	5542	888	755	191	
1370	9258	359	143	273	61	566	566	95	28	
10140	97855	2607	1494	1106	2646	9792	1233	544	193	
4039	67336	1205	1353	82	2287	4158	658	424	121	
92099	1685244	32788	25024	7453	19743	131994	8809	4530	1843	

ANNAPOLIS.

11384	183352	3056	2105	1657	2861	12134	2229	783	294
10199	143767	2318	1679	4200	548	11297	1005	496	217
10057	136515	2774	2840	2218	427	10540	1010	604	318
5446	131956	2020	1208	974	137	3837	589	710	240
4886	101245	2787	1042	1303	367	2601	469	1132	315
2467	66375	2325	621	1013	157	1049	127	525	186
1501	25713	806	58	367	14	291	36	33	56
2123	34674	1488	709	1503	903	1151	790	299	211
3109	31059	1149	598	1300	562	1580	814	74	142
2869	90066	2978	716	787	1674	3563	553	975	226
3026	71163	2085	905	452	435	2507	689	1163	372
6381	103488	2367	2090	872	1063	5353	1016	1292	391
3263	28019	1113	478	588	451	1861	999	100	86
1572	10884	555	182	359	496	1273	482	57	31
1927	12185	594	167	179	328	442	333	13	22
70210	1170461	28424	15398	17865	10423	59482	11105	8256	3107

DIGBY.

4733	70432	1418	865	849	231	2413	1167	261	182
2065	28813	1236	539	672	112	2196	1059	47	87
3456	57585	1262	493	770	5	1522	1273	57	50
125	2567	75	10	121		62	27		1
621	18857	425	41	97	20	334	8		
250	8365	158				72			
1164	23544	1216	346	522		643	968	218	33
1694	40899	1277	151	935	35	1288	565	61	66
192	3198	97	16	81		134		3	5
3831	71723	1623	106	3601	24	705	32	32	158
1937	57661	1224	299	2593	16	789	23	29	52
2467	32996	698	76	536	27	515	49	2	29
22535	416645	10709	2942	10777	500	10643	5173	690	665

No. 6.—RETURN OF AGRICULTURAL PRODUCE,

COUNTY OF

Grain, &c., raised in 1860—*Continued.*

POLLING DISTRICTS.	Bushels Timothy Seed.	Bushels Potatoes.	Bushels Turnips.	Bushels other Roots.	Bushels Apples.	Bushels Plums.
1. Canning	37	132433	2663	283	3493	151
2. Canard	30	127835	3160	845	6161	114
3. Centreville	36	114707	2222	700	4935	41
4. Lakeville	47	84040	3117	258	2314	21
5. Somerset	74	91401	5532	344	2806	100
6. Kentville	34	68372	3854	452	3905	29
7. Gaspereaux	106	22712	1738	199	1223	
8. Wolfville	62	64709	5560	653	2642	87
9. Lower Horton	49	38259	2611	240	765	58
10. Aylesford	59	37616	5683	326	2198	32
11. West Sherbrooke	24	4055	932	71	99	
12. Aylesford	32	38746	7449	650	4085	46
13. Berwick	34	33666	2478	388	1634	
	624	858551	46099	5418	36260	679

COUNTY OF

1. Wilmot	90	44630	10748	572	4532	47
2. Wilmot, Middleton Corner	64	24834	4798	888	4460	9
3. Clarence, Wilmot	74	26991	3903	378	6672	27
4. Bridgetown	28	20325	5533	706	4640	17
5. Bellisle	15	17165	8465	992	8913	14
6. New Caledonia	21	12681	7320	1053	4638	23
7. Broad Cove		5112	1900	545	2035	5
8. Clementsport	25	11467	2614	961	1853	36
9. Hessian Line	14	7880	2072	377	768	1
10. Annapolis Royal	29	27287	11063	1463	9343	70
11. Carleton's Corner	52	24793	5530	472	10064	42
12. Nictaux	24	23810	4934	1432	5901	16
13. Dalhousie	13	7657	1728	273	884	5
14. Maitland	12	3598	857	126	237	2
15. Morse Road	17	6522	1245	30	75	
	469	266732	72710	10268	65405	316

COUNTY OF

1. Hillsburg	35	13571	4758	924	1725	19
2. Head St. Mary's Bay	12	13544	3430	1113	2091	13
3. Digby	8	17179	4739	1490	1952	10
4. Sandy Cove		785	313	63	14	
5. Long Island		5881	897	74		
6. Westport		1566	56	131		
7. On St. Mary's Bay		20309	3694	571	1284	5
8. Weymouth	11	15463	6716	596	1947	5
9. Belivee Cove		2015	180	118	11	
10. Session House, Clare	1	36792	4075	762	1546	2
11. Montegan		46616	3052	290	689	
12. Salmon River		19835	2704	326	45	
	67	195556	34614	6455	11304	54

STOCK, FISHERIES, &c....1860—61.

KING'S, Continued.

Neat Cattle, exclusive of Cows.	Milch Cows.	Horses.	Sheep.	Pigs.	Hand Looms.	Fulled Cloth, y'ds made in 1860.	Not Fulled, yards made in 1860.	Butter, lbs. made in 1860.
857	477	414	1537	352	64	3116	4166	21872
980	461	333	1099	335	16	1882	2906	21252
1042	577	428	1738	339	27	616	6417	29511
979	451	315	1500	231	43	2312	3596	23233
1352	705	404	2283	366	66	3146	5607	30499
986	481	348	1497	326	40	827	4659	23928
858	437	268	1365	208	56	....	4826	23870
1059	431	317	1175	247	15	249	2900	21045
743	364	225	949	199	28	149	3178	18983
793	507	314	1699	288	68	4050	6396	25239
175	83	33	255	36	6	....	1101	3535
945	543	269	2273	281	43	505	6064	25530
403	243	192	769	161	28	583	2781	12029
11172	5760	3860	18199	3369	500	17435	53877	280526

ANNAPOLIS, Continued.

1173	746	383	2474	401	103	1918	11907	32160
915	593	284	2188	351	73	1157	12636	28518
1179	673	285	2349	259	74	2327	6102	24858
725	456	210	1303	146	35	681	2936	19259
888	456	144	1830	168	53	151	5983	17095
888	404	131	1855	150	34	1324	2740	18970
362	207	57	822	88	21	271	1680	8190
591	347	103	1122	111	33	302	3315	12969
482	278	89	793	77	36	238	2343	12261
1077	523	201	1315	201	45	14742	5061	20196
768	363	146	816	136	27	655	2146	10455
864	646	259	1327	274	60	1564	5850	24184
459	247	84	645	65	43	350	3850	9921
246	124	30	328	56	23	214	1264	6427
240	127	46	186	57	12	597	706	5514
10857	6190	2452	19353	2540	672	26491	68519	250977

DIGBY, Continued.

534	335	106	716	147	37	689	2673	16271
615	342	68	822	125	37	152	2393	12027
601	389	103	1333	131	27	504	2751	14967
61	26	6	178	10	5	33	247	1200
203	165	18	1231	43	21	201	2777	6968
29	71	2	581	39	4	10	205	3427
617	331	54	847	42	27	130	2595	15555
638	331	59	1056	141	23	140	3120	15288
48	24	23	74	8	6	....	413	1070
994	446	59	1727	281	143	177	7594	27017
709	337	72	1037	358	96	519	4278	17495
371	244	67	779	100	35	....	2317	15205
5420	3041	637	10381	1424	461	2555	31363	146490

No. 6.—RETURN OF AGRICULTURAL PRODUCE,

COUNTY OF

POLLING DISTRICTS.	Cheese, lbs. made in 1860.	Maple Sugar, lbs. made in 1860.	Bricks made in 1860.		Grindstones made in 1860.	
			M.	Value in Dollars.	No.	Value in Dollars.
1. Canning	2226	174	100	800		
2. Canard	4929	100				
3. Centreville	6087					
4. Lakeville	7490	796	40	246	1	1
5. Somerset	20315	362	25	150		
6. Kentville	2690	1110	40	240		
7. Gaspereaux	2335	1042				
8. Wolfville	4190	400	400	2337		
9. Lower Horton	2849					
10. Aylesford	10330	1548	50	300		
11. West Sherbrooke	250	655	7	45		
12. Aylesford	17265	463	45	240		
13. Berwick	4025	445	68	460		
	84981	7095	775	4818	1	1

COUNTY OF

1. Wilmot	41455	383				
2. Wilmot, Middleton Corner	25086	822	70	500	2	2
3. Clarence, Wilmot	10950	274			1	1
4. Bridgetown	16545	296				
5. Bellisle	16340	365				
6. New Caledonia	9670					
7. Broad Cove	265					
8. Clementsport	1470	415				
9. Hessian Line	928	1736	20	80		
10. Annapolis Royal	5350	315	500	2400		
11. Carleton's Corner	14678	170	257	1068		
12. Nictaux	62714	936	3	17		
13. Dalhousie	9151	1043	18	86		
14. Maitland	318	150	12	102		
15. Morse Road	850	42				
	215770	6947	880	4253	3	3

COUNTY OF

1. Hillsburg	1100	425				
2. Head St. Mary's Bay	362	100				
3. Digby	162		30	200		
4. Sandy Cove						
5. Long Island	180	80				
6. Westport						
7. On St. Mary's Bay	275		110	650		
8. Weymouth	358	249				
9. Belivoe Cove	20					
10. Session House, Clare	1292	53	1	6		
11. Montegan	1012					
12. Salmon River	1235		7	63		
	5996	907	148	919		

STOCK, FISHERIES, &c....1860-61.

KING'S, Continued.

Gypsum quarried in 1860.		Vessels employed in the Fisheries.		Boats engaged in the Fisheries.		No. Nets and Seines.	Fish Cured in 1860.		
Tons.	Value in Dollars.	No.	Men.	No.	Men.		Quintals Dry.	Barrels Mackerel.	Barrels Shad.
		2		6		22	114		528
						22			148
		2	13	10		5	381	50	4
				3	7	3	36		
		1	6	11	14	18	297	44	119
						14	1		44
				1		7	90		28
				7	13	23	15		202
		1	9	5	4	7	9	17	153
				7	5	16	145	21	
						4			48
		6	28	50	43	141	1088	132	1274

ANNAPOLIS, Continued.

		1		16	14	56	211	1	
				24	5	167	399	1	7
				16	6	78	426		24
		2	9	14	2	65	396	81	3
				9	2	42	47		
				26	27	23	93		
				22	36	36	563	19	
				49	19	17	175	2	1
				1			12	3	1
				2		2			
				2		6			2
				3	4	13	2		15
							2		
		3	9	184	109	507	2324	107	53

DIGBY, Continued.

				11	6	3	230	62	
		1	8	8	3	2	45	570	18
		2	9	40	62	84	536	325	125
				7	2	14	61	217	
		15	89	72	74	136	5456	1238	1
		26	135	37	50	176	5041	2411	3
				7	7	4	110	339	5
				1		1	33	148	
				1	2	1	61	36	
		4	18	81	159	42	986	758	1
		3	15	24	33	27	560	232	6
		5	28	6	7	33	905	31	
		56	302	295	405	523	14114	6387	209

No. 6.—RETURN OF AGRICULTURAL PRODUCE,

COUNTY OF

POLLING DISTRICTS.	Barrels Herring.	Barrels Alewives.	Barrels Salmon.	No. Smoked Salmon.	Boxes Herring.	Gallons Fish Oil in 1860.
1. Canning	454				864	72
2. Canard				2		
3. Centreville	110		4			363
4. Lakeville	4					58
5. Somerset	248		1	2	140	103
6. Kentville	2	1				
7. Gaspereaux	6	100	2		227	57
8. Wolfville	56	32			541	73
9. Lower Horton	12	60		32	26	9
10. Aylesford						
11. West Sherbrooke						
12. Aylesford	37	5	6			65
13. Berwick	27		1			
	956	210	14	36	1808	800

COUNTY OF

	Barrels Herring.	Barrels Alewives.	Barrels Salmon.	No. Smoked Salmon.	Boxes Herring.	Gallons Fish Oil in 1860.
1. Wilmot	792			25		63
2. Wilmot, Middleton Corner	894	27				271
3. Clarence, Wilmot	536	50		60	20	324
4. Bridgetown	204					325
5. Belisle	125				6	21
6. New Caledonia	803				4308	20
7. Broad Cove	762				7086	409
8. Clementsport	181		25		11563	59
9. Hessian Line	12				27	4
10. Annapolis Royal	10		3		20	4
11. Carleton's Corner	3		1	18		
12. Nictaux	5		1			10
13. Dalhousie						
14. Maitland						
15. Morse Road						17
	4333	77	30	103	23040	1527

COUNTY OF

	Barrels Herring.	Barrels Alewives.	Barrels Salmon.	No. Smoked Salmon.	Boxes Herring.	Gallons Fish Oil in 1860.
1. Hillsburg	53				6663	34
2. Head St. Mary's Bay	135	8			437	7
3. Digby	662			1	751	308
4. Sandy Cove	98					23
5. Long Island	3186				266	2158
6. Westport	8578				1180	1994
7. On St. Mary's Bay	44				10	50
8. Weymouth	3					
9. Belivoe Cove						
10. Session House, Clare	920			1		571
11. Montegan	9				2	68
12. Salmon River	29	3	1			149
	13717	11	1	2	9309	5362

STOCK, FISHERIES, &c....1860—61.

KING'S, Continued.

Value of Leather manufact'd in 1860.	Carriages made in 1860.	Bush. Lime burnt in 1860.	Gallons Malt Liquor made in 1860.	Boats built in 1860.	Lumber manufactured in 1860.				
					M. feet Deals, Superficial.	M. feet Pine Boards	M. feet Spruce & Hemlock Boards.	Tons Square Timber.	M. Staves.
500	39			2	29	5	124	6	3
12	8				1	20	3		
1110	16		180				87	26	
1600	2					10	290		4
	15			2		12	44	5	
630	8				180	334	553	56	11
	10					117	103	81	
4150	11			2		12	40	5	
197	2					7	38		
240	40				25	616	530	18	14
						43	17		13
2220	22			2		14	71		
400	3					60	253		
11059	176		180	8	234	1250	2153	197	45

ANNAPOLIS, Continued.

5420	44			7		67	194	15	
920	18			2		14	118	6	22
1410	11			2		6	66		2
1200	21			3		2	23		58
	4			1		10	39		14
775	1			5		5	45		
	2			9	1		93		12
	6			19		52	58	15	
16						39	102	5	
1814	4			4	14	117	215		60
4	10			1	9	89	91	11	
800	67				3	448	274		49
	3				2	385	80		6
						192	55		
					66	94	135		37
12359	191			53	95	1520	1588	52	260

DIGBY, Continued.

2000	22			8	20	584	289	100	
	1			4		51	186	20	18
4200	18			13		12	64		7
				2			12		
				7		1	56		
237				14					2
20				11		96	128		3
900	1				1873	1304	758	1101	
				2	5	20	70		
100	6			8	20	134	746	40	11
				2		16	275		
100	3			3	75	8	273	23	32
7557	51			74	1993	2226	2857	1284	73

No. 6.—RETURN OF AGRICULTURAL PRODUCE,

COUNTY OF

POLLING DISTRICTS.	Dyke Marsh.		Salt Marsh.		Cultivated Intervale.	
	Acres.	Value in Dollars.	Acres.	Value in Dollars.	Acres.	Value in Dollars.
1. Ohio	68	2480	7	136	505	11347
2. Yarmouth	768	23231	392	5495	391	34575
3. Chebogue	167	3400	1709	16365	214	3620
4. Carleton	2	60			252	4441
5. Plymouth	107	1488	569	9670	201	2294
6. Tusket	239	3911	713	13169	451	8934
7. Argyle	62	771	561	7250	144	1012
8. Pubnico	26	470	294	5080	534	15170
9. Kempt					351	3918
10. West side Tusket River	1	40	64	1538	114	2071
	1440	35851	4309	58706	3157	87382

COUNTY OF

1. Carleton Village			119	3460	111	3361
2. Shelburne	43	1250	138	2507	52	2510
3. Ragged Islands	13	900	120	3514	28	2820
4. Louis Head	15	600	161	2671	117	1528
5. Shag Harbor	3	30	113	1579	243	6919
6. Cape Sable Island	2	40	18	393	110	2910
7. Barrington	16	380	79	2090	42	2180
8. Port LaTour	4	120	194	4682	133	1917
	96	3320	942	20896	836	24145

COUNTY OF

1. Liverpool	4	520	17	316	26	4630
2. Bristol	16	800	17	548	88	5975
3. Port Medway			105	2450	276	11800
4. Port Mouton	33	866	88	2388	29	710
5. Brookfield	13	100			489	4263
6. Caledonia					340	3570
7. Greenfield					262	6715
	66	2286	227	5702	1510	37662

COUNTY OF

1. Lunenburg	1	320	9	158	16	640
2. Ritcey's Cove			67	1029	19	2928
3. Mahone Bay	6	80	3	33	2206	92825
4. LaHave			2	70	25	724
5. New Germany					243	3999
6. Chester			1	10	18	324
7. Sherbrooke					23	208
8. Petite Riviere			122	5470	46	3085
9. Bridgewater	10	400			307	2896
10. Tancook Island						
11. Mill Cove, St. Margaret's Bay.					1	30
	17	800	204	6770	2904	106959

STOCK, FISHERIES, &c....1860—61.

YARMOUTH.

Cultivated Upland Acres.	Value in Dollars.	Tons of Hay cut in 1860.	Bushels Wheat.	Bushels Barley.	Bushels Rye.	Bushels Oats.	Bushels Buckwheat.	Bushels Indian Corn.	Bushels Peas and Beans.
11760	182232	2602	472	3319	271	2546	529	43	225
5804	215638	2801	217	1525	65	2007	48	23	35
4122	82798	2303	113	1047	99	1032	2	9	45
2876	35346	903	78	473	93	370	421	60	194
1135	14480	1074	28	362	16	72	.....	2	5
2653	61062	1746	71	141	6	164	2	58	65
4518	30227	892	76	332	136	358	9	2	19
829	16481	847	4	31	.....	355	.....	4	2
1018	13170	452	12	90	10	40	66	69	32
489	7978	378	59	84	.....	94	19	37	38
35204	659402	13998	1130	7404	696	7044	1096	307	660

SHELBURNE.

Acres	Value	Hay	Wheat	Barley	Rye	Oats	Buckwheat	Indian Corn	Peas/Beans
439	19139	584	.....	307	.....	151	.....	.....	2
1788	69522	1114	116	688	11	479	15	19	23
727	56448	718	24	452	7	514	.....	3	8
803	26630	934	9	367	.....	832	.....	.....	9
765	17774	483	.....	4	.....	245	.....	.....	
813	22487	480	.....	10	.....	162	.....	.....	10
1028	62289	746	16	23	.....	438	1	1	23
866	32393	710	12	149	.....	184	2	.....	11
7229	306682	5769	177	2000	18	3005	18	23	85

QUEEN'S.

Acres	Value	Hay	Wheat	Barley	Rye	Oats	Buckwheat	Indian Corn	Peas/Beans
819	92955	790	31	571	40	541	16	.....	29
1272	105208	978	6	649	.....	381	.....	10	28
931	52953	777	47	422	43	181	6	.....	20
669	32177	640	24	102	.....	246	.....	12	13
3710	42390	1496	181	2199	316	2212	633	73	141
6589	51496	2390	838	2885	1023	6723	1150	97	219
751	14841	359	150	284	112	313	134	15	32
14741	392020	7439	1277	7112	1534	10597	1939	207	482

LUNENBURG.

Acres	Value	Hay	Wheat	Barley	Rye	Oats	Buckwheat	Indian Corn	Peas/Beans
3286	169745	2256	708	13709	240	2319	44	.....	191
2375	204978	1429	50	10017	21	1811	.....	2	77
8396	99070	3285	322	10732	1580	2448	329	16	174
710	36807	1097	95	2771	326	740	17	6	53
11278	118438	3511	857	5937	5482	4453	1128	64	240
2476	131364	1854	390	9010	48	1857	67	.....	19
3081	19897	1290	471	842	239	1553	451	8	31
3359	209528	2406	184	9892	332	1279	8	.....	48
8267	126403	2496	517	6098	2799	2702	225	51	116
398	15377	277	130	1910	10	41	.....	2	6
218	12595	111	6	160	5	28	.....	.....	2
43844	1144202	20012	3730	71078	11082	19231	2269	149	957

No. 6.—RETURN OF AGRICULTURAL PRODUCE,

COUNTY OF

POLLING DISTRICTS.	Grain, &c., raised in 1860—*Continued.*					
	Bushels Timothy Seed.	Bushels Potatoes.	Bushels Turnips.	Bushels other Roots.	Bushels Apples.	Bushels Plums.
1. Ohio	19	31382	15391	3480	616	3
2. Yarmouth		20069	9839	4505	53	12
3. Chebogue	1	19811	8248	1043	478	12
4. Carleton	11	8374	4325	1844	640	4
5. Plymouth		23983	896	340	170	
6. Tusket		26723	2817	615	671	11
7. Argyle		15206	1100	160	232	
8. Pubnico		28082	583	220	127	
9. Kempt		4102	1596	254	177	
10. West side Tusket River		3090	460	271	753	6
	31	180822	45255	12732	3917	48

COUNTY OF

POLLING DISTRICTS.	Bushels Timothy Seed.	Bushels Potatoes.	Bushels Turnips.	Bushels other Roots.	Bushels Apples.	Bushels Plums.
1. Carleton Village		6843	246	61	210	
2. Shelburne		18235	1270	327	1404	11
3. Ragged Islands	1	7470	476	285	115	
4. Louis Head		6909	1404	146	96	
5. Shag Harbor		12034	373	12		2
6. Cape Sable Island		8253	358	83		
7. Barrington		9378	1140	235	150	3
8. Port LaTour		7301	269	56	199	
	1	76423	5536	1205	2174	16

COUNTY OF

POLLING DISTRICTS.	Bushels Timothy Seed.	Bushels Potatoes.	Bushels Turnips.	Bushels other Roots.	Bushels Apples.	Bushels Plums.
1. Liverpool	1	11119	993	1092	338	2
2. Bristol		9797	1358	261	457	
3. Port Medway		8689	864	156	334	12
4. Port Mouton		6482	778	136	126	
5. Brookfield	20	6767	4244	1891	1191	2
6. Caledonia	20	10828	4328	1678	2100	30
7. Greenfield		3158	244	169	26	
	41	56840	12809	5383	4572	46

COUNTY OF

POLLING DISTRICTS.	Bushels Timothy Seed.	Bushels Potatoes.	Bushels Turnips.	Bushels other Roots.	Bushels Apples.	Bushels Plums.
1. Lunenburg	5	16864	10821	4357	2644	· 21
2. Ritcey's Cove	14	16165	3679	979	1402	26
3. Mahone Bay	6	16399	7223	2243	4482	2
4. LaHave	1	6740	1498	855	736	
5. New Germany	30	16938	6787	879	599	13
6. Chester	12	12471	3630	864	753	
7. Sherbrooke	20	12490	1001	160	132	
8. Petite Riviere	4	28890	3378	766	3364	8
9. Bridgewater	53	21614	2676	661	968	
10. Tancook Island	1	1529	1163	774	34	
11. Mill Cove, St. Margaret's Bay.	2	3854	347	55	81	
	148	153954	42203	12593	15195	70

STOCK, FISHERIES, &c....1860—61.

YARMOUTH, Continued.

	Cattle.				Hand Looms.	Fulled Cloth, y'ds made in 1860.	Not Fulled, yards made in 1860.	Butter, lbs. made in 1860.
Neat Cattle, exclusive of Cows.	Milch Cows.	Horses.	Sheep.	Pigs.				
1332	938	207	2172	332	72	98	6295	71080
787	707	198	1153	268	30	389	3119	46841
787	545	125	1648	192	41	125	3407	34507
554	284	56	697	77	29	50	2168	19400
463	235	51	974	143	109	984	3287	9256
802	454	76	1099	185	53	2289	3489	18567
438	308	21	866	115	35	180	2716	14800
423	280	18	1210	207	77	815	4262	11290
257	113	23	278	42	9	150	969	5575
309	116	20	239	55	6	30	533	5820
6152	3980	801	10336	1616	461	5105	30245	237136

SHELBURNE, Continued.

262	242	25	1240	162	36	90	2295	10351
748	530	45	1610	309	47	2637	1449	19062
344	266	30	867	122	41	426	3405	11038
518	305	39	1391	90	67	237	3663	11776
290	236	30	431	106	32	50	545	11504
257	279	8	950	167	68	152	1582	13857
281	327	56	780	132	43	99	2139	22854
319	232	49	1294	147	66	....	2606	14883
3019	2417	282	8563	1235	400	3691	17684	115325

QUEEN'S, Continued.

373	369	84	370	193	30	1427	284	15693
403	268	73	519	154	28	120	2366	16971
368	257	49	620	160	15	466	2106	11168
366	235	23	821	103	57	30	3100	13773
666	309	70	655	91	33	419	2493	18022
1123	553	147	1470	178	67	202	6152	30673
197	89	14	136	17	8	57	735	3854
3496	2080	460	4591	896	238	2721	17237	110154

LUNENBURG, Continued.

898	622	42	2265	445	117	125	15553	26119
846	419	18	1327	287	144	469	6918	14211
1593	856	58	2182	432	132	1064	9280	26050
565	313	36	756	120	66	193	5057	10226
2061	898	187	2454	311	128	1549	14562	27309
1066	617	58	1789	652	111	61	6980	31813
606	287	73	945	146	39	200	4752	5616
1372	712	43	2346	421	138	1252	13719	31045
1292	637	105	2012	247	94	30	9894	24643
148	79	....	631	81	29	1182	912	2162
44	45	1	79	48	1	86	....	1619
10491	5485	621	16786	3190	999	6211	87627	200813

No. 6.—RETURN OF AGRICULTURAL PRODUCE,

COUNTY OF

POLLING DISTRICTS.	Cheese, lbs. made in 1860.	Maple Sugar, lbs. made in 1860.	Bricks made in 1860.		Grindstones made in 1860.	
			M.	Value in Dollars.	No.	Value in Dollars.
1. Ohio	51363					
2. Yarmouth	27343	120	1200	6000		
3. Chebogue	23402					
4. Carleton	7625	30				
5. Plymouth	800					
6. Tusket	260	6				
7. Argyle	6759					
8. Pubnico	1024					
9. Kempt	1098	4				
10. West side Tusket River	790	25				
	120464	185	1200	6000		

COUNTY OF

1. Carleton Village	80					
2. Shelburne	458					
3. Ragged Islands	109					
4. Louis Head	235					
5. Shag Harbor	155					
6. Cape Sable Island	50					
7. Barrington	65					
8. Port LaTour	355					
	1507					

COUNTY OF

1. Liverpool	250					
2. Bristol	750					
3. Port Medway	470					
4. Port Mouton	300					
5. Brookfield	1592	416	25	150		
6. Caledonia	4040	118				
7. Greenfield	305	46				
	7707	580	25	150		

COUNTY OF

1. Lunenburg						
2. Ritsey's Cove	371					
3. Mahone Bay	180					
4. LaHave	65	330				
5. New Germany	7043	962	10	55	2	8
6. Chester		5				
7. Sherbrooke	115	592				
8. Petite Riviere	254					
9. Bridgewater	390	179	80	500		
10. Tancook Island						
11. Mill Cove, St. Margaret's Bay						
	8418	2068	90	555	2	8

STOCK, FISHERIES, &c....1860—61.

YARMOUTH, Continued.

Gypsum quarried in 1860.		Vessels employed in the Fisheries.		Boats engaged in the Fisheries.		No. Nets and Seines.	Fish Cured in 1860.		
Tons.	Value in Dollars.	No.	Men.	No.	Men.		Quintals Dry.	Barrels Mackerel.	Barrels Shad.
....	....	2	9	48	63	182	2465	648	7
....	....	33	213	29	45	268	5993	686	3
....	....	9	31	31	14	99	2210	119	20
						7			
....	....	2	11	52	4	382	4840	1063	16
....	....	5	35	23	22	335	4276	635	....
....	....	2	25	6	2	23	3511	825	2
....	....	29	283	72	86	254	15256	692	5
....	....					5			
....	....	1	8	5	....	57	2	20	....
....	....	83	615	266	236	1612	38553	4688	53

SHELBURNE, Continued.

....	....	3	16	75	123	447	4654	204	....
....	....	15	92	99	108	589	5925	291	....
....	....	16	119	91	138	507	14112	304	....
....	....	11	87	48	33	188	7368	5	....
....	....	8	49	60	50	587	3306	962	....
....	....	20	102	172	242	659	8711	1171	3
....	....	9	56	28	43	130	3298	191	....
....	....	14	96	207	226	610	14001	279	....
....	....	96	617	780	963	3717	61375	3407	3

QUEEN'S, Continued.

....	....	11	95	45	78	154	5151	184	....
....	....	17	159	49	68	144	8175	33	....
....	....	18	153	103	150	205	6468	83	37
....	....	9	45	81	46	171	5316	15	10
....	....								
....	....								
....	....								
....	....	55	452	278	342	674	25110	315	47

LUNENBURG, Continued.

....	....	36	364	207	383	472	20898	431	....
....	....	44	383	169	209	617	20567	892	9
....	....	18	127	8	8	33	3814	28	....
....	....	9	83	19	30	36	3285	3	4
....	....			1	....	3	180	....	9
....	....	15	113	150	225	596	969	2148	2
....	....	29	290	238	125	549	13962	780	7
....	....	1	9	1	....	2	1264	....	12
....	....	4	6	80	19	425	686	453	....
....	....	2	5	96	108	305	166	1257	....
....	....	158	1380	969	1107	3038	65791	5992	43

No. 6.—RETURN OF AGRICULTURAL PRODUCE,

COUNTY OF

POLLING DISTRICTS.	Fish Cured in 1860—*Continued.*					Gallons Fish Oil in 1860.
	Barrels Herring.	Barrels Alewives.	Barrels Salmon.	No. Smoked Salmon.	Boxes Herring.	
1. Ohio	1239					1148
2. Yarmouth	3188					700
3. Chebogue	247	85			16	288
4. Carleton		16				
5. Plymouth	1166	31	10		20	751
6. Tusket	255	1305			156	2059
7. Argyle	9	83		1	175	2184
8. Pubnico	345	15				7557
9. Kempt						
10. West side Tusket River	6	332	2	11		
	6455	1927	12	12	367	14687

COUNTY OF

1. Carleton Village	3079	8				5452
2. Shelburne	7268	46	5		30	2248
3. Ragged Islands	5291	129	11		150	3101
4. Louis Head	1488	12			15	4621
5. Shag Harbor	1052				100	1156
6. Cape Sable Island	4114	29				3582
7. Barrington	779	258				1938
8. Port LaTour	2730	34			10	13028
	25801	516	16		305	35126

COUNTY OF

1. Liverpool	1028			4	4	2604
2. Bristol	1522	15		12		5014
3. Port Medway	1901	314	5	123	45	4499
4. Port Mouton	949	4			28	2608
5. Brookfield		1		26		
6. Caledonia		9				
7. Greenfield		115	1	2		
	5400	458	6	187	77	14815

COUNTY OF

1. Lunenburg	6676	5		2		15117
2. Ritcey's Cove	6484		30	296		13665
3. Mahone Bay	984	89		16		2422
4. LaHave	87	9	1	188		1731
5. New Germany	3	76		189		59
6. Chester	4230	969	9	140		805
7. Sherbrooke						
8. Petite Riviere	8059	28	2	327		11083
9. Bridgewater	15	1	1	20		480
10. Tancook Island	1066					1476
11. Mill Cove, St. Margaret's Bay.	1061		3			229
	28665	1177	46	1178		47067

STOCK, FISHERIES, &c....1860—61.

YARMOUTH, Continued.

Value of Leather manufact'd in 1860.	Carriages made in 1860.	Bush. Lime burnt in 1860.	Gallons Malt Liquor made in 1860.	Boats built in 1860.	Lumber manufactured in 1860.				
					M. feet Deals, Superficial.	M. feet Pine Boards	M. feet Spruce & Hemlock Boards.	Tons Square Timber.	M. Staves.
2514	20			23	7	6	309	97	91
12600	12	3500		89	5	30	24		
	7			1		5	4		
800					3	454	803	68	25
	1			1					
1055	1		200	3	20	139	97	630	237
20				2			12		4
800	1			8					
					34	574	203	57	2
12	1					97	45	173	17
17801	43	3500	200	127	69	1305	1397	1025	376

SHELBURNE, Continued.

				121		630	20		8
1054				45		1428	75	24	92
600				31		239	60		70
				7		45	126		70
180				26					
	1			47		1			
1540	11			36		483	2	5	7
				17		256	20	4	34
3374	12			320		3082	303	33	281

QUEEN'S, Continued.

17380	7			13		5405	160		6
165	6			50	10	7033	354	131	40
70				23	627	11646	551		80
				2	2	67	144	2	28
600				1		614	55	6	
	10					115	11		
	1					481	43		60
18215	24			89	639	25361	1318	139	214

LUNENBURG, Continued.

1000	30			300	90	89	237	1	5
620	2		150	18					2
2150		1500		18	93	450	1036	44	88
1600	14			23	12	680	747	41	9
					186	1329	952		73
4680	4	1600		35		185	104		485
	1				20	49	53		342
1890	1			30	17	111	1877	10	4
1484	29			3	121	2372	2469		34
				4				3	140
22424	81	3100	150	431	539	5265	7475	99	1182

GENERAL ABSTRACT.

COUNTIES.	Lands—Area Occupied.								Tons of Hay cut in 1860.
	Dyke Marsh.		Salt Marsh.		Cultivated Intervale.		Cultivated Upland.		
	Acres.	Value in Dollars.	Acres.	Value in Dollars.	Acres.	Value in Dollars.	Acres.	Value in Dollars.	
1. { Halifax (City)					28	9800	1730	361160	1258
" (Outside City)	489	11993	736	12771	3727	103298	22674	543859	19614
Total in County	489	11992	736	12772	3755	113098	24306	905019	20872
2. Colchester	2069	273112	1834	39628	10846	370073	61583	1068217	13101
3. Cumberland	11608	697540	3910	70594	5048	140200	80430	1319151	21582
4. Pictou	658	3860	727	8089	5665	107130	106751	1448855	27494
5. Sydney	466	3006	262	4485	6438	165388	82078	730081	23320
6. Guysborough	84	490	127	1703	2666	58378	12892	192660	9617
7. Inverness	910	5426	592	10910	7129	118533	86908	742240	21962
8. Richmond	1338	2965	104	1187	1186	14841	21302	232297	4827
9. Victoria	5	20	132	1603	1086	28993	26075	225858	1983
10. Cape Breton	180	701	288	1086	1068	19708	43549	377206	8631
11. Hants	3012	488616	2135	52631	3902	129895	53759	860696	23680
12. King's	6806	793085	1734	53065	9245	344977	80099	1085344	32786
13. Annapolis	2375	100897	2109	124525	8342	250362	70810	1170461	28424
14. Digby	84	1074	519	14262	1878	19911	22533	436245	10700
15. Yarmouth	1440	35851	4369	58703	3157	47482	35204	659402	13898
16. Shelburne	76	3330	963	29884	636	24143	7229	308882	5760
17. Queen's	46	2286	237	5702	1516	37042	14741	302020	7439
18. Lunenburg	37	800	204	6770	2904	100939	43844	1144268	20012
	35487	2902548	20729	508937	77192	2117044	894714	13941935	334287

GENERAL ABSTRACT, Continued.

COUNTIES.	Grain, &c., raised in 1860									
	Bushels Wheat	Bushels Barley	Bushels Rye	Bushels Oats	Bushels Buckwheat	Bushels Indian Corn	Bushels Pease and Beans	Bushels Timothy Seed	Bushels Potatoes	Bushels Turnips
1. Halifax (City)	177	302	100	7932	12	1	61	4	9834	8549
" (Outside City)	2296	11967	436	59879	8341	61	419	181	107777	36193
Total in County	2413	12269	536	60765	8353	62	480	185	111611	44674
2. Colchester	17950	3808	3508	193078	38511	168	2651	900	358002	48310
3. Cumberland	54412	13619	4817	136503	79043	259	1962	1709	326857	55315
4. Pictou	85487	21703	1592	582713	15606	205	4983	2485	288100	31530
5. Sydney	43855	12282	1174	183973	6431	121	1385	651	146206	12880
6. Guysborough	2417	2964	44	51880	5794	32	291	172	89653	3655
7. Inverness	16554	33694	1304	256006	2814	191	919	700	249851	7849
8. Richmond	1181	2714	57	48755	96	1	84	55	64005	4638
9. Victoria	2345	13780	384	117063	293	20	36	134	72847	4080
10. Cape Breton	5472	19765	628	110181	519	48	145	358	108772	10454
11. Hants	39217	9100	1596	128294	8379	302	943	1032	166384	38002
12. King's	23094	7453	19743	131984	8909	4530	1843	624	858651	40099
13. Annapolis	15598	12966	10638	50492	11105	8276	3367	499	566753	72710
14. Digby	8943	10777	500	10843	5173	890	665	67	193596	34624
15. Yarmouth	1130	7294	696	7044	1096	360	660	31	180822	45855
16. Shelburne	177	2000	18	3005	18	23	45	1	76423	5595
17. Queen's	1277	7112	1584	10097	1920	200	482	41	50840	12809
18. Lunenburg	3730	71008	12392	18231	2909	149	957	149	153054	42703
	312081	269528	39706	1978137	195390	15926	21382	9882	3824864	514318

No. 6.—RETURN OF AGRICULTURAL PRODUCE, STOCK, FISHERIES, &c...1860—61.

GENERAL ABSTRACT, Continued.

COUNTIES	Grain, &c., raised in 1860—Continued.			Cattle						Hard Linens.	Fulled Cloth, yds. made in 1860.	Not Fulled yards made in 1860.
	Bushels other Roots.	Bushels Apples.	Bushels Flour.	Neat Cattle, exclusive of Cows.	Milch Cows.	Horses.	Sheep.	Pigs.				
1. { Halifax (City)	7164	490	44	68	445	527	65	169	2	103	90
" (Outside City)	7072	3009		7676	6200	1865	19855	2863	498	4373	55275
Total in County	14236	3499	44	7741	6645	2392	19730	3032	500	4476	55865
2. Colchester	7652	4318	39	12585	8789	3929	27494	3757	1927	14905	114845
3. Cumberland	2899	7492	32	19514	7674	3708	23129	4265	1573	13443	95972
4. Pictou	1973	5697	762	14005	13390	6163	26453	5079	1463	45128	110058
5. Sydney	587	3604	1010	13503	6789	2665	27113	4531	948	37786	72541
6. Guysborough	563	2230	256	5086	3912	3048	11758	2270	328	5573	37476
7. Inverness	653	2222	309	12828	11905	4396	38143	6483	1560	38880	73851
8. Richmond	278	491	38	3428	3437	1111	13703	1807	689	13580	30334
9. Victoria	190	1361	51	5051	6697	1337	14928	1845	544	17524	28056
10. Cape Breton	635	2432	966	6165	6762	3087	20170	4071	873	20266	30485
11. Hants	4097	12106	189	8260	5974	2810	19655	3309	487	9633	63179
12. King's	5418	36260	679	11172	5760	3960	18199	3369	399	17435	53677
13. Annapolis	10368	65490	316	10857	6290	2452	19853	2546	672	26491	68539
14. Digby	6455	11304	54	5420	3941	627	10961	1434	461	3553	51363
15. Yarmouth	12772	3917	48	6157	3980	864	10536	1674	481	5205	30245
16. Shelburne	1905	2174	16	3919	2437	382	8660	1235	400	3691	17684
17. Queen's	5383	4572	49	3496	3080	469	4081	896	228	2771	17237
18. Lunenburg	12693	55196	70	10498	5485	631	16786	3190	999	6211	87827
	87727	186484	4385	151793	110604	41287	332053	53217	13330	281709	1032014

No. 4.—RETURN OF AGRICULTURAL PRODUCE, STOCK, FISHERIES, &c...1860—61.

GENERAL ABSTRACT, Continued.

	COUNTIES.	Butter. lbs. made in 1860.	Cheese, lbs. made in 1860.	Maple Sugar, lbs. made in 1860.	Bricks made in 1860.		Grindstones made in 1860.		Gypsum quarried in 1860.		Vessels employed in the Fisheries.	
					M.	Value in Dollars.	No.	Value in Dollars.	Tons.	Value in Dollars.	No.	Men.
1.	Halifax (City)	4316	40								26	205
	" (Outside City)	216277	2660	3464	1092	7944	14	14	58	58	149	662
	Total in County	220593	2690	3464	1092	7944	14	14	58	58	175	867
2.	Colchester	398229	20736	26578	760	4905	936	608	6026	5417		
3.	Cumberland	382954	17869	130210	335	3465	43706	40166	209	206	6	15
4.	Pictou	471485	73248	30096	411	3286	1268	990	70	46	2	37
5.	Sydney	337836	105763	16019	180	1309	49	49	10	10	3	37
6.	Guysborough	154148	4773	3186	180	1212	763	1196	230	190	85	340
7.	Inverness	467172	123829	9696	47	237	128	188	19	21	38	216
8.	Richmond	92449	4441	295			4	6	1470	1926	109	583
9.	Victoria	186179	10193	804	6	30	48	85			3	15
10.	Cape Breton	210367	12662	1331	5	30	47	58	30	24	23	137
11.	Hants	258835	18224	9239	1556	13509	892	818	118215	77893	1	4
12.	King's	286026	84981	7095	775	4818	1	1			6	28
13.	Annapolis	250977	216770	6947	580	4353	3	3			5	9
14.	Digby	146490	5906	905	148	919					56	302
15.	Yarmouth	237136	120464	185	1200	6000					83	615
16.	Shelburne	113822	1607								96	617
17.	Queen's	116134	7707	580	25	150					65	452
18.	Lunenburg	200815	8413	2068	90	555	2	8			138	1380
		4532711	905296	248849	7502	51703	46496	44100	120400	85073	900	5653

GENERAL ABSTRACT, Continued.

COUNTIES.	Boats engaged in the Fisheries.		No. Nets and Seines.	Fish Cured in 1860.							
	No.	Men.		Quintals Dry.	Barrels Mackerel.	Barrels Shad.	Barrels Herring.	Barrels Alewives.	Barrels Salmon.	No. Smoked Salmon.	Boxes Herring.
1. { Halifax (City)	60	106	156	1695	172	15	8900	93	130		
{ " (Outside City)	1872	1373	11870	43050	14965	441	35299	995	230	758	307
Total in County	1932	1479	12006	44645	15137	456	44199	968	360	758	307
2. Colchester	118	163	155	56	56	3691	387	437	33	74	43
3. Cumberland	99	85	485	200	44	652	753	1240	23	21	49
4. Pictou	81	17	422	757	268		1500	58	148	74	25
5. Sydney	213	280	990	1385	427	9	1613	152	155	85	4
6. Guysborough	1080	631	7991	29734	12519	91	36805	2700	329	90	44
7. Inverness	434	716	1267	18398	716		7617	1871	147	21	31
8. Richmond	684	1190	5424	53905	7384		9361	435	26	4	33
9. Victoria	413	330	1298	7813	3874		2532	29	213	12	
10. Cape Breton	679	598	1422	20429	4393		4137	368	406	139	45
11. Hants	82	72	192	23	80	1078	86	151	3		76
12. King's	50	43	141	1068	132	1274	908	210	14	36	1806
13. Annapolis	184	109	507	2038	107	53	5733	77	30	108	23040
14. Digby	386	405	523	14114	6397	209	13717	11	1	2	3209
15. Yarmouth	395	296	1612	38503	4798	53	6455	1927	12	12	367
16. Shelburne	780	963	3727	61373	3407	3	25801	316	16		305
17. Queen's	274	352	674	25115	315	47	5400	458	6	187	77
18. Lunenburg	969	1107	9038	85791	5892	43	29665	1177	40	1178	
	8946	8689	48966	396426	66106	7849	194170	13868	2481	2728	35587

GENERAL ABSTRACT, Continued.

COUNTIES.	Gallons Fish Oil in 1960.	Value of Lumber manufac'd in 1960.	Carriages made in 1860	Bush. Lime burnt in 1960.	Gallons Malt Liquor made in 1860.	Boats built in 1960.	Lumber manufactured in 1960.				
							M. feet Deals, &c. perhaps'd.	M. feet Pine Boards	M. feet Spruce & Hemlock Boards.	Tons Square Timber.	M. Staves.
1. { Halifax (City)	10154	16000	23	600	100000	3		50			139
" (Outside City)	20816	22844	51	25450		289	315	1212	3138	2532	3097
Total in County	30970	38844	74	26000	100000	292	315	1262	3138	2532	3236
2. Colchester	58	16284	489	4560		26	1662	759	3409	3515	123
3. Cumberland	208	6829	265	19635		51	17794	955	2749	1150	155
4. Pictou	410	41933	117	35990	500	58	237	606	3297	5189	58
5. Sydney	1259	9447	106	3223		39	60	323	1460	1919	125
6. Guysborough	20070	4663	72	720	500	265	823	533	1134	1857	1031
7. Inverness	27234	10828	168	6486	50	98	193	325	815	1769	186
8. Richmond	14622	1893	14	406		214	11	91	47	694	101
9. Victoria	4834	2863	39	4303	12	114	77	328	295	80	71
10. Cape Breton	15004	8675	45	20092	95	149	70	417	891	535	51
11. Hants	55	5990	158	77474		21	945	992	2175	742	15
12. King's	800	11035	176		180	8	294	1250	2153	195	45
13. Annapolis	1507	12589	191			53	95	1520	1588	52	260
14. Digby	5992	7597	51			74	1993	2326	2637	1284	73
15. Yarmouth	14687	17991	45	3000	200	127	69	1305	1397	1955	376
16. Shelburne	32126	3374	19			230		3082	505	30	281
17. Queen's	16815	18015	24			89	639	25361	1318	130	214
18. Lunenburg	47067	22628	61	3500	150	431	539	3265	7475	99	1182
	230979	249586	2131	136948	100967	2408	25073	40607	36422	22593	7639

RETURN

OF

HOUSES, PLACES OF WORSHIP, &c.

No. 7.—RETURN OF HOUSES,

COUNTY OF

POLLING DISTRICTS.	Inhabited.	Vacant.	Building.	Stores and Shops.	Barns & Outhouses.	School Houses.	Temperance Halls.	Value in Dollars.	Schools in operation 30th March, 1861.
1. Ward 1, (City)	414	24	29	2	222	1			6
2. do. 2, do.	306	11	2	6	156	3			4
3. do. 3, do.	314	5		147	56	3			5
4. do. 4, do.	165	2	2	13	64	5			
5. do. 5, do. { 1st Section	285	6	2	34	61	1	1	16000	1
{ 2d do.	608	11	10	1	282	5			5
6. do. 6, do.	392	46	16	2	78	5			4
Total in City	2484	105	46	422	920	23	1	16000	25
7. Ferguson's Cove	122	12	10		60	2			1
8. Portuguese Cove	95	12	2		50	2			2
9. Sambro	90	1	4	2	122	2			
10. Prospect	201	22	20		324	3			3
11. Hagget's Cove	121	3	3		11	6			4
12. French Village	95	6	3	3	9	2			
13. Drysdale's	46	5			5	2			1
14. North West Arm	52	6	2	1	6	1			
15. Piers' Mill	54	11	2	3	76	2			1
16. Hammond's Plains	122	5	5	1	167	3	1	1200	3
17. Windsor Road	135	5		4	18	4			4
18. Truro Road	91	3			128	4			3
19. Guy's River	93	11		1	119	3			3
20. Wise's Corner	89	5	2	1	161	4			1
21. Middle Musquodoboit	204	9	6	7	257	7	1	400	5
22. Upper Musquodoboit	150	5	8	2	35	4			3
23. Caledonia	35		3		45	2			1
24. Salmon River	136	6	11	10	160	8			2
25. Sheet Harbor	90	9	3	1	182	4			3
26. Pope's Harbor	149	5	2	3	26	5			4
27. Jeddore	283	10	10	3	387	6			4
28. Chezetcook	281	3	9	3	269	4			4
29. Lawrencetown	61	4	2		76	3			2
30. Preston	124	3	3		87	3			2
31. Dartmouth	483	37	4	53	309	2			11
32. Black Point	114	7	1	4	13	3			1
33. Eastern Passage	121	1	4		125	5			3
	6130	311	165	524	5099	119	3	17600	96

COUNTY OF

	Inhabited.	Vacant.	Building.	Stores and Shops.	Barns & Outhouses.	School Houses.	Temperance Halls.	Value in Dollars.	Schools in operation 30th March, 1861.
1. Truro	458	10	15	21	564	12			11
2. Old Barns	154	4	3	4	295	5			2
3. Lower Stewiacke	245	18	11	7	484	9	1	200	4
4. Upper Stewiacke	306	13	8	8	731	11	1	400	4
5. Upper Onslow and Kemptown	272	8	4	2	472	11			7
6. Onslow	135	9	3	3	283	6			3
7. Earltown	187	1	14	3	274	7			4
8. New Annan	187	3	4	7	215	6			5
9. Waugh's River	173	6	3	3	195	6			3
10. Tatamagouche	202	10	12	21	258	5			3
11. Upper Londonderry	263	7	15	6	564	8			4
12. Lower Londonderry	316	13	6	9	380	11			4
13. Economy and Five Islands	225	3	10	3	450	5	1	200	3
	3123	105	103	97	5165	102	3	800	57

PLACES OF WORSHIP, &c....1860—61.

HALIFAX.

				Places of Worship.									Vessels.		
Church of England	Church of Rome	Church of Scotl'd.	Presbyterian Ch. of L. P.	Associated Baptist	Other Baptist	Methodist	Congregationalist	Universalist	Union	Other Places of Worship	Total	Launched in 1860	Tonnage	Building 30th March, 1861	Probable Tonnage
1	2										3				
	1	1		1		1					4				
1		1									2				
			1			1				1	3				
1			1	1		2		1			6				
1	1		1	1							4				
1	1										2				
5	5	2	3	3		4		1		1	24				
1	2										3				
	1										1				
						1					1				
1	2										3				
2	1			1		2					6				
1					1						2				
1			1	1							3				
1	1			4							6				
1				1		1					3				
1				2							3				
									1		1				
1		1	1								4				
			1								1				
			1								1				
1											1			3	124
1	1		1								3	1	34	3	210
1	1										2				
2	1		1	2		1					7	2	130	5	221
1	1		1								3				
		1	1								2	1	30		
1				4							5				
2	1		1	2		2					8	1	100		
2											2				
1	1										2				
27	18	4	12	21		12		1	1	1	97	5	294	11	555

COLCHESTER.

Church of England	Church of Rome	Church of Scotl'd.	Presbyterian Ch. of L. P.	Associated Baptist	Other Baptist	Methodist	Congregationalist	Universalist	Union	Other Places of Worship	Total	Launched in 1860	Tonnage	Building 30th March, 1861	Probable Tonnage
1		1	3	2		1			1		9				
1			2								3	2	396	9	1915
2			2	1							5				
			3	1							4				
			1	2		1					4				
			1			1			1		3				
			1								1				
			2	1		1					4				
	1					1					2	1	80	2	80
			2						1		3	6	432	7	800
			3						1		4	1	190	3	780
			2	1							3	1	110	3	400
			2	2		1					5	2	400	2	450
4	1	1	24	10		6			4		50	13	1608	26	4425

No. 7.—RETURN OF HOUSES,

COUNTY OF

POLLING DISTRICTS.	Inhabited.	Vacant.	Building.	Stores and Shops.	Barns & Outhouses.	School Houses.	Temperance Halls.	Value in Dollars.	Schools in operation 30th March, 1861.
1. Amherst	447	12	5	23	837	15			10
2. Westchester	121	12			170	4			
3. Head of Amherst	253	7	3	2	481	11			4
4. River Philip	230	8	8	5	314	12			5
5. River Hebert	246	9	2	7	260	9			6
6. Maccan	135	6	1	2	224	6			1
7. Pugwash	470	21	10	21	675	10	1	1000	9
8. Wallace	378	15	9	27	420	10	1	600	7
9. Wentworth	110	10	2	3	120	3			2
10. Advocate Harbor	168	6	1	1	130	4			2
11. Mill Village	374	10	17	16	450	10			10
	2932	116	58	107	4081	94	2	1600	56

COUNTY OF

	Inhabited.	Vacant.	Building.	Stores and Shops.	Barns & Outhouses.	School Houses.	Temperance Halls.	Value in Dollars.	Schools in operation 30th March, 1861.
1. Pictou	347	12	3	56	231	6			11
2. Carriboo	189	10	6		210	4			2
3. Cape John	224		5	3	221	5			4
4. West side River John	197	5	9	10	238	8	1	400	4
5. West branch River John	141	10	11	3	163	5			3
6. Rogers Hill	186	6	3	4	242	7			
7. Hardwood Hill	178	13	6	6	260	6			5
8. Green Hill and West River	154	13	15	5	344	6			4
9. Mount Thom	194	10	8	5	371	4			3
10. Gairloch	134	2	7	3	223	3			2
11. New Lairg	92	9	2		150	4			4
12. Albion Mines	371	4	4	6	250	4			5
13. New Glasgow	315	7	7	72	359	4	1	700	5
14. Little Harbor	129	4	4		179	4			2
15. McLellan's Mountain	163	2	13	1	244	5			3
16. East branch East River	209	4	4	3	280	5			4
17. Hopewell, W. branch E. River	235	7	8	15	268	7	1	880	5
18. Middle River	165	5		3	318	5			3
19. Gulf Shore	157	6	6	7	196	6			3
20. Barney's River	198	2	7	5	209	5			
21. Merrigomish	240	10	7	4	260	8	1	100	3
22. Blue Mountain, St. Mary's, &c.	127	6	7		146	5			3
	4345	147	142	211	5362	116	4	2080	78

COUNTY OF

	Inhabited.	Vacant.	Building.	Stores and Shops.	Barns & Outhouses.	School Houses.	Temperance Halls.	Value in Dollars.	Schools in operation 30th March, 1861.
1. Arisaig	213	8	5	4	230	7			5
2. Cape George	163	5	5	3	174	4			4
3. Morristown	146		4	4	200	4			2
4. Antigonish	421	5	9	23	531	9			8
5. Lochaber	246	7	11	7	310	6			5
6. Upper South River	162	3	12	5	205	5			3
7. St. Andrew's	303	2	6	11	369	10			9
8. Tracadie	253	5	5	8	280	8			8
9. Harbor Bouche	237	4	28	3	339	4			4
	2144	39	85	68	2638	57			48

PLACES OF WORSHIP, &c...1860—61.

CUMBERLAND.

				Places of Worship.									Vessels.		
Church of England.	Church of Rome.	Church of Scotl'd.	Presbyterian Ch. of L. P.	Associated Baptist.	Other Baptist.	Methodist.	Congregationalist.	Universalist.	Union.	Other Places of Worship.	Total.	Launched in 1860.	Tonnage.	Building 30th March, 1861.	Probable Tonnage.
2	1			4		6				2	15	1	130		
				1				1			2				
		3	2			2					7				
		1	1			4					6				
	2		1	2			1				6			2	260
			2	2		3					7				
1	1	1	1	2		2					8	2	281	4	231
1	1	1	2			2					7	3	383	4	563
		1	1			1					4				
				1		1					2	1	64	6	1030
5	1		1	2		4			1		14	2	157	15	2355
9	6	3	12	18		25		1	2	2	78	9	1015	31	4439

PICTOU.

Church of England.	Church of Rome.	Church of Scotl'd.	Presbyterian Ch. of L. P.	Associated Baptist.	Other Baptist.	Methodist.	Congregationalist.	Universalist.	Union.	Other Places of Worship.	Total.	Launched in 1860.	Tonnage.	Building 30th March, 1861.	Probable Tonnage.
1	1	1	2							1	6	2	437	3	980
			1								1				
1		1		1							3				
			1		1						2	3	947	3	1196
			1								1				
			1								1				
			1								1			1	130
		1									1				
			2								2				
		1	1								2				
			1								1				
1											1				
		1	3								4	3	764	5	2150
			2								2				
		1									1				
		1	2								3				
		1	1								2				
	1										1			1	300
		1	1								2	1	60		
	2		3								5	1	156	1	200
		1	2								3				
3	4	11	24	1		1				1	45	10	2364	14	4956

SYDNEY.

Church of England.	Church of Rome.	Church of Scotl'd.	Presbyterian Ch. of L. P.	Associated Baptist.	Other Baptist.	Methodist.	Congregationalist.	Universalist.	Union.	Other Places of Worship.	Total.	Launched in 1860.	Tonnage.	Building 30th March, 1861.	Probable Tonnage.
	2										2	1	137		35
	2		1								3	1	97	1	141
1	1										2	1	93	2	180
1	1		2	1							5			2	
	2	1	2								5				
											2	1	40	1	90
	2										8	2	250	1	200
1	5			1		1					2			4	325
1	1														
4	16	1	5	2		1					29	6	617	11	971

No. 7.—RETURN OF HOUSES,

COUNTY OF

POLLING DISTRICTS.	Inhabited	Vacant	Building	Stores and Shops	Barns & Outhouses	School Houses	Temperance Halls	Value in Dollars	Schools in operation 30th March, 1861.
1. Guysborough	360	5	5	24	424	5	1	400	5
2. Intervale	148	3	4	2	159	2			1
3. Manchester	229	4	3	15	270	4			3
4. Melford	248	12	20	59	224	3			4
5. Crow Harbor	117	10	6	60	100	2			
6. Cape Canso	120	29	5	78	66	2			2
7. Country Harbor	134	3	10	6	230	3			2
8. Sherbrooke	159	6	5	13	178	7			4
9. Marie Joseph	103	3	12	28	129	3			
10. Forks, St. Mary's	188	3	10	3	279	9			5
11. Molasses Harbor	142		3	72	88	4			1
	1948	78	83	360	2125	44	1	400	27

COUNTY OF

1. Plaster Cove	240	9	11	32	313	4			2
2. Judique	210	3	14	5	301	4			4
3. River Inhabitants	204		14	6	213	6			6
4. Port Hood	141	7	20	19	170	4			3
5. Mabou	406		5	18	507	12			12
6. Broad Cove (Intervale)	185	4	10	2	198	7			5
7. Broad Cove	107	3	13	5	159	3			3
8. Margaree	57	2	1	8	77	2			1
9. Young's Bridge	117	7	14	4	160	3			3
10. Friar's Head	106	12	13	2	148	4			2
11. Cheticamp	210	8	25	13	469	2			3
12. Whycocomagh	336	2	11	10	348	8			9
13. Lake Ainslie	114		6	2	105	4			4
14. River Dennis	168	3	21	3	200	8			4
15. North-east Margaree	186		7	7	248	6	1	100	
	2817	60	185	136	3616	77	1	100	60

COUNTY OF

1. Arichat	201	8	6	30	189	3			3
2. Petit Degrate	273	17	33	185	97	2			5
3. D'Escouse	196	4	15	5	250	2			2
4. Black River	101	4	7	3	117	5			4
5. River Bourgeoise	139	22	14	51	150	3			3
6. St. Peter's	133	4	14	19	214	2			1
7. L'Ardoise	236	6	8		292	1			1
8. Grand River	122	1		1	200	2			
9. Red Islands	105	1	2		115	3			2
10. River Inhabitants	138	8	26	29	139	2			1
11. Little Arichat	200	15	10	17	203	3			4
12. Loch Lomond	63	1	10		90	2			1
13. Flamboise	75	1		8	124	2			
	1972	92	145	346	2180	32			27

PLACES OF WORSHIP, &c....1860—61.

GUYSBOROUGH.

				Places of Worship.										Vessels.		
Church of England.	Church of Rome.	Church of Scotl'd.	Presbyterian Ch. of L.P.	Associated Baptist.	Other Baptist.	Methodist.	Congregationalist.	Universalist.	Union.	Other Places of Worship.	Total.	Launched in 1860.	Tonnage.	Building 30th March, 1861.	Probable Tonnage.
1	1			2		1				1	6	1	23	4	280
1	1										2	1	90		
1				1		1	1				4				
2	2										4			1	120
1									1		2				
	1			1		1	1				4				
2				1							3	5	250	8	400
2	1		1	2							6	4	691	4	800
2											2	2	30	2	90
		1	1	1							3				
3											3			2	70
15	6	1	2	8		3	2		2		39	13	1003	21	1760

INVERNESS.

	2		1	1		1					5	2	197	5	490
	1										1				
	1	1									2				
	1									1	2				
	1		1	1							3			2	150
			1								1				
	1										1				
			1								1			2	81
	1										1				
	1										1	1	32		
	1										1	4	111	1	35
		2									2				
	1	1									2				
	1	2									3				
	1			1		1	1				4				
	13	1	9	3		2	1			1	30	7	340	10	756

RICHMOND.

1	1										2			1	60
	1										1	1	35	1	80
			2								2				
	1										1			3	90
	1										1			1	40
	1										1			2	74
		1									1				
	2										2				
												3	135	3	102
												3	322	7	830
		1									1				
				1							1				
L	7		4			1					13	7	492	18	1276

No. 7.—RETURN OF HOUSES,

COUNTY OF

POLLING DISTRICTS.	Inhabited.	Vacant.	Building.	Stores and Shops.	Barns & Outhouses.	School Houses.	Temperance Halls.	Value in Dollars.	Schools in operation 30th March, 1861.
1. Washabok	161	10	14	.....	185	2	.....	.....	1
2. Middle River	123	4	4	2	148	2	.....	.....	2
3. Baddeck	225	3	7	13	250	6	.....	.....	5
4. Munro's Point, St. Ann's	210	11	7	2	246	9	.....	.....	7
5. Englishtown, St. Ann's	202	3	.....	6	160	4	.....	.....	4
6. Boulardrie	173	12	15	5	181	6	.....	.....	3
7. Ingonish	86	18	6	7	88	2	.....	.....	2
8. Cape North	90	.....	4	3	124	2	.....	.....	2
9. Bay St. Lawrence	55	4	6	2	75	.....	.....	.....	
10. Little Narrows	104	4	.....	.....	98	5	.....	.....	3
	1429	69	63	40	1555	38	.....	.....	29

COUNTY OF

POLLING DISTRICTS.	Inhabited.	Vacant.	Building.	Stores and Shops.	Barns & Outhouses.	School Houses.	Temperance Halls.	Value in Dollars.	Schools in operation 30th March, 1861.
1. Sydney	373	20	16	19	460	4	1	1000	9
2. Ball's Bridge	304	10	9	6	389	9	2	750	7
3. Mira Ferry	142	.....	10	1	210	7	.....	.....	.....
4. Sydney Mines	452	11	4	28	152	7	2	1000	7
5. Mainadieu	232	7	11	15	224	6	.....	.....	6
6. Louisburg	223	8	6	40	212	1	.....	.....	1
7. Gabarus	236	47	33	8	404	6	.....	.....	4
8. East Bay	273	6	18	2	424	6	.....	.....	3
9. Beaver Cove	148	.....	2	2	200	1	.....	.....	.....
10. Howley's Ferry	156	4	1	1	160	3	.....	.....	2
11. Lingan Mines	172	8	4	5	206	4	.....	.....	3
12. Cow Bay	99	4	11	6	108	5	.....	.....	3
13. Big Pond	103	2	12	3	165	3	.....	.....	1
14. Christmas Island	182	5	.....	5	180	3	.....	.....	3
	3095	132	137	141	3494	65	5	2750	49

COUNTY OF

POLLING DISTRICTS.	Inhabited.	Vacant.	Building.	Stores and Shops.	Barns & Outhouses.	School Houses.	Temperance Halls.	Value in Dollars.	Schools in operation 30th March, 1861.
1. Windsor	367	16	8	50	387	2	1	2000	9
2. St. Croix	176	2	.....	2	186	5	.....	.....	3
3. Brooklyn	165	7	4	8	297	4	.....	.....	3
4. Scotch Village	327	21	22	5	627	11	2	860	6
5. Falmouth	211	11	1	14	288	6	1	600	4
6. Kempt	307	8	10	10	350	8	1	200	5
7. Rawdon Church	122	6	1	1	240	3	1	200	2
8. South Rawdon	96	6	1	1	120	2	.....	.....	1
9. Noel	265	12	7	5	487	12	1	250	4
10. Nine Mile River	304	29	5	17	481	6	1	300	6
11. Maitland	295	19	10	13	333	7	1	200	4
12. Chester Road	90	2	.....	.....	161	2	.....	.....	2
	2725	139	69	126	3957	68	9	4610	49

PLACES OF WORSHIP, &c....1860—61.

VICTORIA.

Church of England	Church of Rome	Church of Scotl'd.	Presbyterian Ch. of I. P.	Associated Baptist.	Other Baptist.	Methodist.	Congregationalist.	Universalist.	Union.	Other Places of Worship.	Total.	Launched in 1860.	Tonnage.	Building 30th March, 1881.	Probable Tonnage.
	1										1				
			1								1				
1	1		3							1	6				
			2								2			1	180
			2								2				
			2								2			1	60
	1					1					2				
		1									1				
	1										1				
1	4	1	10			1				1	18			2	240

CAPE BRETON.

Church of England	Church of Rome	Church of Scotl'd.	Presbyterian Ch. of I. P.	Associated Baptist.	Other Baptist.	Methodist.	Congregationalist.	Universalist.	Union.	Other Places of Worship.	Total.	Launched in 1860.	Tonnage.	Building 30th March, 1881.	Probable Tonnage.
2	1		1	1		1					6				
1	1		3	1							6			1	30
			1								1	1	74	2	160
1	3		1			1				1	7	3	300	1	200
2	1		2								5	1	100	2	135
1	1		1			1					4			1	37
	1		1			3					5	7	325		
	1										1				
	1										1				
												1	24	1	20
1	3										4				
1		2		2							5			2	149
	1										1				
	1										1				
9	15	2	9	5		6				1	47	13	823	10	741

HANTS.

Church of England	Church of Rome	Church of Scotl'd.	Presbyterian Ch. of I. P.	Associated Baptist.	Other Baptist.	Methodist.	Congregationalist.	Universalist.	Union.	Other Places of Worship.	Total.	Launched in 1860.	Tonnage.	Building 30th March, 1881.	Probable Tonnage.
2	1		1	1		2					7			1	1300
1											1				
1			1	1		1			1		5	1	227	2	375
2			2	1	3						8	3	1030	3	1175
			2		3	1					6	1	162	2	1500
			2		3						8	1	200	4	1000
1	1		1	2							5				
1			1	1		2					5				
				2							2				
1			2		1	1					5	2	400		
1	3		4			2					10	4	710	7	1870
1	1		3			1					6				
1				1							2				
12	6		13	12	2	18	1		1		65	13	2729	19	7220

No. 7.—RETURN OF HOUSES,

COUNTY OF

POLLING DISTRICTS.	Inhabited.	Vacant.	Building.	Stores and Shops.	Barns & Outhouses.	School Houses.	Temperance Halls.	Value in Dollars.	Schools in operation 30th March, 1861.
1. Canning	384	8	6	19	634	11			10
2. Canard	222	5	4	10	440	6	2	800	6
3. Centreville	375	7	1	8	446	5			5
4. Lakeville	230	6	2	9	350	8	1	300	5
5. Somerset	369	10	4	4	592	7			4
6. Kentville	257	15	10	13	419	5			4
7. Gaspereaux	198	4		1	273	6			4
8. Wolfville	258	15	4	13	575	5	1	1200	3
9. Lower Horton	236	12		8	342	6			3
10. Aylesford	240	7	5	8	417	5	2	800	3
11. West Sherbrooke	31	2	1		43				
12. Aylesford	235	5	2	6	395	5	1	400	3
13. Berwick	137	7	2	3	265	5	1	200	3
	3172	103	41	102	5191	74	8	3700	53

COUNTY OF

POLLING DISTRICTS.	Inhabited.	Vacant.	Building.	Stores and Shops.	Barns & Outhouses.	School Houses.	Temperance Halls.	Value in Dollars.	Schools in operation 30th March, 1861.
1. Wilmot	303	4	3	5	375	6			5
2. Wilmot, Middleton Corner	255	12	2	16	369	8			6
3. Clarence, Wilmot	251	2	2	16	561	5	1	200	3
4. Bridgetown	234	10	1	26	360	5			5
5. Bellisle	191	4	2	4	350	4			3
6. New Caledonia	215	7	17	20	487	6			7
7. Broad Cove	148	8	2	4	197	2			1
8. Clementsport	208	12	7	8	322	6			
9. Hessian Line	164	2	1	7	185	5			3
10. Annapolis Royal	314	6	4	18	335	12			11
11. Carleton's Corner	130	4	1	2	300	3			3
12. Nictaux	210	10	5	5	364	6	2	200	2
13. Dalhousie	75	2	4		144	4			1
14. Maitland	55	1		1	60	4			2
15. Morse Road	57	1			114	2			1
	2810	85	51	132	4523	78	4	400	53

COUNTY OF

POLLING DISTRICTS.	Inhabited.	Vacant.	Building.	Stores and Shops.	Barns & Outhouses.	School Houses.	Temperance Halls.	Value in Dollars.	Schools in operation 30th March, 1861.
1. Hillsburg	217	5	4	8	213	2			4
2. Head St. Mary's Bay	162	3	5	6	208	5	1	700	3
3. Digby	309	28	21	26	534	4			5
4. Sandy Cove	196	4	4	4	241	6	1	1200	5
5. Long Island	155	2	7	4	217	4			3
6. Westport	113	1	7	6	150	2	1	200	2
7. On St. Mary's Bay	232	15	17	12	420	4			1
8. Weymouth	110	6	11	19	225	7			2
9. Belivoc Cove	171	11	3	6	195	3			3
10. Session House, Clare	240	13	14	10	505	9			6
11. Montegan	235	3	20	5	300	7			1
12. Salmon River	148	5	6	2	166	4			3
	2288	96	119	108	3374	57	3	2100	38

PLACES OF WORSHIP, &c....1860--61.

KING'S.

Church of England	Church of Rome	Church of Scotl'd	Presbyterian Ch. of L. P.	Associated Baptist	Other Baptist	Methodist	Congregationalist	Universalist	Union	Other Places of Worship	Total	Launched in 1860	Tonnage	Building 29th March, 1861	Probable Tonnage
				2	2	1	1				6	4	480	6	1600
1	1		1	2							5				
			1		2						3	1	140	2	120
			1								1	1	132	2	300
1				2		2				1	6	2	334	2	310
1			1	2		1					5				
				2				1			3				
1	1		1	1		2					6				
				2		2					4				
				1		1		2			4				
	1										1				
2	1		1	1		2					6	1	40		
			1	1		1					3				
6	4		6	16	4	12	1		3	1	53	9	1126	12	2330

ANNAPOLIS.

Church of England	Church of Rome	Church of Scotl'd	Presbyterian Ch. of L. P.	Associated Baptist	Other Baptist	Methodist	Congregationalist	Universalist	Union	Other Places of Worship	Total	Launched in 1860	Tonnage	Building 29th March, 1861	Probable Tonnage
			1	4		1					6			2	50
1				4		3					8	2	480	3	680
1				4		1					6				
1				3		1					5				
1				2		1				1	5	1	613	1	200
1				2		1			1	1	6	3	737	3	1645
1				1							2			1	350
1				2		2					5	3	153		
1				2		2					5	1	75	1	180
3	1		1	1		1					7				
				1		1					2				
				2		1					3				
				1							1				
1				1							2				
12	1		2	30		15			1	2	63	10	2058	11	3105

DIGBY.

Church of England	Church of Rome	Church of Scotl'd	Presbyterian Ch. of L. P.	Associated Baptist	Other Baptist	Methodist	Congregationalist	Universalist	Union	Other Places of Worship	Total	Launched in 1860	Tonnage	Building 29th March, 1861	Probable Tonnage
	1			2						1	4	2	422	3	280
2						1					3	2	134	2	35
2	1			4	1	1					9	2	294		
1				3		2					6	2	258	1	220
				2							2	1	45	4	180
1				1	1						3	3	90	1	30
1	1			1							3	2	309	9	1585
2				3		1					6	2	298	1	315
	1			1							2	1	125	2	120
	2										2	3	682	3	225
	1										1	1	25	6	1225
	1										1	3	1015	1	700
9	8			17	2	5				1	42	24	3697	33	4915

No. 7.—RETURN OF HOUSES,

COUNTY OF

POLLING DISTRICTS.	Houses, &c.								Schools in operation 30th March, 1861.
	Inhabited.	Vacant.	Building.	Stores and Shops.	Barns & Outhouses.	School Houses.	Temperance Halls.	Value in Dollars.	
1. Ohio	397	20	4	7	650	8	1	400	7
2. Yarmouth	697	53	11	40	430	6			10
3. Chebogue	250	24	10	3	337	7			3
4. Carleton	107	2	4	3	132	3			1
5. Plymouth	150	9	9	7	200	4			1
6. Tusket	340	16	24	17	376	5			3
7. Argyle	190	3	9	3	135	4			3
8. Pubnico	215	4	19	15	273	6			5
9. Kempt	50	4			58	1			1
10. West side Tusket River	50		2	1	65	1			
	2446	135	92	96	2656	45	1	400	34

COUNTY OF

	Inhabited.	Vacant.	Building.	Stores and Shops.	Barns & Outhouses.	School Houses.	Temperance Halls.	Value in Dollars.	Schools in operation 30th March, 1861.
1. Carleton Village	154	10	12	3	240	7			4
2. Shelburne	336	5	16	16	421	7			13
3. Ragged Islands	195	3	7	18	216	3	1	700	2
4. Louis Head	130	7	5	46	166	7			2
5. Shag Harbor	202	4	12	34	169	5			2
6. Cape Sable Island	220	8	18	118	260	6	1	500	1
7. Barrington	292	13	13	38	430	6			4
8. Port LaTour	235	10	6	13	383	7			5
	1764	60	89	286	2285	48	2	1200	33

COUNTY OF

	Inhabited.	Vacant.	Building.	Stores and Shops.	Barns & Outhouses.	School Houses.	Temperance Halls.	Value in Dollars.	Schools in operation 30th March, 1861.
1. Liverpool	476	13	6	100	500	7	2	4000	8
2. Bristol	287	11	18	28	300	4			4
3. Port Medway	295	10	20	30	252	6			4
4. Port Mouton	125	2	2	46	112	3			1
5. Brookfield	98	5	4	1	240	4			3
6. Caledonia	165	2	4	4	233	4			1
7. Greenfield	54	3	1	2	86	2			
	1500	46	55	211	1723	30	2	4000	21

COUNTY OF

	Inhabited.	Vacant.	Building.	Stores and Shops.	Barns & Outhouses.	School Houses.	Temperance Halls.	Value in Dollars.	Schools in operation 30th March, 1861.
1. Lunenburg	403	29	8	29	687	10	1	1600	14
2. Ritsoy's Cove	206	13	1	2	480	10			4
3. Mahone Bay	393	3	6	24	524	9			6
4. LaHave	141	8	6	10	195	4			2
5. New Germany	317	5	10	4	408	8			3
6. Chester	429	12	8	9	576	10			5
7. Sherbrooke	122	5	6	3	122	4			3
8. Petite Riviere	459	16	8	23	746	16			11
9. Bridgewater	339	6	3	27	436	9			7
10. Tancook Island	52	3		44	45	1			1
11. Mill Cove, St. Margaret's Bay	68	5		56	50	2			1
	2929	105	56	231	4269	83	1	1600	57

PLACES OF WORSHIP, &c....1860—61.

YARMOUTH.

			Places of Worship.										Vessels.		
Church of England.	Church of Rome.	Church of Scotl'd.	Presbyterian Ch. of L. P.	Associated Baptist.	Other Baptist.	Methodist.	Congregationalist.	Universalist.	Union.	Other Places of Worship.	Total.	Launched in 1860.	Tonnage.	Building 20th March, 1861.	Probable Tonnage.
.....	.....	.....	.....	5	2	.....	.....	.....	.....	.....	7	2	540	3	437
1	1	.....	1	2	3	3	.....	.....	.....	.....	11	.....	.....	5	4650
.....	.....	1	3	3	.....	1	.....	.....	.....	.....	8	.....	.....	1	54
.....	.....	1	1	2	.....	.....	.....	.....	.....	.....	4	.....	.....	1	15
.....	1	.....	.....	1	.....	.....	.....	.....	.....	.....	2	5	330	6	100
1	2	.....	.....	1	.....	.....	.....	.....	.....	.....	4	7	1039	3	800
.....	1	.....	.....	1	2	.....	.....	.....	.....	.....	4	.....	.....	2	180
.....	1	.....	.....	.....	.....	.....	.....	.....	2	.....	3	1	48	1	45
.....	.....	.....	.....	.....	1	.....	.....	.....	.....	.....	1	.....	.....	.....	.....
2	6	.....	3	13	14	3	1	.....	2	.....	44	15	1957	22	6281

SHELBURNE.

Church of England.	Church of Rome.	Church of Scotl'd.	Presbyterian Ch. of L. P.	Associated Baptist.	Other Baptist.	Methodist.	Congregationalist.	Universalist.	Union.	Other Places of Worship.	Total.	Launched in 1860.	Tonnage.	Building 20th March, 1861.	Probable Tonnage.
.....	.....	.....	1	.....	.....	2	.....	.....	.....	.....	3	1	90	.....	.....
3	.....	.....	2	.....	.....	1	.....	.....	.....	.....	6	11	979	10	962
.....	.....	.....	1	3	.....	.....	.....	.....	.....	.....	4	2	66	.....	.....
.....	.....	.....	2	.....	2	1	.....	.....	.....	.....	5	4	400	3	330
.....	.....	.....	.....	3	.....	.....	.....	.....	.....	.....	3	.....	.....	1	30
.....	.....	.....	.....	2	.....	.....	.....	1	.....	.....	3	1	20	1	10
1	.....	.....	.....	2	2	.....	.....	3	.....	.....	8	2	155	2	90
1	.....	.....	.....	1	2	.....	.....	.....	.....	.....	4	2	96	2	850
5	.....	.....	4	5	8	9	1	.....	4	.....	36	23	1806	19	2272

QUEEN'S.

Church of England.	Church of Rome.	Church of Scotl'd.	Presbyterian Ch. of L. P.	Associated Baptist.	Other Baptist.	Methodist.	Congregationalist.	Universalist.	Union.	Other Places of Worship.	Total.	Launched in 1860.	Tonnage.	Building 20th March, 1861.	Probable Tonnage.
3	1	.....	.....	1	.....	4	2	.....	.....	.....	11	3	100	4	150
1	.....	.....	.....	1	1	1	1	.....	.....	.....	5	8	690	2	110
2	1	.....	.....	3	2	3	.....	.....	.....	.....	11	1	50	1	124
.....	.....	.....	.....	2	.....	2	.....	.....	.....	.....	4	1	52	.....	.....
.....	.....	.....	.....	1	.....	.....	1	.....	.....	.....	2	.....	.....	.....	.....
1	1	.....	.....	2	1	.....	.....	.....	.....	.....	5	.....	.....	.....	.....
.....	.....	.....	.....	1	.....	.....	.....	.....	.....	.....	1	.....	.....	.....	.....
7	3	.....	.....	11	4	10	4	.....	.....	.....	39	13	892	7	384

LUNENBURG.

Church of England.	Church of Rome.	Church of Scotl'd.	Presbyterian Ch. of L. P.	Associated Baptist.	Other Baptist.	Methodist.	Congregationalist.	Universalist.	Union.	Other Places of Worship.	Total.	Launched in 1860.	Tonnage.	Building 20th March, 1861.	Probable Tonnage.
1	1	.....	1	1	.....	1	.....	.....	.....	1	6	5	217	7	463
1	.....	.....	1	.....	.....	1	.....	.....	.....	.....	3	.....	.....	.....	.....
1	.....	.....	2	.....	.....	.....	1	.....	.....	.....	4	5	225	1	48
1	.....	.....	1	.....	.....	.....	.....	.....	.....	.....	2	2	69	3	490
1	.....	.....	.....	1	.....	1	.....	1	.....	.....	4	.....	.....	.....	.....
1	1	.....	.....	2	.....	.....	.....	.....	.....	.....	4	.....	.....	2	60
1	1	.....	.....	1	.....	.....	.....	.....	.....	.....	3	.....	.....	.....	.....
4	.....	.....	1	.....	3	.....	.....	2	.....	.....	10	5	316	4	225
2	.....	.....	1	1	.....	.....	1	1	.....	.....	6	5	2281	1	20
.....	.....	.....	.....	1	.....	.....	.....	.....	.....	.....	1	.....	.....	.....	.....
13	3	.....	4	10	.....	6	.....	.....	5	2	43	22	3138	18	1306

34

No. 7.—RETURN OF HOUSES, PUBLIC BUILDINGS, PLACES OF WORSHIP, &c...1860—01.
GENERAL ABSTRACT.

COUNTIES.	Houses, &c.						Temperance Halls		Public Buildings			Schools in operation	Places of Worship		
1. Halifax (City)	2684	198	46	422	908	58	1	16000	19	705900	15	5	51	2
(Outside City)	3648	206	218	102	4170	96	2	1600	3	160500	71	22	18	2
Total in County	6199	332	305	524	5069	119	5	17600	22	862000	86	27	18	4
2. Colchester	3128	103	505	307	3460	102	3	800	8	1770	51	6	1	1
3. Cumberland	2592	116	58	107	4081	93	2	1800	6	7300	56	9	0	3
4. Pictou	4345	147	142	214	5922	116	8	2080	8	12500	78	35	4	13
5. Sydney	3144	39	85	68	3038	37	3		3	7800	48	4	10	1
6. Guysborough	1908	78	80	389	2124	44	1	400	3	4500	27	10	6	1
7. Inverness	2817	60	189	180	3016	13	1	100	2	6000	60		13	1
8. Richmond	1672	82	145	340	2158	32			2	8200	27	5	7	
9. Victoria	1429	69	65	40	1555	38			2	2000	29	3	4	1
10. Cape Breton	3095	132	187	141	3404	65	6	2050	4	5400	49	9	13	3
11. Hants	2755	133	69	126	3057	68	8	4610	5	4500	49	13	0	
12. King's	3172	902	43	102	3191	74	8	2540	5	8500	53	12	4	
13. Annapolis	2810	85	53	132	4629	78	4	400	4	8400	55	12	3	
14. Digby	2288	95	119	168	3574	37	3	2100	3	7081	38	0	8	
15. Yarmouth	2448	133	95	95	3008	45	1	400	4	7300	34	2	6	
16. Shelburne	1764	68	89	185	2285	48	2	1340	2	5600	25	5		
17. Queen's	1900	86	51	211	1725	30	2	400	4	3800	21	7	3	
18. Lunenburg	3928	160	94	251	4209	83	1	1600	3	5800	45	12	3	
	49569	1916	1728	3326	62267	1225	46	42334	92	984160	805	190	131	25

Note.—The Counties containing a large number of Houses being Fishing Counties, it is supposed that a great proportion of them are only Fish Houses.

COUNTIES	Places of Worship—Continued.									Vessels.			
	Presbyterian Ch. of E.	Associated Baptist	Other Baptist	Methodist	Congregationalist	Unitarian	Other	Other Places of Worship	Total	Launched in 1860	Tonnage	Building their Masts, 1861	Outside Tonnage
1. { Halifax (City)	3	3		4		1		1	24				
" (Outside City)	9	18		8			1		73	5	204	11	555
Total in County	13	21		12		1	1	1	97	5	204	11	555
2. Colchester	24	18		6			4		80	15	1608	26	4425
3. Cumberland	12	18		20		1	12	9	78	9	2015	21	4430
4. Pictou	26	1		2					65	19	2564	19	4006
5. Sydney	8	2		1					29	6	852	11	671
6. Guysborough	3	8		3	2		2		23	14	1095	72	1700
7. Inverness	8	3		3	1				24	7	326	14	756
8. Richmond	4			1					14	7	492	18	1218
9. Victoria	10			1				3	18			2	246
10. Cape Breton	9	5		6				1	47	13	825	16	784
11. Hants	18	12	2	18	1		3		65	12	2125	18	7230
12. King's	6	10	4	12	1		3	1	52	9	1120	17	3550
13. Annapolis	2	30		15			3	1	65	10	946	11	3305
14. Digby		17	2	5				1	42	24	2007	32	4925
15. Yarmouth	3	15	14	5	1		2		44	16	1937	23	6251
16. Shelburne	6	5	8	9	1		4		36	23	1800	10	2279
17. Queen's		13	4	18	4				38	12	892	7	984
18. Lunenburg	4	10		6			5	2	62	22	3198	18	1300
	143	182	34	150	11	2	30	15	821	251	26049	290	47903

APPENDIX NO. 8.

RETURN

OF

MILLS, MANUFACTORIES, &c.

No. 8.—RETURN OF MILLS,

COUNTY OF

POLLING DISTRICTS.	Grist Mills.					Saw Mills.				
	No. of Mills.	Propell'd by Water.	Propell'd by Steam.	No. of hands employed.	Value in Dollars.	No. of Mills.	Propell'd by Water.	Propell'd by Steam.	No. of hands employed.	Value in Dollars.
1. Ward 1, (City)										
2. do. 2, do										
3. do. 3, do										
4. do. 4, do										
5. do. 5, do. {1st Section / 2d do.						2		2	20	3200
6. do. 6, do						1	1		2	400
Total in City						3	1	2	22	3600
7. Ferguson's Cove										
8. Portuguese Cove										
9. Sambro										
10. Prospect						1	1		1	200
11. Hagget's Cove	2	2		2	400					
12. French Village						6	6		10	2250
13. Drysdale's										
14. North West Arm	3	3		4	2600	1	1		4	300
15. Piers' Mill	1	1		5	800	4	2	2	13	7000
16. Hammond's Plains						11	11		22	9480
17. Windsor Road						8	8		24	3200
18. Truro Road						5	5		9	2150
19. Gay's River	1	1		1	400	4	4		10	3600
20. Wise's Corner	2	2		2	900	7	7		10	2800
21. Middle Musquodoboit	3	3		3	5200	9	9		9	2160
22. Upper Musquodoboit	3	3		7	3420	4	4		16	14600
23. Caledonia	1	1		1	800	2	2		2	1000
24. Salmon River										
25. Sheet Harbor						4	4		18	13000
26. Pope's Harbor						2	2		6	800
27. Jeddore						17	17		40	7430
28. Chezetcook	1	1		1	160	2	2		2	500
29. Lawrencetown	2	2		2	1000	3	3		5	1600
30. Preston						2	2		8	1600
31. Dartmouth	*6	5		9	16000	1	1		2	400
32. Black Point	1	1		1	320	7	7		10	3510
33. Eastern Passage										
	26	25		38	63600	103	99	4	243	80980

* One Grist Mill propelled by wind.

COUNTY OF

POLLING DISTRICTS.	Grist No. of Mills.	Water.	Steam.	Hands.	Value.	Saw No. of Mills.	Water.	Steam.	Hands.	Value.
1. Truro	3	3		8	2800	16	16		34	6500
2. Old Barns	1	1		2	600	10	10		12	3400
3. Lower Stewiacke	4	4		8	2100	6	5	1	19	3000
4. Upper Stewiacke	4	4		8	5800	10	10		20	6480
5. Upper Onslow and Kemptown						11	11		17	7920
6. Onslow	2	2		2	1200	3	3		3	1120
7. Earltown	2	2		4	2100	8	8		8	3200
8. New Annan	3	3		6	2400	17	17		35	6800
9. Waugh's River	1	1		2	800	5	5		13	2300
10. Tatamagouche	2	2		3	2100	12	12		36	5840
11. Upper Londonderry	3	3		3	1700	9	9		9	5000
12. Lower Londonderry	5	5		5	2500	8	8		8	3000
13. Economy and Five Islands	3	3		3	700	8	8		10	1600
	33	33		54	25400	123	122	1	224	57060

MANUFACTORIES, &c....1860—61.

HALIFAX.

No. of Mills	Carding Mills — Propell'd by Water	Steam	No. of hands employed	Value in Dollars	No. of Mills	Shingle Mills — Propell'd by Water	Steam	No. of hands employed	Value in Dollars	REMARKS.
										Halifax also returns 1 Lath Mill, value $300; 1 Block Factory, $1000; 3 Soap and Candle Factories, $7000; 1 Axe Factory, $1500; 1 Rake Factory, $600; 1 Chair Factory, $400; 1 Pail and Chair Factory, $1000; 1 Cloth Factory, $400; 1 Paper Mill, $1000; 1 Tobacco Factory, $800; 4 Iron Foundries, $38,100; 2 Nail Factories, $6000; 1 Carriage Factory, $800; 8 Tanneries, $36,500; 1 Cabinet Factory, $4800; 1 Brush Factory, $1200; 1 Gas Factory, $180,000; 1 Trunk Factory, $300; 5 Breweries, $46,000; 1 Joiner's Factory, $12,000; 1 Brick Factory, $3200; 1 Steam Bakery, $400.
1	1	....	1	600	1	1	....	3	400	
2	2	....	2	420	2	2	....	2	800	
1	1	....	12	400	3	3	....	12	9000	
					1	1	....	2	600	
1	1	....	2	200						
5	5	....	7	1620	9	9	....	21	11300	

COLCHESTER.

No. of Mills	Water	Steam	No. of hands employed	Value in Dollars	No. of Mills	Water	Steam	No. of hands employed	Value in Dollars	
2	2	....	4	1000	2	2	....	4	250	Colchester also returns 3 Fulling Mills, value $3600; 5 Tanneries, $6000; 1 Shoe Factory, $2000; 1 Saw and Planing Mill, $2000; 1 Iron Foundry, $40,000; 3 Lath Mills, $1500; 1 Plaster Mill, $400.
1	1	....	2	400	12	12	....	40	3600	
2	2	....	5	2800						
1	1	....	2	400	2	2	....	4	280	
2	2	....	4	800						
1	1	....	1	700	3	3	....	3	650	
4	4	....	4	1500						
13	13	....	22	7600	19	10	....	51	4780	

No. 8.—RETURN OF MILLS,

COUNTY OF

POLLING DISTRICTS.	Grist Mills.					Saw Mills.				
	No. of Mills.	Propell'd by Water.	Steam.	No. of hands employed.	Value in Dollars.	No. of Mills.	Propell'd by Water.	Steam.	No. of hands employed.	Value in Dollars.
1. Amherst	5	5		5	1140	25	25		43	6200
2. Westchester	3	3		3	850	16	16		25	6200
3. Head of Amherst	7	7		7	3730	49	49		120	14395
4. River Philip	7	7		7	2400	71	71		200	20660
5. River Hebert	1	1		1	1500	23	23		85	18440
6. Maccan	4	4		4	1700	18	18		34	8840
7. Pugwash	4	4		6	3120	18	17	1	39	6840
8. Wallace	5	4	1	12	12800	6	6		18	1450
9. Wentworth	2	2		2	300	9	9		20	9360
10. Advocate Harbor	1	1		2	200	25	25		50	10000
11. Mill Village	1	1		2	500	32	32		64	9600
	40	39	1	51	28640	292	291	1	698	111985

COUNTY OF

POLLING DISTRICTS.	Grist Mills.					Saw Mills.				
	No. of Mills.	Propell'd by Water.	Steam.	No. of hands employed.	Value in Dollars.	No. of Mills.	Propell'd by Water.	Steam.	No. of hands employed.	Value in Dollars.
1. Picton						*1		1	10	12000
2. Carriboo	1	1		1	400					
3. Cape John	1	1		2	800	7	7		7	1940
4. West side River John	2	2		4	4000	5	4	1	8	4320
5. West branch River John	2	2		4	1460	6	6		9	1386
6. Rogers Hill	1	1		3	400	4	4		12	988
7. Hardwood Hill	3	3		6	7000	7	7		14	3000
8. Green Hill and West River	4	2	2	8	9200	7	7		17	4920
9. Mount Thom	3	3		6	4800	7	7		14	3200
10. Gairloch	1	1		3	1200	2	2		2	400
11. New Lairg						1	1		1	120
12. Albion Mines	2	1	1	4	1000	3	2	1	5	2400
13. New Glasgow						1	1		1	100
14. Little Harbor	2	2		2	1600	2	2		2	1200
15. McLellan's Mountain	3	3		3	3200	7	7		7	2220
16. East branch East River	2	2		4	2000	5	5		5	2600
17. Hopewell, W. branch E. Riv	2	2		2	1900	9	9		11	1530
18. Middle River	3	3		6	2400	9	9		18	4000
19. Gulf Shore	3	3		3	3000	2	2		2	800
20. Barney's River	2	2		4	2600	4	4		8	960
21. Merigomish	5	5		9	4900	8	8		12	3000
22. Blue Mount'n, St. Mary's, &c.						4	4		5	1700
	42	39	3	74	51860	101	98	3	170	53084

* Grist and Carding Mill connected with this.

COUNTY OF

POLLING DISTRICTS.	Grist Mills.					Saw Mills.				
	No. of Mills.	Propell'd by Water.	Steam.	No. of hands employed.	Value in Dollars.	No. of Mills.	Propell'd by Water.	Steam.	No. of hands employed.	Value in Dollars.
1. Arisaig	2	2		4	1600	2	2		4	600
2. Cape George	2	2		3	2520	2	2		2	320
3. Morristown	2	2		4	2300	2	2		4	1040
4. Antigonish	5	5		5	6800	19	19		30	6500
5. Lochaber	4	4		4	2480	12	12		12	1920
6. Upper South River	5	5		10	4000	5	5		10	1600
7. St. Andrew's	4	4		4	4800	4	4		4	1040
8. Tracadie	3	3		6	2400	7	7		10	2800
9. Harbor Bouche						1	1		1	120
	27	27		40	26900	54	54		77	15940

MANUFACTORIES, &c....1860—61.

CUMBERLAND.

No. of Mills.	Carding Mills. Propell'd by Water.	Steam.	No. of hands employed.	Value in Dollars.	No. of Mills.	Shingle Mills. Propell'd by Water.	Steam.	No. of hands employed.	Value in Dollars.	REMARKS.
1	1		2	1200						Cumberland also returns 3 Oat Mills, $1400; 1 Grindstone Factory, $4000, propelled by steam.
1	1		2	600						
1	1		2	600						
1	1		2	1500						
1	1		1	600						
2	2		4	680						
7	7		13	5180						

PICTOU.

No. of Mills.	Carding Mills. Propell'd by Water.	Steam.	No. of hands employed.	Value in Dollars.	No. of Mills.	Shingle Mills. Propell'd by Water.	Steam.	No. of hands employed.	Value in Dollars.	REMARKS.
					2	1	1		1000	Pictou also returns 6 Fulling Mills, value $7600; 1 Axe Factory, $30; 3 Iron Foundries, $15,200; 1 Wooden Factory, $800; 1 Cabinet Factory, $800; 12 Tanneries, $17,400; 1 Coal Oil Factory, $1000; 1 Steam Bakery, $2000; 1 Cloth Factory, $2400.
1	1		2	600	5	5		5	1200	
1	1		1	280						
2	2		2	2000						
1	1		2	450	3	3		6	1200	
2	2		2	1200	1	1		2	240	
7	7		9	4530	11	10	1	13	3640	

SYDNEY.

No. of Mills.	Carding Mills. Propell'd by Water.	Steam.	No. of hands employed.	Value in Dollars.	No. of Mills.	Shingle Mills. Propell'd by Water.	Steam.	No. of hands employed.	Value in Dollars.	REMARKS.
					2	2		8	400	Sydney also returns 2 Fulling Mills, value $2400; 1 Lath Mill, $160.
					1	1		1	400	
5	5		9	2400	1	1		2	250	
2	2		2	480						
					3	3		7	640	
1	1		2	800						
8	8		13	3680	7	7		18	1690	

35

No. 8.—RETURN OF MILLS,

COUNTY OF

POLLING DISTRICTS.	Grist Mills.					Saw Mills.				
	No. of Mills.	Propell'd by		No. of hands employed.	Value in Dollars.	No. of Mills.	Propell'd by		No. of hands employed.	Value in Dollars.
		Water.	Steam.				Water.	Steam.		
1. Guysborough	2	2		2	1400	3	3		8	1200
2. Intervale						3	3		6	720
3. Manchester						2	2		3	480
4. Melford	1	1		1	1000	1	1		1	200
5. Crow Harbor										
6. Cape Canso										
7. Country Harbor	1	1		1	200	6	6		12	2400
8. Sherbrooke						3	3		12	5400
9. Marie Joseph						2	2		7	880
10. Forks, St. Mary's	5	5				10	10			
11. Molasses Harbor										
	9	9		4	2600	30	30		49	11280

COUNTY OF

POLLING DISTRICTS.	No. of Mills.	Water.	Steam.	No. of hands employed.	Value in Dollars.	No. of Mills.	Water.	Steam.	No. of hands employed.	Value in Dollars.
1. Plaster Cove	3	3		6	2400	3	3		6	1600
2. Judique	3	3		3	1600					
3. River Inhabitants	1	1		2	800	2	2		5	840
4. Port Hood	1	1		1	500					
5. Mabou	6	6		9	8500	7	7		7	1680
6. Broad Cove (Intervale)	2	2		3	1200	3	3		4	720
7. Broad Cove	1	1		2	1000	1	1		2	320
8. Margaree						1	1		2	230
9. Young's Bridge	2	2		2	800					
10. Friar's Head	1	1		1	480	1	1		1	240
11. Cheticamp	2	2		2	200					
12. Whycocomagh	5	5		7	4000	5	5		5	1400
13. Lake Ainslie	3	3		6	3000					
14. River Dennis	3	3		3	1800	3	3		3	520
15. North-east Margaree	4	4		8	2400	4	4		8	820
	37	37		55	28680	30	30		43	8370

COUNTY OF

POLLING DISTRICTS.	No. of Mills.	Water.	Steam.	No. of hands employed.	Value in Dollars.	No. of Mills.	Water.	Steam.	No. of hands employed.	Value in Dollars.
1. Arichat										
2. Petit Degrate										
3. D'Escouse										
4. Black River	3	3		3	4000	1	1		1	320
5. River Bourgeoise										
6. St. Peter's										
7. L'Ardoise										
8. Grand River	2	2		4	1800					
9. Red Islands	2	2		4	1200					
10. River Inhabitants										
11. Little Arichat										
12. Loch Lomond	2	2		2	1120					
13. Flamboise										
	9	9		13	8120	1	1		1	320

MANUFACTORIES, &c....1860—61.

GUYSBOROUGH.

Carding Mills.					Shingle Mills.					REMARKS.
No. of Mills.	Propell'd by Water.	Steam.	No. of hands employed.	Value in Dollars.	No. of Mills.	Propell'd by Water.	Steam.	No. of hands employed.	Value in Dollars.	
2	2	....	2	800	....	....	....	....	....	Guysborough also returns 1 Fulling Mill, value $1000.
1	1	....	1	300	....	....	....	....	....	
1	1	....	1	120	....	....	....	....	....	
....	....	....	....	....	....	....	....	....	....	
....	....	....	....	....	....	....	....	....	....	
....	....	....	....	....	....	....	....	....	....	
2	2	....	....	....	1	1	....	3	400	{ Value not returned in this district.
					2	2				
6	6	....	4	1280	3	3	....	3	400	

INVERNESS.

										Inverness also returns 2 Fulling Mills, value $3000; 1 Tannery, $600; 1 Factory, kind not designated, $1600.
2	2	....	4	400	....	....	....	....	....	
....	....	....	....	....	....	....	....	....	....	
....	....	....	....	....	1	1	....	2	200	
....	....	....	....	....	....	....	....	....	....	
....	....	....	....	....	....	....	....	....	....	
....	....	....	....	....	....	....	....	....	....	
....	....	....	....	....	3	3	....	5	720	
....	....	....	....	....	2	2	....	4	450	
....	....	....	....	....	....	....	....	....	....	
2	2	....	4	400	6	6	....	11	1370	

RICHMOND.

....	....	....	....	....	....	....	....	....	....	
....	....	....	....	....	....	....	....	....	....	
1	1	....	1	350	....	....	....	....	....	
....	....	....	....	....	....	....	....	....	....	
....	....	....	....	....	....	....	....	....	....	
....	....	....	....	....	....	....	....	....	....	
....	....	....	....	....	....	....	....	....	....	
....	....	....	....	....	....	....	....	....	....	
....	....	....	....	....	....	....	....	....	....	
....	....	....	....	....	....	....	....	....	....	
1	1	....	1	350	....	....	....	....	....	

No. 8.—RETURN OF MILLS,

COUNTY OF

POLLING DISTRICTS.	Grist Mills.					Saw Mills.				
	No. of Mills.	Propell'd by Water.	Steam.	No. of hands employed.	Value in Dollars.	No. of Mills.	Propell'd by Water.	Steam.	No. of hands employed.	Value in Dollars.
1. Washabok						2	2		4	400
2. Middle River	3	3		6	2350	1	1		3	160
3. Baddeck	3	3		3	1400	2	2		2	400
4. Munro's Point, St. Ann's	3	3		6	2300	4	4		7	2680
5. Englishtown, St. Ann's						2	2		4	1280
6. Boulardrie	4	4		8	4000					
7. Ingonish										
8. Cape North	2	2		2	200	2	2		2	140
9. Bay St. Lawrence	1	1		1	80					
10. Little Narrows	2	2		2	1880	1	1		1	200
	18	18		28	12710	14	14		23	5260

COUNTY OF

POLLING DISTRICTS.	Grist Mills.					Saw Mills.				
	No. of Mills.	Propell'd by Water.	Steam.	No. of hands employed.	Value in Dollars.	No. of Mills.	Propell'd by Water.	Steam.	No. of hands employed.	Value in Dollars.
1. Sydney	4	3	1	8	7440	4	4			260
2. Ball's Bridge	2	2		6	1600	9	9		28	3500
3. Mira Ferry	1	1		3	400	3	3		3	1000
4. Sydney Mines	1	1		2	1400	2	1	1	4	500
5. Mainadieu	1	1		1	200					
6. Louisburg						1	1		1	160
7. Gabarus	2	2		7	2000	2	2		5	800
8. East Bay	2	2		4	2600	1	1		2	1000
9. Beaver Cove	1	1		2	300	5	5		8	800
10. Howley's Ferry	3	3		3	2800	1	1		12	400
11. Lingan Mines						1	1		1	100
12. Cow Bay	2	2		3	600					
13. Big Pond										
14. Christmas Island	1	1		2	600					
	20	19	1	41	19040	29	28	1	54	8670

COUNTY OF

POLLING DISTRICTS.	Grist Mills.					Saw Mills.				
	No. of Mills.	Propell'd by Water.	Steam.	No. of hands employed.	Value in Dollars.	No. of Mills.	Propell'd by Water.	Steam.	No. of hands employed.	Value in Dollars.
1. Windsor										
2. St. Croix	2	2		2	3200	5	4	1	38	13600
3. Brooklyn	2	2		3	2000	6	6		10	1800
4. Scotch Village	2	2		3	2400	3	3		7	1300
5. Falmouth	2	2		2	1080	2	2		2	400
6. Kempt	1	1		2	1000	9	8	1	33	5100
7. Rawdon Church	1	1		1	800	6	6		16	3500
8. South Rawdon	1	1		1	800	6	6		10	1850
9. Noel	3	3		4	4800	6	5	1	22	5400
10. Nine Mile River	3	3		3	2000	11	10	1	20	6700
11. Maitland	1	1		2	500	6	6		8	2620
12. Chester Road	1	1		1	800	7	7		14	3000
	19	19		24	19380	67	63	4	180	45270

MANUFACTORIES, &c...1860—61.

VICTORIA.

No. of Mills.	Carding Mills.				No. of Mills.	Shingle Mills.				REMARKS.
	Propell'd by		No. of hands employed.	Value in Dollars.		Propell'd by		No. of hands employed.	Value in Dollars.	
	Water.	Steam.				Water.	Steam.			
					2	2	.....	4	800	Victoria also returns 1 Fulling and Dying Mill, employing 4 hands, value $1200.
					2	2		4	800	

CAPE BRETON.

										Cape Breton also returns 1 Iron Foundry, value $8000; 2 Tanneries, $1000; 1 Engine Factory, $4000; 1 Oat Mill, $200.
1	1	.....	1	400	1	1	.....	1	400	
1	1	.....	1	400	1	1	.....	1	400	

HANTS.

										Hants also returns 1 Iron Foundry, value $10,000; 1 Tannery, $800; 2 Factories, kind not designated, $22,000; 3 Carriage Factories, $16,540; 1 Block Factory, $400; 1 Brick and Pottery Factory, $5000.
1	1	.....	2	800						
1	1	.....	2	1000	2	2	.....	3	800	
2	2	.....	5	1200						
					1	1	.....	1	500	
					1	1	.....	1	200	
2	2	.....	4	1000						
					3	3	.....	4	1200	
					1	1	.....	1	400	
6	6	.....	13	4000	8	8	.....	10	3100	

No. 8.—RETURN OF MILLS,

COUNTY OF

POLLING DISTRICTS.	Grist Mills.					Saw Mills.				
	No. of Mills.	Propell'd by		No. of hands employed	Value in Dollars.	No. of Mills.	Propell'd by		No. of hands employed.	Value in Dollars.
		Water.	Steam.				Water.	Steam.		
1. Canning	1	1	......	1	1000	8	8	......	16	3200
2. Canard										
3. Centreville						4	3	1	9	2760
4. Lakeville	1	1	......	3	500	7	7	......	15	1075
5. Somerset						5	5	......	5	2000
6. Kentville	3	3	......	3	3000	5	5	......	10	3720
7. Gasperaux	3	3	......	5	1800	12	12	......	18	4000
8. Wolfville	2	2	......	3	980	2	2	......	2	400
9. Lower Horton	1	1	......	1	480	2	2	......	3	600
10. Aylesford	4	4	......	4	1500	15	15	......	30	4500
11. West Sherbrooke	1	1	......	1	160	2	2	......	2	350
12. Aylesford						3	3	......	3	600
13. Berwick	4	4	......	4	3700	8	8	......	8	4650
	20	20	......	24	13120	73	72	1	121	27855

COUNTY OF

1. Wilmot	4	4	......	4	3500	7	7	......	14	4000
2. Wilmot, Middleton Corner	2	2	......	2	800	7	7	......	9	2040
3. Clarence, Wilmot	2	2	......	2	300	7	7	......	14	1100
4. Bridgetown	2	2	......	2	1300	5	5	......	5	800
5. Bellisle	1	1	......	1	400	7	7	......	7	1000
6. New Caledonia	2	2	......	3	600	7	7	......	14	1820
7. Broad Cove						4	4	......	16	2200
8. Clementsport	3	3	......	3	480	6	6	......	6	620
9. Hessian Line	2	2	......	2	1000	10	10	......	10	2000
10. Annapolis Royal	3	3	......	3	1200	8	8	......	8	2000
11. Carleton's Corner	3	3	......	3	200	4	4	......	4	2400
12. Nictaux	5	5	......	5	1000	7	7	......	8	1000
13. Dalhousie	4	4	......	4	640	7	7	......	14	1440
14. Maitland						4	4	......	21	2250
15. Morse Road						1	4	......	10	1480
	33	33	......	34	13220	94	94	......	168	26150

COUNTY OF

1. Hillsburg	2	2	......	4	1300	8	8	......	36	10000
2. Head St. Mary's Bay	2	2	......	2	600	7	7	......	10	1400
3. Digby	2	2	......	2	600	4	4	......	4	900
4. Sandy Cove	2	2	......	2	800	4	4	......	4	800
5. Long Island						2	2	......	3	280
6. Westport										
7. On St. Mary's Bay						9	9	......	18	1270
8. Weymouth	1	1	......	1	600	11	11	......	65	7880
9. Belivee Cove						21	21	......	21	3470
10. Session House, Clare	2	2	......	2	900	23	23	......	23	6520
11. Montegan	1	1	......	1	1000	16	16	......	34	6400
12. Salmon River						3	3	......	9	1850
	12	12	......	14	5700	108	108	......	221	40770

MANUFACTORIES, &c....1860—61.

KING'S.

Carding Mills.					Shingle Mills.					REMARKS.
No. of Mills.	Propell'd by		No. of hands employed.	Value in Dollars.	No. of Mills.	Propell'd by		No. of hands employed.	Value in Dollars.	
	Water.	Steam.				Steam.				
.....	.....	.....	.....	.....	.....	.....	.....	.....	.....	King's also returns 1 Tannery, value $1000; 5 Factories, kind not designated, $10,800.
1	1	.....	2	1200	.....	.....	.....	.....	.....	
.....	.....	.....	.....	.....	2	2	.....	2	800	
1	1	.....	2	300	.....	.....	.....	.....	.....	
1	1	.....	1	500	.....	.....	.....	.....	.....	
2	2	.....	3	1000	7	7	.....	14	1400	
.....	.....	.....	.....	.....	2	2	.....	3	800	
2	2	.....	2	800	2	2	.....	2	200	
7	7	.....	10	3800	13	13	.....	21	3200	

ANNAPOLIS.

										REMARKS.
.....	.....	.....	.....	.....	.....	.....	.....	.....	.....	Annapolis also returns 1 Iron Foundry, value $3000; 1 Cabinet Factory, $1500; 1 Cloth Factory, $12,000; 1 Pottery, $500; 1 Rake Factory, $80.
1	1	.....	1	200	1	1	.....	3	160	
1	1	.....	2	1200	.....	.....	.....	.....	.....	
3	3	.....	3	1200	1	1	.....	2	600	
.....	.....	.....	.....	.....	4	4	.....	8	830	
5	5	.....	6	2600	6	6	.....	13	1590	

DIGBY.

										REMARKS.
1	1	.....	2	200	.....	.....	.....	.....	.....	Digby also returns 4 Tanneries, value $3000; 4 Carriage and Cabinet Factories, $2200.
1	1	.....	1	400	.....	.....	.....	.....	.....	
1	1	.....	1	200	.....	.....	.....	.....	.....	
.....	.....	.....	.....	.....	1	1	.....	1	130	
1	1	.....	2	600	.....	.....	.....	.....	.....	
1	1	.....	1	800	4	4	.....	4	880	
.....	.....	.....	.....	.....	5	5	.....	10	1800	
5	5	.....	7	2200	10	10	.....	15	2810	

No. 8.—RETURN OF MILLS,

COUNTY OF

POLLING DISTRICTS.	Grist Mills.					Saw Mills.				
	No. of Mills.	Water.	Steam.	No. of hands employed.	Value in Dollars.	No. of Mills.	Water.	Steam.	No. of hands employed.	Value in Dollars.
1. Ohio	*1	1		2	2400	4	4		4	300
2. Yarmouth	1	1		3	2000					
3. Chebogue										
4. Carleton						9	9		17	3120
5. Plymouth										
6. Tusket						4	4		12	1600
7. Argyle						3	3		6	400
8. Pubnico										
9. Kempt						13	13		39	2810
10. West side Tusket River	†1	1		4	400	3	3		6	800
	3	3		9	8400	36	36		84	9030

* Combining Last, Planing, and other machinery.
† Combining the manufacture of Laths, Shingles, Staves, &c.

COUNTY OF

1. Carleton Village						4	4		14	3400
2. Shelburne	1	1		1	1200	11	11		34	16000
3. Ragged Islands	1	1		1	200	3	3		5	1400
4. Louis Head						4	4		12	1300
5. Shag Harbor										
6. Cape Sable Island										
7. Barrington	1	1		1	1000	1	1		2	800
8. Port LaTour						3	3		12	3600
	3	3		3	2400	26	26		79	26500

COUNTY OF

1. Liverpool	1	1		1	600	7	7		70	10500
2. Bristol	1	1		1	400	13	13		38	20000
3. Port Medway						13	13		50	4400
4. Port Mouton						5	5		10	1200
5. Brookfield	2	2		2	1100	6	6		25	3000
6. Caledonia	2	2		2	1200	3	3		9	1200
7. Greenfield	1	1		1	400	5	5			3000
	7	7		7	3700	52	52		202	43300

COUNTY OF

1. Lunenburg	12	12		24	5800	8	8		16	5500
2. Rirsey's Cove	3	3		3	900					
3. Mahone Bay	8	8		8	1800	31	31		50	9400
4. LaHave	5	5		5	1240	19	19		44	10600
5. New Germany	7	7		7	2800	37	37		74	22200
6. Chester	8	8		8	3200	11	11		20	1400
7. Sherbrooke	1	1		1	250	3	3		3	600
8. Petite Riviere	4	4		5	2000	28	28		54	16800
9. Bridgewater	8	8		8	4400	28	28		80	22400
10. Tancook Island										
11. Mill Cove, St. Margaret's Bay						3	3		6	360
	56	56		69	22450	168	168		347	89260

MANUFACTORIES, &c....1860—61.

YARMOUTH.

No. of Mills.	Carding Mills. Propell'd by Water.	Steam.	No. of hands employed.	Value in Dollars.	No. of Mills.	Shingle Mills. Propell'd by Water.	Steam.	No. of hands employed.	Value in Dollars.	REMARKS.
					2	2		4	1000	Yarmouth also returns 4 Bark Mills, value $1500; 1 Joiner's Factory, $2400; 2 Block Factories, $250; 5 Tanneries, $4000; 1 Pail Factory, $100; 2 Carriage Factories, $400; 7 Shoe Factories, $2000; 1 Chair, &c. Factory, $3000.
					3	3		6	600	
					1	1		1	160	
					1	1		1	100	
					1	1		3	600	
					8	8		15	2460	

SHELBURNE.

No. of Mills.	Water.	Steam.	No. of hands employed.	Value in Dollars.	No. of Mills.	Water.	Steam.	No. of hands employed.	Value in Dollars.	REMARKS.
					1	1		1	400	Shelburne also returns 1 Tannery, value $1400.
1	1		1	500	1	1		1	500	
1	1		1	500	2	2		2	900	

QUEEN'S.

No. of Mills.	Water.	Steam.	No. of hands employed.	Value in Dollars.	No. of Mills.	Water.	Steam.	No. of hands employed.	Value in Dollars.	REMARKS.
1	1		2	600	1	1		3	250	Queen's also returns 1 Lath Mill, value $50; 1 Bark Mill, $6000; 1 Planing Mill, $5000; 1 Axe Factory, $1600; 2 Factories, kind not designated, $23,000.
					1	1		2	200	
1	1		2	600	2	2		5	450	

LUNENBURG.

No. of Mills.	Water.	Steam.	No. of hands employed.	Value in Dollars.	No. of Mills.	Water.	Steam.	No. of hands employed.	Value in Dollars.	REMARKS.
					5	5		5	1360	Lunenburg also returns 1 Bark Mill, value $400; 4 Tanneries, $3300; 2 Factories, kind not designated, $1600.
1	1		1	200	2	2		2	260	
1	1		2	500	16	16		32	1600	
2	2		3	700	23	23		39	3220	

GENERAL ABSTRACT.

COUNTIES.	Grist Mills.					Saw Mills.					Carding Mills.				
	No. of Mills	Propelled by Water	Steam	No. of hands employed	Value in Dollars	No. of Mills	Propelled by Water	Steam	No. of hands employed	Value in Dollars	No. of Mills	Propelled by Water	Steam	No. of hands employed	Value in Dollars
1. Halifax	*36	25		38	6/8600	103	99	4	243	80900	6	6		7	1820
2. Colchester	53	53		54	25400	129	128	1	224	55900	13	13		22	7600
3. Cumberland	49	39	3	51	28640	202	202	1	696	119885	7	7		15	5180
4. Pictou	42	39	3	74	51900	201	98	3	170	53984	7	7		9	4550
5. Sydney	27	27		40	26000	54	54		177	15940	8	8		13	3600
6. Guysborough	9	9		41	2800	30	30		49	11280	6	6		4	1280
7. Inverness	37	37		53	29030	30	30		43	8370	3	2		4	400
8. Richmond	9	9		13	6130	3	3		3	320	1	1			350
9. Victoria	18	18		29	12710	14	14		23	5200					
10. Cape Breton	29	28	1	41	10040	29	28	1	54	8070	1	1		1	400
11. Hants	19	19		24	16380	65	63	4	180	45250	6	6		13	4000
12. King's	29	29		24	13137	72	73	1	121	27855	7	7		10	3800
13. Annapolis	33	33		34	13250	94	94		163	26150	5	5		6	2000
14. Digby	13	13		16	5700	108	108		225	40770	5	5		7	2200
15. Yarmouth	73	5		9	8400	36	36		84	9050				1	500
16. Shelburne	3	3		3	2800	25	25		70	26500	1	1		2	600
17. Queen's	7	7		7	3700	53	53		202	43300	1	1		2	600
18. Lunenburg	56	56		68	22400	110	158		347	89980	3	3		3	700
	414	406	5	582	396320	1407	1385	15	2959	661084	73	73		115	39440

* 1 Grist Mill propelled by wind.   † 2 combining other machinery.—See County Abstract.

No. 8.—RETURN OF MILLS, MANUFACTORIES, &c. 1860—61.

GENERAL ABSTRACT. Continued.

COUNTIES	Shingle Mills					Lath Mills		Block Factories		Soap and Candle Factories		Axe Factories		Rake Factories	
	No. of Mills	Propelled by Water	Steam	No. of hands employed	Value in Dollars	Number	Value in Dollars	Number	Value in Dollars	Number	Value in Dollars	Number	Value in Dollars	Number	Value in Dollars
1. Halifax	9	9		21	11200	1	300	2	1000	3	7000	1	1500	1	600
2. Colchester	19	19		61	4780	3	1500								
3. Cumberland															
4. Pictou	11	10	1	13	2640							1	30		
5. Sydney	7	7		18	1600	1	160								
6. Guysborough	3	3		3	400										
7. Inverness	6	6		12	1270										
8. Richmond															
9. Victoria	2	2		4	800										
10. Cape Breton	1	1		1	400										
11. Hants	8	8		10	3100										
12. Kings	13	13		21	2200			1	400						
13. Annapolis	6	6		18	1800									1	800
14. Digby	10	10		15	2810										
15. Yarmouth	6	6		10	2460			2	250						
16. Shelburne	2	2		3	900										
17. Queen's	2	2		6	450	1	50					1	1600		
18. Lunenburg	33	28		33	3220										
	180	180	1	243	4500	5	2010	4	1650	3	7000	2	3100	2	1600

No. 8.—RETURN OF MILLS, MANUFACTORIES, &c. 1860—61.

GENERAL ABSTRACT, Continued.

COUNTIES.	Chair Factories.		Cloth Factories.		Paper Mills.		Tobacco Factories.		Iron Foundries.		Nail Factories.		Carriage Factories.	
	Number.	Value in Dollars.	Number.	Value in Dollars.	Number.	Value in Dollars.	Number.	Value in Dollars.	Number.	Value in Dollars.	Number.	Value in Dollars.	Number.	Value in Dollars.
1. Halifax	*2	1400	1	400	1	1200	1	800	4	38400	2	6000	1	800
2. Colchester									1	40000				
3. Cumberland														
4. Pictou			1	2400					3	15200				
5. Sydney														
6. Guysborough														
7. Inverness														
8. Richmond														
9. Victoria														
10. Cape Breton									1	6000				
11. Hants									1	10000			3	16540
12. King's														
13. Annapolis			1	12000					1	8000				
14. Digby													4	2200
15. Yarmouth		3000											2	400
16. Shelburne														
17. Queen's														
18. Lunenburg														
	3	4400	3	14800	1	1000	1	800	11	114000	2	6000	10	19940

* Full Factory connected with one of these.

GENERAL ABSTRACT. Continued.

COUNTIES.	Tanneries.		Cotton Factories.		Brush Factories.		Gas Factories.		Trunk Factories.		Breweries.		Joiners' Factories.	
	Number.	Value in Dollars.	Number.	Value in Dollars.	Number.	Value in Dollars.	Number.	Value in Dollars.	Number.	Value in Dollars.	Number.	Value in Dollars.	Number.	Value in Dollars.
1. Halifax	8	36500	1	4800	1	1200	1	180000	1	300	5	45000	1	12000
2. Colchester	5	5000												
3. Cumberland														
4. Victoria	12	17400	1	900										
5. Sydney														
6. Guysborough														
7. Inverness	1	600												
8. Richmond														
9. Victoria														
10. Cape Breton	2	1000												
11. Hants	1	900												
12. King's	1	1000												
13. Annapolis			1	1800										
14. Digby	6	3600												
15. Yarmouth	5	6000												
16. Shelburne	1	1400											1	2400
17. Queen's														
18. Lunenburg	4	3300												
	48	76500	3	7100	1	1200	1	180000	1	300	5	45000	2	14400

No. 8.—RETURN OF MILLS, MANUFACTORIES, &c...1860—61.

GENERAL ABSTRACT, Continued.

COUNTIES.	Brick Factories.		Fulling Mills.		Shoe Factories.		Saw & Planing Mills.		Plaster Mills.		Gas Mills.		Grindstone Factories.	
	Number.	Value in Dollars.	Number.	Value in Dollars.	Number.	Value in Dollars.	Number.	Value in Dollars.	Number.	Value in Dollars.	Number.	Value in Dollars.	Number.	Value in Dollars.
1. Halifax	1	2000												
2. Colchester			3	3600	1	2000	1	2000	1	400				
3. Cumberland											3	1400	1	4000
4. Pictou			6	7000										
5. Sydney			2	2400										
6. Guysborough			1	1000										
7. Inverness			2	3000										
8. Richmond														
9. Victoria			1	1200										
10. Cape Breton											1	200		
11. Hants	*1	5000												
12. King's														
13. Annapolis														
14. Digby														
15. Yarmouth					7	2000								
16. Shelburne														
17. Queen's									1	5000				
18. Lunenburg														
	2	8200	18	18600	8	4000	2	7000	1	600	4	1600	1	4000

* Pottery connected with this.

GENERAL ABSTRACT, Continued.

COUNTIES	Woolen Factories		Coal Oil Factories		Bakeries		Factories, kind not designated		Engine Factories		Potteries		Sash Mills		Pail Factories	
	Number	Value in Dollars	Number	Value in Dollars	Number	Value in Dollars	Number	Value in Dollars	Number	Value in Dollars	Number	Value in Dollars	Number	Value in Dollars	Number	Value in Dollars
1. Halifax					1	5000										
2. Colchester																
3. Cumberland																
4. Pictou	1	800	1	1000	1	2000										
5. Sydney																
6. Guysborough																
7. Inverness							1	1600								
8. Richmond																
9. Victoria									1	4000						
10. Cape Breton							2	22800								
11. Hants							3	10800								
12. King's																
13. Annapolis											1	500				
14. Digby																
15. Yarmouth													4	1500	1	100
16. Shelburne																
17. Queen's							2	25000					1	6000		
18. Lunenburg							2	1600					1	500		
	1	800	1	1000	2	7000	13	33000	1	4000	1	500	6	7500	1	100

APPENDIX NO. 9.

RETURN

OF

ASSESSED VALUE OF PROPERTY, ASSESSMENTS, &c.

No. 9.—RETURN OF ASSESSED VALUE OF PROPERTY, ASSESSMENTS, &c...1860—61.

COUNTIES.	Assessed Value.		For County Purpose.		No. of Rate Payers.	No. of Poor Families.	No. of Paupers.			Assessment for Poor for 1860.
	Real Estate in Dollars.	Personal Property in Dollars.	Assessment for 1860.	Highest Rate for 1860.			M.	F.	Total.	
1. Halifax (exclusive of City)	2953108	679636	$4427 00	$21 00	3453	3	4	13	17	$980 00
2. Colchester	4100000	260000	6000 00	14 00	3800	14	16	8	24	1696 00
3. Cumberland	3087504	683658	2960 00	14 50	3901	12	17	20	37	1489 00
4. Pictou	2530656	1132184	7914 79	38 80	2636	22	23	52	75	4358 00
5. Sydney	2160967	533248	3200 00	10 00	2004	6	11	6	17	1936 34
6. Guysborough	1053254	388434	1974 86	10 45	3550	22	15	12	27	1375 74
7. Inverness	Not returned.		1745 70	13 00	2717					
8. Richmond	520260	337785	2560 07	37 91	2395					
9. Victoria	480060	105056	1655 00	34 66	1821					
10. Cape Breton	1519480	672850	2601 07	*484 00	3784	5	12	11	23	1740 31
11. Hants	3456014	1137708	1982 00	24 13	3584	9	12	15	27	3204 00
12. King's	3773828	645492	2082 84	9 72	3730	3	56	55	111	4930 77
13. Annapolis	2650601	606204	2083 25	16 00	3293	9	42	49	91	3879 40
14. Digby	1468378	349036	1134 00		2953	13	29	37	66	2404 80
15. Yarmouth	2456080	1388146	1851 55	32 79	2622	2	19	30	49	6274 41
16. Shelburne	1167328	478412	1339 40	17 35	2187	7	13	25	38	1232 60
17. Queen's	1288508	488040	1396 65	11 72	1825	7	12	11	23	1920 00
18. Lunenburg	2415032	990000	3400 00	6 52	4055	10	13	21	34	2897 00
City of Halifax valuation returned	7000000	5600000								

Note.—No return from Inverness, Richmond or Victoria, relative to the poor; or of assessment for the City of Halifax.   * 0. M. Acres's.

APPENDIX NO. 10.

RETURN

OF

THE PROVINCIAL HOSPITAL FOR THE INSANE.

No. 10.—RETURN OF THE PROVINCIAL HOSPITAL FOR THE INSANE, MARCH 30, 1861.

Sex.		Age.	Civil Condition.				Birth Place.	County sent from.	Hosp'l Residence.		
Male.	Female.		Married.	Single.	Widower.	Widow.			Years.	Months.	Days.
1		56	1				Scotland	Colchester	2	2	11
1		47	1				Ireland	Halifax	2	2	5
1		47		1			"	"	2	2	5
1		44		1			Native	"	2	2	5
1		42		1			"	"	2	2	5
1		37		1			Doubtful	"	2	2	5
1		60		1			"	Hants	2	2	5
	1	47	1				Newfoundland	Halifax	2	2	4
	1	37		1			Ireland	"	2	2	4
	1	52	1				"	Pictou	2	2	4
	1	42				1	Native	Halifax	2	2	4
	1	57				1	"	Colchester	2	2	1
	1	37	1				Ireland	Queen's	2	1	21
1		47		1			Newfoundland	Halifax	2	1	16
	1	27		1			Native	"	2	1	15
	1	42				1	"	Hants	2	1	15
	1	47		1			"	Halifax	2	1	14
	1	36		1			"	"	2	1	14
	1	62				1	"	"	2	1	12
	1	57				1	"	"	2	1	12
1		62		1			Ireland	"	2	1	3
1		42		1			Native	Hants	2		15
	1	54			1		"	Halifax	1	11	11
1		33		1			"	"	1	11	10
1		28		1			"	Queen's	1	11	9
	1	45	1				Ireland	Halifax	1	11	1
1		30		1			Uncertain	"	1	10	23
	1	52		1			Ireland	"	1	10	6
	1	44		1			Native	"	1	9	19
1		21		1			"	"	1	9	17
	1	49		1			"	"	1	9	17
	1	26		1			"	"	1	9	17
	1	25		1			Newfoundland	"	1	9	12
	1	21		1			Native	Guysborough	1	9	9
1		24		1			"	Pictou	1	9	6
	1	60	1				Uncertain	"	1	9	6
1		35	1				Ireland	Halifax	1	7	25
1		26	1				Native	Victoria	1	7	9
1		28		1			"	Richmond	1	6	18
1		26		1			"	Annapolis	1	6	4
1		34		1			"	Colchester	1	6	1
1		46		1			Ireland	Annapolis	1	4	28
1		21		1			Native	Hants	1	4	27
1		43		1			"	Yarmouth	1	4	27
1		31		1			"	Colchester	1	1	20
	1	47	1				England	Queen's	1		2
1		72	1				France	Digby		11	24
1		26		1			Native	"		11	18
	1	60	1				Scotland	Pictou		11	16
1		40	1				Native	Cumberland		11	14
	1	36		1			Scotland	Newfoundland		11	
	1	30		1			Native	Pictou		10	27
1		38		1			New Brunswick	Cumberland		10	25
	1	30		1			Native	Halifax		10	18
1		34	1				"	"		9	21
	1	23		1			"	"		9	16
1		30		1			"	"		9	9
	1	40	1				Newfoundland	"		9	8
1		75			1		Ireland	Yarmouth		8	24
	1	43	1				Native	Lunenburg		8	13

No. 10.—RETURN OF THE PROVINCIAL HOSPITAL FOR THE INSANE,
MARCH 30, 1861.—*Continued.*

Male	Female	Age	Married	Single	Widower	Widow	Birth Place	County sent from	Years	Months	Days
1		17		1			"	King's		8	12
	1	23		1			"	"		8	3
	1	30	1				"	Halifax		8	3
1		40	1				Ireland	"		7	10
	1	45			1		Native	Sydney		6	27
	1	30	1				"	"		6	26
1							Unknown.			6	23
1							"			6	22
	1	60		1			Native	Pictou		6	18
1*		32		1			P. E. Island	Halifax		6	10
	1	46	1				Native	"		5	26
1		13		1			Ireland	"		5	18
	1	26	1				Native	"		5	10
	1			1			"	"		5	3
1		30		1			Ireland	"		4	24
	1	43				1	"	"		4	24
1		38		1			Ireland	Halifax		4	24
1		41	1				"	"		4	24
1		46		1			Scotland	"		4	24
1		28		1			Barbadoes	"		4	24
	1	50		1			Native	"		4	17
	1	45	1				"	Colchester		4	9
	1	23		1			"	Halifax		4	3
	1			1			"	"		4	2
1		34		1			"	King's		3	26
1		5		1			"	Halifax		3	26
1		45		1			"	"		3	24
	1	23		1			"	"		3	18
	1	32	1				"	Colchester		3	11
1		66	1				"	Halifax		3	10
	1	50		1			"	Colchester		3	6
1		16		1			"	Pictou		1	28
	1	48	1				"	"		1	24
1		45	1				Ireland	Halifax		1	21
1		20		1			Native	Queen's			1
45	50		*26	59	1	6					

* Three, civil condition not known.   This return is signed by J. R. DeWolf, M. D., Superintendent.

GENERAL ABSTRACT
OF THE INSANE, INCLUDING THOSE IN THE HOSPITAL.

COUNTIES.	Returned by Enumerators.		In Hospital for the Insane.		Total.	
	M.	F.	M.	F.	M.	F.
1. Halifax	25	29	21	31	46	60
2. Colchester	11	9	3	4	14	13
3. Cumberland	6	6	2	....	8	6
4. Pictou	7	11	2	6	9	17
5. Sydney	4	6	....	2	4	8
6. Guysborough	4	4	....	1	4	5
7. Inverness	3	11	....	....	3	11
8. Richmond	7	6	1	....	8	6
9. Victoria	3	2	1	....	4	2
10. Cape Breton	12	4	....	....	12	4
11. Hants	6	3	3	1	9	4
12. King's	8	6	2	1	10	7
13. Annapolis	9	5	2	....	11	5
14. Digby	6	8	2	....	8	8
15. Yarmouth	4	2	2	....	6	2
16. Shelburne	....	4	....	....	....	4
17. Queen's	2	1	2	2	4	3
18. Lunenburg	4	7	....	1	4	8
Newfoundland	....	....	....	1	....	1
Unknown	....	....	2	....	2	....
Totals	121	124	45	50	166	174

ERRATA.

ORIGIN.

Page 98—County of Richmond, line 12, Scotland, for 126 read 136.
" 103— " " Hants, line 9, U. S. of America, for 4 read 14.

CAUSES OF DEATH.

Page 145—County of Cumberland, first line, total, for 26 read 21.

AGRICULTURAL.

Page 210—County of Pictou, line 20, Acres Cultivated Intervale, for 313 read 373.
" 221— " " Richmond, line 4, Butter, for 12,330 read 12,230.
" 234— " " Annapolis, line 2, Value of Dyke Marsh, for 808 read 308.
" 251—General Abstract, County Richmond, Potatoes, for 64,005 read 64,055.
" 251— " " County of Annapolis, Potatoes, for 566,752 read 266,752.

HOUSES, &c.

Page 265—County of Cape Breton, total Probable Tonnage, for 741 read 731.
" 266— " " Annapolis, total Temperance Halls, for 4 read 3.

MILLS, &c.

Page 276—County of Cumberland, for total 28,640 value of Grist Mills, read 28,240.

NOTE.—Of the 393 persons returned from District No. 1, County of Cumberland, as belonging to the Presbyterian Church of the Lower Provinces, 271 should be classed under the head of "Reformed Presbyterian Church." The error occurred in transcribing the figures from the Householders' Schedules to the Abstract form, and was not discovered until after the sheet had gone to press.

www.ingramcontent.com/pod-product-compliance
Lightning Source LLC
Chambersburg PA
CBHW020457270326
41926CB00008B/638